The Sāmaveda

The verses of the *Sāmaveda*, all except 78, are taken from the *Ṛgveda*. They are arranged in a sequence different from that of the *Ṛgveda* and divided into two parts. The first part, called *Pūrvārcika*, has 589 verses; the second, called *Uttarārcika*, has 1225 stanzas. The hymns are invocation addressed to Soma, Agni, and Indra meant for chanting by *Udgātṛ* priests at Soma sacrifices and not devoted chiefly to the worship of Indra who is a blustering braggadocio god, who has to befuddle himself with *Soma* in order to slay demons as a reputed scholar put it. Due to its special reference to *Pitṛs* or deceased forefathers, the sounds of the *Sāmans* are considered by some as impure.

This edition of the *Sāmaveda*, a translation by Devi Chand, is based on the exposition of Swami Dayanand. The translator has furnished references in the footnotes to different interpretations of Indian and foreign scholars. An introduction and glossary-cum-index are added for the benefit of those not acquainted with the *Sāmaveda*. Everyone shall find this an excellent book for a thorough understanding of the *Sāmaveda*.

Devi Chand had a closer understanding of Vedic literature and studied diverse interpretations of the Vedas. He has translated the *Yajurveda*, the *Sāmaveda*, and the *Atharvaveda* which are standard editions. He was the founder of D.A.V. College, Hoshiarpur and a well-known educationist of Punjab.

THE SĀMAVEDA

Sanskrit text with English translation
by
Devi Chand M.A.

with introductory remarks by
M.C. Joshi,
Archaeological Survey of India, New Delhi

WITH GLOSSARY AND INDEX

**Munshiram Manoharlal
Publishers Pvt. Ltd.**

ISBN 978-81-215-0199-6
This edition 2010
First edition 1975
Second thoroughly revised and enlarged edition 1981
Reprint of the second edition 1990; 1995; 2000; 2003; 2004

PRINTED IN INDIA
Published by Vikram Jain *for*
Munshiram Manoharlal Publishers Pvt. Ltd.
PO Box 5715, 54 Rani Jhansi Road, New Delhi 110 055, India

www.mrmlbooks.com

CONTENTS

INTRODUCTORY REMARKS

THE Vedas are known as the oldest scriptures of the Hindus and are regarded as the principal source of the Hindu way of life. Although consisting of four *Saṁhitās*, viz., the *Ṛik*, *Yajuḥ*, *Sāman* and *Atharva*, the Vedas distinctly form two groups; (i) the first three forming the Trayī (Trio) and (ii) the *Atharva*. Scholars have tried to associate these two classes with two groups of people, but so far no clear picture has emerged. The Trayī group, however, is commonly regarded as somewhat superior to *Atharvaveda*.

Of the four Saṁhitās, the Ṛik represents a collection of hymns addressed to different gods; Yajuḥ is regarded as a guide to *adhvaryu*-priest, Sāma, a book of holy songs, and *Atharva* contains popular beliefs, concepts, and references to magico-religious rites.

The Vedic tradition associates the four Vedas with four spheres and four deities viz., Sun (*Ṛik*) Fire (*Yaju*) Wind (*Sāma*) and Moon (*Atharva*).

Some interesting data about the Vedas are preserved in the Puranic tradition which are not totally irrelevant. According to the following verse of *Vishnu-Purāṇa*, the Veda originally consisted of one lakh hymns with four *padas* (feet) and it also served as the source of ten types of sacrifices which accomplished the material desires :

आद्यौ वेदचतुष्पाद: शतसाहस्र सम्मित: ततो दशगुण कृत्स्नो यज्ञोऽयं सर्वकामधुक् ॥

Vishnu Purāṇa, III, IV

This text further states that *Sāmaveda* has thousand *Śākhās* (सहस्र संहिता भेदं), although now only three *śākhās* of this Veda are available, viz., Kauthuma (Gujarat), Rāṇāyanīya (Maharashtra) and Jaiminīya (Karnataka).

Our primary concern here is *Sāmaveda* whereof most hymns are to be chanted by Udgātri priests during the performance of important sacrifices connected with the preparation of Soma juice. The hymns have mainly been collected from the *Ṛigveda* but are arranged in a different order with minor variations. The music during the age of the Vedas appears to be in a developed stage for the Vedic *chhandas* like Gāyatrī, Ushṇik, Anushṭup, Bṛihatī, Paṅkti, Trishṭup and Jagatī, according to Pingala, an early authority on the subject, are associated with seven colours (सित सारङ्गपिशङ्कृष्णनीललोहित वर्णा: । III. 3.65). and seven notes (स्वरा: पड्जर्षभ गान्धार मध्यम पञ्चम धैवतं निषादा: । III. 3.64.(

It is impossible to define, in exact or even approximate terms, the period when Sāma was composed out of *Ṛigveda*. The date of the latter itself is not properly settled; on the other hand, the Hindu traditionalist holds the view that the *Vedas* are divine and eternal books of knowledge.

The following verses of the *Vishnu Purāṇa* give an interesting account of

compilation and expansion of Sāmaveda and Ṛishis associated with it from
Vedavyāsa onwards and their division into northern (*Udīchaya sāmagas*) and
eastern Sama singers (*Prāchya sāmagas*)

सामवेदतरोश्शाखा व्यासशिष्यस्स जैमिनि: क्रमेणयेन मंत्रेय विभेद शृणु तन्मम ॥ १

समन्तुस्तस्यपुत्रोऽभूत्सुकर्मास्याप्यभूत्सुत: अधीतवन्तौ चैकैकां संहिता तौ महामती ॥ २

सहस्रसंहिताभेदं सुकर्मा तत्सुतस्तत: चकारे तं चं तच्छिष्यौ जगृहातेमहाव्रतौ ॥ ३

हिरण्यनाभ: कौसल्य: पौष्पिञ्जिश्चद्विजोत्तम:

उदीच्या स्सामगा शिष्या तस्यपञ्चदशंस्मृता ॥ ४

हिरण्यनाभात्तावत्यस्संहिता यैद्विजोत्तमै: गृहीतास्तेऽपि चोच्यन्ते पण्डितै प्राच्यसाभगा: ॥ ५

लोकाक्षिकौशुमिश्चैव कक्षीवांल्लाङ्गुलिस्तथा पौष्पाञ्जि शिष्यास्तज्द्ये दैस्संहिता बहुलीकृता ॥ ६

हिरण्यनाभ शिष्यस्तु चतुर्विंशति संहिता: प्रोवाच कृतिनामासौ शिष्येभ्यश्च महामुनि: ॥ ७

तैश्चापि सामवेदोऽसौ शाखामि बहुलीकृत: ॥ ८

Vishṇu Purāṇa III, Ch. IV, 1-8,

Translation: "You shall now hear, Maitreya, how Jaimini. the pupil of
Vyāsa, divided the branches of the Sāmaveda. The son of Jaimini was
Sumantu, and his son was Sukarman, who both studied the same *Samhitā*
under Jaimini.

The latter composed the *Sahasra Samhitā* (or compilation of a thousand
hymns), which he taught to two disciples, Hiraṇyanābha, also named
Kausalya (or of Kosala), and Paushyiñji. Fifteen disciples of the latter were
the authors of as many Samhitās: they were called the northern chanters of
the Sāman. As many more, also the disciples Hiraṇyanābha, were termed the
eastern chanters of the Sāman, founding an equal number of schools. Lokakshi
Kuthumi, Kushidi, (*Kakshivan*) and Lāngali were the pupils of Paushyiñji;
and by them and their disciples many other branches were formed. Whilst
another scholar of Hiraṇyanābha, named Kṛti, taught twenty-four Samhitās
to as many pupils; and by them again, was the *Sāmaveda* divided into
numerous branches."[1]

Similar data with variations are also found in some other Purāṇas. These
accounts may not be totally historical or authentic, but certainly these cannot be without some amount of truth in regard to the size of the Vedic texts.
It appears that the Samhitās, as available to us today, represent only part
survivals of the original Vedas. Much of these seem to have been lost at an
early date even before their final compilation. The most difficult aspect of
the history of the Vedic literature, however, is to determine the exact period
of the composition of different groups of hymns, in spite of the fact that the
problem has been studied and investigated by a variety of scholars from
diverse angles. So far we have failed to establish, in archaeological terms,
the proper identity of the Vedic people, who are generally styled as Aryans
by modern writers on the basis of over hundred years old historical knowledge
and outdated concepts. The problem is still treated to be fundamentally of

[1]After H.H. Wilson. *The Vishnu-Purana*, English translation, third ed., Calcutt.., 1961,
p. 277.

a linguistic character. Some archaeologists, who did attempt to solve this problem at times, could not do justice to the subject due to their lack of proper grasp of Vedic Sanskrit as also due to deep impact on their minds of conceptual model of Vedic culture, as popularized by most nineteenth century Indologists and Orientalists and their counterparts in the present century.

Modern scholars have often treated Vedic culture as the culture of only one specific social group which does not seem to be a fact. Probably there were more diversities than common points in it. Otherwise how at the same time the people mentioned in the Vedas should be matriarchal and patriarchal, endogamous and exogamous, sacrificial and non-sacrificial and practising systems of burial as well as cremation. Besides, the Aryans living in India were also different from Iranians and other groups of the same linguistic affinity.

It may not be wrong to speculate that the distribution of the Vedic people, both in time and space, was far greater than what it has generally been supposed.

Plausibly the Aryan expansion into India was gradual, in several stages over a long period of several centuries characterized by the movements of several culturally distinct groups. The theory of organized Aryan invasions, comparable to the Saka-Kushan or Turkish occupation of India, seems to be without much historical substance. There may have been wars between different groups of Vedic people and non-Vedic tribes of the same stock or speakers of the same tongue/dialect, but to think in terms of conflicts between the Vedic people (Aryans) and the so-called pre-Aryan (Draviḍas?) occupants of India seems to be unhistorical. Had it been so, the language of upper India through the centuries, should have been other than Sanskritic, for none of the invading forces, being smaller in numbers than the original inhabitants, could ever replace or uproot the speech of the original settlers in a country like India.

It would therefore not be proper to locate the land of the Vedic hymnal compositions outside the undivided India and the adjoining areas of ancient Afghanistan or eastern Iran. The Vedic people were distributed in smaller areas, conditioned by geography, in tribal units called *Janah*, and probably the hymns were composed by the priests/other individuals of each tribe which perhaps remained the oral possession of a specific group, socio-religious or family, within that tribe for a long time. Perhaps, due to this factor the language of early Vedic hymns was not quite homogenous. Some of the well known families associated with the composition of early *mantras* were the Ātreyas, Vāśishṭhas, Kāṇvas, Bhārgavas, Kāśyapas, Bhāradvājas, Bārhaspatyas, Āṅgirasas, etc., and in some cases lingual or other peculiarities could be observed in the composition of various authors.

Most Vedic hymns were perhaps preserved, as a part of oral tradition, by specific families of priests or teachers and it was probably much later that these were collected and arranged into various groups. Those hymns which could not be preserved in the Śruti tradition or could not be collected due to some other reasons at the stage of compilation were lost for ever. In some cases, even the real authors of hymns were forgotten, and the Vedas as a whole were considered by a large section of ancient Indian Society as a collection of revealed (divine) knowledge.

Yet, diverse views have been expressed about the origin of the Vedas by the Vedic people themselves. In a hymn of *Atharvaveda*, the origin of the Vedas has been connected with *Skambha* or the Cosmic Pillar:

यस्मादृचो अपातक्षन् यजुर्यस्मादपाकषन्
सामानि यस्य लोमान्यथर्वाङ्गिरसो मुखं स्कम्भं तं ब्रूहि कतमः स्विदेव सः ।

Atharva X. vii. 20

Yajurveda associates their birth with Sarvahuta Yajña (*Yajuḥ*. XXXI—7); but another *mantra* of *Atharva* (XIX-XLIV. 2) attributes their emergence to *Time Eternal* (Kāla). The same Veda also preserves conception of a deity called Vedamātā i.e., mother of the Vedas who is stated to be the purifier of all the people of twin births and giver of all that is desired:

स्तुतामयावरदावेदमाता प्रचोदयन्तां पावमानी द्विजानाम् ।
आयु प्राणं प्रजां पशुं कीर्ति द्रविणं ब्रह्मवर्चं सम् मह्यं दत्वा व्रजतु ब्रह्मलोकम् ॥

Atharva XIX. lxxi. 7

The concept of Vedamātā appears to be akin to that of Vedic Vāk (speech). In the *Atharvaveda* itself Vāk is regarded as daughter of *Ṛita* i.e., Truth (God) and mother of the *devas*.

The Vedas thus could be treated as offsprings of Vāk i.e., *Śabda* or sound and thereby *nitya* (eternal) in character (नित्याःशब्दाः) which is also applicable to them (*Vedas*) as source book of knowledge for the term *Veda* itself it derived from verbal root *vid* i.e., to know (*vid-jñāne/vid-vichāre/vid-sattāyāṁ*, etc.). From the foregoing it would thus be apparent that how the Vedic hymns were regarded to be divine expositions, although their contents were parts of only human thought.

Much importance was perhaps being attached to the knowledge of *Sāmaveda* by ancients themselves because it was Sāma-music which served as the source of priesthood or Brahmanhood (सामवेदो ब्राह्मणानां प्रसूति ॥ *Tatt*. III. xii. 9-2); besides its recitation pleased every one. In fact, the Sanskrit term *Sāman* itself, which stands for 'soothing' or 'pleasing,' indicates the melodious quality of *Sāmaveda* and *Sāmagāna*. From a number of hymns of *Rigveda* it is evident that the early Vedic society was well familiar with Sāma music and *Sāmagas* (Sāma-singers). A significant aspect of *Sāmaveda* is the employment of several metres like *Sato-bṛihatī, Prastāra-paṅkti Virāja Śakvarī*, etc., in addition to famous seven Vedic metres.

Sāmaveda was being considered important by the priestly class in the ancient and medieval periods of Indian history, and even today its study has not lost significance totally at least for the reconstruction of the ancient cultures of India. Any translation of this text especially in English would always be well received. The *Sāmaveda* (*Rāṇāyaṇīya*) was perhaps first translated by Stevenson in English as early as 1842 which was followed by the translation of Theodor Benfey in 1848 and Ralph Griffith's in 1893.

Devi Chand's present translation follows a specific School of thought i.e., the one founded by Swāmi Dayānanda Sarasvatī, the great Hindu reformer of the nineteenth century, who regarded every word of the *Vedas* as divine and an authority by itself (*svataḥ-pramāṇa*). It is basically different from the commentaries of Sāyaṇa and other traditional pandits or western scholars, yet quite interesting and thought proving in its contents. I hope this also would be liked by scholars/students and others for its own merits.

M.C. Joshi

New Delhi
1 June 1981

OM

INTRODUCTION

COMPOSITION OF THE SAMAVEDA

THE Sāmaveda, like the other three Vedas, is the Word of God revealed in the beginning of creation for the moral, spiritual, economic and physical guidance and uplift of humanity.

God is infinite, the soul is finite in knowledge. The finite soul cannot contain the infinite knowledge of God. God creates, sustains and dissolves the world. Whenever the world is created, God reveals the Vedas. This process is going on since eternity and will go on for ever.

There are 1875 verses in the *Sāmaveda*. It is a Veda primarily of devotion, worship and contemplation, highly essential for the attainment of God, that is why Lord Krishna says in the 10th Chapter of Gita वेदानाम् सामवेदोऽस्मि । of the Vedas I am the Sāmaveda. This Veda is divided into three parts, (1) Pūrva Ārchika, (2) Uttar Ārchika, (3) Mahā Nāmni Ārchika. Pūrva Ārchika is divided into four parts (1) Āgneya Kāṇḍa, (2) Aindra Kāṇḍa, (3) Pāvmāna Kāṇḍa, (4) Āraṇyaka Kāṇḍa. These four Kāṇḍas are divided further into six Prapāthaks. According to Sāyana these Kāṇḍas are divided into five Adhyayas. Prapāthaks contain Ardh-Prapāthaks and Dashtis (Collection of ten verses). Adhyāyas contain Khaṇḍas.

In Uttar Ārchika there are 21 Adhyāyas and 9 Prapāthakas which are further sub-divided into Ardhprapāthakas. There are no Dashtis in the Uttar Ārchika, but there are Sūktas. In Mahā Nāmni Ārchika there are only ten verses. This division is a bit complicated. Some commentators like Swami Tulsi Ram and Pandit Jaidev Vidyalankar, for the facility of the readers have numbered each verse. I have followed this practice, showing the Prapāthak as Book, Ardh-Prapāthak as Chapter, and Dashti as Decade.

Some scholars are of opinion that Sāmaveda has got only 75 verses of its own, and the rest are taken from the Rigveda. This notion is erroneous. The *Sāmaveda* is an independent Veda by itself like the other three Vedas. Their view can be correct only in case the aim of the *Rigveda* and the *Sāmaveda* be one and the same. The *Rigveda* deals with knowledge, the *Sāmaveda* with Upāsnā, worship and contemplation. The same verse conveys in the Rigveda a sense pertaining to knowledge, and in the *Sāmaveda* to prayer and worship. A verse can have different meanings according to its different devatās (subject-matters). The identity of a verse at different places does not connote repetition. Difference in significance according to change in the devatā makes the verse independent. Maharshi Dayanand has dealt with the subject in the *Rigveda* Adi Bhashya Bhumika at length.

In singing, the verses are still further altered in meaning by prolongations, insertion of syllables, and various modulations, rests, and other modifications prescribed for the guidance of the reciters. In Pūrva-Ārchika there are two song manuals, the Grāmageyagāna or Congregational, and the Āraṇyagāna, which the recluse and seekers after salvation sing in forest solitude. In Uttar Archika there are two song manuals, the Uhagana and the Uhyagāna. For details one should study the *Nāradi Siksha* and *Rāga Vibodha*.

All the ancient commentaries on the *Sāmaveda* are not extant at the present time, Shri Dev Raj Yajwa in his commentary on Nighantu has given the names of eight commentators (1) Skand Swami (2) Bhav Swami (3) Rabdeva (4) Shri Niwas (5) Mādhav Deva (6) Uvat Bhatta (7) Bhaskra Misra (8) Bharta Swami.

I give below the number of syllables in different metres, (Chhandas) used in the *Sāmaveda* (1) Gāyatri 24 (2) Ushnik 28 (3) Anushtup 32 (4) Brihati 36 (5) Pankti 40 (6) Trishtup 44 (7) Jagti 48 (8) Ati-Jagti 52 (9) Shakvari 56 (10) Ati Shakvari 60 (11) Ashti 64 (12) Ati Ashti 68 (13) Dhriti 72 (14) Ati Dhriti 76 (15) Kriti 80 (16) Prakriti 84 (17) Akriti 88 (18) Vikriti 92 (19) Sanskriti 96 (20) Atikriti 100 (21) Utkriti 104.

WHAT BOOKS CONSTITUTE THE VEDAS

Maharshi Dayanand considers the Samhita (text) of Rig, Yajur, Sāma and Atharva as the Vedas. Some scholars however believe the Shatpath, Aitreya etc. Brāhmaṇas and the Upanishads also as the Vedas. The Brāhmaṇā Granthas are commentaries on the Vedas, but do not form a part of the Vedas.

In common parlance the *Rigveda*, *Yajurveda*, *Sāmaveda* and *Atharvaveda* are spoken of as the Vedas. The Upanishads and the Brāhmaṇas are separate books written by learned Rishis. They are not the word of God.

Maharshi Pāniṇi, the well-known grammarian also believes that the Vedas and the Brāhmaṇas are quite different books. In *Aṣṭādhyāyi*, 4.2.66, he writes, छन्दो ब्राह्मणानि च तद्विषयाणि, that the Vedas and Brāhmaṇas have got different terminations i.e., suffixes and affixes. This clearly proves that Pāniṇi considers the Vedas and Brāhmaṇas as separate books; had he considered them to be one and the same, he would have used either छन्दांसि or ब्राह्मणानि and not both of them. Pāniṇi can never be accused of repetition. A grammarian prefers brevity and avoids repetition.

Maharshi Patanjali, the author of Mahābhaṣya also considers the Vedas different from the Brāhmaṇas. He writes शब्दास्तावद् द्विविधाः लौकिकाश्च वैदिकाश्च । लौकिकास्तावद् गौरश्व: पुरुषो हस्तीत्यादय: । वैदिकास्तावत् अग्निमीलेपुरोहितम्, इषे त्वोर्जेत्वा, अग्न आयाहि वीतये, ये त्रिषप्ता: परियन्ति, इत्यादय: । Ordinary words are cow, horse, man and elephant. The first verse of each Veda has been quoted by Maharshi Patañjali in proof of Vedic words. As Patañjali considered the text of the four Vedas as Vedic words, and as he did not believe the Brāhmaṇas to be a part of the Vedas, he has quoted the first four verses of the Vedas, and none from the Brāhmaṇas, which he considered to be different from the Vedas.

Manu, the law-giver also considers the Vedas to be quite apart from the Upanishads and the Brāhmaṇas. Defining an Acharya, he says 'उपनीयतु यं शिष्यम् वेदमध्यापयेद् द्विज:, सकल्पं सरहस्यञ्च तमाचार्यं प्रचक्षते' । An Acharya, learned teacher is he, who after investing his pupil with the sacred thread (Yajño-pavīt) gives him instruction in the Vedas, and other books like the Brāhmaṇas and the Upanishads, which divulge the secrets of the Vedas. This clearly proves that Manu considers the Upanishads and the Brāhmaṇas, as commentaries on the Vedas, but not the Vedas. Had he considered them to be a part and parcel of the Vedas, he would not have used the words सकल्पं सरहस्यञ्च, Swami Shankarācharya always names the Upanishadas as Shruti and the Vedas as Samhitas. He has never named the Upanishadas as Samhita. He considers the Veda as a foremost authority and the Upanishada as secondary. He says वेदानां स्वत: प्रामाण्यं स्वविषये स्वेरिव प्रकाशविषये । Just as the sun is authority for light, so are the Vedas authority for themselves. The Upani-shadas and Brāhmaṇas are authoritative so far as they are in conformity with the teachings of the Vedas but not otherwise. They cannot be termed the Vedas. They simply explain the truths of the Vedas. The internal evidence of the Brāhmaṇa Granthas is sufficient to prove that they are man-made, and different from the Vedas, the word of God. I quote the last sentence of the Shatpatha Brāhmaṇa in support of the proposition "यानीमानि शुक्लानि यजूंषि वाजसानेयेन याज्ञवल्क्येन व्याख्यायन्ते ।" These verses of the Shukla Yajur Vedas have been explained by Yājnavalkya born in the family of Vājasaneya.

When Yājnavalkya himself writes at the end of the Shatpatha Brāhmaṇa, that he has written the book as a commentary on the Yajurveda, no further proof is required to establish the fact that the Brāhmaṇas are not the Vedas. They are merely their commentaries and hence different from the Vedas.

Shri Bhattoji Dikshit, the great grammarian, the author of Sidhānta Kaumudi also considers the Vedas to be different from the Brāhmaṇas. In his commentary on Pānini's aphorisms, i e., Aṣṭādhyāyī, 4.3.105. पुराणप्रोक्तेषु ब्राह्मणकल्पेषु he writes 'पुराण इति किम् याज्ञवल्क्यानि ब्राह्मणानि' । i.e. the Brāhmaṇa Granthas written by Rishi Yājnavalkya. When Yājnavalkya is the writer of a Brāhmaṇa Granth, the question of its being revealed by God does not arise, Yājnavalkya cannot be God, the Revealer of the Vedas.

The multiplicity of the Brāhmaṇa Granthas, coupled with the names of their authors is a proof beyond doubt of their being separate from the Vedas. I give here a few names of the Brāhmaṇas named after their authors. Taitreya Brāhmaṇa, Ārsheya Brāhmaṇa, Kama Brāhmaṇa, Shātyayani Brāhmaṇa, Jaimineya Brāhmaṇa, Shankhayan Brāhmaṇa, Kathaka Brāhmaṇa, Shātyayan Brāhmaṇa, Paingāyana Brāhmaṇa. Brāhmaṇas are the books written by different Rishis, hence they can't be called the Vedas, as they are not the work of man.

There is no history in the Vedas, but the Brāhmaṇas and Upanishadas are replete with historical anecdotes, hence the books which are full of history cannot be termed the Vedas.

Maharshi Yāska, the master of grammar and philology also considers the Vedas to be different from the Brāhmaṇas. Whenever Yāska refers to any Vedic verse in the *Nirukta*, he writes इत्यपि निगमो भवति i.e., this is Vedic Mantra. when he gives any quotation from the Brahmana Granth he writes इति च ब्राह्मणम् i.e., this is quoted from the Brāhamaṇa. This clearly proves that Yāska considered the Vedas and the Brāhmaṇas to be different books. He has never ascribed a quotation from the Brāhmaṇa as Vedic, or one from the Vedas as Brāhmanic.

The foregoing arguments and opinions of various Vedic scholars go a long way to establish the view of Maharshi Dayanand, that the Rig, Yajur, Sāma, and Atharva Saṃhitas (texts) alone constitute the Vedas.

SCHOLAR'S OPINIONS ON THE VEDAS

1. The Persian scholar, Dachanji, B.A., LL.B., D. Th. writes in his book *Philosophy of Zoroastrianism and Comparative Study of Religions*:

'The Veda is a book of Knowledge and Wisdom comprising the Book of nature, the Book of Religion, the Book of Prayers, the Book of Morals and so on. The Word 'Veda' means Wit, Wisdom, Knowledge and truly the Veda is condensed Wit, Wisdom and Knowledge.'

'Readers of the Vedas, who do not know this wonderful characteristic feature of the Veda in determining the physical as well as the spiritual by means of the self same words, are apt to be misled by the false idea that the Veda looks upon fire, air, the dawn, the sun and the other agent forces, phenomena or objects of nature as Divine beings, to whom the Vedic Rishis, prayed for strength, health, wealth, long life, brave sons, rich possession and so on. But Vedas teach nothing but monotheism of the purest kind, the belief that this universe manifests the love, might, wisdom and glory of God, Who eternally evolves and dissolves alternately innumerable systems of worlds, for the benefit, discipline and well-being of jeevatmas, according to the eternal laws of nature (called Rit in the Vedas) and also according to the Laws of Karma.'

2. Jain Acharya Kumudendu writes thus in his book.[1] 'The *Rigveda* alone is eternal and the Word of God in the beginning. Various languages have been derived from it. The message of God is one and the same for the speakers of all languages.'

3. Lāvi an Arabian poet 1700 BC. has sung the praise of the Vedas in Arabic verses, the translation of which is given below:

(i) O blessed land of Hind (India) thou art worthy of reverence for in thee has God revealed True Knowledge of Himself.

(ii) What a pure light do these four revealed books afford to our mind's eyes like the (charming and cool) lustre of the dawn ? These four, God

[1]*Bhoovley*, ch. 6.

revealed upto His prophets (Rishis) in Hind.

(iii) And He thus teaches all races of mankind that inhabit His earth. 'Observe (in your lives) the Knowledge I have revealed in the Vedas' for surely God has revealed them.

(iv) Those treasuries are the Sāma and Yajur which God has preached. O my brothers; revere these, for they tell us the good news of salvation.

(v) The two next, of these four, Rig and Atharva teach us lessons of Universal brotherhood. These two (Vedas) are the beacons that warn us to turn towards that goal (universal brotherhood).

4. Dara Shikoh, the elder brother of Aurangzeb, was a Sanskrit scholar. He translated the *Isopanishad*, the 40th Chapter of the Yajurveda, into Persian. He was a seeker after truth, and in his search for truth, he studied the Qurān, the Old Testament, the New Testament and the Vedas with the help of some Pandits. As the result of his search, he made the following remarks, "After gradual research, I have come to the conclusion, that long before all heavenly books like the Qurān, the Old Testament and the New Testament etc., God had revealed to the Hindus, through the Rishis of yore, of whom Brahma was the Chief, his four books of Knowledge, the *Rigveda*, *the Yajurveda*, the *Sāmaveda* and the *Atharvaveda*." Translated from Dara Shikoh's Persian quotation.

"A fortunate person, who, relinquishing the selfishness of his polluted mind, for the sake of God, being free from bias, will study my translation of the *Isopanishad*, the Word of God, will attain to salvation and be free from death, fear and misery." Translated from Dara Shikoh's Persian remarks.

For such sayings the Muslim Mullahs declared him a heretic and got him murdered.

5. Dr. Alfred Russel Wallace[1] writes: 'In the earliest records which have come down to us from the past, we find ample indications that accepted standard of morality and the conduct resulting from these were in no degree inferior to those which prevail today, though in some respects they differed from ours. The wonderful collection of hymns known as the Veda is a vast system of religious teachings as pure and lofty as those of the finest portions of the Hebrew scriptures. Its authors were fully our equals in their conception of the universe and the Deity expressed in the finest poetic language.'

'In it we find many of the essential teachings of the most advanced religious thinkers.'[2]

'We must admit that the mind which conceived and expressed in appropriate language such ideas as are everywhere present in those Vedic hymns could not have been inferior to those of the best of our religious teachers and poets, to our Milton, Shakespeare and Tennyson.'[3]

6. Rev. Morris Philip[4] writes in his book. 'After the latest researches into the history and Chronology of books of Old Testament, we may safely

[1]*Social Environment and Moral Progress*, p. 11.
[2]ibid.　[3]ibid.
[4]*The Teachings of the Vedas*

call the *Rigveda* as the oldest book, not only of the Aryan humanity, but of the whole world.'

It is evident then (i) That the higher upto the source of the Vedic religion, we push our enquiries, the purer and simpler we find the conception of God; and that (ii) In proportion as we come down the stream of time the more corrupt and complex we find it.[1]

The conclusion therefore, is inevitable viz., that the development of religious thought in India has been uniformly downward, and not upward, deterioration and not evolution. We are justified, therefore in concluding that the higher and purer conceptions of the Vedic Aryans were the results of a primitive Divine Revelation.[2]

7. Professor Heeren[3] writes: 'They (the Vedas) are without doubt the oldest works composed in Sanskrit. Even the most ancient Sanskrit writings allude to the Vedas as already existing. The Vedas stand alone in their splendour, standing as beacon of Divine Light for the onward march of humanity.'

8. Mons Deos Delbos, a French Scholar says, "The Rigveda is the most sublime conception of the great high ways of humanity" Quoted in *the Hindu Superiority* by Har Bilas Sharda, pp. 179, 180.

9. Dr. James Cousins in *Path to Peace* writes: 'I have observed during my travels in India, the effects of Swami Dayananda Saraswati's influence in earnest effects to vitalise life in India with the Vedic ideal, which for thirty years has been a fundamental influence in my own life and in that of Mrs. Cousins, and for this much needed service to India and the world, I offer our joint homage to his memory.'[4]

10. Mr. Boulanger, a Russian scholar writes: 'What struck me in Max-Muller's translation was a lot of absurdities, obscene passages and a lot of what is not lucid.'

As far as I can grasp the teaching of the Vedas, it is so sublime that I would look upon it as a crime on my part, if the Russian public become acquainted with it through the medium of a confused and distorted translation thus not deriving for its soul that benefit which this teaching should give to the people.' Quoted from Sadhu T. L. Vaswani's *Torch Bearer*, p. 163.

11. Mr. Jaccolliot writes: 'Astonishing fact. The Hindu Revelation (Veda) is of all revelations the only one whose ideas are in perfect harmony with Modern Science, as it proclaims the slow and gradual formation of the world.' *The Bible in India*, II, ch. 1.

12. The American lady Mrs. Wheeler Willax writes 'We have all heard and read about the ancient religion of India. It is the land of the great Vedas— the most remarkable works containing not only religious ideas for a perfect

---

[1]*The Teachings of the Vedas*, p. 104.
[2]ibid, p. 231.
[3]*Historical Researches*, II, p. 127.
[4]*Dayananda Commemoration Volume, Ajmer*, p. 56.

life, but also facts which all the science has since proved true. Electricity, Radium, Electrons, Airships, all seem to be known to the seers who found the Vedas.

13. Mr. N. B. Pavgee writes. "I may take this opportunity to remind the Reader, without fear of contradiction, that the Vedas contain many things not yet known to any body, as they form a mine of inexhaustible literary wealth, that has only partially been opened, and, has still remained unexplored."[1]

The same author writes in another book of his: 'The Veda is the fountain head of knowledge, the prime source of inspiration, nay the grand repository of pithy passages of Divine wisdom and even eternal truths.'[2]

'THE VEDIC AGE,' AN OBSCURE AND UNRELIABLE BOOK

The Vedic Age has been published by the Bharatiya Vidya Bhawan, Bombay. Shri K.M. Munshi along with others is its Chief Editor. It is a book replete with misconceptions, misstatements, distortion of facts and probabilities. The writers have followed the western scholars like Bloomfield, Max Müller and Macdonell, whose sole aim is to establish the superiority of the Bible, and lower the loftiness and grandeur of the Vedas in the eyes of the world. It requires a separate book to give a fitting reply to all the charges, accusations and insinuations made in this book. I shall briefly allude to a few charges in this brief introduction, and try to show their hollowness and absurdity.

1. The guests are entertained with the flesh of cows killed on the occasion of marriage, The Vedic Age, p. 389.

This is purely a false accusation. A cow is generally spoken of as अघ्न्या and अदिति, i.e., not worthy of being murdered.

(a) सुयवसाद् भगवती हि भूया अथो वयं भगवन्तः स्याम् ।
अद्धि तृणमघ्न्ये विश्ववदानीं पिब शुद्धमुदकमाचरन्ती ॥   *Rigveda*, 1-164-40

In this verse the cow has been addressed as Aghaneya, i.e., not fit for murder. The cow has been asked to eat grass, drink pure water, and remain healthy. May we, drinking thy good milk be virtuous, learned and prosperous.

(b) In *Rigveda* 1.64.27, the cow is spoken of as अघ्न्या' not fit to be killed.

(c) In *Rig* 4-1-6, the cow is again spoken of as अघ्न्या. Its milk and ghee are recommended for use.

(d) In *Rig* 5-83-8, she is spoken of as अघ्न्या. The earth and the atmosphere should be filled with her pure ghee through Havan.

(e) In *Rig* 7-68-9 the cow is again spoken of as अघ्न्या. A devotee of God is spoken of as an early riser, whom the unassailable cow feeds with her pure milk.

[1]*The Vedic Fathers of Geology*, introduction, p. 6.
[2]*Vedic India Mother of Parliaments*, p. 136.

(f) In *Rig* 8-69-2 and *Samaveda* verse 1512 the cow is spoken of as unworthy of being killed.

(g) In *Rig* 9-1-9 the cow is spoken of as unkillable, whose milk is highly beneficial for the children.

(h) In *Rig* 9-93-3, the cow is spoken of as unmurderable, whose milk is highly efficacious for the wise and learned persons.

(i) In *Rig* 10-6-11, the cow is again mentioned as अघ्न्या whose milk purifies the mind and keeps it free from sin.

(j) In *Rig* 10-87-16, the cow is spoken of as unworthy of murder, and severe punishment is prescribed for him who kills her.

(k)   य: पौरुषेयेण क्रविषा समङ्क्ते यो अश्व्येन पशुना यातुधान: ।

यो अघ्न्याया भरति क्षीरमग्ने तेषां शीर्षाणि हरसापि वृश्च ॥   *Rig*, 10-87-16

If a violent sinner be not amenable to reason, and kills a cow, he should be beheaded for his heinous act.

(l)   विषं गवां यातुधाना भरन्तामा वृश्चन्तामदितये दुरेवा: ।

परैणान् देव: सविता ददातु परा भागमोषधीनां जयन्ताम् ॥   *Atharva*, 8-3-16

Monsters who administer poison to cows and kill them, and if ignoble persons cut a cow to pieces, then the King should expel them out of his Kingdom, and debar them from food and medicine.

(m)   माता रुद्राणां दुहिता वसूनां स्वसादित्यानाम् अमृतस्य नाभि: ।

प्र नु वोचं चिकितुषे जनाय मा गामनागामदिति वधिष्ट ॥   *Rig*, 8-101-15

A cow is like a mother unto the Rudra Brahmchāris, a daughter unto the Vasu Brahmchāris, a sister unto the Āditya Brahmchāris, and the storehouse of valuable milk and ghee. I (God) preach unto all sensible persons, never to kill this innocent, unmurderable cow. *Rigveda* 8-101-15.

(n)   इमं साहस्रं शतधारमुत्सं व्यच्यमानं सरिरस्य मध्ये ।

घृतं दुहानामदिति जनायाग्ने मा हिंसी: परमे व्योमन् ॥   *Yajur*, 13-49

O King, for the benefit of humanity, kill not this cow, the source of innumerable comforts, the yielder of limitless streams of milk, the fountain of diverse nourishment, the furnisher of ghee, and unworthy of murder.

(o) In *Yajurvedas* 30-18 the killer of a cow deserves to be hanged.

अन्तकाय गोघातम् ।

(p) Similar sentiments are expressed in *Atharva* 3-30-1, 4-21-6

यदि नो गां हंसि यद्यश्वं यदि पूरुषम् ।

तं त्वा सीसेन विध्यामो यथा नोऽसो अवीरहा ॥   *Atharva*, 1-16-4

O sinner, if thou wilt kill our cow, horse or man, we will shoot thee with a lead bullet. The copious quotations of Vedic verses by me amply negate and militate against the remarks of the Vedic Age, that beef was served on occasions of marriage in ancient times.

(2) 'As the Rigvedic Aryas were full of the joy of life, they were not particularly interested in the life after death, much less had they any special doctrines about it. We can therefore glean only a few notices of the life beyond, that are scattered throughout the *Rigveda*. In our search for any reference implicit or explicit, to rebirth or transmigration we come across only a few doubtful passages" *The Vedic Age*, p. 381.

The author of *The Vedic Age* do not find in the Vedas clear references to transmigration of soul.

(a) अपश्यं गोपामनिपद्यमानमा च परा च पथिभिश्चरन्तम् ।
स सध्रीची: स विषूचीर्वसान आ वरीवर्ति भुवनेष्वन्त: ॥   *Rig*, 1-164-31

May I have a glance at the indestructible lord of the sense-organs (i.e., the individual soul) which ever walks, through the pathways of coming (birth) and departure (death); it traverses its path with its body and even without it and having covered itself with its actions (i.e., in accordance with its good and evil actions) it comes (takes birth) again and again in the various worlds. No stronger proof of the transmigration of soul can there be had.

(b) त्वं स्त्री त्वं पुमानसि त्वं कुमार उत वा कुमारी ।
त्वं जीर्णो दण्डेन वञ्चसि त्वं जातो भवसि विश्वतोमुख: ॥
उतैषां पितोत वा पुत्र एषामुतैषां ज्येष्ठ: उत वा कनिष्ठ: ।
एको ह देवो मनसि प्रविष्ठ: प्रथमो जात: स उ गर्भे अन्त: ॥ *Atharva*, 10.8.27-28

O Individual soul in accordance with thy actions, thou assumest the form of a woman and that of a man, sometimes thou becomest a virgin, thou walkest with the help of a staff when the body becomes old and frail, thou takest birth again and again as thy face is turned towards all directions (in accordance with thy actions).

The individual soul sometimes becomes their father and sometimes their son too, and sometimes it becomes their elder brother and sometimes it even becomes their younger brother. Verily the oneself or luminous soul dwelling within the mind has taken birth before and verily it again enters the womb of the mother.

These two verses clearly establish the doctrine of the transmigration of soul.

(c) अप्स्वग्ने सधिष्टव सौषधीरनुरुध्यसे ।
गर्भे सन् जायसे पुन: ॥   *Yajur*, 12-36

O self-luminous soul! thou art the endurer of sufferings, thou attainest to the plants within the waters, thou takest birth again and again in the womb of the mother.

(d) प्रसद्य भस्मना योनिमपश्च पृथिवीमग्ने ।
संसृज्य मातृभिष्ट्वं ज्योतिष्मान् पुनरासद: ॥   *Yajur*, 12-38

O self-luminous soul ! thou art full of light, after thy body becomes ashes, thou reachest water and earth, the source of birth, and dwelling within the womb of mother, thou takest birth again and again. *Yajur*, 12-38.

(e) असुनीते पुनरस्मासु चक्षुः पुनः प्राणमिह नो धेहि भोगम् ।
ज्योक् पश्येम सूर्यमुच्चरन्तमनुमते मृडया नः स्वस्ति ॥   *Rig*, X-59-6

O God of life ! Please give us eyes again in our future life and give us breath in this world and confer on us all necessary objects of enjoyment. O most Gracious Being ! may we see the rising sun for a long time, be kind upon us and give us blessing.

(f) पुनर्मनः पुनरायुर्मे आगन् पुनः प्राणः पुनरात्मा म आगन् पुनश्चक्षुः पुनः श्रोत्रम् आगन्
वैश्वानरोऽवधस्तनूपा अग्निनः पातु दुरितादवद्यात् ॥   *Yajur*, 4-15

May I receive, through the grace of God, my mind again in future life, may I have life again, may I get breath again, may my soul return again and may I be the possessor of eyes and ears again in future life. May Self-Refulgent God, the Protector of my body. Who is the Ever-living God keep us safe from misfortune and dishonour.

(g) अन्तर्गर्भश्चरति देवतास्वाभूतो भूतः स उ जायते पुनः ।
स भूतो भव्यं भविष्यत् पिता पुत्रं प्र विवेशा शचीभिः ॥   *Atharva*, 11-4-20

The individual soul wanders within the womb of mother and takes birth again and again in the bodies of enlightened persons. It exists in past, present and future; when it becomes a father, it again enters into the body of a son with the powers of his actions.

(h) पुनर्नो असुं पृथिवी दधातु पुनर्द्यौर्देवी पुनरन्तरिक्षम् ।
पुननः सोमस्तन्वं ददातु पुनः पूषा पथ्यां या स्वस्ति ॥   *Rig*, 10-59-7

May the Earth give us breath again and may the shining heavenly region and the atmosphere restore the same to us; may Soma, All-creating God give us body again after our death, and may the All-Nourishing God lead us on the path of peace and happiness.

(i) पुनर्मेत्विन्द्रियं पुनरात्मा द्रविणं ब्राह्मणं च ।
पुनरग्नयो धिष्ण्या यथास्थाम कल्पयन्तामिहैव ॥   *Atharva*, 7-67-1

May I again receive my sense-organs in my future life and may I receive my spirit, together with worldly possessions and knowledge Divine, so that I may perform fire-offering on the altars and may ever attain prosperity.

3. The hymn (R 10-117) is packed with noble sentiments and its every word is charged with vigour. Yet it should not be forgotten that the hectoring eloquence of this energetic priest was probably directed mainly to the purpose of frightening the wealthy into ceding a part of wealth to the Brahmanas especially, and not to the poor of every class, for of genuine sympathy for the poor, there is not much in the *Rigveda*. *The Vedic Age*, p. 342.

These remarks are highly inappropriate and unjustifiable, for the Vedas sing the glory of charity to the poor.

(a) त्वमग्ने प्रयतदक्षिणं नरं वर्मेव स्यूतं परि पासि विश्वतः ।

स्वादुक्षद्मा यो वसतौ स्योनकृज्जीवयाजं यजते सोपमा दिवः ॥   *Rig*, 1-31-15

O Self-refulgent Lord, like a well-sewn armour Thou dost protect the man from all sides, who is liberal in benefactions to others, the man possessed of tasteful means of subsistence, who remains ever engaged in gratifying others, and who performs sacrifice for all the living beings, is really the type of heaven (on earth)! In this verse a rich man is asked to be charitable not only to the Brahmanas, but to all living beings, be they high or low, rich or poor. The Vedic teachings are free from favouritism, nepotism or sordid low-mindedness.

(b) दक्षिणावतामिदिमानि चित्रा दक्षिणावतां दिवि सूर्यासः ।

दक्षिणावन्तो अमृतं भजन्ते, दक्षिणावन्तः प्रतिरन्ति आयुः ॥   *Rig*, 1-1-5-6

Surely all these wonderful objects of the world belong to such persons as are of Charitable disposition, even the sun and the stars shine in the heaven for the liberal-minded, the benevolent men attain to immortality and fully qualified persons enjoy full life.

In the whole of 117th Sūkta of the tenth Maṇḍal, about which Dr. Ghosh, one of the authors of *The Vedic Age*, has made uncharitable remarks on page 342, there is no reference whatsoever to a priest (Purohit) begging for alms, or a Brahman to whom charity should be given in preference to low-caste poor persons. Below I give a few mantras from R 10-117 to prove the futility of the remarks of Dr. Ghosh in *The Vedic Age*.

(c) य आध्राय चकमानाय पित्वो अन्नवान्त्सन्नफितायोपजग्मुषे ।

स्थिरं मनः कृणुते सेवते पुरोतो चित् स मडितारं न विन्दते ॥   *Rig*, 10-117-2

The man, who, possessing means of subsistence, to whom when any needy person, fallen in miserable condition, comes begging for food, hardens his heart against that poor man and enjoys (his food) in very presence, does not find any comforter when he falls in need.

(d) सइद् भोजो यो गृह्वे ददात्यन्नकामाय चरते कृशाय ।

अरमस्मै भवति यामहूता उतापरीषु कृणुते सखायम् ॥   *Rig*, 10-117-3

Verily that man takes delight in his possession who gives liberally to such a feeble person that comes to his house being in need of food. Such a man gets sufficient means for charity at proper time, and he befriends others on the occasion of his future difficulties.

(e) मोघमन्नं विन्दते अप्रचेताः सत्यं ब्रवीमि वध इत स तस्य ।

नार्यमणं पुष्यति नो सखायं केवलाघो भवति केवलादी ॥   *Rig*, 10-117-6

The foolish man acquires means of subsistence with fruitless labour or in vain. I (God) tell you the truth that the very means of subsistence and his wealth will be the cause of his ruin, for with that he serves neither his friends nor does good to the noble-minded, justice-loving persons. Verily the man who enjoys his wealth alone without utilising it for the good of others is the embodiment of sin only.

4. Absence of evil is not what they pray for most. Their supreme desire is to triumph over poverty and resistance. *The Vedic Age*, p. 343.

This is a highly unjust and unfair criticism, that Vedic Rishis did not pray for sinlessness, they simply wanted to overcome poverty and avoid resistance. In all the four Vedas, if there is one topic for which there is the greatest prayer, it is sinlessness.

In Rigveda Maṇḍal, 1, Sūkta 97 there are eight verses, at the end of each one of which occur the following words, अप न: शोशुचदघम् which mean, O God remove in entirety our sin. I give below a few Vedic verses to prove that Rishis of Vedic times prayed intensely for freedom from sin.

(a) प्र यत् ते अग्ने सूरयो जायेमहि प्र ते वयम् ।
    अप न: शोशुचदघम् ॥   *Rig,* 1-97-4

O God, just as learned persons in obedience to Your behests become great, so may we become virtuous under Thy protection. O God, remove in entirety our sin!

(b) त्वंहि विश्वतोमुख विश्वत: परिभूरसि ।
    अप न: शोशुचदघम् ॥   *Rig,* 1-97-6

O God, Thou are All-pervading and Omnipotent, remove in entirety our sin!

(c) स न: सिन्धुमिव नावयाति पर्षा स्वस्तये ।
    अप न: शोशुचदघम् ॥   *Rig,* 1-97-8

O God, just as an ocean is crossed with a steam boat, so may we complete this journey for acquiring happiness, peace and nobility. Remove Thou in entirety our sin!

(d) युष्माकं मित्रावरुणा प्रणीतो परिश्वभ्रेव दुरितानि वृज्याम् ।   *Rig,* 2-27-5

O teacher and preacher, may I under your leadership, renounce the sins, which take me down to the depth of degradation.

(e) आरे अस्मदमुतिमारे अंह आरे विश्वां दुर्मतिं यन्निपासि ॥   *Rig,* 4-11-6

O God, as Thou art our good Guardian, we pray upto Thee, to keep far away from us, ignorance, sin, and every sort of unwisdom.

(f) अया धिया स्याम देवगोपा अया धिया तुतुर्यामात्यंह: ॥   *Rig,* 5-45-11

O learned persons, may we through this pure intellect become the votaries of God, may we through this pure intellect totally shun sin.

(g) अग्ने रक्षा णो अंहस: प्र तिष्म देव रीषत: । तपिष्ठैरजरो दह ॥   *Rig,* 7-15-13

O Wise God, protect us from sin, guard us against a violent person. O Immortal God burn down sin with Thy powers that punish the ignoble!

(h) त्वं न: पाह्यंहसो दोषावस्तरघायत: । दिवा नक्तमदाभ्य: ॥   *Rig,* 7-15- 5

O Wise God, protect us from sin, always protect us from a sinful person day and night!

(i) ऋतस्य मित्रावरुणा पथा वाम् अपो न नावा दुरिता तरेम ॥   *Rig,* 7-65-3

O teacher and preacher, the lovers of all, and the dispellers of darkness, treading on the path of truth, as preached by Ye, may we cross the stream of sin (be far from sin) as men cross a stream with a boat!

(j) यद् ग्रामे यदरण्ये यत्सभायां यदिन्द्रिये ।
यदेनश्चक्रमा वयमिदं तदवयजामहे ॥   *Yajur,* 3-45

May we forsake each sinful act that we have committed in village or solitude, in an assembly or corporeal sense. Let every man so resolve.

(k) चितपतिर्मा पुनातु वाक्पतिर्मा पुनातु देवो मा सविता पुनात्वच्छिद्रेण पवित्रेण सूर्यस्य रश्मिभिः । तस्य ते पवित्रपते पवित्रपूतस्य यत्काम: पुने तच्छकेयम् ॥   *Yajur,* 4-4

Purify me, the Lord of Purity. Purify me, the Lord of Knowledge, Purify me, the Lord of the Vedas. O Lord, Creator of the universe, purify me through sunbeams and Thy immortal purifying Knowledge. O Master of the purified souls, may I full of lofty sentiments accomplish the desire actuated by which through your grace, I purify myself!

(l) परिमाग्ने दुश्चरिताद् बाधस्वा मा सुचरिते भज ।
उदायुषा स्वायुषोदस्थाममृतां अनु ॥   *Yajur,* 4-28

O God, dissuade me from sin, and establish me firmly in righteousness. May I enjoy the pleasure of final beatitude by leading a long and virtuous life!

(m) अपामीवानप सृधमप सेधत दुर्मतिम् ।
आदित्यासो यूयोतना नो अंहस: ॥   *Sāma,* 397

O learned persons, drive Ye, disease and strife away, drive Ye away malignity; keep us far removed from sin!

(n) यद् विद्वांसो यदविद्वांसो एनांसि चक्रमा वयम् ।
यूयं नस्तस्मान्मुञ्चत विश्वे देवा: सजोषस: ॥   *Atharva,* 6-115-1

O righteous learned persons, release us with your sermon from the sin we have committed, knowingly and unknowingly!

(o) यो न: पाप्मन् न जहासि तमु त्वा जहिमो वयम् ॥   *Atharva,* 6-26-2

O sin, if thou dost not leave us, we leave thee for ever!

(p) ब्रजॆष्माद्यासनामाद्याभूमानागसो वयम् ॥   *Atharva*, 16-6-1

Today shall we conquer sin and enjoy comfort, peace and pleasure.
Today we have become free from sin.

These are a few quotations from the Vedas to refute the allegations of the
writers of *The Vedic Age*, that Vedic Rishis cared little to keep themselves
free from sin.

There are various other wrong allegations made in the Vedic Age, e.g.,
Polygamy, the Atharvaveda being full of charms, spells, magic, sorcery and
witch-craft. Bal Khilya (49th to 56th) Sūktas in the 8th Maṇḍal of the *Rigveda* being interpolations, the ignorance of Panini about the *Shukla Yajurveda*, the 15th, 17th, 18th and 19th Kāṇḍas of the *Atharvaveda* being later
compilations and hence late accretions, the 10th Maṇḍal of the *Rigveda*
being of later origin (vide *The Vedic Age*, p. 229). It is difficult to discuss all
these topics in a brief introduction to my translation.

ANTIQUITY OF THE VEDAS

Maharshi Dayanand believes that the Vedas are as old as the Earth. They
are the Word of God, and were revealed in the beginning of creation. The
Aryan era at present is 1,97,29,49,061.

Kalyug is a period of 4,32,000 years, Dwapar is a period of 8,64,000 years,
Treta is a period of 12,96,000 years. Satyuga is a period of 17,28,000 years.
A Chataryugi (the combined period of all the four yugas) lasts for 43,20,000
years. The world lasts for 1000 Chataryugis, i.e. for 4320000000 years. This
view expressed by Maharshi Dayanand in the *Rigveda Bhashya Bhumika*,
and by the author of *Surya Sidhanta* is corroborated by a Vedic text, शतं
तेऽयुतं हायनान् द्वे युगे त्रीणि चत्वारि कृष्ण: ॥   *Atharva*, 8-2-21

Multiply ten thousand years by one hundred, and place against this
number the digits 2, 3, 4, and we get 43,20,00,0000 years as the period for
which the world lasts. Scholars have expressed different views about the age
of the Vedas and the world. Below I give a few quotations.

(a) "We could not hope to be able to lay down any terminus a quo.
Whether the Vedic hymns were composed in 1000 or 1500 or 2000 or 3000
years BC no power on earth can ever fix."[1]

(b) "Any such attempt (of defining the Vedic antiquity) is absolutely
fruitless."[2]

(c) "In reality nothing more has been known than that the Vedic period
extends from an altogether undefined past to the fifth Century before Christ.
Neither the figures 1200 to 500, nor 1500 to 500, 2000 to 500, which are
often to be met with in the popular account about the age of the Vedic
literature have any justification. The only date justifiable is X to 500 BC.

---

[1]Max Müller's *Physical Religion*, p. 18.
[2]*History of Sanskrit Literature* by Bewer, p. 7.

We must however guard against giving any definite figures, where such a possibility is, by the nature of the case, excluded."[1]

(d) "From what has already been said, it will be evident that no date can be assigned to the origin of the hymns that make up the Vedas. Indeed it is necessary to go further and to say that there is not sufficient evidence to show with any precision when the hymns of the four Vedas were collected together and the Vedas themselves as we have them, formed."[2]

(e) Shri Dina Nath Shastri Chulet, an astrologer, has written in his book *Vedakala Nirneya* that the Vedas are 3 lakh years old. He has corroborated his statement with quotation from books on astrology, Shri Sampurnanand's '*Aryon Kā Ādi Desh*, p.223.'

(f) *Rāmāyaṇa*, Ayodhya Kaṇḍa 1-20 Shri Ram Chandra is spoken of as possessing the knowledge of the Vedas along with their Angas. Rāmāyaṇa was written in Treta Yuga, which means the Vedas existed more than 8 lakh years ago.

(g) The *Rigveda* must be held to be as old as the Miocene or the Pliocene Epoch whose age is to be computed by some hundreds of thousands, if not Millions of years. This at first sight would seem to be extremely incredible. But it may be mentioned here in passing, that the Indo Aryans believe the *Rigvedo* to be as old as the creation of man, in other words, to have emanated from Brahmā; the Creator Himself, and is regarded as Apaurusheya i.e., not ascribable to any human agency, though the Rishis or seers might have clothed the revealed truths and eternal verities in language of their own, from time to time. This bereft of all exaggerations, would mean that the *Rigveda* has existed from time immemorial. To this belief of the Indo Aryans, however absurd it might seem, the results of geological investigations, undoubtedly lend some strong colour.[3]

(h) Some good evidence that the real age of the Earth is two or three thousand million years has been supplied by the study of the proportions of Uranium and an isotope of lead (into which it slowly changes) in the various rocks.[4]

(i) "The weight of scientific evidence is against an infinitely extended past, but the past which we formerly reckoned as six thousand years cannot be shorter than 800 Million and be far longer."[5]

This calculation is approximate to the Vedic viewpoint of Swami Dayanand.

(j) "The age of the Earth is about two thousand Million years." This is exactly what the Arya Samaj believes, and nearly coincides with the Aryan era.[6]

[1] *The Age of the Veda* by Winternitz, translated by N.B. Utgikar, p. 4.
[2] *The Rigveda and Vedic Religion* by A.C. Clayton, p. 45.
[3] *Rigvedic India* by Dr. A. C. Das, p. 21.
[4] *Science Past and Present* by Sherwood Taylor, p. 235.
[5] ibid, p. 237.
[6] *Outline of Modern Knowledge*, p. 152.

(k) "Our globe must be about two thousand Million years old and can in no case be much older."[1]

(l) "Astronomers and Mathematicians give us 2000 Million years as the age of the Earth as a body separate from the Sun."[2]

(m) "This tradition attributes to the vast reservoir of the wisdom that somewhere took shape simultaneously with the origin of man ...... to more spiritual entities, to being less entangled in matter."[3]

Concluding Remarks.

After completing and publishing my translation of the *Yajurveda* in 1959, I took up the self-imposed task of translating the *Sāmaveda* Thank God, through persistent application, constant labour for two years, and iron determination, I have been able to fulfil this resolve of mine, in spite of my multifarious activities. I am not a scholar, nor do I possess a thorough knowledge of Sanskrit. I am a mere devotee of the Vedas. I am a fallible human being and claim no perfection for my work. Errors might have crept into my translation, which, if pointed out by learned scholars, will be acknowledged and rectified in the second edition. The readers should appreciate my sincerity and faith and overlook my shortcomings. I believe in evolution in Vedic translation and not in finality. I sincerely express my obligation to those scholars whose works I copiously consulted and where from derived assistance and information in my translation. My sincere thanks are due to Dr. Dina Nath, B.A., LL.B. Ex-Public Prosecutor Ex-Official-Receiver, Gurdaspur and Ex-Manager D.A.V. High Schools, Behrampur, Gurdaspur, Dhariwal and Qadian, who lent me valuable help in going through the manuscript with me, and making useful suggestions for improving the language of this translation, and Lala Shankar Das Trehan, Jullundur, for valuable assistance rendered in going through the manuscript. But for this help, the publication of the work would have inordinately been delayed.

DEVI CHAND

President

All India Dayanand Salvation Mission.

Hoshiarpur,
23rd April, 1961.

---

[1] *Human History*, p. 48.
[2] *Outline of History* by H.G. Wells, p. 19.
[3] *Great Secret* by Materlink, Prologue, p. 6.

The Samāveda

Pūrvarchika (Chhandarchika)

ĀGNEYA KĀṆDA

BOOK I*

Chapter 1**

DECADE I

१. अग्न आ याहि वीतये गृणानो हव्यदातये । नि होता सत्सि बर्हिषि ॥

1. O God, we realise Thee, as Thou art Lnminous, Pervading and Giver of enjoyable objects. Thou art Worthy of adoration, present in the world and our soul, like a Hota in the Yajna. (1)[1]

२. त्वमग्ने यज्ञानाꣳ होता विश्वेषाꣳ हित: । देवेभिर्मानुषे जने ॥

2. O God, Thou art the Accepter of all prayers. The learned have held Thee Adorable by mankind, like fire in a yajna. (2)

३. अग्निं दूतं वृणीमहे होतारं विश्ववेदसम् । अस्य यज्ञस्य सुक्रतुम् ॥

3. We accept God, the Revealer of the Vedas, as Worshipful, All-knowing, All-Giving, and Maker of the Universe. (3)

४. अग्निर्वृत्राणि जङ्घनद् द्रविणस्युर्विपन्यया । समिद्ध: शुक्र आहुत: ॥

4. May God, the Accepter of the devotion of the learned devotees through prayer, Bright, Pure, worshipped duly, remove the sins that surround the soul. (4)

५. प्रेष्ठं वो अतिथिꣳस्तुषे मित्रमिव प्रियम् । अग्ने रथं न वेद्यम् ॥

5. I praise God, Dearest unto you all, lovable like a friend. All pervading and worthy of respect like a guest. O Effulgent Lord, Thou art the grantor of all objects like a war-chariot. (5)[2]

६. त्वं नो अग्ने महोभि: पाहि विश्वस्या अराते: । उत द्विषो मर्त्यस्य ॥

6. O God, guard us against the malignant foe and the hate of mortal man. (6)

---

*is Prapāthaka I.

**is Ardh Prapāthaka I.

[1]आ याहि literally means 'come.' The coming of God means His realisation. Griffith has translated Agni as material fire, whereas it refers to God.

[2]Just as a war-chariot grants us victory, which secures us worldly wealth, so does God grant us all desired objects.

७. एह्यू षु ब्रवाणि तेऽग्न इत्थेतरा गिरः । एभिर्वर्धास इन्दुभिः ॥

7. O God, come, I utter divine and worldly words for Thee. Thy glory is higher than these worldly splendours. (7)[1]

८. आ ते वत्सो मनो यमत्परमाच्चित्सधस्थात् । अग्ने त्वां कामये गिरा ॥

8. O God, like a devoted son, I receive Thy true knowledge in my highly exalted soul. I long for Thee through praise. (8)

९. त्वामग्ने पुष्करादध्यथर्वा निरमन्थत । मूर्ध्नो विश्वस्य वाघतः ॥

9. O God, a non-violent learned person realises Thee, the Driver of all through meditation in his heart like fire through churning. (9)[2]

१०. अग्ने विवस्वदा भरास्मभ्यमूतये महे । देवो ह्यसि नो दृशे ॥

10. O God, for our full protection, grant us a grand, comfortable house, Thou alone art the Supreme Lord to show us the right path. (10)

DECADE II

१. नमस्ते अग्न ओजसे गृणन्ति देव कृष्टयः । अमैरमित्रमर्दय ॥

1. O God, we bow unto Thee; energetic people sing reverent praise to Thee for strength. With Thy might eclipse Thou the foe. (11)

२. दूतं वो विश्ववेदसꣳ हव्यवाहममर्त्यम् । यजिष्ठमृञ्जसे गिरा ॥

2. O God, Admirable like a messenger, Omniscient, Giver of the fruit of our actions, Immortal, Worthy of highest respect, I sing Thy praise through Vedic verses. (12)

३. उप त्वा जामयो गिरो देदिशतीर्हविष्कृतः । वायोरनीके अस्थिरन् ॥

3. O God, the hymns of a devotee, unfolding Thy traits, find a repose in Thee, and realise Thee, the Omnipresent Lord. (13)

४. उप त्वाग्ने दिवेदिवे दोषावस्तर्धिया वयम् । नमो भरन्त एमसि ॥

4. O God, may we daily, morning and evening, with our intellect, worship Thee, offering Thee reverence. (14)

---

[1]The language is figurative, Coming of God means realising Him through contemplation. The soul prays to God for spiritual and worldly progress.

[2]Just as fire is kindled by rubbing together two wooden sticks, so is God realised by the soul through deep and intense meditation. Griffith translates Atharvan as the sage who was the first to obtain fire, to institute sacrifice, and to offer up prayer and libations of Soma. This interpretation is inadmissible, as there is no history in the Vedas, Pt. Jaidev Vidyalankar has rightly translated the word to mean 'non-violent'.

५. जराबोध तद्विविड्ढि विशेविशे यज्ञियाय । स्तोम꣡ꣳरुद्राय दृशीकम् ॥

5. O God, knowable through praise, for the good of all, abide Thyself in our heart. We sing beautiful laudation, for Thee, the just Chastiser of the wicked and Worthy of adoration. (15)

६. प्रति त्यं चारुमध्वरं गोपीथाय प्र हूयसे । मरुद्भिरग्न आ गहि ॥

6. O God, we invoke Thee, for the protection of the beautiful, non-violent and immortal soul. May Thou be manifested in our hearts by the learned. (16)[1]

७. अश्वं न त्वा वारवन्तं वन्दध्या अग्ने नमोभिः । सम्राजन्तमध्वराणाम् ॥

7. With homage, O God, I revere like a long-tailed steed, Thee, imperial Lord of non-violent religious deeds. (17)[2]

८. और्वभृगुवच्छुचिमप्नवानवदा हुवे । अग्निꣳ समुद्रवाससम् ॥

8. I invoke God All-Pure, residing in the heart, as do the men of knowledge and action. (18)[3]

९. अग्निमिन्धानो मनसा धियꣳ सचेत मर्त्यः । अग्निमिन्धे विवस्वभिः ॥

9. Man, kindling God in mind, develops his intellect, I realise the Effulgent Lord in my heart, in the company of the learned. (19)[4]

१०. आदित्प्रत्नस्य रेतसो ज्योतिः पश्यन्ति वासरम् । परो यदिध्यते दिवि ॥

10. The Sun that shines on the yonder side of heaven, which the people see all the day long, verily receives light from the Refulgent Primeval God. (20)[5]

---

[1]Griffith translates Maruts as the gods of wind and storm, the special friends and allies of Indra. Pt. Jaidev Vidyalankar translates the word as learned persons or breaths. If we take the word to mean breaths then the latter part of the verse will mean, that God is attainable through Pranayam and Yoga.

[2]Just as a horse with the hair of his tail, wards off flies and mosquitoes that bite him, so does God remove from our soul the evil passions of lust and anger.

[3]समुद्र means Antriksha, i.e., the heart.

और्वभृगु means, vide Swami Tulsi Ram's commentary, men of Knowledge, who know the Rgveda. and अप्नवान means the men of action, who knowing the Yajurveda, rightly perform rituals (Karma Kanda).

[4]विवस्वभिः has been translated by Swami Tulsi Ram as rays of the Sun. In early dawn when the rays of the sun begin to shine, one should perform Sandhya, and say his daily prayer. Pt. Jaidev Vidyalankar translates the word in the company of the learned persons.

[5]Which refers to the Sun.

DECADE III

१. अग्नि वो वृधन्तमध्वराणां पुरूतमम् । अच्छा नप्त्रे सहस्वते ।

1. Worship reverently God, the Augmenter of your non-violent philanthropic deeds, the Lord of mighty worlds, Your Friend, and Omnipotent. (21)

२. अग्निस्तिग्मेन शोचिषा यꣳद्विश्वं न्यꣳत्रिणम् । अग्निर्नो वꣳसते रयिम् ॥

2. God, through His lustrous splendour subdues the ignoble foes of men. He alone grants us the wealth of spirituality. (22)

३. अग्ने मृड महाꣳ असयय आ देवयुं जनम् । इयेथ बहिरासदम् ॥

3. O God, be gracious, Thou art great, Thou art attained by a pious man. Thou comest to reside in our heart. (23)[1]

४. अग्ने रक्षा णो अꣳहस: प्रति स्म देव रीषत: । तपिष्ठेरजरो दह ॥

4. O God, save us from sin and disease, O Eternal Lord, consume our mental foes, with Thy austerest dignity. (24)[2]

५. अग्ने युङ्क्ष्वा हि ये तवाश्वासो देव साधव: । अरं वहन्त्याशव: ॥

5. O Effulgent God, harness in the practice of Yoga, the organs, fast like a horse. They nicely lead us to our goal. (25)[3]

६. नि त्वा नक्ष्य विश्पते द्युमन्तं धीमहे वयम् । सुवीरमग्न आहुत ॥

6. We worship Thee, O God, worthy of reverence, Lord of mankind, invoked by all, Refulgent and Supereminently Heroic. (26)

७. अग्निर्मूर्धा दिव: ककुत्पति: पृथिव्या अयम् । अपाꣳरेताꣳसि जिन्वति ॥

7. The self-same God is the Head of all, Pre-eminent like the Sun, the Master of Earth, and the Knower of the seeds of deeds. (27)[1]

८. इममू षु त्वमस्माकꣳ सनि गायत्रं नव्याꣳसम् । अग्ने देवेषु प्र वोच: ॥

8. O God, Thou graciously preachest to the learned, this our reverential effectual prayer of the Gayatri verse. (28)

---

[1]The coming of God is a figurative language for His attainment.

[2]Mental foes: Anger, Avarice, Lust etc.

[3]Goal: Salvation. 'They' refers to the organs. Our organs are fleeting like a horse. The practice of Yoga can cool and calm them down to enable us to reach our destination i.e., salvation.

[4]Griffith translates Apām as waters, whereas it means action. Pt. Jaidev Vidyalankar translates the latter half of the verse as 'God grants life to the animate and inanimate creation of all the worlds'.

९. तं त्वा गोपवनो गिरा जनिष्ठदग्ने अङ्गिरः । स पावक श्रुधी हवम् ॥

9. O God, a devotee who controls his organs and speech, manifests Thee through praise, O Refulgent Lord, Remover of the sin of ignorance, hear Thou my invocation. (29)[1]

१०. परि वाजपतिः कविरग्निर्हव्यान्यक्रमीत् । दधद्रत्नानि दाशुषे ॥

10. God, the Lord of strength and Wisdom, giving precious things to the charity-minded person, accepts our laudations. (30)

११. उदु त्यं जातवेदसं देवं वहन्ति केतवः । दृशे विश्वाय सूर्यम् ॥

11. For the good of humanity, the learned as seers, verily dilate upon God, the Creator of the Vedas, the Embodiment of purity and effulgence. (31)[2]

१२. कविमग्निमुप स्तुहि सत्यधर्माणमध्वरे । देवममीवचातनम् ॥

12. O man, in this Yajna of life, praise God, who is Omniscient, Whose holy laws are true. Who is endowed with divine qualities and is Healer of physical and spiritual diseases. (32)

१३. शं नो देवीरभिष्टये शं नो भवन्तु पीतये । शंयोरभि स्रवन्तु नः ॥

13. May the divine powers of God be kind for our desired happiness and satisfaction. May they rain happiness all round us. (33)

१४. कस्य नूनं परीणसि धियो जिन्वसि सत्पते । गोषाता यस्य ते गिरः ॥

14. O Lord of the saints, Thou graciously fulfillest the various ambitions of him, whose praise for Thee is designed to control his organs. (34)[3]

DECADE IV

१. यज्ञायज्ञा वो अग्नये गिरागिरा च दक्षसे ।
प्रप्र वयममृतं जातवेदसं प्रियं मित्रं न शंसिषम् ॥

1. O men, sing the glory of the Omnipotent God at every sacrifice, with each vedic verse. Let us praise Everlasting God, Creator of the Vedas, as a well-beloved friend. (35)

[1]Griffith has not translated the words 'Gopvan' and 'Angira' and has put them as they are, Gopvan means a devotee who controls his organs and speech. Angira means the 'Refulgent Lord'.

Griffith considers Angiras as a name of Agni regarded as the best or eldest of the primeval priestly family of the Angiras. This interpretation is wide of the mark.

[2]This verse occurs in Yajurveda 7—41, 8—41, 33—37 and Rgveda 1—50—1, with different interpretations.

[3]Pt. Jaidev Vidyalankar interprets this verse as thus:

O God, whose various acts and ambitions dost Thou fulfil? Of him, who sings Thy praise for controlling his organs. The first half of the verse puts a question, which is replied in the latter half. He interprets the word कस्य in an interrogatory sense. Swami Tulsi Ram interprets कस्य as denoting happiness.

कस्य=कमिति सुखनाम निघं० ३।६।

२. पाहि नो ग्रग्न एकया पाह्य्३त द्वितीयया ।
पाहि गीर्भिस्तसृभिरूर्जां पते पाहि चतसृभिर्वंसो ॥

2. O God, protect us by one Veda (Rig), protect us by the second (Yajur). Protect us by the three Vedas, (Rig, Yajur, Sāma).

O All-pervading Lord of power, protect us by the four Vedas (Rig, Yajur, Sāma, Atharva). (36)[1]

३. बृहद्भिरग्ने ग्रर्चिभिः शुक्रेण देव शोचिषा ।
भरद्वाजे समिधानो यविष्ठ्य रेवत्पावक दीदिहि ॥

3. O Resplendent God, Embodiment of Charity, most Youthful, the lord of riches, Purifier of all, with Thy pure brilliancy, Kindled in the heart of a man of knowledge, strength and action, shine with Thy lofty beams. (37)[2]

४. त्वे ग्रग्ने स्वाहुत प्रियासः सन्तु सुरयः ।
यन्तारो ये मध्वानो जनानामूर्व दयन्त गोनाम् ॥

4. O God, Who art worshipped well, let the learned be dear to Thee. Let the wealthy governors of men, who are great protectors of their organs. Kine and Vedic lore be loved by all. (38)[3]

५. ग्रग्ने जरितर्विश्पतिस्तपानो देव रक्षसः ।
ग्रप्रोषिवान् गृहपते महाँ ग्रसि दिवस्पायुर्दुरोणयुः ॥

5. O Effulgent God, the Instructor of humanity, Lord of men, Thou consumest our evil intentions.

O Lord of universe, Ever-present, Protector of the sky, Well-wisher of the homes and bodies of all, mighty art Thou. (39)

६. ग्रग्ने विवस्वदुषसश्चित्रँ राधो ग्रमर्त्य ।
ग्रा दाशुषे जातवेदो वहा त्वमद्या देवाँ उपर्बुधः ॥

6. O God, prevading Dawn, Thou grantest us various pleasures. Grant knowledge and wealth of diverse nature to him who is charitably disposed.

O Immortal, O Creator of the Vedas, grant to him, the organs, which awaken and receive knowledge with the rise of Sun. (40)[4]

---

[1]Sāyaṇ also interprets चतसृभिः as the four vedas.

[2]Griffith translates Bhardwaj as Bhardwaj, the name of an individual. There is no history in the Vedas, hence there can be no historical reference.

भरद्वाजे means भरद्वब पुरुषार्थिनि पुरुषे ।

[3]'Governors of men' mean Kings.

[4]Those who rise early in the morning and worship God at dawn, receive knowledge from Him, and get their organs of perception awakened. Morning is the best time for prayer. 'Him' in the latter half refers to the charitably disposed person.

७. त्वं नश्चित्र ऊत्या वसो राधाꣳसि चोदय ।
अस्य रायस्त्वमग्ने रथीरसि विदा गाधं तुच्चे तु नः ॥

7. O gracious God, the abode of all, Thou art Wonderful, with The benign help, send us Thy bounties. Thou art the charioteer of earthly wealth, find rest and safety for our progeny. (41)

८. त्वमित्सप्रथा अस्यग्ने त्रातऋ॑तः कविः ।
त्वां विप्रासः समिधान दीदिव आ विवासन्ति वेधसः ॥

8. O God, the Protector, Famed art Thou alone. Thou alone art Righteous, Omniscient. O Enkindled, Radiant God, the learned singers worship Thee. (42).

९. आ नो अग्ने वयोवृध꣠ रयिं पावक शꣳस्यम् ।
रास्वा च न उपमाते पुरुस्पृह꣠ सुनीती सुयशस्तरम् ॥

9. O Purifying Lord, give us wealth which is praise-worthy and life-prolonging. O Creator of the universe, bestow on us through righteousness, wealth which many crave for, and makes us extremely glorious. (43)

१०. यो विश्वा दयते वसु होता मन्द्रो जनानाम् ।
मधोनं पात्रा प्रथमान्यस्मै प्र स्तोमा यन्त्वग्नये ॥

10. God, the Giver of pleasures and the fruits of actions, grants mankind the manifold wealth of knowledge. To Him, like vessels filled with honey, let the primeval Vedic songs go forth. (44)[1]

DECADE V

१. एना वो अग्निं नमसोर्जो नपातमा हुवे ।
प्रियं चेतिष्ठमरति꣠ स्वध्वरं विश्वस्य दूतममृतम् ॥

1. I preach unto Ye, O men, with this verse, "I am the Guardian of strength, Friend unto all, the Giver of knowledge, the Supreme Lord, praiseworthy, the Bestower of the fruits of actions on all, and Immortal." (45)[2]

२. शेषे वनेषु मातृषु सं त्वा मर्तास इन्धते ।
अतन्द्रो हव्यं वहसि हविष्कृत आदिद्देवेषु राजसि ॥

---

[1]Just as vessels are filled with honey, so we should with our mouths filled with the sweet vedic songs of God's praise, recite them.

[2]I refers to God.

Pt. Harish Chandra Vidyalankar translates एना नमसा as with the spirit of self-abnegation, and Pt. Jaidev Vidyalankar interprets the phrase, as 'with this food'. Swami Tulsi Ram interprets it as 'with this vedic verse'. Both Pt. Harish Chandra and Pt. Jaidev interpret आ हुवे as I pray unto God, whereas Pt. Tulsi Ram interprets it as "I (God) preach."

2. O God, Thou liest in our ephemeral bodies and hearts, Reflective Yogis Kindle Thee.

Thou art free from laziness. Thou rewardest the actions of men. Moreover Thou shinest in material objects. (46)

३. अदर्शि गातुवित्तमो यस्मिन्व्रतान्यादधुः ।
उपो षु जातमार्यस्य वर्धनमग्नि नक्षन्तु नो गिरः ॥

3. God appears unto the best knowers of Yogic postures, who dedicate all their acts to Him. May our songs of praise go nigh to Him, Who gives an Arya strength, and reveals Himself to the Yogis. (47)

४. अग्निरुक्थे पुरोहितो ग्रावाणो बहिरध्वरे ।
ऋचा यामि मरुतो ब्रह्मणस्पते देवा अवो वरेण्यम् ॥

4. In the Yajna of speech, a learned person is the chief priest, and his lauds are the grass.

O divine learned persons.

O knower of the Vedas, I crave with vedic song the protection that is most excellent. (48)[1]

५. अग्निमीडिष्वावसे गाथाभिः शीरशोचिषम् ।
अग्निं राये पुरुमीढ श्रुतं नरोऽग्निः सुदीयते छर्दिः ॥

5. O soul, sing with songs of praise, for protection and wealth, the praise of God, whose glory is vast, and Who is well-sung in the Vedas. Ye men, God is a house for nice protection. (49)[2]

६. श्रुधि श्रुत्कर्ण वह्निभिर्देवैरग्ने सयावभिः ।
आ सीदतु बर्हिषि मित्रो अर्यमा प्रातर्यावभिरध्वरे ॥

6. Hear, O man, who hast ears to hear. Just as God, Prāna and Apāna reside in Sushumnā and worshippers, early in the morning practise Yoga, so shouldst thou practise concentration. (50)[3]

७. प्र देवोदासो अग्निर्देव इन्द्रो न मज्मना ।
अनु मातरं पृथिवीं वि वावृते तस्थौ नाकस्य शर्मणि ॥

7. The light of knowledge residing in God, like the Sun, with its might, spreads itself over the Mother Earth, and then culminates in the blessing of salvation. (51)[4]

[1]Just as in a sacrifice, there is the purohit (priest) and grass (kusha) for Hota Adhwaryu, Udgata and Brahma to sit on, so in mental yajna, a learned person is the priest, and praises are the grass.

[2]Just as a house affords us shelter against storm and rain, and inclement weather, so does God protect us from the evil passions of lust, anger, pride and avarice.

[3]Sushumna is a particular artery of the human body in the vicinity of the heart, said to lie between Ida and Pingla, two of the arteries of the body. In this verse God exhorts man to control his breaths and practise Yoga.

[4]Earth is spoken of as Mother, as it gives birth to animate and inanimate creation.

८. अ्रध ज्मो अ्रध वा दिवो बृह्तो रोचनादधि ।
अ्रया वर्धस्व तन्वा गिरा ममा जाता सुक्रतो पृण ॥

8. O God, Thou art extended beneath the Earth, and over the lofty lucid
realm of Heaven, with the same beauty.

O Maker of the beautiful world, with thy Vedic lore, strengthen Thou my
subjects. (52)

६. कांयमानो वना त्वं यन्मातॄरजगन्न्रप: ।
न तत्ते अ्रग्ने प्रमृषे निवर्तनं यद् दूरे सन्निहाभुव: ॥

9. O God, planning the creation of enjoyable worlds, when Thou controllest
the atoms of the mother Matter, we do not realise the significance of Thy
Inscrutable performance, how, Thou, being distinctly apart from Matter, pervadest it and createst the universe. (53)

१०. नि त्वामग्ने मनुदंधे ज्योतिर्जनाय शश्वते ।
दीदेथ कण्व ऋतजात उक्षितो यं नमस्यन्ति कृष्टय: ॥

10. O God, I, a reflective Yogi, realise Thee, the Resplendent, for Thy
acquisition, the Eternal Entity, Whom the people worship.

Shed Thy lustre on me, a learned person, so that I may become great through
Vedic lore. (54)

Chapter 2

DECADE I

१. देवो वो द्रविणोदा: पूर्णा विवष्ट्वासिचम् ।
उद्वा सिञ्चध्वमुप वा पृणध्वमादिद्वो देव श्रोहते ॥

1. O men, God is the Giver of wealth unto Ye. He demands complete self-
abnegation as an oblation. Pour out the oblation in full, fill it again. Then will
Divine God give Ye speedily the desired fruit. (55)[1]

God is the respository and source of all knowledge. He spreads it on the Earth through
the revelation of the Vedas in the beginning of creation, Soul finally attains to the bliss
of salvation through that knowledge.

Griffith interprets Diwodasa as a liberal prince who especially worshipped Agni his
tutelary god.

The interpretation is wrong, as there is no history in the Vedas. He considers the stanza
to be obscure. This view is unjustified. The verse is clear like day light. Pt. Jaidev Vidyalankar, translates Dewodasa as Resplendent God.

[1]Charity given in the name of God, for a noble cause is a kind of oblation. Just as
oblations poured into the fire again and again satisfy it, so does self-abnegation for a
public cause, or charity, given disinterestedly satisfy God, Who gives speedily its reward
or fruit.

२. प्रंतू ब्रह्मणस्पति: प्र देव्येतु सूनृता ।
अच्छा वीरं नयं पङ्क्तिराधसं देवा यज्ञं नयन्तु न: ॥

2. May we attain to God and His righteous Vedic speech. May divine forces rightly guide the Yajna of our life, the Yajna which secures us heroic offspring, is beneficial to humanity, and is performed by five. (56)[1]

३. ऊर्ध्वं ऊ षु ण ऊतये तिष्ठा देवो न सविता ।
ऊर्ध्वो वाजस्य सनिता यदञ्जिभिर्वाघद्भिर्विह्वयामहे ॥

3. O God, for our protection, be nobly steady like the Sun. Be the grand donor of spiritual force. We extol Thee along with beloved learned persons. (57)[2]

४. प्र यो राये निनीषति मर्तो यस्ते वसो दाशत् ।
स वीरं धत्ते अग्न उक्थशंसिनं त्मना सहस्रपोषिणम् ॥

4. O All-pervading God, the man who aspires after eternal wealth, and dedicates himself to Thee, begets a brave son, who knows the Vedas, and affords protection to thousands of men. (58)[3]

५. प्र वो यह्वं पुरूणां विशां देवयनीनाम् ।
अग्नि सूक्तेभिर्वचोभिर्वृणीमहे यं समिदन्य इन्धते ॥

5. With Vedic hymns and holy eulogies, we supplicate the Great God, the Benefactor of Ye, His devoted subjects, Whom others too worship. (59)

६. अयमग्नि: सुवीर्यस्येशे हि सौभगस्य ।
राय ईशे स्वपत्यस्य गोमत ईशे वृत्रहथानाम् ॥

6. This God is the Lord great prosperity, riches, wealth, noble off-spring, store of kine, and the means for the eradication of diseases and sins. (60)[4]

७. त्वमग्ने गृहपतिस्त्व होता नो अध्वरे ।
त्वं पोता विश्ववार प्रचेता यक्षि यासि च वार्यम् ।

7. O God, Thou art the Lord of our abode. Thou art our Protector in virtuous deeds. Thou art the Remover of all impediments. Thou art the Scrutiniser of all actions and passing wise. Thou grantest us enjoyable prosperity and possessest it Thyself. (61)

---

[1]Five means either five organs of perception or five organs of action. Some commentators say, five refers to the worshipper, Hota, Adhwaryu, Udgata and Brahman.
Griffith makes five to refer to the oblations of grain, gruel, curdled milk, rice-cake and curds. Griffith takes the yajna in the physical and not spiritual sense.
[2]Sayan Acharya interprets Urdhwa as "Yupa" the sacrificial post to which the victims at an animal sacrifice were tied. This rendering is irrelevant.
[3]Eternal wealth means knowledge, which is indestructible and lasts for ever.
[4]Noble offspring means His subjects.

८. सखायस्त्वा ववृमहे देवं मर्तासि ऊतये ।
अपां नपातऀ सुभगऀ सुदऀससऀ सुप्रतूर्तिमनेहसम् ॥

8. O God we mortals, Thy friends, accept Thee, as the Guardian of our actions, the most Mighty, the Doer of noble deeds, the Destroyer of sins, Immaculate and Divine. (62)[1]

DECADE II

१. आ जुहोता हविषा मर्जयध्वं नि होतारं गृहपतिं दधिध्वम् ।
इडस्पदे नमसा रातहव्यऀ सपर्यता यजतं पस्त्यानाम् ॥

1. O men, worship constantly in temples and Ida artery, God, the Lord of our dwelling place. Dedicate yourselves to Him with prayer. Purify body and soul. Honour Him with homage, Who accepts our devotion and rewards our acts. The teacher and pupil should thus worship Him. (63)[2]

२. चित्र इच्छिशोस्तरुणस्य वक्षथो न यो मातरावन्वेति धातवे ।
अनूधा यदजीजनदधा चिदा ववक्षत्सद्यो महि दूत्यां३ चरन् ॥

2. God pervades the universe calmly, as does the child sleep. He is ever-young due to His Might. Wondrous is His act of sustaining the universe.
For the acquisition of His power, He does not depend upon the Sun and the Earth, the mothers of creatures. Having created the universe, He himself sustains it. He is incessantly bearing the burden of the universe, imparting intense warmth to it. (64)

३. इदं त एकं पर उ त एकं तृतीयेन ज्योतिषा सं विशस्व ।
संवेशनस्तन्वे३चारुरेधि प्रियो देवानां परमे जनित्रे ॥

3. O God, Thy one manifestation is this visible world, the Sun is the second, with Thy third resplendent beauty Thou pervadest the universe. Being All-pervading, Thou spreadest Thyself for expanding the universe, Thou art dear to the emancipated souls in their sublimest home. (65)[3]

४. इमऀ स्तोममर्हते जातवेदसे रथमिव सं महेमा मनीषया ।
भद्रा हि नः प्रमतिरस्य सऀसद्यग्ने सख्ये मा रिषामा वयं तव ॥

4. We offer with our mind this praise-song, like a car, to God, the Creator

[1]Griffith translates Apamnapat as offspring of the waters, as born in the form of lightening from the watery clouds of the aerial ocean or firmament. Pt. Jaidev Vidyalankar translates the word as God, Who does not let our deeds fall and is their Guardian and Rewarder.
[2]Yogis concentrate upon God in Ida artery.
[3]Sublimest home: State of salvation.
Sayan has explained this verse as spoken by the Rishi Brihaduktha to his deceased son Vajinam, which is meaningless.

of the Vedas and Worthy of reverence. In His company may our understanding be propitious. O God, may we never suffer harm in Thy friendship. (66)[1]

५. मूर्धानं दिवो अरति पृथिव्या वैश्वानरमृत श्रा जातमग्निम् ।
कविएं सम्राजमतिथि जनानामासन्न: पात्रं जनयन्त देवा: ॥

5. The learned speak of God, as the Head of Heaven, the Lord of Earth, the Pervader in the universe, Omnipresent, Omniscient, the King of all, the Guest of men, Foremost of all, and Worthy of praise. (67)[2]

६. वि त्वदापो न पर्वतस्य पृष्ठादुक्थेभिरग्ने जनयन्त देवा: ।
तं त्वा गिर: सुष्टुतयो वाजयन्त्याजि न गिर्वंवाहो जिग्युरश्वा: ॥

6. O God, the learned receive inspiration from Thee with lauds, like waters from the mountain ridges. Just as intelligent horses acting on mere hint, win the battle, so do hymns and eulogies glorify Thee. (68)[3]

७. आ वो राजानमध्वरस्य रुद्र एं होतारएं सत्ययज एं रोदस्यो: ।
अग्निं पुरा तनयित्नोरचित्ताद्धिरण्यरूपमवसे कृणुध्वम् ॥

7. O mortals, before thunder-like death overtakes Ye, for your preservation worship the Resplendent God, the Lord of Yogic sacrifice, the Giver of the fruit of actions, the Chastiser of the sinners, the effectual Sacrificer between Heaven and Earth and the Master of effulgence. (69)[4]

८. इन्धे राजा समर्यो नमोभिर्यस्य प्रतीकमाहुतं घृतेन ।
नरो हव्येभिरीडते सबाध आग्निरग्रमुषसामशोचि ॥

8. May God, Whose nature is full of brilliance all round. Whose praise is sung with devotion by those who practise Yogic exercises, Who manifests himself in the heart, when we offer reverential salutations unto Him ; Who is Effulgent and Lord of the animate and inanimate creation, shed holiness at dawn, in the hearts of the worshippers. (70)

९. प्र केतुना बृहता यात्यग्निरा रोदसी वृषभो रोरवीति ।
दिवश्चिदन्तादुपमानदानडपामुपस्थे महिषो ववर्ध ॥

9. God manifests Himself with the high light of knowledge. He preaches to the denizens of the Earth and Heaven. He hath come nigh to our heart from the sky's forthest limit. In the midst of actions, He, the Omnipotent, is higher than all in name and fame. (71)

---

[1]Like a Car: Just as a car leads us through intricate and difficult paths to our destination, so Vedic hymns act as a chariot to lead us to God, our final goal.

[2]Guest of all: Just as a guest is respected, is God should be revered and honoured by all like a guest.

[3]Mountain ridges: Just as waters flow from the cloud, so do the learned inspired by God perform noble deeds.

[4]Men should worship God for spiritual advancement before death overtakes them, for after death none can worship Him.

१०. अग्नि नरो दीधितिभिररण्योर्हस्तच्युतं जनयत प्रशस्तम् । दूरेदृशं गृहपतिमथव्युम् ॥

10. O men, realise the manifested God in your heart, with the powerful fingers of action and knowledge, and the fire-sticks of mind and intellect. He is Far-seeing the Lord of our spiritual excellence and constant dweller in our soul. (72)[1]

DECADE III

१. अबोध्यग्नि: समिधा जनानां प्रति धेनुमिवायतीमुषासम् ।
यह्वा इव प्र वयामुज्जिहाना: प्र भानव: सस्रते नाकमच्छ ॥

1. Just as fire is kindled by the people's fuel, and a milch cow yields milk at each coming Dawn, so our soul, with the fuel of breaths, is kindled each morning through Prāṇāyāma. Just as birds flying high reach a tree, and great men follow a liberal policy, and Sun's rays pervade the atmosphere, so mighty souls, soaring aloft, proceed to the Omnipresent God, and with the light of knowledge, the emancipated Yogis attain to the lofty abode of bliss. (73)[2]

२. प्र भूर्जयन्तं महां विपोधां मूरेरमूरं पूरां दमणिम् ।
नयन्तं गीर्भिर्वना धियं धा हरिश्मश्रुं न वर्मणा धनर्चिम् ॥

2. Realize in your heart God, the Subduer of different worlds, the Destroyer through salvation, of the bodies held by infatuated souls, Free from delusion, worshipful through Vedic Verses, the Guide of our intellect on the path of virtue, the Possessor of superhuman power, with the gold-hued rays of the Sun as His armour. (74)

३. शुक्रं ते अन्यद्यजतं ते अन्यद्विषुरूपे अहनी द्यौरिवासि ।
विश्वा हि माया अवसि स्वधावन्भद्रा ते पूषन्निह रातिरस्तु ॥

3. O God, the Nourisher of the world, Thy one bright form is of knowledge and the other of action. Both the forms are dissimilar in colour like Day and Night. Thou art like the Sun. O Lord of food and life, Thou nourishest the extraordinary powers of the universe. Auspicious be Thy bounty here. (75)[3]

४. इडामग्ने पुरुदंसꣳ सनि गो: शश्वत्तमꣳ हवमानाय साध ।
स्यान्न: सूनुस्तनयो विजावाग्ने सा ते सुमतिर्भूत्वस्मे ॥

4. O God, the Giver of cattle wealth, speech and Vedic learning, grant perpetually to the worshipper, knowledge, endowed with manifold actions. To us

---

[1]Just as by rubbing together with fingers the two fire sticks, fire is produced, so by the concentration of mind and the use of intellect our two mental fire-sticks, God is realised. Action and knowledge are the fingers of our soul for the realization of God. अरण्यो: and दीधितिभि: are used figuratively.

[2]Our breaths are the fuel of our soul in Prāṇāyāma i.e., exercise of breaths. Lofty abode of bliss is the state of salvation, in which happiness reigns supreme.

[3]Here: in this world.

be born a son, who procreates the offspring and produces many children. May Thy will be gracious towards us. (76)

५. प्र होता जातो महान्नभोविन्नृषद्य सीददपां विवर्ते ।
दधद्यो धायि सुते वयाꣳसि यन्ता वसूनि विधते तनूपाः ॥

5. God, who is the Giver of the fruit of actions, present in the heart of a devotee, Adorable, the Pervader in the atmosphere, Omnipresent, the Preserver of bodies, Glorious, grants us food and wealth, brings to thee the worshipper wished for objects, and is present in the midst of all mortals. (77)

६. प्र सम्राजमसुरस्य प्रशस्तं पुꣳसः कृष्टीनामनुमाद्यस्य ।
इन्द्रस्येव प्र तवसस्कृतानि वन्दद्वारा वन्दमाना विवष्टु ॥

6. O men, just as Ye know the attributes of the Sun, brilliant, life-infusing, possessing the powers of attraction and retention, the Giver of happiness to humanity, powerful, worthy of praise and eulogy, so shouldst Ye long for the knowledge of the mighty deeds of God. (78)[1]

७. अरण्योर्निहितो जातवेदा गर्भ इवेत्सुभृतो गर्भिणीभिः ।
दिवेदिव ईड्यो जागृवद्भिर्हविष्मद्भिर्मनुष्येभिरग्निः ॥

7. Just as well-cherished germ is preserved in pregnant women, so is God, the Creator of the Vedas, preserved in the two kindling blocks of mind and intellect. Cautious souls worship Him day by day with the oblations of action and devotion. (79)

८. सनादग्ने मृणसि यातुधानान्न त्वा रक्षाꣳसि पृतनासु जिग्युः ।
अनु दह सहमूरान्कयादो मा ते हेत्या मुक्षत दैव्याया: ॥

8. O God, from times immemorial Thou hast been punishing the sinners. Evil forces have never overcome Thee in fights. Burn up the raw flesh devourers. Let none of them escape the edge of Thine divine weapon. (80)

DECADE IV

१. अग्न आजिष्ठमा भर द्युम्नमस्मभ्यमध्रिगो । प्र नो राये पनीयसे रत्सि वाजाय पन्थाम् ॥

1. O God, Resistless on Thy way, bring us most mighty splendour. Prepare for us the path that leads to glorious opulence and strength. (81)

२. यदि वीरो अनु ष्यादग्निमिन्धीत मर्त्यः । आजुह्वद्धव्यमानुषक् शर्म भक्षीत दैव्यम् ॥

2. The man who worships God, and then incessantly dedicates his deeds to Him, becomes a hero, and attains to the happiness of salvation. (82)

---

[1]God preaches to all, that they should long for knowing His superhuman powers, as they know the attributes of the Sun.

३. त्वेषस्ते धूम ऋण्वति दिवि सं च्छुक्र आततः । सूरो न हि द्युता त्वं कृपा पावक रोचसे ॥

3. O Purifying God, Thy Resplendent Superhuman power is visible in the Sun. That light is far-extended in heaven. Like the Sun, Thou beamest with Thy strength and radiant glow. (83)

४. त्वꣳहि क्षैतवद्यशोऽग्ने मित्रो न पत्यसे । त्वं विचर्षणे श्रवो वसो पुष्टि न पुष्यसि ॥

4. O God, Thou possessest, like the Sun, the renown of supremacy. O All-seeing, the Giver of habitation to all, Thou nourishest us by granting us the support of Vedic knowledge. (84)

५. प्रातरग्निः पुरुप्रियो विश स्तवेतातिथिः । विश्वे यस्मिन्नमर्त्ये हव्यं मर्तास इन्धते ॥

5. O men, worship at dawn God, Who is loved by all and is Omnipresent. All mortals dedicate the oblation of their actions to Him, the Immortal. (85)

६. यद्वाहिष्ठं तदग्नये बृहदर्च विभावसो । महिषीव त्वद्रयिस्त्वद्राजा उदीरते ॥

6. O Rich in radiant light, may Thou shine on high. Just as this great Earth yields food and gold, so dost Thou grant riches and all edibles. Our best offering is for Thee, O God. (86)

७. विशोविशो वो अतिथि वाजयन्तः पुरुप्रियम् ॥ अग्नि वो दुर्यं वचः स्तुषे शूषस्य मन्मभिः ॥

7. O men, Ye always worship God, who pervades all His subjects and is loved by all. For Ye, I expatiate on Him, the Abode of happiness, with words of Vedic verses. (87)[1]

८. बृहद्रयो हि भानवेऽर्चा देवायाग्नये । यं मित्रं न प्रशस्तये मर्तासो दधिरे पुरः ॥

8. Sing praise for a major part of life for the Refulgent and Illuminating God, Whom men always keep in view for their eulogy. (88)

९. अगन्म वृत्रहन्तमं ज्येष्ठमग्निमानवम् । य स्म श्रुतर्वन्नार्ध्ये बृहदनीक इध्यते ॥

9. May we realise God, the Remover of the sin of ignorance, Most Excellent, the Well-wisher of humanity, the Revealer of the Vedas, and Visible in the great fight amongst the organs of senses. (89)

१०. जातः परेण धर्मणा यत्सवृद्धिः सहाभुवः । पिता यत्क्रश्यपस्याग्निः श्रद्धा माता मनुः कविः ।

10. O Soul, thou becomest manifest through austere penance and force of character. Thou art hence competent to perform thy task with the help of thy companions, the organs of senses. Thou art the father of mind, the recipient of knowledge. Faith is Thy mother, and a reflective person thy preceptor. (90)

---

[1]The word Atithi अतिथि has been used for God, as He is respected by all like a guest, or pervades all His subjects as a learned guest goes to the house of each house-holder.
  I: a learned person. It is the bounden duty of learned persons to preach to humanity the Vedic doctrines.

4

SĀMAVEDA

DECADE V

१. सोम॑ राजानं वरुणमग्निमन्वारभामहे । आदित्यं विष्णु॑ सूर्यं ब्रह्माणं च बृहस्पतिम् ॥

1. We daily remember God, the Giver of happiness, the Creator of the universe, Effulgent, the Remover of all sins. Indivisible, Omnipresent, the Urger of all, the Encyclopaedia of Knowledge and the Lord of the Vedas. (91)

२. इत एत उदारुहन्दिवः पृष्ठान्या रुहन् । प्र भज्जयो यथा पथोद्यामङ्गिरसो ययुः ॥

2. Just as conquerors of the world attain to salvation through the path of domestic life, so do these Yogis go up to the height of blissful salvation. (92)[1]

३. राये अग्ने महे त्वा दानाय समिधीमहि । ईडिष्वा हि महे वृषं द्यावा होत्राय पृथिवी ॥

3. O God, the Rainer of happiness on the soul, for ample wealth and self-dedication, we kindle Thee through Yoga. Both Heaven and Earth are a great oblation to Him. Worship Him, O spiritually advanced men. (93)

४. दधन्वे वा यदीमनु वोचद्ब्रह्मेति वेरु तत् । परि विश्वानि काव्या नेमिश्चक्रमिवाभुवत् ॥

4. With God as goal, the disciples hear of Him from the preceptor, and recite vedic verses. This all is for Him.
He holds all knowledge in His grasp even as the felly rounds the wheel. (94)

५. प्रत्यग्ने हरसा हरः श्रृणाहि विश्वतस्परि । यातुधानस्य रक्षसो बलं न्युब्जवीर्यम् ॥

5. O God, demolish with Thy righteous indignation, the might of a violent sinner in the world. Break down the strength and vigour of a devil. (95)

६. त्वमग्ने वसू॑रिह रुद्रा॑ आदित्या॑ उत । यजा स्वध्वरं जनं मनुजातं घृतप्रुषम् ॥

6. O God, let Vasus, Rudras, Adityas, reflective souls, men replete with knowledge and action, and benefactors of humanity be Thy companions. (96)[2]

---

[1]It is possible to attain salvation by disinterested saviours of humanity, who lead a married life, and rule selflessly, as it is for the Yogis who don't marry and enter domestic life. Marriage in itself is no bar to the attainment of final beatitude. The underlying spirit for the attainment of salvation is disinterested service. Raj Rishis and Brahm Rishis both are qualified for salvation One follows the path of celibacy, the other of domestic life.

Griffith has translated the word 'Angirasas' as children of Angiras, regarded as a race of higher beings between Gods and men, the typical first sacrificers whose ritual is the pattern which later priests should follow. This interpretation is in-applicable, as there is no history in the Vedas. The word means learned Yogis. Pt. Jawala Prasad has used the word पथा instead of पर्था, and एत has been mentioned as एत. The word भूर्जेय: has been mentioned by him as भू: जय:. The grammatical errors have been pointed out by Swami Tulsi Ram, and Pt. Satyavrat Sam-Ashrami, the well known scholar of the Vedas.

[2]*Vasus*: Persons who observe celibacy for 24 years.
Rudras: Persons who observe celibacy for 36 years.
Adityas: Persons who observe celibacy for 48 years.

Out of the 33 devatas, forces of nature, there are 8 Vasus, 11 Rudras and 12 Adityas, the months, besides Indra, (Lightning) and Prajapati (Yajna). These forces of nature are also the companions of God.

BOOK II

Chapter 2

DECADE I

१. पुरु त्वा दाशिवाँ̐वोचेऽरिरग्ने तव स्विदा । तोदस्येव शरण आ महस्य ॥

1. O Bounteous God, I highly extol Thee, as a servant serves his great master. (97)

२. प्र होत्रे पूर्व्यं वचोऽग्नये भरता बृहत् । विपां ज्योतीँ̐षि बिभ्रते न वेधसे ॥

2. O men, preach to humanity, the immemorial lofty Vedic speech, for glorifying God, the Engulfer of the world at the time of its dissolusion, the Guardian of the Knowledge, celibacy and austerity of the learned, and the Creator of all. (98)

३. अग्ने वाजस्य गोमत ईशानः सहसो यहो । अस्मे देहि जातवेदो महि श्रवः ॥

3. O God, Thou art the Lord of kine, Sun's rays, organs and Vedic speech. Thou art the Master of foodstuffs, wealth, knowledge and prowess, Thou art the embodiment of strength.
O Omniscient God, bestow on us high renown. (99)

४. अग्ने यजिष्ठो अध्वरे देवां देवयते यज । होता मन्द्रो वि राजस्यति स्रिधः ॥

4. O God, Thou art the great Benefactor. In noble deeds of charity, bring the learned to the pious worshipper. O joyful Donor, Thou driving our foes afar, shinest splendidly. (100)[1]

५. जज्ञानः सप्त मातृभिर्मेधामाशासत श्रिये । अयं ध्रुवो रयीणां चिकेतदा ॥

5. The Unchangeable God, creating the universe with seven mothers, controls His strength for His Superhuman manifestation. The same Lord full well knows all forms of supremacy. (101)[2]

६. उत स्या नो दिवा मतिरदितिरूत्यागमत् । सा शन्ताता मयस्करदप स्रिधः ॥

6. May the irrevocable Will of God, daily come nigh unto us for our protection. May that, the bestower of peace and spiritual happiness, chase our mental foes. (102)[3]

---

[1]*Foes*: Our physical and spiritual foes e.g., lust, anger and avarice.

[2]*Seven Mothers*: Seven forces of Nature, i.e., five elements, fire, air, water, earth, atmosphere, Mahat-Tatva, intellect and Ahankar, Ego. Some commentators describe seven mothers to be seven breaths which are spoken of in the Upanishads as seven Rishis, seven sparks, seven fires and seven metres.

[3]That refers to Will. Mental foes mean the diseases of the mind like ignorance, hatred, envy, wrath, lust and greed.

७. ईडिष्वा हि प्रतीव्या३ यजस्व जातवेदसम् । चरिष्णुधूममगृभीतशोचिषम् ।

7. O man, worship the Omniscient, Omnipresent, Originator, Immortal, All-pervading God, and dedicate thyself to Him. (103)

८. न तस्य मायया च न रिपुरीशीत मर्त्यः । यो अग्नये ददाश हव्यदातये ॥

8. No mortal foe can ever by deceit prevail over him, who resigns himself to God, the Bestower of Knowledge. (104)

९. अप त्यं वृजिनꣳ रिपुꣳ स्तेनमग्ने दुराध्यम् । दविष्ठमस्य सत्पते कृधी सुगम् ।

9. O God, Lord of the virtuous, drive far away the sinful foe, the troublesome thief, and make him pursue the right path. (105)[1]

१०. श्रुष्टयग्ने नवस्य मे स्तोमस्य वीर विश्पते । नि मायिनस्तपसा रक्षसो दह ॥

10. O brave God, the Nourisher of His subjects, on hearing the new laud of mine extirpate my fraudulent evil intentions. (106)[2]

DECADE II

१. प्र मꣳहिष्ठाय गायत ऋताब्ने बृहते शुक्रशोचिषे । उपस्तुतासो अग्नये ॥

1. Ye worshippers, sing forth to God, the Holy, most Munificent, and Sublime with His refulgent glow. (107)

२. प्र सो अग्ने तवोतिभिः सुवीराभिस्तरति वाजकर्मभिः । यस्य त्वꣳ सख्यमाविथ ॥

2. O God, he, whom Thou choosest as Thy friend, conquers all obstacles, aided by Thy heroic safeguards and deeds of supremacy. (108)

३. तं गूर्धया स्वर्णरं देवासो देवमरति दधन्विरे । देवत्रा हव्यमूहिषे ।

3. Sing praise to God, the Leader of all. The learned acknowledge Him, the Omniscient. He imparts strength, knowledge and edibles to the pious seekers after knowledge. (109)

४. मा नो हृणिथा अतिथिं वसुरग्निः पुरुप्रशस्त एषः । यः सुहोता स्वध्वरः ॥

4. Be not angry with God, Who is worthy of respect by us a guest. He deserves full praise. He dwells in all and is full of brilliance like fire. He is the Bestower of nice objects and the Guardian of non-violent deeds. (110)

५. भद्रो नो अग्निराहुतो भद्रा रातिः सुभग भद्रो अध्वरः । भद्रा उत प्रशस्तयः ॥

5. May God duly worshipped bring us bliss. O supreme Lord, may our charity, non-violent deeds and eulogies bring us bliss. (111)

[1]God can change the nature of wicked foes, and evil-hearted thieves, and make them tread the path of virtue.
[2]Evil intentions are the deadly foes of soul. God through His Kindness can remove them.

६. यजिष्ठं त्वा ववृमहे देवं देवत्रा होतारममर्त्यम् । अस्य यज्ञस्य सुक्रतुम् ।

6. O God, we worship Thee, the greatest Donor, God amongst the gods, the Bestower of all objects, Immortal, the Fine Finisher of this sacrifice of life. (112)

७. तदग्ने द्युम्नमा भर यत्सासाहा सदने कं चिदत्रिणम् । मन्युं जनस्य दूढ्यम् ॥

7. O God, bring us that splendour, which may overcome in our house each fiend, and sinner who deserves the wrath of every man. (113)

८. यद्वा उ विश्पतिः शितः सुप्रीतो मनुषो विशे । विश्वेदग्निः प्रति रक्षाꣳसि सेधति ॥

8. Whenever God, the Lord of men, eagerly manifests Himself in the soul of man, all devilish tendencies are cast aside. (114)

AYENDRA KĀṆḌA

DECADE III

१. तद्वो गाय सुते सचा पुरूहूताय सत्वने । शं यद्गवे न शाकिने ॥

1. O men, sing together the praise of God, Who is Everlasting, worshipped by many, and grants bliss to the Earth like a King. (115)

२. यस्ते नूनꣳ शतक्रतविन्द्र द्युम्नितमो मदः । तेन नूनं मदे मदः ॥

2. O Resplendent God, the Possessor of hundreds of powers or wise designs, let me rejoice with Thy joy, which is most glorious of all. (116)

३. गाव उप वदावटे मही यज्ञस्य रप्सुदा । उभा कर्णा हिरण्यया ॥

3. O words, go unto God, and express your aim. Heaven and Earth lend beauty to the Yajna. Knowledge and action are two excellent accomplishments. (117)[1]

४. अरमश्वाय गायत श्रुतकक्षारं गवे । अरमिन्द्रस्य धाम्ने ॥

4. O retainer of the Vedas in thy heart, sing adequately the praise of God and the active soul. Expatiate on the learned soul. Extol fully the strength of soul, the master of organs. (118)[2]

---

[1]Griffith writes, the meaning of rapsuda is unknown. Rishi Dayananda in his commentary on Yajur 33-19 translates the word as givers of beauty. रप्सु रूपं दत्तस्ते. As the word गो means speech, earth, cow, stream, Sun's ray, so different commentators have interpreted the verse differently. Just as cows go to the cowshed, rays to the Sun, and streams to the ocean, so do the words of applause go to God.

[2]Griffith has not been able to translate the word 'Shrutkaksha and has mentioned it as a proper noun, There is no historical reference in the Vedas, hence Griffith's explanation is unacceptable. The word means a learned person who possesses the knowledge of the Vedas in his bosom or heart.

५. तमिन्द्रं वाजयामसि महे वृत्राय हन्तवे । स वृषा वृषभो भुवत् ॥

5. We praise God for destroying the mighty forces of evil that overshadow knowledge. He, the Bestower of learning and happiness is All-powerful. (119)[1]

६. त्वमिन्द्र बलादधि सहसो जात ओजस: । त्वꣳसन्वृषन्वृषेदसि ॥

6. O God, Thou manifestest Thyself with Thy strength, patience and lustre. Being powerful, Thou bestowest power. (120)

७. यज्ञ इन्द्रमवर्धयद्यद्भूमि व्यवर्तयत् । चक्राण ओपशं दिवि ॥

7. The united force of knowledge and action, coupled with deliberation, makes the body perform diverse deeds and lends strength to the soul. (121)

८. यदिन्द्राहं यथा त्वमीशीय वस्व एक इत् । स्तोता मे गोसखा स्यात् ॥

8. O King just as thou alone controllest wealth, knowledge and power, if I also be powerful to subdue my passions and breaths, my soul, renowned like the organs, will become the singer of the praise of God. (122)

९. पन्यंपन्यमित्सोतार आ धावत मद्याय । सोमं वीराय शूराय ॥

9. O learned persons, run hard for achieving excellent joy ; after the source of commendable pleasure, the Inspirer of bravery and heroism. (123)[2]

१०. इदं वसो सुतमन्ध: पिबा सुपूर्णमुदरम् । अनाभयित्रिरिमा ते ॥

10. O soul, enjoy to thy entire satisfaction, this well-earned excellent pleasure. We offer it to thee. (124)[3]

DECADE IV

१. उद्घेदभि श्रुतामघं वृषभं नर्यापसम् । अस्तारमेषि सूर्यं ॥

1. O God, verily Thou alone elevatest the hero, who is famous for his wealth, knowledge and renown, is the distributor of happiness, the benefactor of humanity, and the subduer of foes like lust and anger. (125)[4]

२. यदद्य कच्च वृत्रहन्नुदगा अभि सूर्य । सर्वं तदिन्द्र ते वशे ॥

2. O God, the slayer of sin, whatever exists in the world at present, has been promoted by Thee, and is under Thy control. (126)[5]

---

[1]He refers to God.

[2]Source refers to God. Learned persons should make haste to go towards God for the attainment of pleasure.

[3] वसो Means soul, as it dwells in the body.

[4]Surya means God, as He sheds lustre to souls, as Sun gives light to the earth.
Hero may refer to the King or any philanthropic learned person who works disinterestedly for the good of others.

[5]Swami Tulsi Ram interprets Surya as God. I have accepted his interpretation. Pt. Jaidev Vidyalankar interprets Surya as soul. According to his interpretation, the verse

३. य म्रानयत्परावत: सुनीती तुर्वंशं यदुम् । इन्द्र: स नो युवा सखा ॥

3. God is our Youthful friend, Who brings from afar on the right path, the man who is a slave to passions, and has gone astray. (127)[1]

४. मा न इन्द्राभ्या३ दिश: सूरो म्रक्तुष्वा यमत् । त्वा युजा वनेम तत् ॥

4. O God, let not lust or anger, our foe, overpower us stealthily from any direction, due to our ignorance. May we, with Thee as our Friend subdue that. (128)

५. एन्द्र सानसिꣳरयिꣳसजित्वानꣳसदासहम् । वर्षिष्ठमूतये भर ॥

5. O God, grant me that adequate spiritual wealth, which is nicely distributed, is the conqueror of passions, and is competent to endure onslaughts. (129)[2]

६. इन्द्रं वयं महाधन इन्द्रमर्भे हवामहे । युजं वृत्रेषु वज्रिणम् ॥

6. In mighty or lesser struggle we invoke the aid of God, the Friend, Who wit His chastising might removes obstacles. (130)[3]

७. म्रपिबत्कद्रुव: सुतमिन्द्र: सहस्रबाह्वे । तत्राददिष्ट पौꣳस्यम् ॥

7. A king, for overpowering the foe in a thousand ways, drinks deep the knowledge of a learned scholar, and thereby enhances his strength. (131)[4]

will mean thus. 'O soul, the remover of the darkness of ignorance, whatever object thou aspires after, the same comes under thy control.' A strong soul achieves through iron determination, whatever he sets his heart upon.

[1]Indra means God or Preceptor.

तुर्वंश may mean the person who kills others and is a Prey to diseases, तुर्वि हिसायाम्. It may also mean a slave to passions. It can be interpreted as a man who controls Dharma, Arth, Kām and Moksha.

Yadu means a person who abandons the path of virtue and rectitude and goes astray.

Sayana has interpreted तुर्वंश and यदु, as two Kings. This interpretation is inapplicable, as there is no history in the Vedas. Pt. Jawala Prashad interprets Yadu as incarnation of Nar Rup. This is humbug as Veda does not support the doctrine of incarnation.

Griffith translates Turvaśa and Yadu as two Aryan tribes. This is inapplicable as Vedas are free from historical references. Griffith is of the view that some expedition against a distant King appears to be referred to. This is meaningless.

[2]Nicely distributed means spread throughout all the organs of the body.

Onslaughts means mental and physical tortures.

[3]Indra may refer to a King as well.

[4]Ishwar Chandra Vidyalankar, interprets Indra as bright intellect, and, translates the verse thus. Our bright intellect having drunk deep the juice of the knowledge of a scholar, becomes multi-faced, and thereby illumines its intensity.

Sayan, has interpreted Kadru as the name of a Rishi. Pt. Jawala Prasad interprets Indra as Parshu Ram, God's incarnation. Both interpretations are inapplicable as Vedas are free from historical references. Western scholars interpret Kadru as a daughter of Daksha and mother of the Nāgas or serpent race. This is pure nonsense. Kadru means a learned person.

कद्र: कवतेऽसौ कद्रु विद्वान् उणा० ३॥१०२॥

८. वयमिन्द्र त्वायवोSभि प्र नोनुमो वृषन् । विद्धी त्वा३ स्य नो वसो ॥

8. O God, the Bestower of joys, we seekers after knowledge, bow unto Thee.

O Omnipresent God, Thou knowest this feeling of ours. (132)

६. श्रा घा ये अग्निमिन्धते स्तृणन्ति बर्हिरानुषक् । येषामिन्द्रो युवा सखा ॥

9. Learned persons, who enkindle the soul, their ever-young and deathless friend, soon cut asunder the bondage of body. (133)[1]

१०. भिन्धि विश्वा अप द्विष: परि बाधो जही मृध: । वसु स्पार्हं तदा भर ॥

10. O God, drive all our enemies away, smite down our violent foes and tormentors. Grant us that wealth of soul for which we long. (134)

DECADE V

१. इहेव शृण्व एषां कशा हस्तेषु यद्ददान् । नि यामं चित्रमृञ्जते ॥

1. When we two converse, together we hear though 'twere close at hand. It shows speech is in their hands, which accomplishes wondrous achievements. (135)[2]

२. इम उ त्वा वि चक्षते सखाय इन्द्र सोमिन: । पुष्टावन्तो यथा पशुम् ॥

2. O God, these spiritually minded friends look to Thee, just as men with fodder look to the cattle. (136)[3]

३. समस्य मन्यवे विशो विश्वा नमन्त कृष्टय: । समुद्रायेव सिन्धव: ॥

3. All men and people bow down before the righteous indignation of God, as rivers bow them to the sea. (137)

४. देवानामिदवो महत्तदा वृणीमहे वयम् । वृष्णामस्मभ्यमूतये ॥

4. We choose the protection of our learned preceptors, the bestowers of pleasure and learning, that it may help and succour us. (138)

५. सोमानाSस्वरणं कृणुहि ब्रह्मणस्पते । कक्षीवन्तं य श्रौशिज: ॥

5. O God, for acquiring the experiences of knowledge through Yoga, make

[1]Those who develop their soul soon attain to salvation and get relief from the pangs of birth and death.

[2]We refers to teacher and pupil. Their refers to teacher and preacher, which refers to speech.

The word कशा has been translated by Swami Tulsi Ram as speech. Literally the word कशा means as whip or hunter. Pt. Jaidev Vidyalankar says that in the hands of breaths i. e., Pranas there is the hunter of Om, which the Yogis use in their contemplation.

[3]Just as cowherds look upon their cattle with affection, so spiritually advanced persons look towards God, and try to approach Him.

strong and free in motion, my breath, which is perfected through control. (139)[1]

६. बोघन्मना इदस्तु नो वृत्रहा भूर्यासुतिः । श्रृणोतु शक्र आशिषम् ॥

6. May the Omnipotent God, the Dispeller of ignorance, the Embodiment of infinite joy, listen to our prayer, and grant wisdom to our mind. (140)

७. अद्य नो देव सवितः प्रजावत्सावीः सौभगम् । परा दुःष्वप्न्यꣳसुव ॥

7. O God, the Creator, grant us ever prosperity and progeny, and drive away poverty. (141)

८. क्वꣳस्य वृषभो युवा तुविग्रीवो ग्रनानतः । ब्रह्मा कस्तꣳसपर्यति ॥

8. Where is that Ever-Almighty God, the Bestower of joys, the Master of manifold achievements, and Unbending in nature. Which knower of the Vedas prays unto Him ? (142)

९. उपह्वरे गिरीणाꣳसङ्गमे च नदीनाम् । धिया विप्रो ग्रजायत ॥

9. In the solitude of mountains and confluence of streams, a sage develops his spiritual force, contemplating on God through Yoga. (143)

१०. प्र सम्राजं चर्षणीनामिन्द्रꣳस्तोता नव्यं गीर्भिः । नरं नृषाहं मꣳहिष्ठम् ॥

10. Praise through Vedic songs, God, the Lord of mankind, Worthy of adoration, the Leader of men, the Controller of humanity and most liberal. (144)

Chapter 2

DECADE I

१. ग्रपादु शिप्रयन्धसः सुदक्षस्य प्रहोषिणः । इन्दोरिन्द्रो यवाशिरः ॥

1. The soul, that moves from one body to the other, is deft in action, properly gives and takes, is enlightened and mixed with food, assumes bodily form. (145)[2]

२. इमा उ त्वा पुरुवसोऽभि प्र नोनुनवुर्गिरः । गावो वत्सं न धेनवः ॥

---

[1]Kakshivan and Aushija are not the names of Rishis as explained by Griffith. कक्षीवान् means breath, as it resides in कक्ष i. e., breast. Pt. Jawala Prasad translates कक्ष as पाप (sin) which is contrary to nirukta and Grammar.

[2]*Gives and takes*: Soul imparts knowledge to some and receives instruction from others. This verse clearly states that the soul enters the womb at the time of conception through what a woman eats and drinks. This explodes the theory that the soul enters the womb a few months after the conception.

2. O God, the Lord of ample wealth, these songs of praise go forth unto Thee, as milch-Kine low to their calves. (146)

३. अत्राह गोरमन्वत नाम त्वष्टुरपीच्यम् । इत्था चन्द्रमसो गृहे ॥

3. It is generally accepted that in the mansion of the Moon, there is a part of the light of the Sun, so there resides the light of God in our delightful superhuman soul. (147)

४. यदिन्द्रो अनयद्रितो महीरपो वृषन्तमः । तत्र पूषाभवत्सचा ॥

4. When soul, the showerer of extreme delight leads us on to progressive deeds, it becomes our nourisher through affinity. (148)[1]

५. गौर्धयति मरुताᳵश्रवस्युमता मघोनाम् । युक्ता बह्वी रथानाम् ॥

5. The Soul, the mother of vital breaths, the sustainers of life, hankering after knowledge, united with vital breaths and conscious organs, elevates them. (149)

६. उप नो हरिभिः सुतं याहि मदानां पते । उप नो हरिभिः सुतम् ॥

6. O soul, the Lord of rapturous joys, enjoy the knowledge derived from our organs. (150)[2]

७. इष्टा होत्रा असृक्षतेन्द्रं वृधन्तो अध्वरे । अच्छावभृथमोजसा ॥

7. In this non-violent sacrifice of life, the Hotas, fed with the oblations of passions enhancing the knowledge, dignity and sublimity of the soul, nicely finish the Yajna (sacrifice) to the end. (151)[3]

८. अहमिद्धि पितुष्परि मेधामृतस्य जग्रह । अहंᳵसूर्य इवाजनि ॥

8. May I verily receive from my Father God, the deep knowledge of eternal law, and thus become resplendent like the Sun. (152)

९. रेवतीनᳵः सधमाद इन्द्रे सन्तु तुविवाजाः । क्षुमन्तो याभिर्मदेम ॥

9. Along with our soul, may our organs of cognition be joyful and strengthened. Equipped with them may we rejoice. (153)[4]

---

[1]Griffith describes Indra and Pushan as two deities. This explanation is unacceptable, as the Vedas are free from historical reference.

[2]The repetition here is for the sake of emphasis.

[3]Hotas are seven Rishis, i.e., two eyes, two nostrils, two ears and mouth. These seven organs add to the knowledge and grandeur of the soul, and carry on this Yajna throughout life to the end. अवभृथ is the cleansing bath taken at the end of a Yajna.

[4]Organs of cognition means Gyan Indriyas. If our soul feels happiness, our organs too are full of joy.

Them refers to the organs.

१०. सोमः पूषा च चेततुर्विश्वासाᳵसुक्षितीनाम् । देवत्रा रथ्योहिता ॥

10. God, the Urger and Creator of all, the Nourisher of all and soul, that pervades all organs of the body, being friendly to active and passive life, impart us the knowledge of how to behave in life. (154)[1]

DECADE II

१. पान्तमा वो अन्धस इन्द्रमभि प्र गायत । विश्वासाहᳵशतक्रतुं मᳵहिष्ठं चर्षणीनाम् ॥

1. O men sing the praise of God, the Guardian of our foodstuffs, the Subduer of all, the Master of hundreds of achievements, the Object of adoration by all learned persons. (155)

२. प्र व इन्द्राय मादनᳵहर्यश्वाय गायत । सखायः सोमपाᳶने ॥

2. O friends, for the sake of spiritual enjoyment, sing the glory of God, the Embodiment of captivating characteristics, and the Saviour of His devotees. (156)

३. वयमु त्वा तदिदर्था इन्द्र त्वायन्तः सखायः । कण्वा उक्थेभिर्जरन्ते ॥

3. O God, learned persons, Thy friends, worship Thee with Vedic verses. We Thy sincere devotees, longing for Thee, also worship Thee. (157)

४. इन्द्राय मद्वने सुतं परि ष्टोभन्तु नो गिरः । अर्कमर्चन्तु कारवः ॥

4. May admirers admire God. May our Vedic sayings divulge knowledge. (158)

५. अयं त इन्द्र सोमो निपूतो अधि बर्हिषि । एहीमस्य द्रवा पिब ॥

5. O soul, this pure joy residing in the mind is for thee, Run hither, come and drink it. (159)[2]

६. सुरूपकृत्नुमूतये सुदुघामिव गोदुहे । जुह्ममसि द्यविद्यवि ॥

6. Just as a good cow calls him who milks, so we for safety from sin invoke day by day God, the Rewarder of our actions. (160)

७. अभि त्वा वृषभा सुते सुतᳵसृजामि पीतये । तृम्पा व्यश्नुही मदम् ॥

7. O soul, the showerer of happiness on the attainment of knowledge, I pour it for thee to drink. State thee, and enjoy pleasure in full. (161)[3]

---

[1]Soma and Pushan have been translated by Griffith as names of deities. Both words are epithets of God. Soma is God as He urges and creates us. He is Pushan, as He nourishes us.

Active life is Karma Yoni of sentient beings. Passive life is Bhog Yoni of beasts and birds.

[2]Drink means enjoy, realise.

[3]I means Yogi. A Yogi addresses the soul in a state of trance. 'It' refers to knowledge. 'To drink' means to enjoy.

८. य इन्द्र चमसेष्वा सोमश्चमूषु ते सुतः । पिबेदस्य त्वमीशिषे ॥

8. O soul, whatever knowledge there is retained in the cells and arteries of the brain is for thee. Drink thou that, for thou art lord thereof. (162)

९. योगेयोगे तवस्तरं वाजेवाजे हवामहे । सखाय इन्द्रमूतये ॥

9. In every deep meditation, in every search for knowledge, we call, as friends to succour us, God, the Mightiest of all. (163)

१०. आ त्वेता नि षीदतेन्द्रमभि प्र गायत । सखायः स्तोमवाहसः ॥

10. O companions, bringing hymns of praise, come Ye hither, sit Ye down, and sing forth your song to God. (164)[1]

DECADE III

१. इदꣳह्यन्वोजसा सुतꣳराधानां पते । पिबा त्वा३स्य गिर्वणः ॥

1. O soul, the lord of affluence, this knowledge has been gained with great exertion. O worthy of praise, enjoy this knowledge. (165)

२. महाꣳइन्द्रः पुरश्च नो महित्वमस्तु वज्रिणे । द्यौर्न प्रथिना शवः ॥

2. Great is our soul. May we always keep in view the soul, the extinguisher of fears. Wide as the heaven extends in might. (166)

३. आ तू न इन्द्र क्षुमन्तं चित्रं ग्राभꣳसं गृभाय । महाहस्ती दक्षिणेन ॥

3. O soul, full of exertion, gather intelligently the knowledge worthy of acquisition, that equips thee with food and habitation. (167)

४. अभि प्र गोपतिं गिरेन्द्रमर्चं यथा विदे । सूनुꣳसत्यस्य सत्पतिम् ॥

4. O man, sing with thy speech, for true knowledge, the praise of soul, the lord of light, the son of Truth, and the protector of Truth. (168)[2]

५. कया अश्चित्र आ भुवदूती सदावृधः सखा । कया शचिष्ठया वृता ॥

5. With what unique protection, with what mighty force, in what manner, will soul that feeds on truth and acquires knowledge, become our friend. (169)

६. त्यमु वः सत्रासाहं विश्वासु गीष्वायतम् । आ च्यावयस्यूतये ॥

---

[1]In Tandya Brahman nine kinds of stomas have been mentioned, as Trivrit त्रिवृत्, Panchdash पञ्चदश, Saptdash सप्तदश, Ekvinsha, एकविंश Trinava त्रिनव, Trayastrinsh त्रयस्त्रिंश Chaturvinsh चतुर्विंश, Chatvarinsh चत्वारिंश Ashtchatvarinsh अष्टचत्वारिंश ।
Stoma means praise. The method of singing these stomas has been mentioned in the Tandya Brahman.

[2]The son of Truth means the embodiment of truth.

6. Manifest for your advancement, the soul, the conqueror of all evil intentions, and the goal of all praises. (170)

७. सदसस्पतिमद्भूतं प्रियमिन्द्रस्य काम्यम् । सनि मेधामयासिषम् ॥

7. May I hanker after the realisation of God, the Sustainer of the universe, Unrivalled, Lovely, Worthy of adoration by soul, and the Bestower of firm intellect. (171)

८. ये ते पन्था अधो दिवो येभिर्व्यश्ववमैरय: । उत श्रोषन्तु नो भुव: ॥

8. O soul, may all thy paths beneath the skull whereby thou impellest various organs, and our organs of action listen to thy behest. (172)

९. भद्रंभद्रं न आ भरेषमूर्जं ॐशतक्रतो । यदिन्द्र मृडयासि न: ॥

9. O Omnipotent God, when Thou art kind to us, Thou bestowest on us excellent things like food and strength. (173)

१०. अस्ति सोमो अयं ॐसुत: पिबन्त्यस्य मरुत: । उत स्वराजो अश्विना ॥

10. Here is ready this fine essence of knowledge. The intelligent, talented persons, and learned husband and wife drink it. (174)[1]

DECADE IV

१. ईड्वयन्तीरपस्युव इन्द्रं जातमुपासते । वन्वानास: सुवीर्यम् ।

1. Our intellect full of knowledge and willing to act, and enterprising, meditative persons worship God, when He manifests Himself in the heart. (175)

२. नकि देवा इनीमसि न क्या योपयामसि । मन्त्रश्रुत्यं चरामसि ॥

2. O God, let us Thy worshippers be non-violent, and free from illusion. Let us act on the commandments of the Vedas. (176)

३. दोषो आगाद् बृहद्गाय ह्यमद्गामन्नाथर्बण । स्तुहि देव ॐसवितारम् ॥

3. O soul, the singer of Brihat Sāma, the non-destroyer of life, the master of action, the Effulgent God, the Remover of all sorts of ignorance, has manifested Himself in thee. Sing His praise, the Persuader of all. (177)[2]

४. एषो उषा अपूर्व्या व्युच्छति प्रिया दिव: । स्तुषे वामश्विना बृहत् ।

4. This unique and bright intellect emanates from the resplendent soul. I admire both the forces of knowledge and determination. (178)

---

[1] Ashwina means heaven and earth, day and night, sun and moon as well, vide **Nirukta** 12-1.

[2] Brihat Sama is a part of the Sāmaveda.

५. इन्द्रो दधीचो अस्थभिर्वृत्राण्यप्रतिष्कुतः । जघान नवतीनंव ॥

5. Soul, with the aid of ignorance-dispelling forces of God, Attainable through contemplation, Unvanquished by any earthly power, overcomes eight hundred and ten impediments that overshadow knowledge. (179)[1]

६. इन्द्रेहि मत्स्यन्धसो विश्वेभिः सोमपर्वभिः । महाँ अभिष्टिरोजसा ॥

6. O soul, manifest thyself. Delight thee with all the vigour-infusing forces of fine breath. With thy strength, thou art filled with mighty desires. (180)

७. आ तू न इन्द्र वृत्रहन्नस्माकमर्धमा गहि । महान्महीभिरूतिभिः ॥

7. O God, the Slayer of the forces of darkness, come hither to our side. Thou art Mighty with Thy mighty aids. (181)

८. श्रोजस्तदस्य तित्विष उभे यत्समवर्तयत् । इन्द्रश्चर्मेव रोदसी ।

8. God's is that might which is blazing and revolving Heaven and Earth, as a hero revolves the shield. (182)

९. अयमु ते समतसि कपोत इव गर्भधिम् । वचस्तच्चिन्न ओहसे ॥

9. Just as a pigeon goes near his pregnant mate, so does this devotee go near God, Who listens to this prayer of ours. (183)

१०. वात आ वातु भेषजँशभु मयोभु नो हृदे । प्र न आयूँषि तारिषत् ॥

10. May God instil in our heart His blissful, healthful and healing balm. May He prolong the days of our life. (184)

DECADE V

१. यँ रक्षन्ति प्रचेतसो वरुणो मित्रो अर्यमा । न किः स दभ्यते जनः ॥

1. Never does he suffer mentally whom wisdom, purity, love and justice protect. (185)

---

[1]Eight hundred and ten impediments are enumerated below. Three forces of matter, Satva, (Truth) Rajas (Possession). Tamas (Darkness) become nine, multiplied by three divisions of time, past, present and future. They become twenty seven, multiplied by the three attributes of प्रभाव (Power), उत्साह (perseverance) मन्त्र (Counsel). Multiplied by three stages of उत्तम, मध्यम, अधम i.e. High, Medium and Low, the number becomes 81. Taking into consideration the ten directions, the number becomes 810. This is a plausible explanation offered by Pt. Jaidev Vidyalankar, and Swami Tulsi Ram. Some commentators have translated the word नवतीनंव as many. Sayana has fabricated a historical story on this verse, which is unacceptable as Vedas are free from historical references, being the word of God in the beginning of creation.

Griffith translates Dadhicha as a Rishi, son of Atharvan, with his bones converted into a thunderbolt. Indra is said to have slain the host of vritras or demons who withhold the rain. Vritras are impediments of ignorance in the way of knowledge. Dadhicha means God attainable through contemplation.

Griffith's translation is not plausible.

२. गव्यो षु णो यथा पुराश्वयोत रथया । वरिवस्या महोनाम् ॥

2. For the acquisition of knowledge and prosperity it is essential to first control organs, mind and body. (186)

३. इमास्त इन्द्र पृश्नयो घृतं दुहत आशिरम् । एनामृतस्य पिप्युषी: ॥

3. O soul, these organs of thine, enjoying true knowledge, produce bursting lustre, as do the kine yield milk, after taking water. (187)

४. अया धिया च गव्यया पुरुणामन्पुरुष्टुत । यत्सोमेसोम आभुव: ॥

4. O much-lauded ; multi-named ; God, when Thou graciously manifestest Thyself in each exalted soul, we are filled with a desire to sharpen our intellect and acquire spiritual wealth. (188)

५. पावका न: सरस्वती वाजेभिर्वाजिनीवती । यज्ञं वष्टु धियावसु: ॥

5. O Vedic speech, our purifier, powerful through knowledge and action, residing in our mind through contemplation and light of knowledge, beautify the Yajna of our life. (189)

६. क इमं नाहुषीष्वा इन्द्रꣴसोमस्य तर्पयात् । स नो वसुन्या भरात् ॥

6. Who amidst mortals, bound by the ties of action, can gratify the soul with knowledge? God alone grants us the wealth of knowledge. (190)[1]

७. आ याहि सुषुमा हि त इन्द्र सोमं पिबा इमम् । एदं बर्हि: सदो मम ॥

7. Come O soul, we are gleaning divine pleasure for thee. Enjoy it. Illumine this heart of mine. (191)

८. महि त्रीणामवरस्तु द्युक्षं मित्रस्यार्यम्ण: । दुराधर्षं वरुणस्य ॥

8. May great, unassailable, heavenly favour of God, possessing the triple qualities of Love, Praiseworthiness and Justice, shower on us. (192)

९. त्वावत: पुरूवसो वयमिन्द्र प्रणेत: । स्मसि स्थातर्हरीणाम् ॥

9. O God, the Lord of mortals, the Supreme Guide, the Settler of many, we depend on one like Thee ! (193)[2]

---

[1]Griffith considers Nahusha to be a tribe, apparently different from the five great Aryan tribes and dwellers on or near the Indus? This is absurd as there is no history in the Vedas नहुष इति मनुष्यनाम् निघ: 2-3-6 नहुष means man vide Nighantu.

[2]Griffith has translated हरीणाम् as of tawny steeds. It means, 'of men'.

BOOK III

Chapter 2

DECADE I

१. उस्वा मन्दन्तु सोमा: कृणुष्व राधो अद्रिव: । अव ब्रह्मद्विषो जहि ॥

1. O God, let mild worshippers make Thee glad. Grant us wealth of knowledge, cast aside anti-vedic feelings. (194)'

२. गिर्वंण: पाहि न: सुतं मधोर्धाराभिरज्यसे । इन्द्र त्वादातमिद्यश: ॥

2. O God, praised through Vedic hymns, protect the worshipper midst us. Thou art worshipped with Vedic verses. Glory is Thy gift. (195)

३. सदा व इन्द्रश्चकृषदा उपो नु स सपर्यन् । न देवो वृत: शूर इन्द्र: ॥

3. God always attracts you near Him. Why don't you acknowledge Him, Who loves you, is Powerful and Divine. (196)

४. आ त्वा विशन्त्विन्दव: समुद्रमिव सिन्धव: । न त्वामिन्द्राति रिच्यते ॥

4. Let the intellectuals plunge in God, as the rivers flow into the sea. O God, naught excelleth Thee ! (197)

५. इन्द्रमिद्गाथिनो बृहदिन्द्रमर्केभिरर्किण: । इन्द्रं वाणीरनूषत ॥

5. Udgathas, the singers of the Samaveda glorify God through Brihat Sama. Hotas the reciters of the Rigveda, glorify God with the verses of the Rigveda. Adhvaryus glorify God with the verses of the Yajurveda. (198)

६. इन्द्र इषे ददातु न ऋभुक्षणमृभुँरयिम् । वाजी ददातु वाजिनम् ॥

6. May God, according to our desire grant us mighty and handy wealth, May Omniscient God grant us knowledge and action. (199)[1]

७. इन्द्रो अङ्ग महद्भयमभी षदप चुच्यवत् । स हि स्थिरो विचर्षणि: ॥

7. O man, God drives away mighty fear from all sides. For firm is He and Seer of all. (200)

---

[1]Grassman says, the verse may originally have been taken from a hymn addressed to the Ribhus, the eldest of whom was Ribhukshan and the youngest Vāja. This is incorrect, as there is no history in the Vedas. Wilson, following Sayana translates the verse in the Rigveda differently:

"May Indra bring to us the bounteous Ribhu Ribhukshna to partake of our sacrificial viands; may he the mighty bring the mighty." This explanation is untenable, as it refers to history in the Vedas.

८. इमा उ त्वा सुतेसुते नक्षन्ते गिर्वणो गिर: । गावो वत्सं न धेनव: ॥

8. O God ! when spiritual sentiments arise, these Vedic songs reach Thee as milch Kine fondly hasten to their calves. (201)[1]

९. इन्द्रा नु पूषणा वयꣳसख्याय स्वस्तये । हुवेम वाजसातये ॥

9. For friendship, prosperity and wealth of knowledge, we invoke the Omnipotent and Fostering God. (202)

१०. न कि इन्द्र त्वदुत्तरं न ज्यायो अस्ति वृत्रहन् । न क्येवं यथा त्वम् ॥

10. O God ! the Remover of ignorance, none is better, mightier than Thee, verily there is none like Thee. (203)

DECADE II

१. तरणि वो जनानां त्रदं वाजस्य गोमत: । समानमु प्र शꣳसिषम् ॥

1. O men, I praise God, your Saviour, the Banisher of sufferings, the Master of animal world, the Lord of wealth, knowledge and food, and the Dispenser of impartial justice. (204)

२. असृग्रमिन्द्र ते गिर: प्रति त्वामुदहासत । सजोषा वृषभं पतिम् ॥

2. O God, I praise Thee with Vedic songs. Just as a loving wife goes to her husband, so are these songs proceeding towards God, the Fosterer of all. (205)

३. सुनीथी घा स मर्त्यो यं मरुतो यमर्यमा । मित्रास्पान्त्यद्रुह: ॥

3. Verily the mortal man hath good guidance, whom the learned persons free from guile, and just God, the Friend of all afford protection. (206)

४. यद्वीडाविन्द्र यत्स्थिरे यत्पर्शाने पराभृतम् । वसु स्पार्हं तदा भर ॥

4. O God, bring us the wealth for which we long, which is found in a man who does not yield to foes, who is unflinching and reflective ! (207)

५. श्रुतं वो वृत्रहन्तमं प्र शर्ध चर्षणीनाम् । आशिषे राधसे महे ॥

5. O men, for the sake of great munificence and fulfilment of the desires of mankind, worship the Mighty God, highly spoken of in the Vedas ! (208)

६. अरं त इन्द्र श्रवसे गमेम शूर त्वावत: । अरꣳशक्र परेमणि ॥

6. O Valiant God, may we continue singing Thy fame, the fame of one like Thee. O Omnipotent God, may we fully realise Thee through deep meditation ! (209)[2]

---

[1]Full of love the soul sings Vedic songs in praise of God, as kine lovingly go to their calves.

[2]The fame of one like Thee means Thy fame alone, as none else is like God who is Unique and Incomparable. Griffith says the meaning of the words 'Premani' is uncertain. Stevenson translates this as 'In our most solemn sacrifice'. The word प्रेमाणि means परमुत्कृष्टं मोक्षपदं गम्यने येन तस्मिनसमाधौ i.e., deep meditation.

७. धानावन्तं करम्भिणमपूपवन्तमुक्थिनम् । इन्द्र प्रातर्जुषस्व न: ॥

7. O God, accept at day-break our soul, absorbed in meditation, full of pleasure, present in all places far and near, and full of knowledge ! (210)[1]

८. अपां फेनेन नमुचे: शिर इन्द्रोदवर्तय: । विश्वा यदजय स्पृध: ॥

8. O soul, when thou overcomest all evil propensities, cut thou asunder the head of Death through the force of contemplation and action ! (211)[2]

९. इमे त इन्द्र सोमा: सुतासो ये च सोत्वा: । तेषां मत्स्व प्रभूवसो ॥

9. O soul, thine are these pleasures and knowledge derived and which are still to be derived. O Lord of strength, remain ever glad, through their enjoyment ! (212)[3]

१०. तुभ्यꣳसुतास: सोमा: स्तीर्ण बर्हिविभावसो । स्तोतृभ्य इन्द्र मृडय ॥

10. For Thee, O God, Lord of light, have we purified our minds, and spread our hearts. Be gracious to Thy worshippers. (213)

DECADE III

१. आ व इन्द्रं कृवि यथा वाजयन्त: शतक्रतुम् । मꣳहिष्ठꣳसिञ्च इन्दुभि: ॥

1. O men, Ye seeking strength should please with songs of praise, God, Most liberal, Lord of boundless might, just as a cultivator waters the field with water from a well ! (214)

२. अतश्चिदिन्द्र न उपा याहि शतवाजया । इषा सहस्रवाजया ॥

2. Hence, O God, come unto us with food that gives a hundred, Yea a thousand powers ! (215)[4]

३. आ बुन्दं वृत्रहा ददे जात: पृच्छाद्वि मातरम् । क उग्रा: के ह श्रृण्विरे ॥

3. A powerful King, the remover of impediments, being trained in military science, and armed with a shaft, asks his subjects, "who are your fierce tormentors, who are engaged in the pursuit of Violence ?" (216)

४. बृबदुक्थꣳहवामहे सृप्रकरस्नमूतये । साध: कृण्वन्तमवसे ॥

4. O King, for the protection of the people, and for self-protection, we call thee who is highly lauded, and is long armed. (217)

---

[1]For fuller explanation see Pt. Jaidev Vidyalankar's commentary.

[2]Griffith describes Namuchi as one of the numerous demons of draught conquered by Indra. Namuchi means death which follows us and doesn't release the soul till the end. Some commentators have interpreted the word as 'cloud' which does not easily release water. Cutting the head of death means becoming free from the fear of death.

[3]Lord of strength means soul.

[4]Come unto us with food means grant us food.

५. ऋजुनीती नो वरुणो मित्रो नयति विद्वान् । अर्यमा देवैः सजोषाः ॥

5. O God, the Dispeller of all afflictions, the Friend of all, Omniscient, Just, Lover of the learned, Thou leadest us straight on the path of virtue like a King! (218)

६. दूरादिहेव यत्सतोऽरुणप्सुरशिशिवितत् । वि भानुं विश्वधातनत् ॥

6. Just as the Sun from afar sheds his lustre on all objects, as if he were near, so does God spread from all sides His light of Justice. (219)

७. आ नो मित्रावरुणा घृतंगंव्यूतिमुक्षतम् । मध्वा रजांसि सुक्रतू ॥

7. O Prāṇa and Apāna, with your lustres, water the soul with pleasure derived from Yoga. O men of action and knowledge, fill our organs with consciousness! (220)

८. उदु त्ये सूनवो गिरः काष्ठा यज्ञेष्वत्नत । वाश्रा अभिज्ञु यातवे ॥

8. Airs, the source of speech, thus, tread on their paths, in organs, their residence, as cows bend on the knees for walking at the time when they bellow for the calf. (221)

९. इदं विष्णुर्वि चक्रमे त्रेधा नि दधे पदम् । समूढमस्य पांसुले ॥

9. The soul moves thus, and establishes its powers in three ways. Its power is finely manifest in the body. (222)[1]

DECADE IV

१. अतीहि मन्युषाविणं सुषुवांसमुपेरय । अस्य रातौ सुतं पिब ॥

1. O soul, thou shunnest the wrathful and approachest the devotee. Enjoy the height of pleasure derived through his self-dedication! (223)[2]

२. कदु प्रचेतसे महे वचो देवाय शस्यते ॥ तदिद्ध्यस्य वर्धनम् ॥

2. Whatever word however little is addressed to God, Great and excellently Wise, the same exalteth the worshipper. (224)

३. उक्थं च न शस्यमानं नागो रयिरा चिकेत । न गायत्रं गीयमानम् ॥

3. Doesn't God know the prayer offered by an ignorant person. Doesn't He know the recitation of the Gayatra Sama. He does know. (225)[3]

४. इन्द्र उक्थेभिर्मन्दिष्ठो वाजानां च वाजपतिः । हरिवांत्सुतानां सखा ॥

4. O God, Thou art pleased with praise-songs. Thou art the Lord of the learned. Thou Controllest the five elements and art the Friend of the created worlds. (226)

---

[1]The verse is applicable to God as well. See Yajurveda 5-15.
In three ways: (1) Acquiring essence from food (2) Knowledge from organs (3) Spreading breath in the body.
[2]His means devotee's.
[3]Gayatra Sāma is a part of the Sāmaveda.

५. श्रा याह्यद्ध ̐ प न: सुतं वाजेभिर्मा हृणीयथा: । महाँ ̐इव युवजानि: ॥

5. O God, come unto our soul. Don't deprive us of food, knowledge and strength. Thou art venerable like a grandfather before a grandson. (227)

६. कदा वसो स्तोत्रँ ̐हर्यंत आ अव श्मशा रुधद्वा: । दीर्घँ ̐सुतं वाताप्याय ॥

6. O Omnipresent God, when do'st Thou impede the flow of life in the body of the recipient of the knowledge of the Vedas? Thou grantest long life to him who controls his breath. (228)[1]

७. ब्राह्मणादिन्द्र राधस: पिबा सोममृतूँ ̐रनु । तवेदँ ̐सख्यमस्तृतम् ॥

7. O soul, drink deep with thy breaths and organs, the essence of knowledge from a learned person who is the worshipper and knower of God. Invincible is thy friendship! (229)[2]

८. वयं घा ते श्रपि स्मसि स्तोतार इन्द्र गिर्वण: । त्वं नो जिन्व सोमपा: ॥

8. O God, Lover of the song, we are the singers of Thy praise, O Master of knowledge, gratify us! (230)

ए. एन्द्र पृक्षु कासु चिन्नृम्णं तनूषु धेहि न: । सत्राजिदुग्र पौँ ̐स्यम् ॥

9. O Omnipotent God, to some bodies Thou grantest spiritual strength. Strong Lord, to some Thou grantest ever-conquering might! (231)

१०. एवा ह्यसि वीरयुरेवा शूर उत स्थिर: । एवा ते राध्यं मन: ॥

10. O soul, thou art verily the brave man's friend. A hero art thou. Thou art firm, calm and steady. Hence thy power of reflection is worthy of emulation! (232)

DECADE V

१. श्रभि त्वा शूर नोनुमोऽदुग्धा इव धेनव: । ईशानमस्य जगत: स्वद् ̍शमीशानमिन्द्र तस्थुष: ॥

1. O Omnipotent God, the Illuminator of Sun, Lord of this moving world, Lord of what moveth not, we bow before Thee, as unmilked kine bow before the calves! (233)

२. त्वामिद्धि हवामहे सातौ वाजस्य कारव: ।
त्वां वृत्रेष्विन्द्र सत्पतिं नरस्त्वां काष्ठांस्वर्वंत: ॥

2. O God, we, Thy worshippers, call on Thee for the acquisition of the wealth of knowledge. In adversity we contemplate on Thy True, Protecting Nature. We remember Thee alone for success, after exerting to the best of our mite. (234)

---

[1] When dost Thou impede means Thou never impedest.
[2] The friendship of the soul with a learned person is unconquerable.

३. अभि प्र व: सुराधसमिन्द्रमर्चं यथा विदे ।
यो जरितृभ्यो मघवा पुरूवसु सहस्त्रेणेव शिक्षति ॥

3. O men, for the acquisition of knowledge, duly worship God, the Master of wealth. He being ubiquitous and rich in treasure, imparts instructions to His singers in a thousand ways. (235)

४. तं वो दस्ममृतीषहं वसोर्मन्दानमन्धस: ।
अभि वत्सं न स्वसरेषु धेनव इन्द्रं गीर्भिनंवामहे ॥

4. As cows bow to their calves in stalls, so we glorify that God of the people, Who is the Remover of our foes, the Subduer of our passions, the Establisher of soul in the body, and takes delight in the essence of knowledge. (236)

५. तरोभिर्वो विदद्वसुमिन्द्रꣳसबाध ऊतये ।
बृहद्गायन्त: सुतसोमे अध्वरे हुवे भरं न कारिणम् ॥

5. In a Yajna performed for acquiring intense pleasure, when obstacles stand in your way, with full vigour invoke knowledge-bestowing God, singing Brihat Sāma for safety. I too applaud that Nourishing and Propitious God. (237)[1]

६. तरणिरित्सिषासति वाजं पुरन्ध्या युजा ।
आ व इन्द्रं पुरुहूतं नमे गिरा नेमि तष्टेव सुद्रुवम् ॥

6. Soul, coupled with perception soon perceives knowledge in full. Just as a carpenter bends the wheel for swift motion, so do I make you bend with Vedic song before God, much-invoked. (238)[2]

७. पिबा सुतस्य रसिनो मत्स्वा न इन्द्रगोमत: ।
आपिर्नो बोधि सधमाद्ये वृधेꣳस्माꣳअवन्तु ते धिय: ॥

7. O soul, enjoy the knowledge derived from us, the active organs; and be thus delighted. Grant us knowledge, being ever present in our body as a friend. May thy acts of wisdom guard us well for our prosperity! (239)[2]

८. त्वꣳह्येहि चेरवे विदा भगं वसुत्तये ।
उद्वावृषस्व मघवन् गविष्टय उदिन्द्राश्वमिष्टये ॥

8. O God, approach the worshipper for the grant of knowledge. O Master of infinite knowledge, grant us strength to control our organs. Strengthen our breath for the performance of Yoga. Grant us the supremacy of Yoga! (240)

---

[1] I means a learned, devout person, a preacher.
  Brihat Sāma is a part of the Sāmaveda.
[2] 'I' means a preacher.
  You: Worshippers.
  तरणि: means soul that makes us cross the ocean of sufferings and miseries of the world.
  पुरन्धि means perception or intellect that bears the burden of the fortress of our body.

९. न हि वश्चरमं च न वसिष्ठ: परिमꣳसत ।
अस्माकमद्य मरुत: सुते सचा विश्वे पिबन्तु कामिन: ॥

9. God never abandons even the most degraded one of you. O men, let all lovers of divine essence amongst us, unitedly drink it in deep meditation! (241)

१०. मा चिदन्यद्वि शꣳसत सखायो मा रिषण्यत ।
इन्द्रमित्स्तोता वृषणꣳ सचा सुते मुहुरुक्था च शꣳसत ॥

10. Glorify none else but God, O friends. Be non-violent. Sing together in your pure heart the glory of God, the Bestower of Dharma, Arth, Kāma and Moksha. Recite again and again, Vedic hymns in His praise. (242)[1]

Chapter 2

DECADE I

१. नकिष्टं कर्मणा नशद्यश्चकार सदावृधम् ।
इन्द्रं न यज्ञैर्विश्वगूर्तमृभ्वसमधृष्टं धृष्णुमोजसा ॥

1. None can harm the man who, by his deeds and sacrifices renders himself fit to ever tread on the path of progress, like a King, praised of all, full of knowledge, unconquerable by his might, and endurer of afflictions with patience. (243)

२. य ऋते चिदभिश्रिष: पुरा जत्रुभ्य आतृद: ।
सन्धाता सन्धिं मघवा पुरूवसुर्निष्कर्ता विह्रुतं पुन: ॥

2. God, residing in all bodies without ligature, even before blood is produced, joins together the joints of the neck, and at His will soon dissevers them. (244)[2]

३. आ त्वा सहस्रमा शतं युक्ता रथे हिरण्यये ।
ब्रह्मयुजो हरय इन्द्र केशिनो वहन्तु सोमपीतये ॥

3. O God, may hundreds and thousands of learned and talented persons, realising Thee in meditation, for the acquisition of delight, remember Thee, in their body united with soul! (245)

---

[1](1) *Dharma*: Virtuous life.
(2) *Arth*: Desired riches and wealth of knowledge.
(3) *Kāma*: Achievement of noble ambitions.
(4) *Moksha*: Emancipation, Final beatitude.
[2]How wondrous is the power of God, that embryo in the womb, before the creation of blood, and without, any ligature, gets the joints of his neck closed up.
God at His will in a trice dissevers the joints and sends the strongest man to death. This process of birth and death is eternal through the potency of God.

४. आ्रा मन्द्रेरिन्द्र हरिभिर्याहि मयूररोमभिः ।
मा त्वा के चिन्नि येमुरिन्न पाशिनोऽति धन्वेव ता^ॐ इहि ॥

4. O soul, come with pleasure-giving cobwebs of knowledge, brilliant like the peacock's plumes, and with instruments of learning. No alluring temptations can entrap thee, as a hunter does the bird. Thou rather overcomest them, as an archer does an animal! (246)[1]

५. त्वमङ्ग प्र श^ॐसिषो देवः शविष्ठ मर्त्यम् ।
न त्वदन्यो मघवन्नस्ति मडितेन्द्र ब्रवीमि ते वचः ॥

5. O God, the Mightiest, the Illuminator of all, Thou verily infusest life in the mortal body. O All-Powerful, there is no comforter but Thee. I speak my words to Thee! (247)

६. त्वमिन्द्र यशा अस्यृजीषी शवसस्पतिः ।
त्वं वृत्राणि ह^ॐस्यप्रतीन्येक इत्पूर्वन्नुत्तश्चर्षणीधृतिः ॥

6. O God, Thou art far-renowned, the Leader of Thy devotees free from crookedness, on the path of virtue, the Lord of power and might. Alone, Thou, unconquered by many, art the Guardian of mankind. Thou smitest down resistless impediments! (248)[2]

७. इन्द्रमिद्देवतातय इन्द्रं प्रत्यध्वरे ।
इन्द्र^ॐसमीके वनिनो हवामह इन्द्रं धनस्य सातये ॥

7. All worshippers invoke God alone, for the prosperity of the learned, at the commencement of a non-violent undertaking, in a moral struggle, and for the acquisition of spiritual knowledge. (249)

८. इमा उ त्वा पुरूवसो गिरो वर्धन्तु या मम ।
पावकवर्णाः शुचयो विपश्चितोऽभिस्तोमैरनूषत ॥

8. May these my songs of praise exalt Thee, O God, Who hast abundant wealth ! Pure, learned persons, the purifiers of all, also laud Thee with hymns of praise! (250)

९. उदु त्ये मधुमत्तमा गिर स्तोमास ईरते ।
सत्राजितो धनसा अक्षितोतयो वाजयन्तो रथा इव ॥

9. These songs of ours, exceeding sweet, these hymns of praise come out of our heart unto God, like ever conquering chariots that display their strength, gain wealth, and afford unfailing protection! (251)

१०. यथा गौरो अपा कृतं तृष्यन्नेत्यवेरिणम् ।
आपित्वे नः प्रपित्वे तूयमा गहि कण्वेषु सु सचा पिब ॥

[1]*Them*: Temptations.
[2]*Impediments*: Foes like passions.

10. Just as a thirsty deer reaches a watery pool in the desert, so shouldst thou, O soul, acquiring the friendship of us, the devotees of God, awake quickly, and enjoy with us divine felicity! (252)[1]

DECADE II

१. शग्ध्यू३षू शचीपत इन्द्र विश्वाभिरूतिभिः ।
भग न हि त्वा यशसं वसुविदमनु शूर चरामसि ।

1. O God, Lord of knowledge and action, fulfil our aim with all Thy powers of protection. We follow Thee, the Embodiment of glorious bliss, Hero and Giver of wealth. (253)

२. या इन्द्र भुज आभरः स्ववर्पुंअसुरेभ्यः ।
स्तोतारमिन्मघवन्नस्य वर्धय ये च त्वे वृक्तबर्हिषः ॥

2. O Wealthy God, Lord of light, whatever enjoyable things, Thou takest away from the degraded people, prosper therewith Thy obedient worshipper, and them who perform philanthropic deeds in Thy name! (254).

३. प्र मित्राय प्रार्यम्णे सचथ्यमृतावसो ।
वरूथ्ये३वरुणे छन्दं वचः स्तोत्रपुंराजसु गायत ॥

3. O learned lover of truth, sing the praise of God, Your Friend in the heart. Sing well with Vedic praiseworthy, enjoyable words, the glory of God, Who is Just, Ever-present in the heart, the Well-wisher of the body, His residence, the Remover of all impediments, and the King of Kings! (255)[2]

४. अभि ह्र ुवपातय इन्द्र स्तोमेभिरायवः ।
समीचीनास ऋभवः समस्वरन् रुद्रा गृणन्त पूर्व्यम् ॥

4. O God, men aspiring after longevity, for the sake of enjoying life to its full span, realise Thee through Vedic songs. Wise and learned persons praise Thee. The preachers of knowledge sing Thee as the Immemorial! (256)

५. प्र व इंद्राय बृहते मरुतो ब्रह्मार्चंत । वृत्रपुं हनति वृत्रहा शतक्रतुर्वज्रेण शतपर्वणा ॥

5. O men, sing for your lofty God, a holy Vedic hymn. He, the Lord of hundreds of deeds and judgments, the Slayer of sins, removes vice with His hundred-sided power of knowledge! (257)

६. बृहदिन्द्राय गायत मरुतो वृत्रहन्तमम् । येन ज्योतिरजयन्नृतावृधो देवं देवाय जागृवि ॥

---

[1]Griffith considers the meaning of apitve—prapitve as uncertain. He has adopted Grassman's interpretation of morning and evening but does not consider it satisfactory. Ludwig translates these two words as 'near and far away'. Sayana assigns to apitve a different meaning of 'at the time of banquet'. The words mean, having acquired friendship.

[2]Griffith translates Aryama, Mitra and Varuna as different deities, This is unacceptable as the Vedas are free from historical references. These are the significant names of God:

6. O learned persons sing for the Great God, the sin-dispelling hymns of the Sāmaveda ; whereby the advancers of true knowledge, create for the attainment of God, the ever vigilant divine Light! (258)

७. इन्द्र क्रतुं न आ भर पिता पुत्रेभ्यो यथा ।
   शिक्षा णो अस्मिन्पुरुहूत यामनि जीवा ज्योतिरशीमहि ॥

7. O God, give us wisdom as a sire gives wealth and knowledge to his sons! O much-invoked God, instruct us in this divine path. May we souls receive Thy divine light! (259)

८. मा न इन्द्र परा वृणग्भवा न: सधमाद्ये ।
   त्वं न ऊती त्वमिन्न आप्यं मा न इन्द्र परा वृणक् ॥

8. O God, turn us not away. Be present with us in our virtuous deed. Thou art our only refuge. Thou alone art our goal. O God, turn us not away! (260)

९. वयं घ त्वा सुतावन्त आपो न वृक्तबर्हिष: ।
   पवित्रस्य प्रस्रवणेषु वृत्रहन्परि स्तोतार आसते ॥

9. O God, the Remover of the coverings of ignorance, we worshippers, having acquired knowledge, cutting asunder the bond of body, like water overflowing its bank, sit against the banks of the streams of the sacred Vedic knowledge! (261)

१०. यदिन्द्र नाहुषीष्वा ओजो नृम्णं च कृष्टिषु ।
    यद्वा पञ्चक्षितीनां द्युम्नमा भर सत्रा विश्वानि पौंस्या ॥

10. O God, whatever spiritual or physical strength there exists in men and subjects ; whatever beauty there lies in five sheaths of the soul, grant us ever these and all manly powers! (262)[1]

DECADE III

१. सत्यमित्था वृषेदसि वृषजूतिर्नोऽविता ।
   वृषा ह्युग्र श्रृण्विषे परावति वृषो अर्वावति श्रुत: ॥

1. O Mighty God, Thou verily art the showerer of happiness. Thou, served by noble persons, art our Guardian. Thou art spoken of as Vrisha in the Vedas. Thou art the Fulfiller, of our desires far and near ! (263)[2]

---

[1]Pt. Harish Chandra Vidyalankar translates Panch Kshiti as five organs of cognition (Gyan Indriyas).

Griffith translates Nahushas as people different from the five Aryan tribes, Turvas, Yadus, Anavas, Drubyus and Purus.

Panch-Kshitinam has been translated by Griffith as five tribes. This interpretation is wrong, as there is no history in the Vedas. Five sheaths of the soul are Anna, Pran, Mana, Gyan, Vigyan Koshas.

[2]*Vrisha*: The embodiment of virtue and Dharma.

२. यच्छक्राशि परावति यदर्वावति वृत्रहन् ।
अतस्त्वा गीर्भिर्द्युगदिन्द्र केशिभिः सुतावाँ॒आ विवासति ॥

2. O Mighty God, whether Thou be far or near at hand, Thou art the Remover of obstacles!

Hence a worshipper with his eulogies full of knowledge desires to realise Thee. (264)

३. अभि वो वीरमन्धसो मदेषु गाय गिरा महा विचेतसम् ।
इन्द्रं नाम श्रृत्यँ॒शाकिनं वचो यथा ॥

3. Ye men, on occasions of spiritual and physical joy, praise with Vedic verse, as ordained in the Vedas, God, the Valiant, the Most wise, the Subduer, sung in the Vedas, the Omnipotent! (265)

४. इन्द्र त्रिधातु शरणं त्रिवरूथँ॒स्वस्तये ।
च्छर्दियँच्छ मघवद्द्भ्यश्च महां च यावया दिद्युमेभ्यः ॥

4. O God, remove the bondage of three-humoured house. Grant me and these devotees of Thine, for their good, Thy lustrous shelter that wards off triple miseries. (266)[1]

५. श्रायन्त इव सूर्यं विश्वेदिन्द्रस्य भक्षत ।
वसूनि जातो जनिमान्योजसा प्रति भागं न दीधिमः ॥

5. Resorting to His shelter, as rays do to the Sun, all beings born and still to be born should enjoy with vigour, God's gifts, which we should take as our heritage. (267)[2]

६. न सीमदेव आप तदिषं दीर्घायो मर्त्यः ।
एतग्वा चिद्य एतशो युयोजत इन्द्रो हरी युयोजते ॥

6. O immortal soul, a godless mortal reacheth not his desired goal. As a driver alone can yoke his steeds, so a Yogi alone can control his organs! (268)

---

[1]Three-humoured house means the body, that has got three humours of wind, bile and phlegm, i.e., वात, पित्त and कफ.
Triple miseries: Spiritual, Physical and Elemental i.e., Adhyatmik, Adhibhautik, Adhidaivic.
[2]Shri Sayanacharya and Pt. Satyavrat Samashrami have taken जाते in place of जातो as given in the text. This has changed the interpretation.
Ludwig remarks that the reading of the Sāmaveda is almost impossible to interpret. Cowell in his note to Wilson's translation of the Rigveda, writes 'As I can make nothing of Jato Janimani of the text I borrow the Jate Janamane, meaning, when he who will be born is born! There is no need of changing, the text. The word जातो means 'born' and, जनिमानि means 'will be' born. European scholars following Satyavrat Samashrami have unnecessarily been at pains to change the text, and alter the meaning.

७. आ नो विश्वासु हव्यमिन्द्रꣿसमत्सु भूषत ।
उप ब्रह्माणि सवनानि वृत्रहन्परमज्या ऋचीषम: ॥

7. On all occasions of affliction, let our songs of praise glorify God. O Banisher of sins, Conqueror of obstacles, Worthy of adoration, may our Vedic hymns and prayers glorify Thee! (269)

८. तवेदिन्द्रावमं वसु त्वं पुष्यसि मध्यमम् ।
सत्रा विश्वस्य परमस्य राजसि न किष्टꣳवा गोषु वृण्वते ॥

8. O God, the lowest Earth is Thine. Thou cherishest the middle region. Thou rulest the highest region. Thou art verily the Lord of the whole universe. None in all the worlds resisteth Thee! (270)[1]

९. क्वेयथ क्वेदसि पुरुत्रा चिद्धि ते मन: ।
अलर्षि युध्म खजकृत्पुरंदर प्र गायत्रा अगासिषु: ॥

9. O Omnipresent, World-Making-Salvation-Bestowing God, where art Thou, whither hast Thou gone? Thy All-knowing nature is found in all places. Thou pervadest all objects; singers sing Thy glory! (271)[2]

१०. वयमेनमिदा ह्योऽपीपेमेह वज्रिणम् ।
तस्मा उ अद्य सवने सुतं भरा नूनं भूषत श्रुते ॥

10. We, the knowers of God, have in past life been pleasing this God, the Chastiser of the sinners. In this sacrifice of Vedic prayer, verily, Ye worshippers, in this life, glorify Him, and derive the essence of knowledge and pleasure from Him. (272)

DECADE IV

१. यो राजा चर्षणीनां याता रथेभिरध्रिगु: ।
विश्वासां तरुता पृतनानां ज्येष्ठं यो वृत्रहा गृणे ।

1. I eulogise that Great God, Who is the Lord of men, attainable through Yogic practices, Immutable in nature, the Punisher of the wicked and ignoble, and the Vanquisher of fighting hosts. (273)

२. यत इन्द्र भयामहे ततो नो अभयं कृधि ।
मघवञ्छग्धि तव तन्न ऊतये वि द्विषो वि मृधो जहि ॥

2. O God, give us security from that whereof we are afraid! O Mighty Lord, Thy power is adequate! For our protection, keep away from us the vices of hatred and violence. (274)

---

[1]Harish Chandra Vidyalankar translates the verse thus:
O God Thou art the Lord of wealth achieved in waking state (जाग्रत्). Thou art the Master of our sleeping state (स्वप्न). Thou art our Lord in profound sleep (सुषुप्ति). None resisteth Thee in the fourth तुरीय state.
[2]The question in the first part has been answered in the second.

३. वास्तोष्पते ध्रुवा स्थूणाꣳसत्रꣳसोम्यानाम् ।
द्रप्सः पुरां भेत्ता शश्वतीनामिन्द्रो मुनीनाꣳसखा ॥

3. O God, the Lord of all homes and bodies. Thou art the strong support, and Guardian like armour! Thou art Omniscient. Thou relievest the yogis of this old bondage of mortal frame. Thou art the friend of the sages. (275)

४. बण्महाꣳ अ्रसि सूर्यं बडादित्य महाꣳ अ्रसि ।
महस्ते सतो महिमा पनिष्टम मह्ना देव महाꣳ अ्रसि ॥

4. Verily, O Creator, Thou art Great; truly, O Absorber of all, Thou art Great! O Ever-living God, Thy majesty is Great. O most admired God, Thou art Great by Thy greatness! (276)

५. अश्वी रथी सुरूप इद्गोमाꣳ यदिन्द्र ते सखा ।
श्वात्रभाजा वयसा सचते सदा चन्द्रैर्याति सभामुप ॥

5. O God, when Thy friend becomes strong in action master of organs and senses, beautiful in appearance, and full of knowledge; he with his illustrious life and excellent qualities becomes fit to enter the Assembly of the learned! (277)

६. यद्द्याव इन्द्र ते शतꣳ शतं भूमीरुत स्युः ।
न त्वा वज्रिन्त्सहस्रꣳ सूर्या अ्रनु न जातमष्ट रोदसी ॥

6. O God, not even a hundred heavens or a hundred earths can match Thee. O Chastiser of the impious, not even a thousand suns and the universe created by Thee, can match Thee! (278)[1]

७. यदिन्द्र प्रागपागुदङ् न्यग्वा हूयसे नृभिः ।
सिमा पुरू नृषूतो अ्रस्यानवेऽसि प्रशर्धं तुर्वशे ॥

7. O God, Thou art called by men eastward and westward, north and south, O All-powerful, Thou art everywhere near all. O Powerful God invoked by many Thou art present in all men! (279)[2]

८. कस्तमिन्द्र त्वावसुमा मर्त्यो दधर्षति ।
श्रद्धा हि ते मघवन्पार्ये दिवि वाजी वाजꣳ सिषासति ॥

8. O God, the Abode of all, who can be disrespectful unto Thee? O Omnipotent, a yogi, with faith in Thee, depending upon his light of knowledge to finish his journey in the world, surrenders his learning unto Thee! (280)

---

[1]Sun, Earth, Heaven, nay even the whole universe created by God, can not match Him. God is higher than all these.

[2]Griffith translates Anavas and Turvasas as the descendants of the great Aryan eponymi Anu and Turvasa. This interpretation is illogical, as the Vedas are free from historical references.

Anva means man, अ्रन्व इति मनुष्यनाम । निघं॰ २।३।

Turvasha means near, तुर्वश इति अ्रन्तिकनाम् । निघं॰ २।१।

९. इन्द्राग्नी अपादियं पूर्वगात्पद्वतीभ्य: ।
हित्वा शिरो जिह्वया रारपच्चरत्रिव्ँशतपदा न्यक्रमीत् ॥

9. This mental power with the force of breath and soul being footless, moves faster than those with feet. Leaving the field of deliberation, it traverses through the field of speech, whence, it enters the field of action and moves with thirty steps. (281)[1]

१०. इन्द्र नेदीय एदिहि मितमेधाभिरूतिभि: ।
आ शन्तम शंतमाभिरभिष्टिभिरा स्वापे स्वापिभि: ॥

10. O God, come very near to us, with aids of firmly based resolve! Come, Most Auspicious with Thy most valuable gifts. O Good kinsman, come with Thy pleasant powers! (282)

DECADE V

१. इत ऊती वो अजरं प्रहेतारमप्रहितम् ।
आशुं जेतारव्ँहेतारव्ँरथीतममतूर्तं तुग्रियावृधम् ॥

1. O men, call for your protection, God, Undecaying, Urger, Independent, All-pervading, Conqueror, the Giver of knowledge and enjoyment, the Best Master, Immortal, the Dispeller of ignorance! (283)

२. मो षु त्वा वाघतश्च नारे अस्मन्नि रीरमन् ।
आरात्ताद्वा सधमादं न आ गहीह वा सन्नुप श्रुधि ॥

2. O God, we dislike even the learned, who remain far from Thee, and act against the dictates of their conscience. O All-pervading God, verily being near, reside in our heart, and staying there, listen to our prayer! (284)

३. सुनोत सोमपाघ्ने सोममिन्द्राय वज्रिणे ।
पचता पक्तीरवसे कृणुध्वमित्पृणन्नित् पृणते मय: ॥

3. O learned persons, develop happiness for the soul, who hankers after knowledge, and is imbued with asceticism. Imbibe his mature experience. Exert for self-protection. Soul, the giver gives happiness! (285)

४. य: सत्राहा विचर्षणिरिन्द्रं तव्ँहूमहे वयम् ।
सहस्रमन्यो तुविनृम्ण सत्पते भवा समत्सु नो वृधे ॥

---

[1]Thirty steps: According to Sayana these are the thirty divisions of the day and night. A Muhurat is a period of 48 minutes duration. There are thirty Muhurats in a day and night. Pt. Jaidev Vidyalankar explains these as 8 Vasus, Ten Rudras, Pranas barring the soul, and 12 Adityas. Pt. Harish Chandra Vidyalankar considers these words to signify the innumerable powers of the mind.
Mind first deliberates, then speaks, and afterwards acts with its manifold forces. Mind, being without feet, walks faster than those with feet.

4. We call upon that God, Who slays the foes and is Far-seeing. O Master of infinite knowledge, Most Wealthy, Nourisher of noble persons, prosper us in life's struggles. (286)

५. शचीभिर्नः शचीवसू दिवा नक्तं दिशस्यतम् ।
मा वाँरातिरुपदसत्कदाचनास्मद्रातिः कदाचन ॥

5. Ye rich in wisdom and action, with your light of knowledge, vouchsafe us blessings day and night. May not your gifts ever fail. May not our gifts ever fail! (287)

६. यदा कदा च मीढुषे स्तोता जरेत मर्त्यः ।
आदिद्वन्देत वरुणं विपा गिरा धर्तारं विव्रतानाम् ॥

6. Whenever a mortal worshipper will sing the praise of God, the Giver of knowledge and happiness, let him with Vedic song laud God, Who subdues the ignoble, and is the Banisher of sins! (288)

७. पाहि गा यान्धसो मद इन्द्राय मेध्यातिथे ।
यः संमिश्लो हर्योर्यो हिरण्यय इन्द्रो वज्री हिरण्ययः ॥

7. O God, preserve its organs, for the enjoyment of the extreme felicity by the soul, who with the conjunction of the organs of cognition and action derives enjoyable knowledge. The soul, the dispeller of nescience, is the bestower of illuminating knowledge! (289)[1]

८. उभयँश्रृणवच्च न इन्द्रो अर्वागिदं वचः ।
सत्राच्या मघवान्त्सोमपीतये धिया शविष्ठ आ गमत् ॥

8. May soul, listening to both our mental and vocal prayers, equipped with manifold powers, mighty, for enjoying the intense pleasure granted by God, come unto us with the perception of truth! (290)

९. महे च न त्वाद्रिवः परा शुल्काय दीयसे ।
न सहस्राय नायुताय वज्रिवो न शताय शतामघ ॥

9. O soul, the remover of darkness, the possessor of the strength of a thunderbolt, the master of a hundred forms of the wealth of knowledge, I cannot sell thee for a high price, not for a hundred, nor for a thousand, not even for ten thousand! (291)[2]

---

[1]Griffith translates Medhyatithi as the name of a Rishi. This is wrong, as the Vedas are absolutely free from history. The word means God, Who is ever present in the heart, and is fit to be respected like a guest, whose date of arrival is not known. God is present in our heart from undated times immemorial.

[2]The purity of soul should be preserved at all costs. It should not be bartered for a hundred, a thousand or ten thousand sovereigns. Soul is priceless.

१०. वस्याऽऽइन्द्रासि मे पितुरुत भ्रातुरभुञ्जतः ।
माता च मे छदयथः समा वसो वसुत्वनाय राधसे ॥

10. O Ubiquitous God, Thou art more to me than sire or niggard brother is. Thou and my mother are alike in rearing me for acquiring prosperity and success in undertakings! (292)

BOOK IV

Chapter 1

DECADE I

१. इम इन्द्राय सुन्विरे सोमासो दध्याशिरः ।
ताऽऽआ मदाय वज्रहस्त पीतये हरिभ्यां याह्योक आ ॥

1. These juices of knowledge have been acquired for the soul through Yoga.
O soul, come in this body, with the organs of cognition and action, for enjoying excellent pleasure, and drinking them! (293)[1]

२. इम इन्द्र मदाय ते सोमाश्चिकित्र उक्थिनः ।
मधोः पपान उप नो गिरः शृणु रास्व स्तोत्राय गिर्वणः ॥

2. O soul, these juices of divine felicity have been prepared for thee. Enjoy the pleasant divine knowledge, listen to our songs. O God, Worthy of worship through Vedic songs, reward the worshipper! (294)

३. आ त्वाऽद्य सबर्दुघाऽऽहुवे गायत्रवेपसम् ।
इन्द्रं धेनुऽऽसुदुघामन्यामिषमुरुधारामरङ्कृतम् ॥

3. O God, I praise Thee like a milch-cow, who fulfils our desire, yields milk, has an excellent gait, is easy in yielding milk, beautiful in appearance, lovable and richly yielding! (295)[2]

४. न त्वा वृहन्तो अद्रयो वरन्त इन्द्र वीडवः ।
यच्छिक्षसि स्तुवते मावते वसु न किष्टदा मिनाति ते ॥

4. O God, impediments strong and lofty like hills are powerless to bar Thy way. None stays that act of Thine when Thou wouldst fain give wealth to one like me, who sings Thy praise! (296)

५. क ई वेद सुते सचा पिबन्तं कद्वयो दधे ।
अयं यः पुरो विभिनात्योजसा मन्दानः शिप्रयन्धसः ॥

---

[1]Them refers to juices of knowledge.
[2]God has been compared to a cow. Just as a cow does good to humanity by yielding milk, so God works for the uplift of humanity by revealing his knowledge in the form of the Vedas.

5. Who knows the soul, who enjoys happiness along with the organs, in this Yajna of life? Who knows how long will he stay in the body? The strong soul, migrating from one body to the other, enjoying with his dignity, the happiness of knowledge, his food, breaks down the castles of mortal frame and attains to salvation. (297)[1]

६. यदिन्द्र शासो अव्रतं च्यावया सदसस्परि ।
अस्माकमꣳशुं मघवन्पुरुस्पृहं वसव्ये अधि बर्हय ॥

6. O soul, the denizen of our body, control and remove from his seat the person who does not fulfil his vow. Increase in this body, a worthy house, our share, desired by many a one! (298)[2]

७. त्वष्टा नो दैव्यं वचः पर्जन्यो ब्रह्मणस्पतिः ।
पुत्रैर्भ्रातृभिरदितिर्नु पातु नो दुष्टरं त्रामणं वचः ॥

7. May God, the Maker of the universe, the Lover of His subjects, the Lord of the Vedas and their knowers, Invincible, guard our vedic words. May He protect, along with our sons and brothers, our elevating vows, difficult to fulfil. (299)[3]

८. कदा चन स्तरीरसि नेन्द्र सश्चसि दाशुषे ।
उपोपेन्नु मघवन्भूय इन्नु ते दानं देवस्य पृच्यते ॥

8. Never art Thou violent, O God. Thou givest more to the giver. O wealthy God, Thy bounty is poured forth ever more and more! (300)

९. युङ्क्ष्वा हि वृत्रहन्तम हरी इन्द्र परावतः ।
अर्वाचीनो मघवन्त्सोमपीतय उग्र ऋष्वेभिरा गहि ॥

9. O God, the Banisher of sins, yoke to yoga our soul and mind wandering far away from Thee through ignorance. O Mighty God, Wealthy in knowledge, come with Thy grand merits for our equanimity, unto us, who are far from Thee through nescience! (301)

१०. त्वामिदा ह्यो नरोऽपीप्यन्वज्रिन्भूर्णयः ।
स इन्द्र स्तोमवाहस इह श्रुध्युप स्वसरमा गहि ॥

10. O God, the Subduer of the ignoble, the devoted praise-singers had satisfied Thee in the past and are satisfying Thee at present. Listen today here to the lauds of the worshippers and come unto us! (302)[4]

[1]Who knows means none knows.

[2]Our means those who stick to their vow.
Riteless persons should be discouraged and those devoted to their pledge encouraged.
Share means reward, the fruit of our fulfilling the vow.

[3]Griffith translates Tvashta Brahmnaspati and Parjanya as such. He considers Tvashta to be the ideal artist, the divine artisan, the most skilful of workmen, versed in all wonderful contrivances. He describes Aditi, Infinity; the mother of the Adityas.
Words mean prayers.

[4]Today means ever.

DECADE II

१. प्रत्यु अदर्श्यायत्यू३च्छन्ती दुहिता दिवः ।
श्रपो मही वृणुते चक्षुषा तमो ज्योतिष्कृणोति सूनरी ॥

1. O God! Our advancing darkness-dispelling intellect, like the Dawn, the daughter of the Sun, through knowledge removes ignorance. The mighty intellect, leading men on the right path, sheds lustre, and is verily attained daily through Thy grace. (303)

२. इमा उ वां दिविष्टय उस्रा हवन्ते अश्विना ।
अयं वामह्वे ऽवसे शचीवसू विश्विश ऽऽहि गच्छथः ॥

2. O Sun and Moon, the settlers of the world, the subjects hankering after light, want to attain Ye! I too therefore for self-protection want to gain Ye, O giver of intellect and wealth, as Ye visit and reach every man. (304)[1]

३. कुष्ठः को वामश्विना तपानो देवा मर्त्यः ।
घ्नता वामश्मया क्षपमाणो ऽश्नुनेत्यमु श्राद्धन्यथा ॥

3. O Prān and Apān, Ye gods, what mortal man can satisfy Ye? Continual lessening of the quantity of food, harasses Ye with hunger and thirst. Proper feeding keeps Ye intact. (305)[2]

४. अयं वां मधुमत्तमः सुतः सोमो दिविष्टिषु ।
तमश्विना पिबतं तिरोश्न्न्घं धत्त ऽऽरत्नानि दाशुषे ॥

4. O Prāna and Apāna, the sweetest pleasure laid in living beings is meant for Ye. Drink deep that pleasure prepared since long. Grant strength and health to the Yogi, who gives Prāna to Apāna and vice versa. (306)[3]

५. आ त्वा सोमस्य गल्दया सदा याचन्नहं ज्या ।
भूरिणि मृगं न सवनेषु चुक्रुधं क ईशानं न याचिषत् ॥

5. O God, I always pray unto Thee with words full of knowledge. In all acts of sacrifice, Thou art filled with righteous indignation on the sinners like a tiger. Who does not beseech the Almighty One, Who nourishest the universe? (307)

---

[1] Subjects means men.

[2] In the first part there is a question, and in the latter an answer. If the body is not properly fed, Prāna and Apāna, and intellect deteriorate and become weak. Food keeps the vital breaths in order. He who underfeeds himself lowers his intellect and the vitality of his breaths. Prāna is the in-going and Apāna the outgoing breath.

Griffith writes, the stanza is obscure, and some words of the text seem corrupt. These remarks are inapt, as the verse is clear in meaning.

[3] A Yogi has been described as a giver. He uses both the breaths properly giving Prāna to Apāna and Apāna to Prāna.

६. अध्वर्यो द्रावया त्व॑ सोममिन्द्र: पिपासति ।
उपो नूनं युयुजे वृषणाहरी आ च जगाम वृत्रहा ॥

6. O undecaying mind, create sap of happiness, for the soul longs to drink thereof. Soul, the banisher of impediments and darkness, has yoked together strong Prāna and Apāna and hath come nigh! (308)[1]

७. अभीषतस्तदा भरेन्द्र ज्याय: कनीयस: ।
पुरूवसुर्हि मघवन्बभूविथ भरेभरे च हव्य: ॥

7. O Mighty God, O Most Great, fulfil the ideal of this frail soul; as Thou art, rich in treasures and worthy of being invoked in each calamity. (309)

८. यदिन्द्र यावतस्त्वमेतावदहमीशीय ।
स्तोतारमिद्धिषे रदावसो न पापत्वाय र॑सिषम् ॥

8. If I, O God, were the lord of riches ample as Thine own, I would give them, O God Who scatterest wealth; to the saint and never to the sinner. (310).

९. त्वमिन्द्र प्रतूर्तिष्वभि विश्वा असि स्पृध: ।
अशस्तिहा जनिता वृत्रतूरसि त्वं तूर्य तरुष्यत: ॥

9. O God, in spiritual conflicts, Thou art the subduer of all evil propensities. Father art Thou, Conqueror of sins, Averter of the insults and imprecations of our enemies. Thou art the Victor of the violent. (311)

१०. प्र यो रिरिक्ष ओजसा दिव: सदोभ्यस्परि ।
न त्वा विव्याच रज इन्द्र पार्थिवमति विश्वं ववक्षिथ ॥

10. O God, in Thy might Thou stretchest out beyond the mansions of the sky. The earthly region, O God, comprehends Thee not. Thou transcending the whole universe sustainest it. (312)

DECADE III

१. असावि देवं गोऋजीकमन्धो न्यस्मिन्निन्द्रो जनुषेमुवोच ।
बोधामसि त्वा हर्यश्व यज्ञैर्बोधा न स्तोममन्धसो मदेषु ॥

1. We have acquired the essence of intense pleasure through the light of knowledge. Knowledge is the birth-right of the soul. O soul, the lord of the organs of cognition and action, in stages of extreme felicity forget not our eulogies. (313)[2]

२. योनिष्ट इन्द्र सदने अकारि तमा नृभि: पुरुहूत प्र याहि ।
असो यथा नोऽविता वृधश्चिद्दो वसूनि ममदश्च सोम: ॥

---

[1] Hath come nigh: The soul harnessing the two vital breaths has approached to enjoy happiness.
[2] We means Saints, Yogis.

2. O soul, this body is a home made for thee to dwell in. O much invoked soul, go thither with thy powers of meditation. Thou dost guard, increase and give us wealth, and joyest in knowledge. (314)

३. अदर्दरुत्समसृजो वि खानि त्वमर्णवान्बद्बधानाꣳ अरम्णाः ।
महान्तमिन्द्र पर्वतं वि यद्वः सृजद्धारा अव यद्दानवान्हन् ॥

3. O soul, thou cleavest the skull, hast let loose the gates of organs, hast controlled the moving, struggling breaths, hast manifested the huge mountain-wise body full of pores, urgest these breaths, the messengers of knowledge, and impellest the streams of knowledge. (315)

४. सुष्वाणास इन्द्र स्तुमसि त्वा सनिष्यन्तश्चित्तुविनृम्ण वाजम् ।
आ नो भर सुवितं यस्य कोना तना तमना सह्याम त्वोताः ॥

4. O Omnipotent God, we, enjoying the food of knowledge, praise Thee for achieving extreme pleasure. Lead us on to our goal; aspiring after which and uniting ourselves with Thee, we ourselves acquire abundant pleasure. (316)[1]

५. जगृह्मा ते दक्षिणमिन्द्र हस्तं वसूयवो वसुपते वसूनाम् ।
विद्या हि त्वा गोपतिꣳ शूर गोनामस्मभ्यं चित्रं वृषणꣳरयिं दाः ॥

5. O God, Thou art the Knower of all the truths of life. Longing for them, we grasp Thy right hand. We know Thee as Hero and Lord of the rays of divine light. Vouchsafe us mighty and resplendent riches of knowledge! (317)[2]

६. इन्द्रं नरो नेमधिता हवन्ते यत्पार्या युनजते धियस्ताः ।
शूरो नृषाता श्रवसश्च काम आ गोमति व्रजे भजा त्वं नः ॥

6. In life's struggle men invoke God, and utilise His powers of deliberation and action. The Valiant God is the Suppressor of hostile passions, the Distributor of knowledge to mankind, and is Resplendent with knowledge. O God, in the cloud of ignorance, be our companion! (318)

७. वयः सुपर्णा उप सेदुरिन्द्रं प्रियमेधा ऋषयो नाधमानाः ।
अप ध्वान्तमूर्णुहि पूर्धि चक्षुमुमुग्ध्याꣳस्मान्निधयेव बद्धान् ॥

7. Far-seeing, Knowledge-seeking, sacrifice-loving sages, imploring, approach God, and pray unto Him to dispel the darkness of their ignorance, fill full their eye with flow of knowledge, and release them from the snare of infatuation like birds entangled in a net. (319)

८. नाके सुपर्णमुप यत्पतन्तꣳहृदा वेनन्तो अभ्यचक्षत त्वा ।
हिरण्यपक्षं वरुणस्य दूतं यमस्य योनौ शकुनं भुरण्युम् ॥

---

[1] Which refers to goal.
[2] Grasping the right hand means seeking shelter.

8. O soul, we, longing for thee from the core of our heart, look upon thee, as a bird soaring on the painless path of salvation, as equipped with wonderful resources, as a messenger from God, as a denizen of God's space, as full of strength, and as a rearer and nourisher of mankind! (320)[1]

९. ब्रह्म जज्ञानं प्रथमं पुरस्ताद्वि सीमतः सुरुचो वेन आवः ।
स बुध्न्या उपमा अस्य विष्ठाः सतश्च योनिमसतश्च विवः ॥

9. God revealed for the spread of knowledge, the Veda, an encyclopaedia of light, before the creation of the physical world. He created other similar worlds in the space. He created the Sun, the basic asylum of the visible and invisible creation. (321)

१०. अपूर्व्या पुरुतमान्यस्मै महे वीराय तवसे तुराय ।
विरप्शिने वज्रिणे शन्तमानि वचाँस्यस्मै स्थविराय तक्षुः ॥

10. The learned use many matchless words for this highly Heroic, Power-ful, Energetic, Learned, Irrevocable God, the Remover of calamities. (322)

DECADE IV

१. अव द्रप्सो अँशुमतीमतिष्ठदीयानः कृष्णो दशभिः सहस्त्रैः ।
आवत्तमिन्द्रः शच्या धमन्तमप स्नीहितिं नृमणा अधद्राः ॥

1. The black but alluring sentiment of sin, marching forth with its ten: and thousands of propensities, over-powers the strength of mind. The soul, with its power of knowledge and action, catches hold of that sin. Soul, the reflective power in all men, subjugates that terrible demon. (323)[2]

२. वृत्रस्य त्वा श्वसथादीषमाणा विश्वे देवा अजहुर्ये सखायः ।
मरुद्भिरिन्द्र सख्यं ते अस्त्वथेमा विश्वाः पृतना जयासि ॥

2. Flying in terror from the threat of sin, all thy friendly noble traits have forsaken thee. Create, O soul, friendship with thy mental powers. Thus shalt thou be able to achieve victory over the host of passions, thy foes! (324)

३. विध्युं दद्राणाँसमने बहुनाँयुवानँसन्तं पलितो जगार ।
देवस्य पश्य काव्यं महित्वाद्या ममार स ह्यः समान ॥

3. In life's struggle, the aged soul engulfs the youthful demon of sin, the slayer and destroyer of many. Behold God's high wisdom, through whose greatness, the sin that was living yesterday is dead today. (325)[3]

[1]We means good, noble persons, saintly in nature.
[2]Sayana interprets the word Krishna as Lord Krishna of Gita. Griffith, translates Ansumati as a mystic river of the air. These interpretations are inadmissible, as the Vedas are free from historial references.
[3]The verse may also mean.
Just as the Sun engulfs the moon at the time of Amavas, so does the All pervading immemorial God, Mighty in nature, absorb the beautiful, active soul. Look at God's wis-dom, how one who dies today, is reborn the other day. Like the waxing and waning of the moon, the soul leaves and enters the body again and again, till it attains to salvation.

४. त्व॑ऍह॒ त्य॒त्स॒प्त॑भ्यो जाय॑मानोऽश॒त्रु॑भ्यो अ॒भव॑: श॒त्रु॒रिन्द्र॑ ।
गूढे॑ द्यावापृ॑थि॒वी अन्वविन्दो विभुम॑द्भ्यो॒ भुव॑नेभ्यो र॒णं धा॑: ॥

4. O soul, at the time of thy appearance thou alone sendest to slumber those seven slumberless breaths in the head. Hidden in the heart, thou attainest like heaven and earth, the upper and the lower parts of the body, and derivest pleasure from the powerful breaths. (326)[1]

५. मेडि॒ न त्वा॑ व॒ज्रिणं॑ भृ॒ष्टिम॑न्तं पु॒रु॒घ॒स्मानं॑ वृष॒भऍस्थि॒रप्स्नु॑म् ।
करो॒ष्यर्य॒स्तरु॑षी॒र्दुव॒स्यु॒रिन्द्र॑ द्यु॒क्षं वृ॒त्रह॒णं गृ॒णीषे॑ ।

5. O soul, longing for service, thou puttest thy organs in action. Like Vedic speech, I laud thee, as powerful, intellectual, controller of organs, most excellent, Immortal, resplendent and remover of obstacles ! (327)[2]

६. प्र वो॑ म॒हे म॒हे वृ॒धे भ॒रध्वं॑ प्रचे॒तसे॒ प्र सु॒मतिं॑ कृ॒णुध्व॑म् ।
विश॑: पू॒र्वी: प्र च॑र चर्ष॒णिप्रा॑: ॥

6. O men, realise your responsibility for high nay higher progress, devote your mind to excellent consciousness. O soul, the supplier of knowledge to men, go unto noble and virtuous men ! (328)

७. शु॒नऍहु॑वेम म॒घवा॑नमि॒न्द्रम॒स्मिन्भ॒रे नृ॒तमं॒ वाज॑सातौ ।
शृ॒ण्व॒न्तमु॒ग्रमू॒तये॑ स॒मत्सु॒ घ्नन्तं॑ वृ॒त्राणि॑ सं॒जितं॒ धना॑नि ॥

7. In this performance of the source of knowledge, for protection, we call on God, the Omniscient, Auspicious, the best Leader of men, Listener to our supplications, and the sole Remover of obstacles in life's struggles, the Winner and Giver of riches. (329)

८. उदु॒ ब्रह्मा॑ण्येर॑त श्र॒वस्ये॒न्द्रऍस॑म॒र्ये म॑ह॒या व॑सिष्ठ ।
आ यो विश्वा॑नि॒ श्रव॑सा तता॒नोप॑श्रोता म ई॒वतो॑ व॒चांऍसि ॥

8. O learned person, for the acquisition of knowledge, recite aloud the Vedic verses. In struggle for advancement pray unto God, Who in His might creates all the worlds and listens to the words which I, his faithful servant, utter ! (330)

९. च॒क्रं यदस्याप्स्वा निष॒त्तमु॒तो तद॑स्मै॒ मध्व॒च्छद्धा॑त् ।
पृ॒थि॒व्याम॑ति॒षि॒तं यदूध॑: प॒यो गोष्व॒दधा॒ ओष॑धीषु ॥

---

[1]Sendest to slumber means controls, takes within thy grip. Derivest pleasure through Yoga.

[2]Just as the Vedas sing the glory and beauty of the soul, so do I, a seeker after truth. This verse is not found in the Rigveda. Griffith writes that the exact meaning of the word मेडि is uncertain. It means Vedic speech.

9. This visible creation of mankind, according to the actions of souls, possesses a sort of concealed sweetness in it. God, from the firmament which is fastened over the earth, fills the cows with milk and the herbs with sap. (331)[1]

DECADE V

१. त्यमू षु वाजिनं देवजूत॑ᳲ सहोवानं तरुतार॑ᳲरथानाम् ।
अरिष्टनेमि पृतनाजमाशु॑ᳲस्वस्तये ताक्ष्यमिहा हुवेम ॥

1. We invoke for our weal in our heart, God, Full of knowledge, Praised by the sages, highly Tolerant, the Revolver of heavenly bodies, the Leader of mankind on the right path according to His laws, present in the hearts of His subjects, All-pervading and Most active. (332)

२. त्रातारमिन्द्रमवितारमिन्द्र॑ᳲ हवेहवे सुहव॑ᳲ शूरमिन्द्रम् ।
हुवे नु शक्रं पुरुहूतमिन्द्रमिद॑ᳲ हविर्मघवा वेत्विन्द्रः ॥

2. I invoke God, the Rescuer, God the Helper, easily called at each invocation, the Hero, Omnipotent, invoked by many. May He accept this prayer of ours. (333)

३. यजामह इन्द्रं वज्रदक्षिण॑ᳲहरीणा॑ᳲरथ्यां३ विव्रतानाम् ।
प्र श्मश्रुभिर्दोधुवदूर्ध्वधा भुवद्वि सेनाभिर्भयमानो वि राधसा ।

3. We worship the soul, who is expert in warding off calamities, and the lord of turbulent organs. Aided by his mental forces, blowing the evil tendencies, and terrorising them through the armies of noble traits and distinguished resolve, the soul marches on to amelioration. (334)[2]

४. सत्राहणं दाधृषि तुम्रमिन्द्रं महामपारं वृषभ॑ᳲसुवज्रम् ।
हन्ता यो वृत्र॑ᳲ सनितोत वाजं दाता मघानि मघवा सुराधाः ॥

4. We praise God, Who is the Destroyer of misfortunes, the Queller of all, the Impeller of all, Boundless, most Excellent, the Wielder of the weapon of justice, Great, the Banisher of ignorance, the Bestower of Knowledge and food, the Master of vast resources and riches, Bounteous, the Rewarder of the fruit of our actions. (335)

५. यो नो वनुष्यन्नभिदाति मर्तं उगणा वा मन्यमानस्तुरो वा ।
क्षिधी युधा शवसा वा तमिन्द्राभी ष्याम वृषमणस्त्वोताः ॥

---

[1]God pours rain over the earth from clouds in the firmament, which produces milk in cows and sap in the herbs.

[2]Armies means innumerable. The soul struggling against the forces of evil, comes out victorious by means of various noble traits and determination, and continues its march to final beatitude,

5. The man who with a desire to kill us, fights against us, deeming himself a giant or a hero, equipped with a host of warriors, should be conquered by us, O God, protected and strengthened by Thee! (336)

६. यं वृत्रेषु क्षितय: स्पर्धमाना यं युक्तेषु तुरयन्तो हवन्ते ।
यउ शूरसातौ यमपामुपज्मन्यं विप्रासो वाजयन्ते स इन्द्र: ॥

6. He is God, Whom men in adversity, losing self-control pray, Whom the Yogis overcoming mental confusion remember through Yogic practices, Who is remembered by the heroes on the battle-field, Who is invoked by His subjects, Who is remembered for growing more food, Whom the learned persons laud. (337)

७. इन्द्रापर्वता बृहता रथेन वामीरिष श्रा वहतउसुवीरा: ।
वीतउहव्यान्यध्वरेषु देवा वर्धेथां गीर्भिरिड्या मदन्ता ॥

7. O soul and God, through your vast resources, grant us pleasant food, fit to produce nice progeny. Ye gods, accept our offerings in non-violent spiritual sacrifices, wax strong by Vedic hymns, rejoice in our oblation! (338)[1]

८. इन्द्राय गिरो श्रनिशितसर्गा अप: प्रेरयत्सगरस्य बुध्नात् ।
यो श्रक्ष्णेव चक्रियौ शचीभिर्विष्वक्तस्तम्भ पृथिवीमुत द्याम् ॥

8. Let us recite eternal Vedic verses for God, Who pours down waters from the sky, and supports the Earth and Heaven with His acts of wisdom, like the two wheels of a car with an axle. (339)

९. श्रा त्वा सखाय: सख्या ववृत्युस्तिर: पुरू चिदर्णवां जगम्या: ।
पितुर्नपातमा दधीत वेधा श्रस्मिन्क्षये प्रतरां दीद्यान: ॥

9. O God, may worshippers treat Thee as a friend. Outstretching the atmospheric ocean, Thou invisibly art All prevading. May the Disposer grant offspring to the father, and be radiant in this world with special lustre! (340)

१०. को श्रद्य युङ्क्ते धुरि गा ऋतस्य शिमीवतो भामिनो दुहॅणायून् ।
श्रासन्नेषामप्सुवाहो मयोभून्य एषां भृत्यामृणधत्स जीवात् ॥

10. In the pilgrimage for search after Truth undertaken for the acquisition of truth, he who diverts his lascivious, turbulent, sinful organs to philanthropic acts, really enjoys life. (341)

---

[1]'Ye gods' refers to God and soul.

Oblation means the sacrifice we make in life.

Pt. Jawala Prashad in his commentary has wrongly given श्रावहतम् as श्रावहन्तम् and मदन्ता as मदन्ताम् God has been spoken of as i.e., mountain, as he is the final and sublime abode of the soul.

Chapter 2

DECADE I

१. गायन्ति त्वा गायत्रिणोऽर्चन्त्यर्कमर्किण: । ब्रह्माणस्त्वा शतक्रत उद्वँशमिव येमिरे ॥

1. O God, the Doer of innumerable deeds, the singers hymn Thee, they who chant the psalm of praise laud Thee. The knowers of all the four Vedas exalt Thee, as they raise their family to importance! (342)

२. इन्द्रं विश्वा अवीवृधन्त्समुद्रव्यचसं गिर: । रथीतमँरथीनां वाजानाँसत्पतिं पतिम् ॥

2. All Vedic songs magnify God, Diffused like the firmament, the most effi-cient Sustainer of the universe, the true Guardian of the learned, and the Lord of all. (343)

३. इममिन्द्र सुतं पिब ज्येष्ठममर्त्यं मदम् । शुक्रस्य त्वाभ्यक्षरन्धारा ऋतस्य सादने ॥

3. O soul, drink deep the juice of knowledge born of Yoga, which is immor-tal, excellent and gladdening. Struggling for the attainment of ultimate Truth, the pure streams of knowledge have prepared it for thee! (344)[1]

४. यदिन्द्र चित्र म इह नास्ति त्वादातमद्रिव: । राधस्तन्नो विदद्वस उभयाहस्त्या भर ॥

4. O Dispeller of ignorance, O wondrous God, O solitary prop of the lear-ned, whatever wealth of knowledge Thou hast not given me here, give us that bounty filling full both Thy hands! (345)[2]

५. श्रुधी हवं तिरश्च्या इन्द्र यस्त्वा सपर्यति । सुवीर्यस्य गोमतो रायस्पूर्धि महाँ असि ॥

5. O God, hear the call of the learned Yogi, who worships Thee. Fill that self-controlled Brahmchari with the wealth of knowledge. Great art Thou! (346)[3]

६. असावि सोम इन्द्र ते शविष्ठ धृष्णवा गहि ।
आ त्वा पृणक्त्विन्द्रियँरज: सूर्यो न रश्मिभि: ॥

6. O mighty God, the Annihilator of sins, this knowledge has been created for Thy pleasure. Come for our protection. May our mind concentrate on Thee, as the Sun does on the mid-air with its rays! (347)

७. एन्द्र याहि हरिभिरुप कण्वस्य सुष्टुतिम् । दिवो अमुष्य शासतो दिवं यय दिवावसो ॥

7. O God, with Thy means of imparting knowledge, accept soul's eulogy. O soul, the denizen of light, go unto the divine light of God, the Commander of that lustrous firmament. (348)

[1]Which refers to the juice of knowledge.
[2]God has no hands, Giving us wealth of knowledge filling full both Thy hands, is a figurative way of indicating the liberal-mindedness of God.
Here means in this world.
[3]*Brahmchari*: A celibate Yogi.

८. आ त्वा गिरो रथीरिवास्थुः सुतेषु गिर्वणः । अभि त्वा समनूषत गावो वत्सं न धेनवः ॥

8. O God, knowable through Vedic verses, in Yogic practices, the vedic prayers proceed fast unto Thee like a charioteer. Just as mother Kine go unto their calves so do these Vedic prayers go unto Thee as their goal. (349)

९. एतो न्विन्द्रꣳस्तवाम शुद्धꣳशुद्धेन साम्ना । शुद्धैरुक्थैर्वावृध्वाꣳसꣳशुद्धैराशीर्वान्ममत्तु ॥

9. O learned persons come now and let us glorify the Pure. Mighty God with pure Sama hymns and pure Rigveda verses. May He with pure songs of praise be gracious unto us and send us His blessings. (350)

१०. यो रयिं वो रयिन्तमो यो द्युम्नैर्द्युम्नवत्तमः । सोमः सुतः स इन्द्र तेऽस्ति स्वधापते मदः ॥

10. That God, Who is most wealthy and most illustrious in splendour, makes you rich. O God, the Nourisher of soul, may Thy calm and son-like subjects be a source of happiness to Thee. (351)

DECADE II

१. प्रत्यस्मै पिपीषते विश्वानि विदुषे भर । अरङ्गमाय जग्मयेऽपश्चादध्वने नरः ॥

1. O God, grant all sorts of pleasures to the learned and highly educated person, who is thirsty for delight, never retraces his step in the journey of life, and leads others on the right path. (352)

२. आ नो वयो वयःशयं महान्तं गह्वरेष्ठां महान्तं पूर्विणेष्ठाम् । उग्रं वचो अपावधीः ॥

2. We praise the Mighty God, who keeps the world under control since the beginning of creation, ends our life journey, is Great, resides in the inmost recesses of the heart, and grants us life. Bearing Him in mind, we should avoid the use of harsh words. (353)

३. आ त्वा रथं यथोतये सुम्नाय वर्तयामसि । तुविकूर्मिमृतीषहमिन्द्रꣳशविष्ठ सत्पतिम् ॥

3. Just as we assume body again and again for progress and happiness, so do we, O Mighty God again and again approach Thee, the Lord of Mighty deeds, the Subduer of distressing passions and the Guardian of the sages. (354)[1]

४. स पूर्व्यो महोनां वेनः क्रतुभिरानजे । यस्य द्वारा मनुः पिता देवेषु धिय आनजे ॥

4. That learned man, amongst respectable persons, is fit to be honoured first, who urges all to work and acquire knowledge. Through whom, God, The Wise Father, impels the intellects of the learned. (355)[2]

---

[1] In this verse body is spoken of as a kind of रथ car or vehicle, for the sake of progress the soul assumes the body again and again, so for the attainment of salvation, the final beatitude, the soul approaches God again and again. Soul is born and reborn till salvation is attained.

[2] Western scholars consider this to be a difficult verse. Griffith has followed partly Professor Aufrecht's Commentary as given by Dr. Muir, and partly Professor Ludwig's

५. यदी वहन्त्याशवो भ्राजमाना रथेष्वा । पिबन्तो मदिरं मधु तत्र श्रवाँसि कृण्वते ॥

5. Where and when the swift, shining forces of meditation, making us enjoy absorbing delight through senses draw the soul on, that stage is the final goal of knowledge. (356)

६. त्यमु वो अप्रहणं गृणीषे शवसस्पतिम् । इन्द्रं विश्वासाहं नरँ शचिष्ठं विश्ववेदसम् ॥

6. I preach unto You that God, Who is Immortal, the Lord of strength, All-conquering, the Leader, Mightiest and Omniscient. (357)

७. दधिक्राव्णो अकारिषं जिष्णोरश्वस्य वाजिनः ।
सुरभि नो मुखा करत्प्र ण आयूँषि तारिषत् ॥

7. Let us praise the Victorious, All-pervading, Powerful God, Who leads us on the right path, and prolongs the days of our life. (358)[1]

८. पुरां भिन्दुर्युवा कविरमितौजा अजायत । इन्द्रो विश्वस्य कर्मणो धर्ता वज्री पुरुष्टुतः ॥

8. God is the Bestower of Salvation by dissolving our bodies into Causal Matter, Ever Young, the Wise, Unmeasured in strength, the Sustainer of the working of the whole universe, the Dissolver, aud Extolled by many. (359)

DECADE III

१. प्रप्र वस्त्रिष्टुभमिषं वन्दद्वीरायेन्दवे । धिया वो मेधसातये पुरन्ध्या विवासति ॥

1. For acquiring supreme happiness realised by spiritual giants, I draw your attention to Jagrat, Swapna and Sushupti stages of the soul. For the attainment of that pure wealth, cultivate a versatile and steady intellect. (360)[2]

२. कश्यपस्य स्वर्विदो यावाहुः सयुजाविति । ययोर्विश्वमपि व्रतं यज्ञं धीरा निचाय्य ॥

2. Yogis, the seers of illuminated joy, consider Pran and Apan as the eternal companions of the soul. They define all their movements as a kind of Yajna (sacrifice). (361)[3]

३. अर्चंत प्रार्चता नरः प्रियमेधासो अर्चंत । अर्चन्तु पुत्रका उत पुरमिद् घृष्ण्वर्चंत ॥

Commentary. The verse is simple and not difficult. Wilson and other Western scholars have translated वेन as friend, पूर्व्यों as ancient, and महोनाम् as mighty gods and consider the verse to refer to Soma and not Indra. It is regrettable the Western scholars have not rightly grasped the significance of the verse. The Devta of the verse is Indra and not Soma.

[1]Western scholars have translated Dadhikravan as a most distinguished race-horse, whereas the word means God, Who absorbs the universe in Himself and regulates it.

[2]There are three stages of the soul, Jagrat i.e., wakeful, Swapna, dreamy, sleepish, sushupti i.e., profound sleep. Pt. Jaidev Vidyalankar translates it as thought, word and action.

[3]Western scholars consider this verse to be obscure. The significance of the verse is clear like day light. Benfy and Stevenson call यो as Indra's pair of courageous horses. This is incorrect. The word means Prān and Apān, the in-going and out-going breaths.

3. Sing, sing Ye forth Your songs of praise, O men of fine intellect, sing your songs for God, the Sustainer of the universe, Yea, deliverers of humanity from sufferings, sing Your lauds for Him. (362)[1]

४. उक्थमिन्द्राय शव्स्यं वर्धनं पुरुनिष्षिधे । शक्रो यथा सुतेषु णो रारणत्सख्येषु च ॥

4. We should recite Vedic verses to testify to the glory of the soul that pervades the body. May God, whereby keep us busy with scientific researches and acts of comradeship. (363)

५. विश्वानरस्य वस्पतिमनानतस्य शवसः । एवैश्च चर्षणीनामूती हुवे रथानाम् ॥

5. O men, I, the Leader of humanity, the Master of unbending strength, preach unto Ye for the dealings of men and the protection of bodily conveyances! (364)

६. स घा यस्ते दिवो नरो धिया मर्तस्य शमतः । ऊती स बृहतो दिवो द्विषो अव्ंहो न तरति ॥

6. O God, the man enkindled like the Sun with knowledge, meditating on Thee, behaves like a calm person. He, under the protection of the Almighty Father, overcomes all forthcoming inimical forces, as he does overcome sin! (365)

७. विभोष्ट इन्द्र राधसो विभ्वी रातिः शतक्रतो । अथा नो विश्वचर्षणे द्युम्न व्सुदत्र मव्हय ॥

7. O God, wide spreads the bounty of Thine, ample grace. So, good and liberal Giver, the Master of innumerable deeds and sciences, the Seer of all, grant us splendid wealth! (366)

८. वयश्चित्ते पतत्रिणो द्विपाच्चतुष्पादर्जुनि । उषः प्रारन्नृतूव्रनु दिवो अन्तेभ्यस्परि ॥

8. Bright Dawn, on thy rise, all quadrupeds and bipeds stir, and round about flock together winged birds, from all the boundaries of heaven. (367)

९. अमी ये देवा स्थन मध्य आ रोचने दिवः । कद्ध ऋतं कदमृतं का प्रत्ना व आहुतिः ॥

9. These worlds are found amid the luminous realm of heaven. Are the Vedas prevalent in them ? Is there provision for the performance of Yajnas? Is ancient system of Yajnas found there? (368)[2]

१०. ऋचव्ं साम यजामहे याभ्यां कर्माणि कृण्वते । वि ते सदसि राजतो यज्ञं देवेषु वक्षतः ॥

---

[1]Repetition of the word 'sing is made for intensifying and emphasising the necessity of offering prayer unto God.

[2]These are so many planets in the solar system. Swami Dayanand writes in the Satyarth Prakash, that all these planets like Mars, Mercury, Venus, Neptune etc. are worlds like the Earth, where living beings inhabit, and where God has revealed the Vedas for the spiritual guidance of their inhabitants. The same question has been raised in this verse which is answered in the next. Swami Tulsi Ram of Meerut has thus interpreted the verse. Pt. Jaidev Vidyalankar and Pt. Harish Chandra Vidyalankar have interpreted it differently. Present day science has proved that there is life on the Moon and other planets.

10. With the assistance of the Sam and Rigvedas, all acts are performed. We study them. They are prominent in all Yajnas and societies. They preach the performance of Yajnas in all the planets. (369)[1]

DECADE IV

१. विश्वाः पृतना अभिभूतरं नरः सजूस्ततक्षुरिन्द्रं जजनुश्च राजसे ।
क्त्वे वरे स्थेमन्यामुरीमुतोग्रमोजिष्ठं तेरसं तरस्विनम् ॥

1. For power and firm, excellent skill in action all men in accord, select and declare him as their Lord, who is the conqueror of violent armies, their destroyer, fierce, exceeding strong, stalwart and free from indolence. (370)[2]

२. श्रत्ते दधामि प्रथमाय मन्यवेऽहन्यदृस्युं नर्यं विवेरपः ।
उभे यत्वा रोदसी धावतामनु भ्यसाते शुष्मात्पृथिवी चिदद्रिवः ।

2. O Omniscient God, I have faith in Thee, Most Excellent and powerful, as Thou hast destroyed the violent tendencies of the mind, and manifested the deeds for man's welfare. Both Heaven and Earth fly for refuge unto Thee. Earth even trembles at Thy strength! (371)

३. समेत विश्वा ओजसा पति दिवो य एक इद्भूरतिथिर्जनानाम् ।
स पूर्व्यो नूतनमाजिगीषं तं वर्तनीरनु वावृत एक इत् ॥

3. Ye men, take shelter under Him, Who is the one Lord of lustrous heaven, and pervades all living beings. He is the ardent Conqueror of all past and present feelings of the mind. All pathways follow Him alone. (372)

४. इमे त इन्द्र ते वयं पुरुष्टुत ये त्वारभ्य चरामसि प्रभूवसो ।
न हि त्वदन्यो गिर्वणो गिरः सघत्क्षोणीरिव प्रति तद्धर्यं नो वचः ॥

4. O God, praised of many, excellently Rich, Thine are we, who, trusting in Thy help draw near to Thee. None but Thou, Song-lover, shalt receive our lauds; as the Earth loves all her creatures, so welcome this our hymn ! (373)

५. चर्षणीधृतं मघवानमुक्थ्याइमिन्द्रं गिरो बृहतीरभ्यनूषत ।
वावृधानं पुरुहूतँसुवृक्तिभिरमत्यं जरमाणं दिवेदिवे ॥

5. May our high hymns sound forth the praise of God, the Supporter of mankind, the Lord of Wealth, Meet for laud, Who hath waxen mighty, is much invoked with prayers, Immortal, One whose praise each day is sung aloud. (374)

---

[1]This verse clearly establishes that the Vedas are found in all the worlds besides the Earth. Enumeration of the Sam and Rig is symbolical of all the four Vedas. They refer to the Vedas.

[2]*Lord* : King.

६. अच्छा व इन्द्रं मतयः स्वर्युवः सध्रीचीर्विश्वा उशतीरनूषत ।
परि ष्वजन्त जनयो यथा पतिं मर्यं न शुन्ध्युं मघवानमूतये ॥

6. Just as wives embrace for protection, their pure, prosperous and strong lords, so do the forces of meditation, in their march to profound delight, in full unison, all hankering after God, offer their praise unto Him. (375)

७. अभि त्यं मेषं पुरुहूतमृग्मियमिन्द्रं गीर्भिर्मदता वस्वो अर्णवम् ।
यस्य द्यावो न विचरन्ति मानुषं भुजे म्ँहिष्ठमभि विप्रमर्चत ॥

7. Praise for your nourishment, that ever memorable God, the Bestower of all pleasures, sung in Vedic verses, the Ocean of wealth, Charitable, Full of knowledge, Whose rays of knowledge spread throughout mankind. (376)

८. त्यँ सु मेषं महया स्ववर्विद्ँशतं यस्य सुभुवः साकमीरते ।
अत्यं न वाजँ हवनस्यदँ रथमिन्द्रं ववृत्यामवसे सुवृत्तिभिः ॥

8. O man, worship God, the Showerer of nice pleasures, the Bestower of Salvation, hundreds of Whose created worlds, revolve simultaneously. I, for safety, with hymns of praise, worship again and again, God, the Master of supernatural powers, Most Beautiful, the Percolator in our hearts, through songs of praise; like a fast, beautiful horse! (377)[1]

९. घृतवति भुवनानामभिश्रियोर्वी पृथ्वी मधुदुघे सुपेशसा ।
द्यावापृथिवी वरुणस्य धर्मणा विष्कभिते अजरे भूरिरेतसा ॥

9. Full of light and water, encompassing all things that be wide, spacious, pleasant, beautiful in their form, the Heaven and the Earth, by God's decree, undecaying, rich in germs, stand apart. (378)

१०. उभे यदिन्द्र रोदसी आपप्राथोषा इव । महान्तं त्वा महीना्ँ सम्राजं चर्षणीनाम् ।
देवी जनित्र्यजीजनन्द्रद्रा जनित्र्यजीजनत् ॥

10. As, like the Dawn, O God, Thou fillest with light both the Earth and Heaven, so, as Mightier than the mighty, great King of human beings, the divine mother Veda, describes Thee thus, the propitiating mother Veda dilates thus upon Thee ! (379)[2]

११. प्र मन्दिने पितुमदर्चता वचो यः कृष्णगर्भा निरहन्नृजिश्वना ।
अवस्यवो वृषणं वज्रदक्षिणं मरुत्वन्तँ सख्याय हुवेमहि ॥

11. Recite laudatory words for God, the Embodiment of joy, Who with His knowledge drives away the evil tendencies, the mother of sin. Let us, desiring help call Him for friendship, Showerer of happiness, the Foremost Remover of obstacles, the Mainstay of His subjects. (380)

---

[1]According to Griffith hundreds' refers to the plentiful draughts of Soma juice. This is not a nice interpretation.
[2]Repetition of the 'mother Veda' is for the sake of emphasis.

DECADE V

१. इन्द्र सुतेषु सोमेषु क्रतुं पुनीष उक्थ्यम् । विदे वृधस्य दक्षस्य महाँ हि षः ।

1. O soul, on maturity of knowledge, thou actest upon Vedic behests and teachings, for the gain of advanced spiritual strength. Great indeed is that God! (381)

२. तमु अभि प्र गायत पुरुहूतं पुरुष्टुतम् । इन्द्रं गीर्भिस्तवीषमा विवासत ॥

2. Sing forth to Him Whom many a man invokes, to Him whom many laud. Worship the Mighty God with Your songs of praise! (382)

३. तं ते मदं गृणीमसि वृषणं पृक्षु सासहिम् । उ लोककृत्नुमद्रिवो हरिश्रियम् ॥

3. O Omniscient God, we expatiate upon that supreme happiness of Thine which nourishes mankind, is undecayable in all struggles. Thou art the Creator of ths universe, and worthy of resort by the learned! (383)

४. यत्सोममिन्द्र विष्णवि यद्वा घ त्रित आप्त्ये । यद्वा मरुत्सु मन्दसे समिन्दुभिः ॥

4. O God, whatever nectar of immortality there exists in Thee, the Omnipresent, or collectively in the Ida, Pingla, Sushumna of the Yogis, or in breaths, or in fact wherever there is found divine delight, Thou art the source of all that. (384)[1]

५. एदु मघोर्मदिन्तरँ सिञ्चाध्वर्यों अन्धसः । एवा हि वीरस्तवते सदावृधः ॥

5. O Yogi, acquire the highly gladdening elixir of devotion. None but an ever-progressing brave person hankers after it! (385)

६. एन्दुमिन्द्राय सिञ्चत पिबाति सोम्यं मधु । प्र राधाँसि चोदयते महित्वना ।

6. O learned persons, acquire knowledge for the realisation of God, Who enjoys the sweetness of tranquillity. He through His majesty sends forth His bounteous gifts! (386)

७. एतो न्विन्द्रँ स्तवाम सखायः स्तोम्यं नरम् । कृष्टीर्यो विश्वा अभ्यस्त्येक इत् ॥

7. O friends, come, let us sing praise to God, the Leader Who deserves the laud. He with none to aid overcomes all men! (387)

८. इन्द्राय साम गायत विप्राय बृहते बृहत् । ब्रह्मकृते विपश्चिते पनस्यवे ॥

8. Sing a great psalm to the Almighty, Omniscient God, the Revealer of the Vedas, the Bestower of knowledge, and Worthy of adulation. (388)

---

[1]Ida, Pingla and Sushumna are the three arteries through which the Yogis perform Yoga. Whatever ambrosia अमृत or divine delight there exists in the world, it emanates from God.

९. य एक इद्विदयते वसु मर्ताय दाशुषे । ईशानो अप्रतिष्कुत इन्द्रो अङ्ग ॥

9. He, Who alone speedily bestoweth wealth on mortal man, Who is charitably disposed, is God, potent Lord, Whom none can resist. (389)

१०. सखाय आ शिषामहे ब्रह्मेन्द्राय वज्रिणे । स्तुष ऊ षु वो नृतमाय धृष्णवे ॥

10. Companions, let us preach the divine Vedic knowledge, for expounding God, the Chastiser of the sinners. Unto Ye. I expatiate upon God, the Highest Entity, the Conqueror of all. (390)[1]

BOOK V

Chapter 1

DECADE I

१. गृणे तदिन्द्र ते शव उपमां देवतातये । यद्धॅसि वृत्रमोजसा शचीपते ।

1. O God, Thou banishest ignorance with Thy might. O Omnipotent Lord, I praise most highly this might of Thine for acquiring divinity. (391)

२. यस्य त्यच्छम्बरं मदे दिवोदासाय रन्धयन् । अयॅस सोम इन्द्र ते सुतः पिब ॥

2. O God, Thou hast removed the mountain of obstacles in the way of the joy of a worshipper of divinity. That Yogi is prepared for Thy acquisition. Pray take him under Thy protection. (392)[2]

३. एन्द्र नो गधि प्रिय सत्राजिदगोह्या । गिरिनं विश्वतः पृथुः पर्तिर्दिवः ॥

3. Come unto us, O God, Dear, still Conquering, Unconcealable. Wide as a mountain spread on all sides, Lord of heaven! (393)

४. य इन्द्र सोमपातमो मदः शविष्ठ चेतति । येना हॅसि न्याऽत्रिणं तमीमहे ॥

4. O Almighty, Father highly satisfied, Thou perceivest the greatest joy, whereby Thou smitest down the mind full of thirst, lust, anger and avarice! That joy we crave! (394)

५. तुचे तुनाय तत्सु नो द्राघीय आयुर्जीवसे । आदित्यासः समहसः कृणोतन ।

5. O very mighty, learned preceptors, grant to our sons and grandsons, this lengthened term of life that they may live long days! (395)

६. वेत्था हि निऋॅतीनां वज्रहस्त परिवृजम् । अहरहः शुन्ध्युः परिपदामिव ॥

6. O learned person, strong like a hero equipped with arms, thou knowest how to avoid the evil tendencies of the mind, just as a detective knows the thieves who daily roam about in all directions! (396)

---

[1] I refers to a highly learned person.
[2] That Yogi refers to the worshipper of divinity.

७. अ्रपामीवामप स्निधमप सेघत दुर्मतिम् । आदित्यासो युयोतना नो अ्रँहस: ॥

7. O learned persons, drive Ye disease and strife away, drive Ye away malignity. Keep us far removed from sin! (397)

८. पिबा सोममिन्द्र मन्दतु त्वा यं ते सुषाव हर्यश्वात्रि: । सोतुर्बाहुभ्याँ सुयतो नार्वा ॥

8. O soul, enjoy supreme happiness, May it gladden thee. O soul, coupled with fleeting breaths, deep meditation (Samadhi) has established it for thee. May it afford thee pleasure, like a well-disciplined horse led by the arms of a skilled driver! (398)

DECADE II

१. अ्रभ्रातृव्यो अ्रना त्वमनापिरिन्द्र जनुषा सनादसि । युधेदापित्वमिच्छसे ॥

1. O God, from times immemorial, Thou art ever Rivalless, Leaderless, Companionless: Thou seekest friendship through Yoga alone! (399)

२. यो न इदमिदं पुरा प्र वस्य आनिनाय तमु व स्तुषे । सखाय इन्द्रमूतये ॥

2. O friends, I praise unto Ye, for potection, the same God, Who hast been granting us in previous births, different forms of bodies worth living! (400)

३. आ गन्ता मा रिषण्यत प्रस्थावानो माप स्थात समन्यव: । दृढा चिद्यमयिष्णव: ॥

3. O learned persons come hither, do not feel distressed, Ye ever active persons, in a fit of rage, abandon not the path of rectitude. Ye can tame even what is firm! (401)

४. आ याह्ययमिन्दवेऽश्ववपते गोपत उर्वरापते । सोमँ सोमपते पिब ॥

4. O lord of senses, lord of speech, lord of the strength of procreation, lord to knowledge, come hither, acquire knowledge for supreme happiness! (402)[1]

५. त्वया ह स्विद्युजा वयं प्रति श्वसन्तं वृषभ ब्रवीमहि । सँस्थे जनस्य गोमत: ॥

5. O God, the Bestower of knowledge, with Thee for friend, we magnify Thee, in the company of the learned persons, unto living beings! (403)

६. गावश्चिद् घा समन्यव: सजात्येन मरुत: सबन्धव: । रिहते ककुभो मिथ: ॥

6. O learned persons, full of alertness, equipped with the strength of acquiring knowledge, full of amity, Kin by common ancestry, Ye contact one another in wide quarters! (404)

---

[1]A learned person should seek the company of other learned persons to advance his knowledge. Lord refers to a learned person.

७. त्वं न इन्द्रा भर ओजो नृम्णॐशतक्रतो विचर्षणे । आ वीरं पृतनासहम् ॥

7. O God, the Master of hundreds of sciences, the Seer of all worlds, bring us strength and wealth, a hero conquering in war! (405)

८. अधा ह्रीन्द्र गिर्वण उप त्वा काम ईमहे ससृग्महे । उदेव ग्मन्त उदभिः ॥

8. O laudable God, just as waters are united with waters, so we draw nigh unto Thee with aspirations and are absorbed in Thee! (406)

९. सीदन्तस्ते वयो यथा गोश्रीते मधौ मदिरे विवक्षणे । अभि त्वामिन्द्र नोनुमः ॥

9. O God, verily do we sing Thy praise, realising Thy nature, resplendent like knowledge, the giver of delight, and the bestower of final beautitude. (407)[1]

१०. वयमु त्वामपूर्व्य स्थूरं न कच्चिद्रन्तोऽवस्यवः । वज्रि चित्रॐहवामहे ॥

10. O Mighty, Most Primordial God, we longing for protection, serving Thee, Adorable, sing Thy praise, just as one nourishes a virtuous man! (408)

DECADE III

१. स्वादोरित्था विषूवतो मधोः पिबन्ति गौर्यः ।
या इन्द्रेण सयावरीवृष्णा मदन्ति शोभथा वस्वीरनु स्वराज्यम् ।

1. The organs of senses enjoy the all-pervading, efficacious, satisfying, supreme delight. They thus rejoice in the company of the strong soul and add grandeur to the body with their inherent lustre. (409)

२. इत्था हि सोम इन्मदो ब्रह्मा चकार वर्धनम् ।
शविष्ठ वज्रिन्नोजसा पृथिव्या निः शशा अहिमर्चन्नु स्वराज्यम् ॥

2. O Mighty, Omnipotent God, just as a contented learned person, verily, on the strength of his spiritual force, through the study of the Vedas, thus enhances his knowledge, just as the sun rends asunder the cloud, so dost Thou, establishing Thy supremacy, with Thy vigour remove the covering of stupefying Matter! (410)[2]

३. इन्द्रो मदाय वावृधे शवसे वृत्रहा नृभिः ।
तमिन्महत्स्वाजिषूतिमर्भे हवामहे स वाजेषु प्र नोऽविषत् ॥

3. God is highly great for joy and strength. He, the Banisher of all obstacles along with his subjects, aids us in all scientific pursuits. For our protection we remember Him alone in undertakings great or small. (411)

[1]Final beautitude means salvation.
[2]Covering means hurdle, impediment. In the way of spiritual advancement, Matter sometimes proves an obstacle.

४. इन्द्र तुभ्यमिदद्रिवोनुत्तं वज्रिन्वीर्यम् ।
यद्ध एयं मायिनं मृगं तव एयन्मायायावधीरर्चन्ननु स्वराज्यम् ॥

4. O strong, mighty God, unconquered strength is only Thine. With Thy
surpassing wisdom, Thou affordest shelter to the thirsty soul bewitched by
Matter, and thus establishest Thy splendour. All this redounds to Thy glory
alone! (412)

५. प्रेह्यभीहि धृष्णुहि न ते वज्रो नि यँसते ।
इन्द्र नृम्णँहि ते शवो हनो वृत्रं जया अपोर्चन्ननु स्वराज्यम् ॥

5. O soul, striving after emancipation, go forward, face opposition, overcome obstacles. Thy force is unassailable. Thou wilt certainly attain to prosperity. Slay ignorance with thy strength. Have full mastery over thy actions!
(413)

६. यदुदीरत आजयो धृष्णवे धीयते धनम् ।
युङ्क्ष्वा मदच्युता हरी कँहन: कं वसौ दधोस्माँइन्द्र वसौ दध: ॥

6. When battles and wars are on foot, booty is offered to the conqueror.
Yoke thou, O soul, thy wildly rushing bays of Prān and Apān. Which spiritual weakness wilt thou slay? Which limb of Yoga wilt thou practice? O soul,
keep us under control with thy inner spiritual force. (414)[1]

७. अक्षन्नमीमदन्त ह्यव प्रिया अधूषत ।
अस्तोषत स्वभानवो विप्रा नविष्ठया मती योजा न्विन्द्र ते हरी ॥

7. The sages illumined with Yoga and penance, enjoy all sorts of pleasure
and feel regaled. Thy renounce all desires. O God, they praise Thee with
their most laudable hymns, Yoke Thy two bay steeds for them. (415)[2]

८. उपो षु श्रृणुही गिरो मघवन्मातथा इव ।
कदा न: सूनृतावत: कर इदर्थयास इद्योजा न्विन्द्र ते हरी ॥

8. O soul, graciously listen to our prayers, be not negligent! When wilt
thou make us truthful and sweet in speech? This is our request unto thee.
Control thou thy two bay steeds of Prāna and Apāna. (416)

९. चन्द्रमा अप्स्वाइन्तरा सुपर्णो धावते दिवि ।
न वो हिरण्यनेमय: पदं विन्दन्ति विद्युतो वित्तं मे अस्य रोदसी ॥

9. In all resolves and doubts, the delightful, active soul moves on to the
Refulgent God. O beauties of Nature, bewitching the heart like gold, ignorant

[1]Prāna and Apāna are in-going out-going breaths. Us means the organs of senses. Bays
may refer to organs of action and cognition as well.
[2]Bay steeds means conscious and super conscious samadhi, i.e., सम्प्रज्ञात and असम्प्रज्ञात
concentration or knowledge and action, ज्ञान and कर्म God grants such sages knowledge
and action, and deep meditation and concentration.

persons cannot appreciate Ye. O Prāna and Apāna, let me gain the knowledge of this secret! (417)[1]

१०. प्रति प्रियतम ᳵ रथं वृषणं वसुवाहनम् ।
स्तोता वामश्विनावृषि स्तोमेभिर्भूषति प्रति माध्वी मम श्रुत ᳵ हवम् ॥

10. O Prāna and Apāna, a seer and expounder of truth, through Vedic verses, wants to grace Ye both, in each body, the vehicle of soul, the reaper of the fruit of action and most lovely. O masters of the knowledge of God, listen to My instruction! (418)[2]

DECADE IV

१. आ ते अग्न इधीमहि द्युमन्तं देवाजरम् ।
यद्ध स्या ते पनीयसी समिद्दीदयति द्यवीष ᳵ स्तोतृभ्य आ भर ॥

1. O Resplendent God, we kindle Thee, Refulgent and Immortal. This glorious lustre of Thine is shining in Heaven. Grant knowledge and food to those who sing Thy praise. (419)

२. आग्निं न स्ववृक्तिभिर्होतारं त्वा वृणीमहे ।
शीरं पावकशोचिषं वि वो मदे यज्ञेषु स्तीर्णबर्हिषं विवक्षसे ॥

2. O God Thou art great. Just as the performers of sacrifice in Yajnas, choose fire, prevalent everywhere, full of purifying lustre, the developer of Yajna, so, we the devotees of knowledge, solicit Thee, the Bestower to all of good things for life! (420)

३. महे नो अद्य बोधयोषो राये दिवित्मती ।
यथा चिन्नो अबोधयः सत्यश्रवसि वाय्ये सुजाते अश्वसूनृते ।

3. O heavenly Dawn, in whose silence words are clearly audible, whose birth is full of grandeur, in which sweet words travel fast, full of expansion, awaken us to ample opulence today, just as thou didst awaken us before! (421)

४. भद्रं नो अपि वातय मनो दक्षमुत क्रतुम् ।
अथा ते सख्ये अन्धसो वि वो मदे रणा गावो न यवसे विवक्षसे ॥

4. O God, Thou art great. Grant us a delightful mind, grant us energy and mental power. Let us joy in the pleasant love of God, the Dispeller of darkness, just as kine do in pasturage! (422)

५. कृत्वा महा ᳵ अनुष्वधं भीम आ वावृते शवः ।
श्रिय ऋष्व उपाकयोनि शिप्री हरिवां दधे हस्तयोर्वज्रमायसम् ॥

[1]Ordinary ignorant persons cannot appreciate the beauty of nature, a self controlled, intellectually advanced person alone can do it.
[2]My refers to God.

5. The Great, Awe-inspiring God, through His wisdom, urges His force of knowledge towards Soul and Matter. For the protection of humanity, the Great Omnipotent, Fascinating, Nearest God, grasps in His hands the armour of love and determination for preventing degradation and sin. (423)[1]

६. स घा तं वृषण॒ रथमधि तिष्ठाति गोविदम् ।
य: पात्र॒ हारियोजनं पूर्णमिन्द्राचिकेतति योजा न्विन्द्र ते हरी ॥

6. O soul, the devotee who knows full well the application of the organs of knowledge and action, assumes control over the vehicle of his body, the source of happiness, and the bestower of knowledge through senses. O soul yoke thy organs to deep meditation (Yoga)! (424)

७. अग्नि तं मन्ये यो वसुरस्तं यं यन्ति धेनव: ।
अस्तमर्वन्त आशवोऽस्तं नित्यासो वाजिन इष॒ स्तोतृभ्य: आ भर ॥

7. I look upon Him as God, Who affords dwelling to all, Whom the learned resort to, as Kine to their shed, Whom the five pervading elements consider as their home, Who is the refuge of eternal immortal, learned emancipated souls. O God, bestow knowledge on those who sing Thy praise! (425)[2]

८. न तम॒हो न दुरितं देवासो अष्ट मर्त्यम् ।
सजोषसो यमर्यमा मित्रो नयति वरुणो अति द्विष: ॥

8. No sin or depravity affects the mortal man, O learned persons, whom the Just, Affectionate, Sin-Protecting God, through intense love, removes far from foes! (426)

DECADE V

१. परि प्र धन्वेन्द्राय सोम स्वादुमित्राय पूष्णे भगाय ॥

1. O Tranquil God, the Bestower of supreme felicity, rain happiness on the lovely, strong and prosperous soul! (427)

२. पर्यू षु प्र धन्व वाजसातये परि वृत्राणि सक्षणि: । द्विषस्तरध्या ऋणया न ईरसे ॥

2. O God, for the acquisition of knowledge, wealth and food, remove all obstacles through Thy forbearance. O Discharger of obligations, goad us to quell foes like lust! (428)

३. पवस्व सोम महान्त्समुद्र: पिता देवानां विश्वाभि धाम ॥

3. O God, Thou art the mighty Ocean of delight, the Progenitor of noble traits, purify the hearts of all! (429)

[1]The language is figurative.
[2]Answer to the question is, that they are Ritwijas i.e., priests devoted to action and contemplation.

४. पवस्व सोम महे दक्षायाइवो न निक्तो वाजी धनाय ।

4. O God, just as a pure, learned, well-disciplined person goes to earn money, so shouldst Thou be gracious unto a devoted soul full of energy! (430)

५. इन्दु: पविष्ट चारुमंदायापामुपस्थे कविर्भंगाय ॥

5. May the Benevolent, Prosperous, Wise God, purify us, in the lap of action, for acquiring happiness and riches. (431)

६. अनु हि त्वा सुतꣳ सोम मदामसि महे समर्यंराज्ये । वाजाꣳ अभि पवमान प्र गाहसे ॥

6. O God, under Thy Majestic Sovereignty, where all men are given equal treatment, following in Thy wake, realizing Thee in the heart, we enjoy happiness. O Purifier, Thou enterest into mighty deeds! (432)

७. क ई व्यक्ता नर: सनीडा रुद्रस्य मर्या अथा स्वश्वा: ॥

7. Who are these kind-hearted ethical persons, dwelling together, fine controllers of breath? (433)[1]

८. अग्ने तमद्याश्वं न स्तोमें: क्रतुं न भद्रꣳ हृदिस्पृशम् । ऋध्यामा त ओहै: ॥

8. O Resplendent God, with hymns that extol Thee, we adore Thee, our Carrier to destination like a horse, the Creator of the universe like an artisan, Auspicious, the Dweller in the immost recesses of the heart! (434)

९. आविर्मर्यां आ वाजं वाजिनो अग्मं देवस्य सवितु: सवम् । स्वर्गाꣳ अर्वन्तो जयत ॥

9. Learned mortal men evidently obey the wise command of God, the Creator. O devotees of knowledge, attain to the exhilarating joys of salvation! (435)

१०. पवस्व सोम द्युम्नी सुधारो महाꣳ अवीनामनुपूर्व्य: ॥

10. O God, the Primordial Cause, Refulgent, the nice Sustainer of the universe, Mightiest among the waking souls, purify us, and lead us on the right path! (436)

Chapter 2

DECADE I

१. विश्वतोदावन्विश्वतो न आ भर यं त्वा शविष्ठमीमहे ।

1. O God, the Giver from all sides, Thou, Whom as Strongest we entreat, nourish us from every side! (437)

२. एष ब्रह्मा य ऋत्विय इन्द्रो नाम श्रुतो गृणे ॥

---

[1]Answer to the question is, that they are Ritwijas i.e., priests devoted to action and contemplation.

2. I praise God. Who is gracious in all seasons, Mightiest of all, and Well-renowned. (438)

३. ब्रह्माण इन्द्रम् महयन्तो अर्कैरवर्धयन्नहये हन्तवा उ ॥

3. The Knowers of the Vedas for slaughtering the serpent of sin, exalting God, sing His glory. (439)

४. अनवस्ते रथमश्वाय तक्षुस्त्वष्टा वज्रं पुरुहूत द्युमन्तम् ॥

4. Men, for speedy attainment of salvation, use Him as a vehicle. O God, invoked by many, a man of highly illumined knowledge, uses Thee as a lustrous armour! (440)

५. शं पदं मघऽ रयीषिणो न काममन्वतो हिनोति न स्पृशद्रयिम् ॥

5. Mental peace, knowledge, wealth are attained by him who longs for riches to be given in charity. A vowless person, not disposed to charity, acquires not the cherished desire, nor wins his way to riches. (441)

६. सदा गाव: शुचयो विश्वधायस: सदा देवा अरेपस: ॥

6. The Vedic hymns are ever pure and all-supporting. The charitably disposed learned persons are ever free from stain and blemish. (442)[1]

७. आ याहि वनसा सह गाव: सचन्त वर्तनि यदूधभि: ॥

7. O Dawn, with all thy beauty come! Our Vedic verses, full of sweetness, like cows with udders full of milk, follow on thy path. (443)[2]

८. उप प्रक्षे मधुमति क्षियन्त: पुष्येम रयिं धीमहे त इन्द्र ॥

8. May we, inhabiting a dwelling full of spiritual happiness, increase our wealth of knowledge, and meditate on Thee, O God! (444)[3]

९. अर्चन्त्यर्कं मरुत: स्वर्का आ स्तोभति श्रुतो युवा स इन्द्र: ।

9. The brilliant learned persons, chant their praise for God, Who Famed and Mighty protects them. (445)

१०. प्र व इन्द्राय वृत्रहन्तमाय विश्राय गाथं गायत यं जुजोषते ॥

10. Sing to God, the sage, the subduer of lust and anger, the song that He accepteth. (446)

---

[1]The word गाव: has been interpreted differently, as cows, waters, sun's rays, learned persons and Vedic Verses.

[2]At dawn, just as kine with udders full, yield milk, so should devotees sing the praise of God with Vedic verses full of sweetness.

[3]See Brihad-Aranyak Upanishad 4/5—(13—16), where soul is spoken of as a sweet object. This sweetness of the soul can be realised by the learned alone, and not by ignorant persons. The Chhandogya Upanishad also makes its mention.

DECADE II

१. अचेत्यग्निश्चिकितिर्हव्यवाड्न सुमद्रथ: ॥

1. God, full of resplendent, beautiful lustre, like oblation-bearing fire, is realised by His worshippers. (447)

२. अग्ने त्वं नो अन्तम उत त्राता शिवो भुवो वरूथ्य: ॥

2. O God, be Thou our nearest Friend, Yea our Protector, our Kind Deliverer, and worthy of worship by us! (448)

३. भगो न चित्रो अग्निर्मंहोनां दधाति रत्नम् ॥

3. Among the mighty forces, God, resplendent like the ṣun, grants us wondrous treasure of knowledge. (449)

४. विश्वस्य प्र स्तोभ पुरो वा सन्यदि वेह नूनम् ।

4. O Most Adorable God, Thou wast with me in the past, and art so in the present! (450)[1]

५. उषा अप स्वसुष्टम: सं वर्तयति वर्तनि सूजातता ॥

5. Just as Dawn drives away the darkness of sister Night, and shows the right path to the traveller; so does the dawn of intellect, remove the darkness of ignorance, and shows the soul the right path unto God. (451)

६. इमा नु कं भुवना सीषधेमेन्द्रश्च विश्वे च देवा: ॥

6. O God, may our soul and organs of senses, derive delight from all these existing worlds! (452)

७. वि स्तुतयो यथा पथा इन्द्र त्वद्यन्तु रायत: ॥

7. Like streams of water on their way, let bounties, God, flow from Thec! (453)

८. अया वाजं देवहित सनेम मदेम शतहिमा: सुवीरा: ॥

8. With this prayer may we obtain strength granted by God, and remain happy with brave sons for a hundred years. (454)

९. ऊर्जा मित्रो वरुण: पिन्वतेडा: पीवरीमिषं कृणुही न इन्द्र ॥

9. Just as the sun and cloud fill the fields with water, so may Thou, O God, grant us vast spiritual knowledge! (455)

१०. इन्द्रो विश्वस्य राजति ।

10. God is King of the universe. (456)

---

[1]At all times in the past, present and future, God is present with man. So one should always remember God.

DECADE III

१. त्रिककुकेषु महिषो यवाशिरं तुविशुष्मस्तृम्पत्सोममपिबद्विष्णुना सुतं यथावशम् ।
स इं ममाद महि कर्म कर्तवे महामुरुꣳ सैनꣳसश्चद्देवो देवꣳसत्य इन्दुः सत्यमिन्द्रम् ॥

1. The great and strong soul, in its three stages, enjoys to its fill the supreme felicity produced by God through Yajna, and is satiated therewith. The same soul, always remains happy for the performance of mighty deeds. The soul through its knowledge, attains to Great, Vast, Mighty God. The true, supreme soul, reaches the virtuous God. (457)[1]

२. अयꣳ सहस्रमानवो दृशः कवीनां मतिज्योतिर्विधर्म ।
ब्रध्नः समीचीरुषसः समैरयदरेपसः सचेतसः स्वसरे मन्युमन्तश्चिता गोः ॥

2. This God, worshipped by thousands of contemplative sages, Handsome, the sole Object of meditation by the wise, Resplendent, the Nourisher of His manifold subjects, the Infuser of life in all, the Excellent Dweller in the heart during our life's journey, Immaculate, Learned, nicely impels pure intellects. He is lustrous like the brilliant rays of the sun. (458)

३. एन्द्र याह्युप नः परावतो नायमच्छा विदथानीव सत्पतिरस्ता राजेव सत्पतिः ।
हवामहे त्वा प्रयस्वन्तः सुतेष्वा पुत्रासो न पितरं वाजसातये मꣳहिष्ठं वाजसातये ॥

3. O God, come unto us, who have gone far astray from Thee, just as the sun, the protector of the Earth through attraction, goes to the Yajnas through his pervading rays, and just as a King, the guardian of noble persons goes to his seat of justice. Striving for the means of attaining supreme happiness, we invoke Thee, O most Adorable God, for acquiring the wealth of knowledge, just as sons invoke a sire for riches! (459)

४. तमिन्द्रं जोहवीमि मघवानमुग्रꣳ सत्रा दधानमप्रतिष्कुतꣳ श्रवाꣳसि भूरि ।
मꣳहिष्ठो गीर्भिरा च यज्ञियो ववर्त राये नो विश्वा सुपथा कृणोतु वज्री ॥

4. I invoke that God, Who is Opulent, Agile, the Preserver of the good, the Master of many glories, Resistless, most Liberal, Worthy of remembrance, in Yajnas through Vedic verses. May He, the Remover of all impediments, make our pathways pleasant. (460)

५. अस्तु श्रौषट् पुरो अग्नि धिया दध आ नु त्यच्छर्धो दिव्यं वृणीमह इन्द्रवायू वृणीमहे ।
यद्ध क्राणा विवस्वते नाभा सन्दाय नव्यसे ।
अध प्र नूनमुप यन्ति धीतयो देवाꣳअच्छा न धीतयः ॥

5. Heard be our prayer. In thought manifestly I honour God. In His Might we realise His Refulgence. We realise both soul and breath. They both nicely arrange all human bodies through the ever fresh strength of God. We,

---

[1]Three stages of the soul are its stages of जाग्रत, स्वप्न, सुषुप्ति i.e., waking, sleeping and profound repose.

the gleaners of knowledge through study, go near the sages, as do the disciples to their preceptors. (461)

६. प्र वो महे मतयो यन्तु विष्णवे मरुत्वते गिरिजा एवयामरुत् ।
प्र शर्धाय प्र यज्यवे सुखादये तवसे भन्ददिष्टये धुनिव्रताय शवसे ॥

6. Just as lightnings flash for the cloud, so should your praises, born of learned orators, be offered to the Omnipresent, Mighty God, the Master of myriads of subjects. O Knower of the Vedas! the encyclopaedia of knowledge, absorb yourself in search after God, Almighty, the Accomplisher of life's journey, Equipped with efficient resources, Vital, Worthy of homage, the Great Actor, and the Embodiment of strength. (462)

७. प्रया रुचा हरिण्या पुनानो विश्वा द्वेषाꣳसि तरति सयुग्वभि: सूरो न सयुग्वभि: ।
धारा पृष्ठस्य रोचते पुनानो ꣳरुषो हरि: ।
विश्वा यद्रूपा परियास्यृक्वभि: सप्तास्येभिऋ्ꣳ क्वभि: ॥

7. Just as an energetic leader, with his own allies, subdues all enemies, so an active, highly learned soul, with the help of Yogic practices, and this lustre of his, competent to remove ignorance, sweeping away the dirt of sin, overcomes all evil propensities. The sustaining and nourishing power of God is apparent everywhere. The All-Pervading, Refulgent, Impelling God, encompasses all globes in the atmosphere with seven vital, lustrous airs. (463)

८. ꣳभि त्यं देवꣳसवितारमोण्यो: कविक्रतुमर्चामि सत्यसवꣳ रत्नधामभि प्रियं मतिम् ।
ऊर्ध्वा यस्यामतिर्भा ꣳदिद्युत्सवीमनि हिरण्यपाणिरमिमीत सुक्रतु: कृपा स्व: ॥

8. I praise this God, Father of Heaven and Earth, the Revealer of truth, exceeding Wise, Possessed of charming superhuman powers, Dear to all, Worthy of adoration, Whose splendour is sublime, Who is Peerless, Whose light shines brilliant in creation, Who agile-handed, Wise Creator, with His might, makes the Sun and other luminous planets. (464)

९. ꣳग्निꣳहोतारं मन्ये दास्वन्तं वसो: सूनुꣳ सहसो जातवेदसं विप्रं न जातवेदसम् ।
य ऊर्ध्वया स्वध्वरो देवो देवाच्या कृपा ।
धृतस्य विभ्राष्टिमनु शुक्रशोचिष ꣳाजुह्वानस्य सर्पिष: ॥

9. I deem God, the Creator of the universe, the munificent Wealth-Giver, the Urger of the in-dwelling powerful soul, the Knower of all that is born, like the sage who knoweth the wealth he creates.

The Refulgent God, performing a non-violent sacrifice (Yajna) high in the atmosphere, and mastering all the forces of nature, is Self-luminous, just as clarified butter shines, when put in the blazing and active fire. (465)

१०. तव त्यन्नर्यं नृतोऽप इन्द्र प्रथमं पूर्व्यं दिवि प्रवाच्यं कृतम् ।
यो देवस्य शवसा प्रारिणा ꣳसु रिणन्नप: ।
भुवो विश्वमभ्यदेवमोजसा विदेदूर्जꣳशतक्रतुर्विदेदिषम् ॥

10. O God, the Revolver of luminous bodies like the Sun, it is Thy humanitarian, diffused in space, immemorial, well-performed, laudable deed, that a worshipper of Thine, with Thy power, undertakes tasks in his life-time, and being the lord of hundred powers conquers all that is godless with his exertion, procures strength and food! (466)[1]

PĀVAMĀNAM KĀNDA

DECADE IV

१. उच्चा ते जातमन्धसो दिवि सद्भुम्या ददे । उग्र^ꣻशर्म महि श्रव: ॥

1. O God, the denizens of Earth obtain the vast knowledge and great shelter, created by Thy inspiring strength, and set in the universe ! (467)

२. स्वादिष्ठया मदिष्ठया पवस्व सोम धारया । इन्द्राय पातवे सुत: ॥

2. O God, with Thy sweetest and most gladdening power of sustenance, Thou art present in all. Thou hast created pleasant knowledge for the use of the soul ! (468)

३. वृषा पवस्व धारया मरुत्वते च मत्सर: । विश्वा दधान ओजसा ॥

3. O God, the Bestower of comforts, the satisfier of all, nourishing all the people with Thy strength and power of protection, shine for the soul ! (469)

४. यस्ते मदो वरेण्यस्तेना पवस्वान्धसा । देवावीरघश^ꣻसहा ॥

4. O God, Thy supreme delight is acceptable, shine forth with that. Thou art the Guardian of virtues and the Slayer of sins ! (470)[2]

५. तिस्रो वाच उदीरते गावो मिमन्ति धेनव: । हरिरेति कनिक्रदत् ॥

5. Just as the milch-kine low, so do the three vedas manifest their import. We perceive God, proclaiming His laws ! (471)[3]

६. इन्द्रायेन्दो मरुत्वते पवस्व मधुमत्तम: । अर्कस्य योनिमासदम् ॥

6. O lofty person, for God, the Lord of all active and powerful objects, thou being highly rich in sweetness, manifest thyself for sitting in the place of a holy Yajna ! (472)

७. असाव्य^ꣻशुर्मंदायाप्सु दक्षो गिरिष्ठा: । श्येनो न योनिमासदत् ॥

7. All-pervading God, the companion of the learned, Mighty in the performance of deeds and imparting knowledge, manifests Himself for the enhancement of joy. He resides in the heart like the soul. (473)

---

[1] A worshipper sings in this verse the glory and grandeur of God.
[2] That refers to supreme delight.
[3] The Vedas are four in number, but taking into consideration the knowledge, action and contemplation; ज्ञान, कर्म, उपासना they preach, they are often spoken of as three. All these three subjects are treated in each of the four Vedas. God proclaims His laws and edicts in the Vedas.

८. पवस्व दक्षसाधनो देवेभ्यः पीतये हरे । मरुद्भ्यो वायवे मदः ॥

8. O All pervading God, the Banisher of sin, the Accomplisher of all deeds, the Embodiment of joy, manifest Thyself for enjoyment of soul and charitable persons ! (474)

९. परि स्वानो गिरिष्ठाः पवित्रे सोमो अक्षरत् । मदेषु सर्वधा असि ।

9. The Joyful God, the Impeller of all, the Dweller in speech, manifests Himself in a pure heart. He is competent to keep all absorbed in His Supreme joy. (475)

१०. परि प्रिया दिवः कविर्वया ॐसि नप्त्योर्हितः । स्वानैर्याति कविक्रतुः ॥

10. The wise soul, manifest between Prāna and Apāna, acting intelligently towards other souls, fond of light, is discussed everywhere by the learned, who expatiate on the knowledge of God. (476)

DECADE V

१. प्र सोमासो मदच्युतः श्रवसे नो मघोनाम् । सुतां विदथे अक्रमुः ॥

1. The rapture-shedding learned persons, mild in nature, appointed to officiate at a Yajna, advance the wealth of our knowledge. (477)

२. प्र सोमासो विपश्चितोपो नयन्त ऊर्मयः । वनानि महिषा इव ॥

2. Just as the waves of the ocean take travellers to distant places ; just as powerful conveyances take goods to different countries, so do the active learned persons of affable nature, procure for men objects worth enjoying. (478)[1]

३. पवस्वेन्दो वृषा सुतः कृधी नो यशसो जने । विश्वा अप द्विषो जहि ॥

3. O God, the Accomplisher of our desires, Realizable in the inmost recesses of the heart, manifest Thyself, glorify us among the folk. Drive all our enemies away ! (479)[2]

४. वृषा ह्यसि भानुना द्युमन्तं त्वा हवामहे । पवमान स्वद्ऱ्शम् ॥

4. O Purifying God, Thou art competent in fulfilling our desires. We invoke Thee, as Thou art Resplendent with the lustre of knowledge, and the Bestower of happiness ! (480)

५. इन्दुः पविष्ट चेतनः प्रियः कवीनां मतिः । सृजदश्व ॐरथीरिव ॥

5. The Conscious God, Friend of the learned, Reflective, determines our journey on the path of progress, as a charioteer prepares the horses for the journey. (481)

[1]Powerful conveyances means aeroplanes or buses.
[2]Enemies : Spiritual weaknesses like lust and anger.

६. असृक्षत प्र वाजिनों गव्या सोमासो ग्रश्वया । शक्रासो वीरयाशव: ॥

6. Potent, swift, brilliant Yogis exert, with a desire to have mastery over speech, control over senses, and acquire virility. (482)

७. पवस्व देव ग्रायुषगिन्द्रं गच्छतु ते मद: । वायुमा रोह धर्मणा ॥

7. O God, manifest Thyself, working with mankind, may Thy gladdening juice reach the soul. Be Thou the Master of our life's force, as Thy Law commands ! (483)

८. पवमानो अजीजनद्दिवश्चित्रं न तन्यतुम् । ज्योतिर्वेश्वानरं बृहत् ॥

8. A pure, wise Yogi, like the wonderful thundering of the sky, realises in his soul, the lofty light of God, the Leader of mankind. (484)

९. परि स्वानास इन्दवो मदाय बर्हणा गिरा । मधो अर्षन्ति धारया ॥

9. Highly accomplished, prosperous, learned persons, for imparting intense pleasure, with lofty Vedic speech, like the stream of honey, manifest themselves all over the world. (485)

१०. परि प्रासिष्यदत्कवि: सिन्धोरूर्मावधि श्रित: । कारुम् बिभ्रत्पुरुस्पृहम् ॥

10. A far-seeing scholar, reposing on the wave of his mind's ocean, loved by many, and bearing the skilful soul, roams about rapidly in the world, like a ship in the ocean. (486)

BOOK VI
Chapter 1
DECADE I

१. उपो षु जातमप्तुरं गोभिर्भंङ्गं परिष्कृतम् । इन्दुं देवा ग्रयासिषु: ॥

1. The learned people, attain to the beautitude of God, the Banisher of afflictions, equipped with excellent qualities, devoted to action, and adorned with eloquence. (487)

२. पुनानो ग्रक्रमीदभि विश्वा मृधो विचर्षणि: । शुम्भन्ति विप्रं धीतिभि: ॥

2. A seer, transgresses all conflicts by reconciling them mutually. The learned deck such a sage with holy hymns. (488)

३. आविशन्कलशꣴ सुतो विश्वा अर्षन्नभि श्रिय: । इन्दुरिन्द्राय धीयते ॥

3. A calm Yogi, diffusing all the accomplishments of Yoga, and considering himself as united with God, contemplates upon Him. (489)

४. ग्रसर्जि रथ्यो यथा पवित्रे चम्वो: सुत: । काष्मेन्वाजी न्यक्रमीत् ॥

4. Just as a powerful car-horse, standing in the midst of two armies displays heroism in a battle, so does the soul, placed between Prāna and Apāna in life's journey, display heroism in life's struggle. (490)

५. प्र यद्गावो न भूर्णयस्त्वेषा आयासो अक्रमुः । घ्नन्तः कृष्णामप त्वचम् ॥

5. Just as the impetuous, bright, unwearied rays, come forth driving far away the black covering of the night, so should the soul do. (491)[1]

६. अपघ्नन्पवसे मृधः क्रतुवित्सोम मत्सरः । नुदस्वादेवयुं जनम् ॥

6. O God! Thou art the Ocean of happiness and the Bestower of intellect, suppressing the feelings of sin, Thou lettest loose the stream of holiness. Drive Thou the godless folk afar! (492)

७. अया पवस्व धारया यया सूर्यमरोचयः । हिन्वानो मानुषीरपः ॥

7. O God! urging the actions of man with lustre, with which Thou hast illumined the sun, make the stream of purity flow in the world. (493)

८. स पवस्व य आविथेन्द्रं वृत्राय हन्तवे । वन्निवाँसं महीरपः ॥

8. O God! may we realise Thee, Who helpest the soul in overpowering the sin that opposes mighty virtuous deeds. (494)

९. अया वीती परि स्रव यस्त इन्दो मदेष्वा । अवाह्नन्नवतीनँव ॥

9. O God, Shower Thy blessings on the soul, wherewith revelling in Thy delights, it may sojourn in the body for more than ninety nine years! (495)

१०. परि द्युक्षँ सनद्रयिं भरद्वाजं नो अन्धसा । स्वानो अर्ष पवित्र आ ॥

10. O God, through life's force, grant us lovely wealth, food and knowledge. May Thou reside in a pure heart, in Thy full Majesty! (496)

DECADE II

१. अचिक्रदद्वृषा हरिर्महान्मित्रो न दर्शतः । सँसूर्येण दिद्युते ॥

1. God, the Showerer of happiness, Mightiest of all, Beautiful like the Sun, exhibits His strength and shines with His lustre. (497)

२. आ ते दक्षं मयोभुवं वह्निमद्या वृणीमहे । पान्तमा पुरुस्पृहम् ॥

2. O God, we pray for Thy vigour, the generator of peace, virtue and happiness, the afforder of protection, and desired by all! (498)

३. अध्वर्यो अद्रिभिः सुतँ सोमं पवित्र आ नय । पुनाहीन्द्राय पातवे ॥

3. O priest, establish in a pure heart, the knowledge derived from the sages, and purify it for the enjoyment of the soul. (499)

४. तरत्स मन्दी धावति धारा सुतस्यान्धसः । तरत्स मन्दी धावति ॥

---

[1]Just as the rays of Sun remove the darkness of the night, so should the soul drive away its sins and short-comings.

4. The satisfied soul crosses the bondage of the body. With the force of knowledge acquired for the removal of ignorance, the soul elevates itself. Overcoming ignorance, full of happiness, the purified soul attains to God. (500)

५. आ पवस्व सहस्रिणᵕ रयिᵕ सोम सुवीर्यम् । अस्मे श्रवाᵕसि धारय ॥

5. O God, grant us wealth in thousand, full of strength. Keep all sorts of knowledge secure for us ! (501)

६. अनु प्रत्नास आयव: पदं नवीयो अक्रमु: । रुचे जनन्त सूर्यम् ॥

6. Aspirants after eternal life, probe into knowledge worth acquiring. For self-effulgence they realise God. (502)[1]

७. अर्षा सोम द्युमत्तमोऽभि द्रोणानि रोरुवत् । सीदन्योनौ वनेष्वा ॥

7. O God, exceeding bright, reside in our hearts, Thy home. Resting in our hearts, inculcate the Vedic teachings ! (503)

८. वृषा सोम द्युमाᵕ असि वृषा देव वृषव्रत: । वृषा धर्माणि दध्रिषे ॥

8. O Divine God, Thou art Happiness-Giver, Bright, Strength-Infuser and Master of excellent deeds. Thou Mighty One ordainest laws ! (504)

९. इषे पवस्व धारया मृज्यमानो मनीषिभि: । इन्द्रो रुचाभि गा इहि ॥

9. O God, sought after by the worshippers, mayest Thou be realised through steady abstraction of the mind, for the delight of contemplation !
Approach all round the eulogiser, with the lustre of knowledge. (505)

१०. मन्द्रया सोम धारया वृषा पवस्व देवयु: । अव्या वारेभिरस्मयु: ॥

10. O God, the Showerer of happiness, the Friend of the learned, our Well-wisher, protect us with Thy praiseworthy fine qualities, and shower on us the pleasant stream of ambrosia ! (506)

११. अया सोम सुकृत्यया महान्त्सन्नभ्यवर्धथा: । मन्दान इद्वृषायसे ॥

11. O soul, with this lofty character, being great, hast thou progressed ? Full of happiness, Thou desirest to spread knowledge. (507)

१२. अयं विचर्षणिर्हित: पवमान: स चेतति । हिन्वान आप्यं बृहत् ॥

12. God is Far-seeing, Benevolent and Purifier. He, offering lofty friendship develops the intellect. (508)

१३. प्र न इन्दो महे तु न ऊर्मि न बिभ्रदर्षसि । अभि देवाᵕ अयास्य: ॥

13. O God, Thou art fully realised by the worshippers. For our wealth of knowledge, Thou manifestest Thyself like a wave creating pleasure ! (509)[2]

[1] Eternal life means salvation.
[2] The pleasure derived from the attainment of God, creates a kind of wave in the hearts of the worshippers.

१४. अपघ्नन्पवते मृघोऽप सोमो अराव्णः । गच्छन्निन्द्रस्य निष्कृतम् ॥

14. A highly developed soul, overcomes the internal foes like lust and anger, removes the uncharitable sinners and marching on to God's final beautitude realizes Him. (510)

DECADE III

१. पुनानः सोम धारयापो वसानो अर्षसि ।
आ रत्नधा योनिमृतस्य सीदस्युत्सो देवो हिरण्ययः ॥

1. O God, through Thy stream of benevolence, purifying our souls and actions, residing therein through pervasion, Thou approachest us. Thou, the Sustainer of all luminous heavenly bodies, Resplendent, Deep like a well, Divine, the Origin of the Vedas, art ever calm and steady ! (511)

२. परीतो षिञ्चता सुतꣳ सोमो य उत्तमꣳ हविः ।
दघन्वाꣳ यो नर्यो अप्स्वाꣳन्तरा सुषाव सोममद्रिभिः ॥

2. God is the best of sacred gifts. The worshipper, who, through Yogic exercises, realises God, the Seer of actions, is the benefactor of humanity. Ye men, retaining in your mind the Almighty God, realised by the Yogis, spread spiritual knowledge all round in the world. (512)

३. आ सोम स्वानो अद्रिभिस्तिरो वाराण्यव्यया ।
जनो न पुरि चम्वोर्विशद्धरिः सदो वनेषु दधिषे ॥

3. O All-Sustaining God, Thou, eclipsing the undecaying rays of the Sun, art fully pervading the Heaven and Earth ; just as men reside in a city. In solitary places of contemplation, Thou art retained in the inmost recesses of the heart ! (513)

४. प्र सोम देववीतये सिन्धुर्न पिप्ये अर्णसा ।
अꣳशोः पयसा मदिरो न जागृविरच्छा कोशं मधुश्चुतम् ॥

4. O Immortal God, just as the ocean is full of water, so art Thou full of the nectar of Immortality. Gladdening and Sentient as Thou art, for the contentment of the devotees, reside in the heart, the developer of the soul ! (514)

५. सोम उ ष्वाणः सोतृभिरधि ष्णुभिरवीनाम् ।
अश्वयेव हरिता याति धारया मन्द्रया याति धारया ॥

5. O soul, thou art grasped by the Yogis through channels of organs. Thou manifestest Thyself in the heart in a fast, conscious and pleasant stream. Thou revealest Thyself like an excellent horse in a joyous current ! (515)[1]

---

[1]Just as a King riding on a fast horse goes throughout the capital, so does the soul reveal itself full of pleasure, in the heart.

६. तवाहꣳ सोम रारण सख्य इन्दो दिवेदिवे ।
पुरूणि बभ्रो नि चरन्ति मामव परिधीꣳ रति ताꣳइहि ।

6. O Omnipresent, Glorious, Immortal God, every day Thy friendship hath been my delight. Manifold agonies of birth torment me. Kindly release me from these barriers and grant salvation ! (516)

७. मृज्यमान: सुहस्त्या समुद्रे वाचमिन्वसि । रयि पिशङ्गं बहुलं पुरुस्पृहं पवमानाभ्यर्षसि ॥

7. O Purifying, Refulgent God, Thou, when sought for, preachest the Vedas in the ocean-like heart. Thou makest riches flow unto us, yellow like gold, abundant, and much desired ! (517)

८. अभि सोमास आयव: पवन्ते मद्यं मदम् ।
समुद्रस्याधि विष्टपे मनीषिणो मत्सरासो मदच्युत: ॥

8. Austere, aged, ecstatic, rapturous, self-controlled Yogis, stationed in the extreme boundary of the ocean of joy, spread gladdening delight all round. (518)

९. पुनान: सोम जागृविरव्या वारें: परि प्रिय: ।
त्वं विप्रो अभवोऽङ्गिरस्तम मध्वा यज्ञं मिमिक्ष ण: ॥

9. O Immortal, Most Learned God, Thou art Pure, Conscious, Lovable, Omniscient, Pray protect us from all sides with Thy excellent qualities, and fill our life with pleasure ! (519)[1]

१०. इन्द्राय पवते मद: सोमो मरुत्वते सुत: । सहस्रधारो अत्यव्यमर्षति तमी मृजन्त्यायव: ॥

10. The purified, delightful soul goes unto God, the Lord of Creation. With thousand-fold strength, transgressing the mind, the soul manifests itself. The aged Yogis polish the same soul. (520)

११. पवस्व वाजसातमोभि विश्वोऽनि वार्या । त्वꣳ समुद्र: प्रथमे विधर्मं देवेभ्य: सोम मत्सर: ॥

11. O God, manifest Thyself, overcoming all impediments, being endowed with knowledge and strength. Thou art the vast ocean of happiness. O Sustainer, Thou art the Fountain of delight for imparting noble virtues. (521)

१२. पवमाना असृक्षत पवित्रमति धारया ।
मरुत्वन्तो मत्सरा इन्द्रिया हया मेधामभि प्रयाꣳसि च ॥

12. The pure souls, immersed in happiness, attain to God through steady abstraction of the mind. Abandoning the horse-like restless organs of senses, discrimination, mind, desire, egoism and worldly belongings, they get salvation. (522)[2]

---

[1]Life has been spoken of as यज्ञ, as life is meant to be spent in the service of others. A life of sacrifice is the true, real life.

[2]An emancipated soul is free from desire, ego, and material organs of sense.

DECADE IV

१. प्र तु द्रव परि कोशं नि षीद नृभिः पुनानो अभि वाजमर्ष ।
अश्वं न त्वा वाजिनं मर्जयन्तोऽच्छा बर्हीं रशनाभिर्नयन्ति ॥

1. O soul, go forward, reside in the heart and being purified by the sages, acquire knowledge. Just as a powerful and swift horse, being cleansed, and led by reins is taken to the battle-field by horsemen, so is a purified soul, filled with knowledge, taken by the sages to God through Yogic accomplishments.
(523)[1]

२. प्र काव्यमुशनेव ब्रुवाणो देवो देवानां जनिमा विवक्ति ।
महिव्रतः शुचिबन्धुः पावकः पदा वराहो अभ्येति रेभन् ॥

2. The Author of Vedic-speech, the Friend of the noble, the Embodiment of purity, God of the gods, desiring for world's welfare, preaching the Vedas, reveals the attributes, action and nature of divine objects. In the beginning of Creation, He reveals the hymns of the Vedas in the hearts of the Rishis. (524)[2]

३. तिस्रो वाच ईरयति प्र वह्निऋंतस्य धीति ब्रह्मणो मनीषाम् ।
गावो यन्ति गोपतिं पृच्छमानाः सोमं यन्ति मतयो वावशानाः ॥

3. A learned soul preaches in the world the three-fold hymns of the Vedas, the notion of truth, and the wisdom of God. Just as cows go to the cowherd, so do the mental faculties, aspiring after purification, go seeking for a philosopher. (525)[3]

४. अस्य प्रेषा हेमना पूयमानो देवो देवेभिः समपृक्त रसम् ।
सुतः पवित्रं पर्येति रेभन् मितेव सद्म पशुमन्ति होता ॥

4. Observing the precious teachings of the Veda, purifying itself thereby, the brilliant soul, along with the organs of senses, affords us pleasure. Thus manifesting itself, like a learned preacher, it reaches a pure lofty stage. Just as a peasant comes to a cattle-shed, and yokes the cattle to a conveyance, so does a sage, advancing his knowledge, control this body, coupled with the organs of senses. (526)

---

[1]The word तु in the text has been taken by Sāyanāchārya as नु and translated thus. In all the well known five Editions of the Samaveda, and in the exegesis of Shri Jiva Nand and that of Pt. Guru Dutta, the word तु is used. Sāyana seems to have mistaken it for नु.

[2]God reveals in the beginning of each cycle of creation the Veyas, in the hearts of the Rishis. The Vedas were revealed in the present cycle to Agni, Vayu, Aditya, Angiras, the great seers. God is free from desire, but He is spoken of here figuratively as if desirous for the good of humanity. Some commentators take the word वराहः to mean the incarnation of God. No where in the Vedas is there any mention of an incarnation of God. Sāyana, Yaska, Satyavrat Samashrami do not take the word to mean an incarnation of God in the form of a boar. In fact no ancient commentator of the Vedas has interpreted the word as an incarnation.

[3]The Vedas are four, but they are spoken of as three to denote the division of their hymns.

५. सोम: पवते जनिता मतीनां जनिता दिवो जनिता पृथिव्या: ।
जनिता।'नेर्जनिता सूर्यस्य जनितेन्द्रस्य जनितोत विष्णो: ॥

5. God, the Father of mental functions, the Father of the Earth, the Father of Heaven ; the Father of fire, Sun's Generator, the Father, Who begat lightning and space, is realised by the sacrificers. (527)

६. अभि त्रिपृष्ठं वृषणं वयोधामङ्गोषिणमवावशन्त वाणी: ।
वना वसानो वरुणो न सिन्धुर्वि रत्नधा दयते वार्याणि ॥

6. Vedic hymns always dilate upon God, the Dweller in the firmament, space and earth, the Fulfiller of desires, the Bestower of life, and Worthy of adoration. The All-pervading God, the Lord of wealth, residing in all material objects, like an ocean, the mine of gold, distributes blessings. (528)

७. अक्रांत्समुद्र: प्रथमे विधर्मं जनयन् प्रजा भुवनस्य गोपा: ।
वृषा पवित्रे अधि सानो अव्ये बृहत्सोमो वावृधे स्वानो अद्रि: ॥

7. The mighty soul, manifesting itself, grows in the proximity of God, Who is Eternal, the Bestower of happiness, Immortal, Purifier and the Embodiment of joy. God, the solitary Resort of humanity like the ocean, the Guardian of the world, creating His subjects in eminent places of shelter in the space, is farther away from all. (529)[1]

८. कनिक्रन्ति हरिरा सृज्यमान: सीदन्वनस्य जठरे पुनान: ।
नृभिर्यत: कृणुते निर्णिजं गामतो मति जनयत स्वधाभि: ॥

8. The All-pervading, Pure God, residing in the midst of the heart, adored by men, purifies the speech for the pronunciation of Vedic Verses. Hence, Ye men, contemplate on Him through mental faculties. (530)

९. एष स्य ते मधुमाँ इन्द्र सोमो वृषा वृष्ण: परि पवित्रे अक्षा: ।
सहस्रदा: शतदा भूरिदावा शश्वत्तमं बहिरा वाज्यस्थात् ॥

9. O Happiness-Bestowing God, the soul, a showerer of joy, full of the sweetness of divine knowledge, in its radiant beauty flows unto Thee.
Soul, the bestower of thousands of delights, hundreds of powers, immense joy, and eternal in nature, resides in God, the Great Soul, coupled with a knowledge ! (531)

१०. पवस्व सोम मधुमाँ ऋतावापो वसानो अधि सानो अव्ये ।
अव द्रोणानि घृतवन्ति रोह मदिन्तमो मत्सर: इन्द्रपान: ॥

10. O God, the Embodiment of sweetness and knowledge, in the midst of the heart, covering the mind with diverse forms of consciousness, gladdening

[1]Just as all rivers and streams finally go to the ocean, so all human beings finally resort to God for shelter and protection.

the kindled heads, and filling the heart with happiness, descend down to the
soul for its enjoyment ! (532)

DECADE V

१. प्र सेनानी: शूरो अग्ने रथानां गव्यन्नेति हर्षते अस्य सेना ।
भद्रान् कृण्वन्निन्द्रहवान्त्सखिभ्य आ सोमो वस्त्रा रभसानि दत्ते ॥

1. Just as a Valiant Commander, but on conquering the enemy's territory,
goes forth in front of the cars, and his army is pleased thereby ; and just as a
brave King, announcing his benevolent behests for his associates, wards off
the formidable, overpowering onslaughts of the enemy ; so does the soul, the
leader of all organs, ruling over bodies and controlling all faculties march onward ; whereby all its breaths and senses are gratified. Bestowing manifold,
useful knowledge on its votaries, it discards the powerful coverings of ignorance. (533)

२. प्र ते धारा मधुमतीरसृग्रन्वारं यत्पूतो अत्येष्यव्ययम् ।
पवमान पवसे धाम गोनां जनयन्त्सूर्यमपिन्वो अर्कैः ॥

2. O happy soul, thy streams of divine knowledge flow forth, when thou
being purified manifestest thyself crossing the respiratory sheath !
O purifier, in the midst of the organs, thou revealest thy radiant beauty,
and with thy pure beams, like the Sun, fillest thy votary with supreme delight !
(534)[1]

३. प्र गायताभ्यर्चाम देवान्त्सोमꣳ हिनोत महते धनाय ।
स्वादु: पवतामति वारमव्यमा सीदतु कलशं देव इन्दु: ॥

3. O learned persons, recite Vedic verses for acquiring mighty riches. Let
us revere the sages. Enjoy the exquisite happiness of the soul. Crossing the
respiratory sheath, let the soul flow. Let the luminous soul reside in the
inmost recesses of the heart ! (535)

४. प्र हिन्वानो जनिता रोदस्यो रथो न वाजꣳ सनिष्यन्नयासीत् ।
इन्द्रं गच्छन्नायुधा सꣳशिशानो विश्वा वसु हस्तयोरादधानः ॥

4. The pure soul of a Yogi, the urger of all, the impeller of Prāna and
Apāna, the bestower of knowledge, strength and food, charming like the sun,
behaves in an excellent way. Equipped with the weapon of Yoga, going
towards God, sharpening itself, taking in its hands all the wealth of knowledge,
it continues marching on and on. (536)

५. तक्षद्यदी मनसो वेनतो वाग् ज्येष्ठरय धर्मं द्युक्षोरनीके ।
आदीमायन् वरमा वावशाना जुष्टं पति कलशे गाव इन्दुम् ॥

_____
[1]Respiratory sheath is प्राणमय कोश, one of the five sheaths which enshrine the soul.

5. When the utterance of a learned and contemplative Yogi, reveals in the foremost place of lustre, the joy felt by the mighty soul, then mental faculties go to their lord, the excellent, acceptable joy of the heart, as loudly lowing cows go to their master. (537)[1]

६. साकमुक्षो मर्जयन्त स्वसारो दश धीरस्य धीतयो धनुत्री: ।
हरि: पर्यंद्रवज्जा: सूर्यस्य द्रोणं ननक्षे ग्रत्यो न वाजी ॥

6. The ten impelling organs of a contemplative Yogi, like ten sisters, united-ly relishing the pleasure of knowledge, purify the soul. Soul's joy, the dispeller of all afflictions, flows towards the mental faculties, its dependents, and itself pervades the soul like a fleet vigorous courser. (538)

७. ग्रधि यदस्मिन् वाजिनीव शुभ: स्पर्धन्ते धिय: सूरे न विश: ।
ग्रपो वृणान: पवते कवीयान् व्रजं न पशुवर्धनाय मन्म ॥

7. Just as trappings on a horse vie with one another, or as subjects emulate one another in offering presents to their noble King, so do the internal auspicious mental faculties try to excel one another in their reverence unto the soul. Just as a cow-herd goes to the fascinating cattle-herd for the amelioration of cows, so does a learned soul, mastering his mental propensities, for strengthening his organs, goes in search after God, with an iron determination. (539)

८. इन्दुर्वाजी पवते गोन्योघा इन्द्रे सोम: सह इन्वन्मदाय ।
हन्ति रक्षो बाधते पर्यराति वरिवस्कृण्वन् वृजनस्य राजा ॥

8. Endowed with knowledge, the elixir of spiritual happiness, running in the heart, for the enhancement of joy, infusing strength in the soul, flows letting loose a flood of knowledge. It quells the foes of spiritual advancement and slays its moral enemies, and being the lord of strength, fulfils all desires.
(540)[2]

९. ग्रया पवा पवस्वेना वसूनि माँश्चत्व इन्दो सरसि प्र धन्व ।
ब्रध्नश्चिद्यस्य वातो न जूति पुरुमेधाश्चित्तकवे नरं धात् ॥

9. O soul, with Thy well-known purity, purifying the resources of life, fulfil the ocean of my heart. A self-controlled, wise, calm person alone realizes Thy wind-like speed. (541)

१०. महत् तत् सोमो महिषश्चकारापाँ यद्गर्भोऽवृणीत देवान् ।
ग्रदधादिन्द्रे पवमान ग्रोजोऽजनयत् सूर्ये ज्योतिरिन्दु: ॥

10. God, the Observer of our actions, welcomes the learned. The Supreme God performs this mighty deed. God, the Purifier, grants strength to the soul, and generates light in the Sun. (542)

---

[1]Foremost place of lustre means the heart.

[2]Sayana has mistakenly translated ग्ररातिम् of the verse as ग्रराती: as occurs in Rigveda 9-97-10.

११. प्रसर्जि वक्वा रथ्ये यथाजौ धिया मनोता प्रथमा मनीषा ।
दश स्वसारो अधि सानो अग्र्ये मृजन्ति वह्निꣳसदनेष्वच्छ ॥

11. Just as in a battle fought with chariots, an intelligent Commander is appointed, so in a struggle of Yogic practices, through contemplation and abstraction, a sage, the reciter of praise-verses, is destined to play the role of a commander. All mental functions are intertwined with the foremost intellectual power. Ten vital breaths like sisters decorate the soul on a high level, and function in their respective spheres. (543)

१२. अपामिवेदूर्मयस्तर्तुराणाः प्र मनीषा ईरते सोममच्छ ।
नमस्यन्तीरुप च यन्ति सं चाच विशन्त्युशतीरुशन्तम् ॥

12. Hastening onward like the waves of waters our intellectual forces are proceeding towards the soul. To him they go with lowly adoration, and longing, enter him who longs to meet them. (544)[1]

Chapter 2

DECADE I

१. पुरोजिती वो अन्धसः सुताय मादयित्नवे ।
अप श्वानꣳ शनथिष्टन सखायो दीर्घजिह्व्यम् ॥

1. Ye friends ! for protecting the accomplished and gladdening soul, that subdues devotion to external objects, and is endowed with life-preserving force, control this long-tongued dog. (545)[2]

२. अयं पूषा रयिर्भगः सोमः पुनानो अर्षति । पतिर्विश्वस्य भूमनो व्यख्यद्रोदसी उभे ॥

This Strengthening, Adorable, Wealth-Bestowing, Purifying God, the Lord of all beings, illumines both the Earth and Heaven. (546)

३. सुतासो मधुमत्तमाः सोमा इन्द्राय मन्दिनः ।
पवित्रवन्तो अक्षरन् देवान् गच्छन्तु वो मदाः ॥

3. The renowned learned persons, relishing the beauty of the soul, spreading joy, pure in nature, long for the soul. May your pleasures go forth to the learned. (547)[3]

४. सोमाः पवन्त इन्दवोऽस्मभ्यं गातुवित्तमाः । मित्राः स्वाना अरेपसःस्वाध्यः स्वविदः ॥

4. For us roam the Yogis, the Knowers of the right path, lovely, friendly, self-reliant, immaculate, contemplative, and imparters of all sorts of knowledge. (548)

[1]Him refers to the soul.
[2]Long-tongued dog, means the mind, that is thirsty, avaricious and voluptuous like a dog.
[3]Your refers to the performers of a Yajna.

५. अभी नो वाजसातम꣸रयिमर्ष शतस्पृहम् । इन्दो सहस्रभर्णसं तुविद्युम्नं विभासहम् ॥

5. O learned person, stream on us the wealth of knowledge, the bestower of strength, craved by hundreds, the sustainer of thousands, full of great dignity and lustre, surpassing extreme loveliness. (549)[1]

६. अभी नवन्ते अद्रुह: प्रियमिन्द्रस्य काम्यम् ।
वत्सं न पूर्व आयुनि जात꣸ रिहन्ति मातर: ॥

6. The guileless ones bow before God's well-beloved friend, as in the morning of its life, the mothers lick the new-born calf. (550)[2]

७. आ हर्यताय धृष्णवे धनुष्टन्वन्ति पौ꣸स्यम् ।
शुक्रा वि यन्त्यसुराय निर्णिजे विपामग्रे महीयुव: ॥

7. Just as soldiers extend the powerful bow for their beloved King, so do the learned persons control their formidable passions for the attainment of the Beautiful God. Strong souls, hankering after greatness, approach the learned and wise persons, for purifying the soul, the urger of vital breaths. (551)[3]

८. परि त्य꣸ हर्यत꣸हरि बभ्रुं पुनन्ति वारेण ।
यो देवान् विश्वा꣸ इत्परि मदेन सह गच्छति ॥

8. Sages discern through their soul, that God, beloved by all, and Sustainer of all, Who verily fills all the forces of nature with joy. (552)

९. प्र सुन्वानायान्धसो मर्तो न वष्ट तद्वच: । अप श्वानमराधस꣸ हता मखं न भृगव: ॥

9. The unimpaired Word of God is meant for him who accomplishes the truth of life. An ordinary mortal cannot achieve it. O learned persons, shun him who is avaricious and uncharitable like a dog, but not the spirit of sacrifice ! (553)

DECADE II

१. अभि प्रियाणि पवते चनोहितो नामानि यह्वो अधि येषु वर्धते ।
आ सूर्यस्य बृहतो बृहन्नधि रथं विश्वञ्चमरुहद् विचक्षण: ॥

1. God, accepted for His mature knowledge, manifests Himself in all those highly lovely attributes, through which He rules over the hearts of His subjects. God, the Great Seer, rules over this body, acquired by all mortals, and shaped by Him, the Developer of all. (554)

---

[1]Satyavrat Samashrami is of the view that the word विभासह: occurs only here in all the Vedas.

[2]Mother means kine.

[3]धनु: may also mean the bow of Om. Learned persons recite Om and contemplate upon it.

Extending the bow by learned persons, means the observance of celibacy, and comradeship with the sages.

२. अचोदसो नो धन्वन्त्विन्दव: प्र स्वानासो बृहद् देवेषु हरय: ।
वि चिदश्नाना इषयो अरातयोऽर्यो न: सन्तु सनिषन्तु नो धिय: ॥

2. Let active, spontaneous souls, visibly, elegantly approach us, in the midst of the learned. Let our foe-like, distressing, thirsty and lascivious passions be unsuccessful, and our noble resolves succeed. (555)[1]

३. एष प्र कोशे मधुमाꣳ अचिक्रददिन्द्रस्य वज्रो वपुषो वपुष्टम: ।
अभ्यृ३तस्य सुदुघा घृतश्चुतो वाश्रा अर्षन्ति पयसा च धेनव: ॥

3. God, the Queller of the obstacles and sins of the soul like a thunderbolt, most Bounteous of the bounteous, in the inmost recesses of the heart, nicely reveals His undecaying Word, full of the sweet elixir of divine joy.

Just as lowing milch-kine shed streams of milk, so do the juices of supreme joy, recipients of knowledge, shedders of the streams of loveliness, ooze in the heart. (556)

४. प्रो अयासीदिन्दुरिन्द्रस्य निष्कृतꣳ सखा सख्युर्न प्र मिनाति सङ्गिरम् ।
मर्यइव युवतिभि: समर्षति सोम: कलशे शतयामना पथा ॥

4. Soul, the friend of God, even after the attainment of final beautitude, does not transgress the injunction of God's Vedic speech. Just as a youth moves with pleasure with youthful maids, so does the soul with its intellectual functions, roam in God by a course of hundred paths. (557)

५. धर्ता दिव: पवते कृत्व्यो रसो दक्षो देवानामनुमाद्यो नृभि: ।
हरि: सृजानो अत्यो न सत्वभिर्वृ॑था पाजाꣳसि कृणुषे नदीष्वा ।ꞌ

5. Soul, the sustainer of knowledge, the acquirer of learning through Yogic practices and the strengthener of organs, in fulness of joy, enjoyed by men, like a fleeting horse, spontaneously exhibits its multitudinous force, in our arteries and veins, as water flows freely without exertion in the streams. (558)

६. वृषा मतीनां पवते विचक्षण: सोमो अह्नां प्रतरीतोषसाꣳ दिव: ।
प्राणा सिन्धूनाꣳ कलशाꣳ अचिक्रददिन्द्रस्य हार्द्याविशन्मनीषिभि: ॥

6. God, the Showerer of joys, the Displayer of mental faculties in diverse ways, the Furtherer of days, of mornings and of heaven, the Infuser of life in the arteries of the body, entering the soul's receptacles of the heart, through mind's goadings, purifies and urges the soul. (559)

७. त्रिरस्मै सप्त धेनवो दुदुह्रिरे सत्यामाशिरं परमे व्योमनि ।
चत्वार्यन्या भुवनानि निर्णिजे चारूणि चक्रे यदृतैरवर्धत ॥

---

[1]Griffith writes, the meaning of इषय: is unknown. The word means thirsty, lascivious passions. I wonder why Griffith failed to understand the meaning of the word.

7. When the soul develops itself with true sorts of knowledge, then the seven cows in the loftiest head, in three stages, yield real knowledge for it. It fills the other four sheaths of the body with beauty and strength for their purification. (560)[1]

८. इन्द्राय सोम सुषुतः परि स्रवापामीवा भवतु रक्षसा सह ।
मा ते रसस्य मत्सत द्र्याविनो द्रविणस्वन्त इह सन्त्विन्दवः ॥

8. Flow on to soul, O God, carefully worshipped. Let sickness stay afar along with evil-mindedness. Let not the double-tongued sinners enjoy Thy beauty. Let those devoted to Thy contemplation prosper in the world. (561)[2]

९. असावि सोमो अरुषो वृषा हरी राजेव दस्मो अभि गा अचिक्रदत् ।
पुनानो वारमत्येष्यव्ययᵒ श्येनो न योनि घृतवन्तमासदत् ॥

9. The lustrous, gladdening, attractive soul, handsome like a King, being accomplished, produces sensation in the organs. Being purified, it overcomes even the impenetrable obstacle, and like a swift falcon, attains to the Refulgent God. (562)

१०. प्र देवमच्छा मधुमन्त इन्दवोऽसिष्यदन्त गाव आ न धेनवः ।
बर्हिषदो वचनावन्त ऊधभिः परिस्रुतमुस्रिया निर्णिजं धिरे ॥

10. Just as milch-kine go to the calf and yield their milk, so do the God-knowing Yogis directly go unto God. They, the revellers in Mighty God, following the teachings of the Vedas, shining like the rays of the Sun, enjoy the pure, heartening delight, oozing out of cerebral abodes. (563)

११. अञ्जते व्यञ्जते समञ्जते क्रतुᵒ रिहन्ति मध्वाभ्यञ्जते ।
सिन्धोरुच्छ्वासे पतयन्तमुक्षणᵒ हिरण्यपावाः पशुमप्सु गृभ्णते ॥

11. The Yogis realise, manifest God, and identify themselves with Him. They relish the supreme bliss of the soul, and intermingle it with their internal joy. They, the decorators of the soul with knowledge, revelling in God's attractive force, perceive the gladdening soul with their powers of discernment. (564)[3]

१२. पवित्रं ते विततं ब्रह्मणस्पते प्रभुर्गात्राणि पर्येषि विश्वतः ।
अतप्ततनूर्न तदामो अश्नुते श्रुतास इद् वहन्तः सं तदाशत ॥

[1]Seven cows are two eyes, two ears, two nostrils, and mouth, which are placed in the head, the highest part of the body and serve as channels to furnish knowledge to the soul.
Three stages: Jagrat (waking), Swapna (sleeping) Sushupti (Profound repose).
Other four sheaths are the प्राणमय कोश, मनोमय कोश, ज्ञानमय कोश, आनन्दमय कोश, besides the अन्नमय कोश. These five vestures or cases successively make the body, enshrining the soul.
[2]Double-tongued sinners means persons who sometimes speak the truth and sometimes untruth, who do not always stick to the truth. Or it may mean, who suffer both from physical and mental diseases.
[3]They refers to the Yogis.

12. O God, the Master of the Vedas, vast is Thy pure knowledge. O God, Thou pervadest all physical bodies. An immature soul devoid of penance cannot realise the true nature of God. Only the learned, ripened in the furnace of austerity can perceive Thee. (565)

DECADE III

१. इन्द्रमच्छ सुता इमे वृषणं यन्तु हरयः । श्रुष्टे जातास इन्दवः स्वविदः ॥

1. These accomplished, charming Yogis, acquiring pleasure, absorbing themselves in God, nicely realise Him, the Showerer of happiness. (566)

२. प्र धन्वा सोम जागृविरिन्द्रायेन्दो परि स्रव । द्युमन्तꣲ शुष्ममा भर स्वविदम् ।

2. O tranquil Yogi, ever vigilant, with God as thy goal, proceed forward, and achieve Him. Hoard the illuminating, instructive strength of spiritual knowledge ! (567)

३. सखाय आ नि षीदत पुनानाय प्र गायत । शिशुं न यज्ञैः परि भूषत श्रिये ॥

3. O Comrades, come, sit down, and sing the virtues of the soul, the purifier. Just as mothers adorn the child for elegance, so should Ye, for acquiring spiritual wealth, beautify the soul with knowledge and deeds ! (568)

४. तं व: सखायो मदाय पुनानमभि गायत । शिशुं न हव्यैः स्वदयन्त गूर्तिभिः ॥

4. O Comrades, sing for your happiness, the praise of the Yogi, who purges his impurities through penance. Just as a child is appeased by offering him sweets and nice play-things, so should the soul be controlled through noble ideas and the nectar of spiritual knowledge ! (569)

५. प्राणा शिशुर्महीनाꣲ हिन्वन्नृतस्य दीधितिम् । विश्वा परि प्रिया भुवदध द्विता ॥

5. Of all the mighty forces of God, the soul-force, the infuser of life in the bodies, shedding the lustre to true knowledge, doubly comprehends all excellent lovely objects ! (570)[1]

६. पवस्व देववीतय इन्दो धाराभिरोजसा । आ कलशं मधुमान्त्सोम नः सदः ॥

6. O calm God, for enhancing the knowledge of the learned, manifest Thyself with Thy strength and powers of preservation and sustenance. O Omniscient God reside in our heart ! (571)

७. सोम: पुनान ऊर्मिणाव्यं वारं वि धावति । अग्रे वाचः पवमानः कनिक्रदत् ॥

7. Soul, the purifier and self-purified, through mental elevation, transgresses the covering of ignorance, and absorbs itself in the lofty mysteries of the Vedas. (572)

[1]Double means individually व्यष्टिरूपे and collectively, समष्टिरूपे, or in subtle सूक्ष्म and rough स्थूल ways.

८. प्र पुनानाय वेधसे सोमाय वच उच्यते । भृति न भरा मतिभिर्जुजोषते ॥

8. All spiritual teachings are preached for the wise, pure soul. A worshipper, through his reflective functions, enjoys his soul. O worshippers, just as a labourer is paid his wages according to law, so should ye develop mental faculty, which elevates the soul ! (573)

९. गोमन्न इन्दो अश्ववत्सुतः सुदक्ष धनिव । शुचि च वर्णमधि गोषु धारय ॥

9. O Mighty God, being contemplated in the heart, grant us the wealth of knowledge and physical strength. Grant our organs a lustrous beauty ! (574)

१०. अस्मभ्यं त्वा वसुविदमभि वाणीरनूषत । गोभिष्टे वर्णमभि वासयामसि ॥

10. O God, the Vedas sing for our welfare, the virtues of Thee, the Bestower of knowledge and riches. Through Vedic verses we know Thy true nature ! (575)

११. पवते हर्यतो हरिरति ह्वराँसि रँह्या । अभ्यर्ष स्तोतृभ्यो वीरवद्यशः ॥

11. God, Attainable by all, shines forth, after rapidly transgressing all formidable obstacles. O God, grant hero-like glory to Thy eulogisers ! (576)

१२. परि कोशं मधुश्चुतँसोमः पुनानो अर्षति । अभि वाणीऋषीणाँसप्ता नूषत ॥

12. The sinless soul attains to the sheath of supreme joy. The seven metres of the Vedic verses clearly praise the soul. (577)[1]

DECADE IV

१. पवस्व मधुमत्तम इन्द्राय सोम क्रतुवित्तमो मदः । महि द्युक्षतमो मदः ॥

1. O happiest and most learned God, excellent amongst the preachers of knowledge and actions, Embodiment of joy, manifest Thyself for the soul. Being full of delight, of all divine objects, Thou art the most Mighty and Pre-eminent ! (578)

२. अभि द्युम्नं बृहद्यश इषस्पते दिदीहि देव देवयुम् । वि कोशं मध्यमं युव ॥

2. O Lord of food, knowledge and mental urges, O Refulgent God, Master of the learned and all the forces of nature, we pray unto Thee, to grant us ample glory and wealth, and remove the middle mental and intellectual coverings and take the soul direct to the last sheath of supreme joy ! (579)[2]

___

[1]Sheath of supreme joy means आनन्दमय Kosha, the last of the five coverings which enshrine the soul.

Seven metres are: 1. Gayatri, 2. Ushnik, 3. Anushtup, 4. Brihati, 5. Pankti, 6. Trishtup, 7. Jagati.

[2]Mental and intellectual coverings refer to मनोमय and विज्ञानमय Koshas. The sheath of supreme joy is आनन्दमय Kosha.

३. आ सोता परि षिश्चताश्वं न स्तोममप्तुरॐ रजस्तुरम् । वनप्रक्षमुदप्रुतम् ॥

3. O Yogi, realise in the heart, and pour into it again and again the delightful elixir of God, who is Adorable, Attainable through knowledge and noble deeds. All-pervading, constantly Present in all souls, and replete with knowledge ! (580)

४. एतमु त्यं मदच्युतॐ सहस्रधारं वृषभं दिवोदुहम् । विश्वा वसूनि बिभ्रतम् ॥

4. The Yogis verily attain to this God, Who is, the Showerer of joy, the Sustainer of innumerable worlds, the Bestower of ease, the Giver of knowledge, and the Lord of all sorts of wealth. (581)

५. स सुन्वे यो वसूनां यो रायामानेता य इडानाम् । सोमो यः सुक्षितीनाम् ॥

5. God, Who is, the Giver of glories, the Lord of the forces of nature, the Master of all sorts of knowledge, and the Maker of handsome bodies, is realised in the heart. (582)

६. त्वं ह्यां३ङ् देव्यं पवमान जनिमानि द्युमत्तमः । अमृतत्वाय घोषयन् ।

6. O dear, holy, Most Refulgent God, Thou alone preachest to the learned, the assumption of several births, for the attainment of salvation ! (583)

७. एष स्य धारया सुतोऽव्या वारेभिः पवते मदिन्तमः । क्रीडन्नूमिरपामिव ।

7. The accomplished soul, transgressing the coverings of the mind, endowed with supreme joy, plays in this world with knowledge and actions, backed by its internal strength, just as ripples play on water. He, Who is sought after, shines in the heart. (584)[1]

८. य उस्रिया अपि या अन्तरश्मनि निर्गा अक्रन्तदोजसा ।
   अभि व्रजं तत्निषे गव्यमश्व्यं वर्मीव धृष्णवा रुज ॥
   श्रो३म् वर्मीव धृष्णवा रुज ॥

8. The soul creates in the heart with its strength, the active, developing organs of cognition and action. It spreads the organs of cognition and action all around it.

O God, the Conqueror of all, remove all obstacles like an armoured hero! (585)

Āranyak Kānda

Chapter 3

DECADE I

१. इन्द्र ज्येष्ठं न आ भर ओजिष्ठं पुपुरि श्रवः ।
   यद्धिध्ध्रुक्षेम वज्रहस्त रोदसी उभे सुशिप्र पप्राः ॥

[1]He refers to God.

1. O God, Grant us excellent, most vigorous, full knowledge. O God, equipped with the weapon of knowledge and asceticism, Mighty and Omniscient, grant us in this world and the next, the knowledge we desire to gain ! (586)[1]

२. इन्द्रो राजा जगतश्चर्षणीनामधिक्षमा विश्वरूपं यदस्य ।
ततो ददाति दाशुषे वसूनि चोदद्राघ उपस्तुतं चिदर्वाक् ॥

2. God is the Lord of cattle and men, and whatever there exists on this earth. The All-Pervading God provides all necessities of life for a charitably disposed person. May He grant us the wealth and knowledge, desired by all. (587)

३. यस्येदमा रजोयुजस्तुजे जने वनꣳ स्व: । इन्द्रस्य रन्त्यं बृहत् ॥

3. The Refulgent God, Who endows a charitably disposed person with serviceable, supreme bliss and prosperity, possesses a vast, beautiful glory. (588)

४. उदुत्तमं वरुण पाशमस्मदवाधमं वि मध्यमꣳश्रथाय ।
अथादित्य व्रते वयं तवानागसो अदितये स्याम ॥

4. O Holiest God, cut asunder our fetters of uppermost, medium and low sins. O Mighty God, in obedience to Thy Law, being free from sin, may we be competent to acquire full light ! (589)

५. त्वया वयं पवमानेन सोम भरे कृतं वि चिनुयाम शश्वत् ।
तन्नो मित्रो वरुणो मामहन्तामदिति: सिन्धु: पृथिवी उत द्यौ: ॥

5. O God, with the help of Thee, the Purifier of the world, let us in this life determine our constant actions. O Loving God, the Remover of sins, Indivisible, All-pervading like the ocean, the Sustainer of all like the Earth, Lustrous like the Sun, grant us the desired fruit ! (590)

६. इमं वृषणं क्रणुतैकमिन्माम् ॥

6. O God, make me the helpless one, the accomplisher of all desires ! (591)

७. स न इन्द्राय यज्यवे वरुणाय मरुद्भ्य: । वरिवोवित् परिस्रव ॥

7. May God, the Giver of wholesome objects for our prosperous soul, the performer of the Yajna of life; for our Prāṇas, manifest Himself unto us. (592)

[1]Some Commentators are of opinion, that, पूर्वार्चिक the first part, concludes with the last verse 'य उस्रिया'. According to their view the 55 verses of the Aranyak Kanda do not form a part of the पूर्वार्चिक, but is the third अर्धप्रपाठिक (chapter) of the sixth Prapathik. Others differ from this view, and consider these verses forming a separate Aranyak Kanda. I have translated them as a separate fourth Kanda, the Agneya, Ayndra and Pavamana forming the first three. These 55 verses have been treated as the 3rd Ardhprapathik (Chapter) of the 6th Prapathak (Book).

८. एना विश्वान्यर्य आ द्युम्नानि मानुषाणाम् । सिषान्सतो वनामहे ॥

8. O God, the Lord of all, grant us all these riches of the people. We ask for these for distribution amongst all ! (593)[1]

९. ब्रह्मास्मि प्रथमजा ऋतस्य पूर्वं देवेभ्यो अमृतस्य नाम ।
यो मा ददाति स इदेवमावदहमन्नमन्नमदन्तमद्मि ॥

9. I exist before the creation of this world. I exist before the forces of Nature. Imperishable am I. He who preaches My divine knowledge to others, is the benefactor of humanity. I, All-pervading God, destroy him, who does not preach My divine knowledge to others. (594)[2]

DECADE II

१. त्वमेतदधारयः क्रृष्णासु रोहिणीषु च । परुष्णीषु रुशत्पयः ॥

1. O soul, thou preservest this beautiful splendour in the Pinglā, Idā and Sushumna arteries. (595)

२. अररूरुचदुषसः पृश्निरग्रिय उक्षा मिमेति भुवनेषु वाजयुः ।
मायाविनो ममिरे अस्य मायया नृचक्षसः पितरो गर्भमादधुः ॥

2. Source of the loveliness of a Yogi, foremost in gleaning happiness, the delightful soul hankering after spiritual power, intensely manifests itself in all the Prāṇas (breaths). The five elements with the moral force of the soul, put into order, the objects of the earth, which protect all and watch human beings. Finally they dissolve themselves into the womb of God. (596)[3]

३. इन्द्र इद्धर्योः सचा सम्मिश्ल आ वचोयुजा । इन्द्रो वज्री हिरण्ययः ॥

3. God alone, with His Word, keeps the Sun and Moon simultaneously inter-connected. God is Chastiser; and Lustrous like the Sun. (597)

४. इन्द्र वाजेषु नोऽव सहस्रप्रधनेषु च । उग्र उग्राभिरूतिभिः ॥

4. O Invincible God, protect us with Thy unsurpassable safeguards, in ordinary battles and mighty struggles ! (598)[4]

---

[1]Riches are prayed for, not for one's use only, but for the good of humanity, and to be distributed amongst the needy and indigent people.

[2]It is the duty of the learned to preach the Vedas, God's knowledge to humanity, He who enjoys His knowledge alone, and does not share it with others is a sinner, and liable to be punished by God. The message of God revealed in the shape of the Vedas is universal and meant for all high or low. It is the foremost duty of the learned to preach God's message to humanity, vide Yajurveda 25-6 and the third principle of the Arya Samaj. I refers to God.

[3]*Five elements*: air, water, fire, earth and space. They refers to the five elements.

[4]सहस्रप्रधनेषु: Mighty struggles in which thousands of horses and elephants are won.

५. प्रथश्च यस्य सप्रथश्च नामानुष्टुभस्य हविषा हवियंत् ।
धातुर्धुतानात् सवितुश्च विष्णी रथन्तरमा जभारा वसिष्ठ: ॥

5. The Vedic speech, which has got two qualities of proclamation and spreading, and is the best oblation in Anushtup metre, is grasped by a wise sage in the form of Rathantra from God, the Maker, the Creator and Refulgent. (599)[1]

६. नियुत्वान् वायवा गह्ययⓋ शुक्रो श्रयायि ते । गन्तासि सुन्वतो गृहम् ॥

6. O God, Powerful art thou, come, I send this pure soul unto Thee, Thou goest to the heart of a Yogi! (600)[2]

७. यज्जायथा श्रपूर्व्यं मघवन्वृत्रहत्याय । तत् पृथिवीमप्रथयस्तदस्तभ्ना उतो दिवम् ॥

7. O Eternal, Opulent God, Thou manifestest Thyself in the heart, for the eradication of the darkness of ignorance. Thou fillest the Earth with comforts and sustainest the space ! (601)

DECADE III

१. मयि वर्चो श्रथो यशोऽथो यज्ञस्य यत्पय: । परमेष्ठी प्रजापतिर्दिवि द्यामिव दृⓋहतु ॥

1. May the All-pervading God, the Nourisher of the animate and inanimate Creation, strengthen in me, dignity, glory and the soul's supreme bliss of salvation, just as He establishes the Sun in the atmosphere. (602)

२. सं ते पयाⓋसि समु यन्तु वाजा: सं वृष्ण्यान्यभिमातिषाह: ।
श्राप्यायमानो श्रमृताय सोम दिवि श्रवाⓋस्युत्तमानि धिष्व ॥

2. O God, the Chastiser of the proud, may Thy invigorating knowledge, all kinds of food, and forces, nicely be achieved by us. Thou art Mightier than the mighty, endow the soul in final beatitude with knowledge, power and joy ! (603)[3]

३. त्वमिमा श्रोषधी: सोम विश्वास्त्वमपो अजनयस्त्वं गा: ।
त्वमातनोरुर्वा३न्तरिक्षं त्वं ज्योतिषा वि तमो ववर्थ ॥

3. O God, Thou hast created the herbs, the water, the cattle like kine, Thou hast expanded the vast atmosphere and hast cast aside darkness with lustre in diverse ways ! (604)

४. श्रग्निमीडे पुरोहितं यज्ञस्य देवमृत्विजम् । होतारⓋरत्नधातमम् ॥

---

[1]Rathantra is a part of the Samaveda.
[2]The word गृह in the verse means the heart, which is the house of a Yogi, as he always contemplates upon God in this mind.
[3]Final beatitude means the state of salvation.

4. I praise the Omniscient God, Foremost of all through Omnipresence, the Illuminator of Yajna (sacrifice) Adorable in all seasons, the Giver of all joys, the Possessor of all charming objects. (605)

५. ते मन्वत प्रथमं नाम गोनां त्रि: सप्त परमं नाम जानन् ।
ता जानतीरभ्यनूषत क्षा आविर्भुवन्नरुणीर्यशसा गाव: ॥

5. O God, Thy subjects on the Earth, consider Thy name Om as the best amongst the Vedic words, and know it as Thy highest name amongst all the Vedic verses couched in twenty one metres. Those conscious subjects praise Thee. The Vedic verses appear glowing with Thy eulogy ! (606)[1]

६. समन्या यन्त्युपयन्त्यन्या: समानमूर्वं नद्यस्पृणन्ति ।
तमू शुचिꣳ शुचयो दीदिवाꣳसमपान्नपातमुप यन्त्याप: ॥

6. O God, just as some waters mingle together, some exhaust themselves in reaching the ocean, and some fill the ocean in the form of streams, so do these holy Vedic words reach unto Thee, Most Brilliant, the Preserver of actions ! (607)

७. आ प्रागाद्द्रा युवतिरह्न: केतून्त्समीत्संति । अभूद्रा निवेशनी विश्वस्य जगतो रात्री ॥

7. The Night, affording rest to the whole world, was a source of bliss. Now has come this blissful young Dawn, that urges the lights of the day. (608)

८. प्रक्षस्य वृष्णो अरुषस्य नू मह: प्र नो वचो विदथा जातवेदसे ।
वैश्वानराय मतिर्नव्यसे शुचि: सोम इव पवते चारुरग्नये ॥

8. May our tongue nicely utter in the Yajna, the Venerable glory of the All-knowing, Refulgent, Joy-Bestowing, All-pervading God. Pure intellect most excellently manifests itself like supreme bliss, for the Omniscient, Adorable, and All-leading God. (609)

९. विश्वे देवा मम श्रृणवन्तु यज्ञमुभे रोदसी अपां नपाच्च मन्म ।
मा बो वचाꣳसि परिचक्ष्याणि वोचꣳ सुम्नेष्विद्वो अन्तमा मदेम ॥

9. O all learned persons, pray listen to my reflective prayer. May the Earth and Heaven and God even listen to it. May I never disobey Your commands, rather remember them at times of festivity. May we remain in happiness in Your utmost proximity ! (610)

१०. यशो मा द्यावापृथिवी यशो मेन्द्रबृहस्पती ।
यशो भगस्य विन्दतु यशो मा प्रति मुच्यताम् ।
यशस्व्याꣳस्या३स्य: सꣳसदोऽहं प्रवदिता स्याम् ॥

---

[1]*Twenty one metres:* Gayatri, Ushnik, Anushtup, Brihati, Pankti, Trishtup, Jagati, Atijagati, Shakwari, Atishakwari, Ashti, Atiashti, Dhriti, Atidhriti, Kriti, Prakriti, Akriti, Vikriti, Sanskriti, Atikriti, Utkriti.

10. May Heaven and Earth grant me splendour, may the Sun and Air grant me splendour. May I attain the splendour of God. May not splendour renounce me. Being famous, may I be the speaker of this learned assembly. (611)

११. इन्द्रस्य नु वीर्याणि प्रवोचं यानि चकार प्रथमानि वज्री ।
अहन्नहिमन्वपस्ततर्द प्र वक्षणा अभिनत् पर्वतानाम् ॥

11. I describe the heroic deeds of God, which, He, the Severer of atom from atom, performs, with full significance. He destroys the demon of ignorance. He lets knowledge flow. He cuts asunder the bonds of the body for the learned, as streams are cut out of the mountains. (612)[1]

१२. अग्निरस्मि जन्मना जातवेदा घृतं मे चक्षुरमृतं म आसन् ।
त्रिधातुरर्को रजसो विमानोऽजस्रं ज्योतिर्हविरस्मि सर्वम् ॥

12. I am Omniscient, Knowledge is My eye, Immortality is My breath, I sustain all objects in three ways. I am full of Lustre. I make all planets revolve in the universe. I am an Imperishable Light. I, Omnipresent, am the bestower of all enjoyable objects. (613)[2]

१३. पात्यग्निर्विपो अग्रं पदं वेः पाति यह्वश्चरणं सूर्यस्य ।
पाति नाभा सप्तशीर्षाणमग्निः पाति देवानामुपमादमृष्वः ॥

13. The Wise God guards the orbit of the moving Earth, The Almighty Father guards the orbit of the Sun. God alone guards the soul, the master of seven organs in the head. The same Beautiful God, guards the soul, the gladdener of all vital parts of the body. (614)[3]

DECADE IV

१. भ्राजन्त्यग्ने समिधान दीदिवो जिह्वा चरत्यन्तरासनि ।
स त्वं नो अग्ने पयसा वसुविद्रयिं वर्चो दृशेऽदाः ॥

1. O Wise, Refulgent, Lustrous God, like the tongue in the mouth, mental power, the recipient of knowledge, acts in every body. Thou alone, the Bestower of riches, grantest us, for our guidance, life, strength, glory, along with knowledge and invigorating food ! (615)

---

[1]Cuts asunder the bonds of the body means grants salvation to the learned.

[2]I refers to God. Just as breath always moves in the mouth and nostril, so God is ever Immortal.

There ways are सत्, चित्, and आनन्द. All material inanimate objects have got existence alone, souls possess existence and consciousness, but God has got existence, consciousness, supreme joy. All the objects of the world possess one or two of these three qualities. God alone possesses the three.

[3]Seven organs refer to two eyes, two ears, two nostrils, and mouth.

२. वसन्त इन्नु रन्त्यो ग्रीष्म इन्नु रन्त्यः । वर्षाण्यनु शारदो हेमन्तः शिशिरः इन्नु रन्त्यः ॥

2. Just as verily the spring is pleasant, the summer is pleasant, the rainy season is pleasant, the autumn is pleasant, the winter is pleasant, the dewy season is pleasant, so pleasant is God, the Bestower of joys, being the Dweller of all, the Dissolver of all, the Rainer of happiness, the Remover of all afflictions, the Chastiser of all, the Consumer of the age and strength of men. (616)[1]

३. सहस्रशीर्षाः पुरुषः सहस्राक्षः सहस्रपात् । स भूमिँ सर्वतो वृत्वात्यतिष्ठद्दशाङ्गुलम् ॥

3. The Almighty God, hath the power of a thousand heads, a thousand eyes, a thousand feet. Pervading the Earth on every side, He transgresses the universe. (617)[2]

४. त्रिपादूर्ध्व उदैत् पुरुषः पादोऽस्येहाभवत् पुनः । तथा विष्वङ् व्यक्रामदशनानशने अभि ॥

4. God, with three-fourths of His grandeur rises higher than all, separate from the world, enjoying liberation. With one fourth of His grandeur, He creates and dissolves the universe again and again. Then pervading the animate and inanimate creation He resides therein. (618)[3]

५. पुरुष एवेदँ सर्वं यद् भूतं यच्च भाव्यम् । पादोऽस्य सर्वा भूतानि त्रिपादस्यामृतं दिवि ॥

5. God is the Creator of all that exists, existed in the past, and will exist in the future. All worlds are but a part of Him, the rest lies in His Immortal Resplendent Nature. (619)[4]

६. तावानस्य महिमा ततो ज्यायाँश्च पूरुषः । उतामृतत्वस्येशानो यदन्नेनातिरोहति ॥

6. The visible and invisible universe display His grandeur. Yes, He is greater than this universe. God is the Lord of final emancipation and what grows on Earth. (620)[5]

---

[1]God has been compared in this verse to six seasons of the year, on account of His six qualities.

[2]Griffith translates दशांगुलम् as a space of ten fingers, which is meaningless. Thousand means innumerable. Dash Angulam means the world which is made up of ten parts, i.e., five gross and five subtle elements. Five gross elements are earth, water, air, fire and atmosphere, Five subtle elements are sight (रूप), smell (गंध), speech (शब्द), taste (रस), touch (स्पर्श) vide Maharashi Dayanand's commentary on the Yajurveda. 31-1. Some commentators like Sayana and Swami Tulsi Ram have translated दशांगुलम् as heart, and Pt. Jaidev Vidyalankar has translated it as ten quarters and sub-quarters.

[3]What eats is the animate, and what eats not is the inanimate creation. See Yajur 31-4.

[4]God is Indivisible. He can't be spoken of as having parts. The words Pada fourth and Tripad three fourths are used figuratively to show His immensity and world's littleness. See Yajur 31-2-3.

[5]Swami Dayanand interprets अन्न as Earth, out of which grow all trees, vegetables, and food-stuffs vide Yajurveda 31-2.

७. ततो विराडजायत विराजो अधि पूरुष: । स जातो अत्यरिच्यत पश्चाद्भूमिमथो पुर: ॥

7. God creates the universe and lords over it. He, then pre-existent, remains aloof from the world, and afterwards creates the Earth and human
bodies. (621)

८. मन्ये वां द्यावापृथिवी सुभोजसौ ये अप्रथेथाममितमभि योजनम् ।
द्यावापृथिवी भवतॐ स्योने ते नो मुञ्चतमॐहस: ॥

8. O God, Resplendent like the Sun and O Matter, vast like the Earth, I
know Ye as excellent Guardians. Ye both have expanded this immeasurable
world. May Ye God and Matter give us pleasure. May Ye both liberate us
from sin ! (622)

९. हरी त इन्द्र इमश्रूण्युतो ते हरितौ हरी । तं त्वा स्तुवन्ति कवय: परुषासो वनर्गव: ॥

9. O wonderful mind, thy beams of knowledge, and thy powers of action
and contemplation are ever in motion. The wise sages, with beautiful speeches sing thy praise ! (623)

१०. यद्वर्चो हिरण्यस्य यद्वा वर्चो गवामुत । सत्यस्य ब्रह्मणो वर्चस्तेन मा सॐसृजामसि ॥

10. Let us equip our soul with the dignity of gold, the dignity of knowledge and action, and the dignity of the Veda and God. (624)[1]

११. सहस्तन्न इन्द्र दद्धचोज ईशे ह्यस्य महतो विरप्शिन् ।
क्रतुं न नृम्णॐ स्थविरं च वाजं वृत्रेषु शत्रून्सहना कृधी न: ॥

11. O Almighty God, grant us the forbearance and vitality, wherewith
Thou rulest over this vast universe. Grant us the wealth of knowledge coupled with action, and steady strength. Make us strong to overcome the foe-
like lust and anger, waging war against all afflictions ! (625)

१२. सहर्षभा: सहवत्सा उदेत विश्वा रूपाणि विभ्रतीदिव्यूर्धनी: ।
उर: पृथुरयं वो अस्तु लोक इमा आप: सुप्रपाणा इह स्त ॥

12. Ye organs of senses, always remain with us, assuming diverse forms,
possessing the teats of knowledge and action, devoted to gracious God and
dear mind. This body is Your vast extended space. Knowledge and action
alone can allay Your thirst. Remain here. (626)[2]

---

[1] It is a prayer to become rich, learned, active, scholar of the Vedas, and devotees of
God.

[2] Here means in the body. This verse can be interpreted for cows as well, as has been
done by Sayana and other Commentators.

Teats means traits.

DECADE V

१. अग्न आयूंषि पवस आसुवोर्जमिषं च नः । आरे बाधस्व दुच्छुनाम् ॥

1. O God, Thou grantest us longevity, give us strength and food as well. Torment far away from us, the persons blind with avarice and wrath like dogs! (627)[1]

२. विभ्राड् बृहत् पिबतु सोम्यं मध्वायुर्दधद्यज्ञपतावविह् तम् ।
वातजूतो यो अभिरक्षति त्मना प्रजाः पिपर्ति बहुधा वि राजति ॥

2. May God, Lustrous like the Sun, bestowing uncrooked life on the accomplisher of life's Yajna (sacrifice), make him drink the nectar of life, full of extreme felicity. Adored by the Controller of breath, He Himself, protects His subjects, and nourishes them in diverse ways. He lords over all. (628)

३. चित्रं देवानामुदगादनीकं चक्षुर्मित्रस्य वरुणस्याग्नेः ।
आप्रा द्यावापृथिवी अन्तरिक्षं सूर्य आत्मा जगतस्तस्थुषश्च ॥

3. God is Wonderful and Powerful amongst all the forces of nature and learned persons. He is the Manifestor of air, water and fire. He pervades the Sun, Earth and Atmosphere. He is the Creator and Sustainer of all that moveth and moveth not. (629)[2]

४. आयं गौः पृश्निरक्रमीदसदन्मातरं पुरः । पितरं च प्रयन्त्स्वः ॥

4. This Earth revolves in the space. It revolves with its mother water in its orbit. It moves graciously round its father, the Sun. (630)[3]

५. अन्तश्चरति रोचनास्य प्राणादपानती । व्यख्यन्महिषो दिवम् ॥

5. The lustre of this fire goes up and down in the space like exhalation and inhalation in the body. This great fire displays the Sun. (631)[4]

६. त्रिंशद्धाम वि राजति वाक् पतङ्गाय धीयते । प्रति वस्तोरह द्युभिः ॥

6. God's word rules supreme throughout the world. The Vedas are recited for acquiring the knowledge of God. We should resolutely recite and under-

---

[1]See Yajur 19-38, 35-16.
[2]See Yajur 7-42, 13-46.
[3]See Yajur 3-6.
Water is the mother of Earth as Earth is produced by the mixture of the particles of water with its own particles, and remains pregnant with water. Sun is the father of the Earth, as from the Sun, it derives all light and sustenance.
[4]See Yajur 3-7. Lightning is the lustre of fire. Just as Pran and Apan go up and down in the body, so does fire rise in the sky and then it comes down.

stand the Vedas everyday with their illuminating sayings. (632)[1]

७. अप त्येॐतायवो यथा नक्षत्रा यन्त्यक्तुमि: । सूराय विश्वचक्षसे ॥

7. Just as stars along with nights disappear on seeing the All-illuminating Sun, so in the light of the knowledge of God, the Seer of all, disappear the thieves of the heart, like lust, indignation, avarice, madness and pride. (633)

८. अदृश्रन्नस्य केतवो वि रश्मयो जनाॐ अनु । भ्राजन्तो अग्नयो यथा ॥

8. Just as resplendent rays and fires make known the objects of this earth, so do I make known men. (634)[2]

९. तरणिर्विश्वदर्शतो ज्योतिष्कृदसि सूर्य । विश्वमाभासि रोचनम् ॥

9. O God, Thou relievest the worshippers from ailment. All emancipated souls visualise Thee. Thou art the Creator of all luminous planets like the Sun and Moon. Thou illuminest the whole refulgent world ! (635)[3]

१०. प्रत्यङ् देवानां विश: प्रत्यङ्ङुदेषि मानुषान् । प्रत्यङ् विश्वॐ स्वद्र्शे ॥

10. O God, Thou shinest before the intellect of the learned and the contemplative souls. Thou shinest before the whole world for showing the path of salvation ! (636)

११. येना पावक चक्षसा भुरण्यन्तं जनाॐ अनु । त्वं वरुणं पश्यसि ॥

11. O pure God, the Remover of all calamities Thou lookest upon us with the same eye of compassion, with which we look upon Thee as our Guardin ! (637)

१२. उद् द्यामेषि रज: पृथ्वहा मिमानो अक्तुभि: । पश्यञ्जन्मानि सूर्य ॥

12. O God, looking upon the entire Creation with an eye of kindness, and creating days and nights; in this vast space, Thou appearest in the heart of a worshipper, as the sun rises in the sky ! (638)

१३. अयुक्त सप्त शुन्ध्युव: सूरो रथस्य नप्त्य: । ताभिर्याति स्वयुक्तिभि: ॥

13. God, the Urger of all, has yoked with His administrative admonitions the seven purifying organs of senses with this chariot-like body. With those organs He makes the body work. (639)[4]

---

[1]See Yajur 3-8.

त्रिशद्धाम according to Ubhat means the thirty parts मुहूर्त of the day. According to Mahidhar, it means the thirty days of the month. According to Swami Dayanand it means the thirty devtas excluding the space. (Antriksha) Sun and Fire. The phrase thirty realms means all the parts of the world. The number thirty is used to denote many.

[2]I refers to God.

[3]The verse is applicable to the Sun as well.

[4]Sever organs refer to two eyes, two ears, two nostrils, mouth.

१४. सप्त त्वा हरितो रथे वहन्ति देव सूर्य । शोचिष्केशं विचक्षण ।।

14. O All-Creating, Lustrous, Renowned God, in this chariot-like body, seven organs conveying knowledge, derive sustenance from Thee, Refulgent with the beams of knowledge ! (640)

Mahānāmnyārchika*

१. विदा मघवन् विदा गातुमनुष॒ऽ꣡सिषो दिशः । शिक्षा शचीनां पते । पूर्वीणां पुरूवसो ॥

1. O God, Thou art All-knowing, Guide us on the right path. Preach us how to reach our goal. O Lord of all powers, Most Opulent, teach us Thy laws ! (641)

२. अभिष्ट्वमभिष्टिभिः । स्वा꣢ऽन्नऽ꣡शुः । प्रचेतन प्रचेतयेन्द्र द्युम्नाय न इषे ।

2. O most Conscious and Glorious God, All-prevading like the Sun, make us full of knowledge, with these religious meditations, for acquiring life and light of learning ! (642)

३. एवा हि शक्रो राये वाजाय वज्रिवः । शविष्ठ वज्रिन्नृꣳजसे म꣢ऽꣳहिष्ठ वज्रिन्नृꣳजस ।
आ याहि पिब मत्स्व ॥

3. O God, the Greatest Giver, the Remover of sins, Thou verily art Mighty. O All-pervading, Powerful God, equip us with wealth, knowledge and spiritual force. O Mighty God, make us strong. Manifest Thyself in our heart. Accept our praise. May Thou ever remain full of joy ! (643)

४. विदा राये सुवीर्यं भुवो वाजानां पतिर्वंशा꣢ऽ अनु ।
म꣢ऽꣳहिष्ठ वज्रिन्नृꣳजसे यः शविष्ठः शूराणाम् ॥

4. O God, grant us celibacy for acquiring spiritual knowledge. Thou art most Heroic amongst the heroes. O Mightiest, O Sin-Destroyer, Thou art the Lord of all sciences and forces. Thou controllest Thy subjects for their betterment ! (644)

५. यो म꣢ऽꣳहिष्ठो मघोनाम꣢ऽ अंशुर्नं शोचिः ।
चिकित्वो अभि नो नयेन्द्रो विदे तमु स्तुहि ॥

5. He is most charitable amongst all the wealthy people. He is pure like the Sun. O Omniscient and Glorious God, lead us on for acquiring knowledge and strength. Praise Him alone, O man. (645)

*Mahanamniarchika is neither a part of the first part पूर्वार्ध nor of the second part उत्तरार्ध. It is an independent Archika, lying in between the first and second parts of the Samaveda. I wonder how a learned Vedic scholar like Satyavrat Samashrami has described it as an appendix, though it is inserted between the first and second parts in almost all the available texts of the Samaveda. It is a mistake to call this part of ten verses as an appendix. It is a part and parcel of the Samaveda.

६. ईशे हि शक्रस्तमूतये हवामहे जेतारमपराजितम् ।
   स नः स्वर्पदति द्विषः क्रतुश्छन्द ऋतं बृहत् ॥

6. Verily the Almighty Father rules over all. For our protection we invoke
that Unconquerable Conqueror. He totally destroys our feelings of enmity.
He is full of knowledge and action. He is our Protector from sins, the
Embodiment of Truth, and Mightiest of all. (646)

'७. इन्द्रं धनस्य सातये हवामहे जेतारमपराजितम् ।
   स नः स्वर्पदति द्विषः स नः स्वर्पदति द्विषः ॥

7. For acquiring prosperity we invoke God, the Unconquerable Conqueror.
He entirely destroys our feelings of enmity. He entirely destroys our feelings
of enmity. (647)[1]

८. पूर्वस्य यत्ते अद्रिवोꣳ श्शुर्मंदाय । सुम्न श्रा घेहि नो वसो पूर्तिः शविष्ठ शस्यते ।
   वशी हि शक्रो नूनं तन्न्व्यꣳ संन्यसे ॥

8. O Indivisible God, O Settler of all, grant us for our felicity, Thy Immemorial, All-pervading, Gladdening nature. O Mighty Lord, the accomplishment of an action alone is praiseworthy. O Omnipotent God, Thou rulest over all. I praise Thee worthy of adoration ! (648)[2]

९. प्रभो जनस्य वृत्रहन्त्समर्येषु ब्रवावहै । शूरो यो गोषु गच्छति सखा सुशेवो श्रद्वयुः ॥

9. O All-Powerful, Vice-Destroying God, we sing Thy praise in man's pil-
grimages for progress. Thou art Wise, sung in Vedic verses, the Friend of
our soul, Worthy of service, and Peerless. (649)

Panch Purish Padani

१०. एवाह्योꣳ३ऽ३ऽ३ऽ३व । एवां ह्याग्ने । एवाहीन्द्र । एवा हि पूषन् । एवा हि देवाः ॥

10. (i) O God, Thou art the same as described in the first part !
    (ii) O God, Thou art Resplendent as described before !
    (iii) O Refulgent God, Thou art verily the same as mentioned before !
    (iv) O Nourishing God, Thou art the same as delineated before.
    (v) O learned persons, Ye are so through God's grace ! (650)

---

[1]The repetition of the last two sentences is for the sake of emphasis, to convince our
soul that God keeps it apart from hatred and enmity.
[2]Grant us means make us realise and appreciate.

Uttararchika

BOOK I

Chapter 1

I

१. उपास्मैं गायता नर: पवमानायेन्दवे । अभि देवाँ इयक्षते ॥

1. O men, worship the Holy God, the Revealer of His knowledge to the learned ! (651)

२. अभि ते मधुना पयोऽथर्वाणो अशिश्रयु: । देवं देवाय देवयु: ॥

2. The sedate learned persons, for the attainment of God, longing for Him, taste the invigorating joy derived from the reflective knowledge of God. (652)[1]

३. स न: पवस्व शं गवे शं जनाय शमर्वते । शँ राजन्नोषधीभ्य: ॥

3. O God, may thou grant happiness to our cattle, happiness to our offspring, happiness to our horses in the battle, happiness to our powerful and dignified persons ! (653)

II

१. दविद्युतत्या रुचा परिष्टोभन्त्या कृपा । सोमा: शुक्रा गवाशिर: ॥

1. The charming learned Yogis, sinless, self-controlled, brilliant, preaching loveliness and noble virtues, are equipped with praiseworthy capacity. (654)

२. हिन्वानो हेतृभिर्हित आ वाज वाज्यक्रमीत् । सीदन्तो वनुषो यथा ॥

2. Just as violent warriors attack from the positions of advantage, and just as a powerful horse, impelled by hunters, runs in the battlefield ; so does a man of learning, goaded by worldly privations, choose the right course of conduct and tread on the path of knowledge. (655)

३. ऋध क्सोम स्वस्तये संजग्मानो दिवा कवे । पवस्व सूर्यो दृशे ॥

3. O wise, noble, magnanimous, exalted scholar on the strength of know-

---

[1]In the first Prapathik (Book) of the second part, there are 23 verses, each of which is divided into three parts, hence called तृच. Some commentators like Sayana, Swami Tulsi Ram, Pt. Jaidev Vidyalankar, have treated the three parts of each verse as separate verses, and numbered them as such.

ledge, travelling far and wide, for the good of humanity, go everywhere bringing to light all true objects like the Sun ! (656)

III

१. पवमानस्य ते कवे वाजिन्त्सर्गा असृक्षत । अर्वन्तो न श्रवस्यवः ॥

1. O wise, learned fellow, just as horses in a carriage begin to run fast, so do thy efforts for the attainment of knowledge, treading the path of Yoga, spontaneously begin to bear fruit ! (657)

२. अच्छा कोशं मधुश्चुतमसृग्रं वारे अव्यये । अवावशन्त धीतयः ॥

2. Contemplative souls, elegantly realise the sheath of joy, which makes them relish the divine elixir, and is higher than the covering of respiration. They long for that. (658)[1]

३. अच्छा समुद्रमिन्दवोऽस्तं गावो न धेनवः । अगमन्नृतस्य योनिमा ।

3. Just as the milch kine return to their house, so do the tranquil worshippers of God, nicely and joyfully realise Him, Fathomless like an ocean, and Primordial Cause of the Yedas. (659)[2]

IV

१. अग्न आ याहि वीतये गृणानो हव्यदातये । नि होता सत्सि बर्हिषि ॥

1. O Preceptor, casting aside the dirt of ignorance, for spreading knowledge, and preaching the performance of action in a spirit of renunciation, come thou unto me. Remain next to my heart, and ever act as my monitor ! (660)

२. तं त्वा समिद्भिरङ्गिरो घृतेन वर्धयामसि । बृहच्छोचा यविष्ठय ॥

2. O Omnipresent God, we magnify Thee through Yogic practices and love. O Omnipotent God, shine fully in our hearts ! (661)[3]

३. स नः पृथु श्रवाय्यमच्छा देव विवाससि । बृहदग्ने सुवीर्यम् ॥

3. O God, grant us magnificently, the vast, grand, potent knowable knowledge of the Vedas! (662)

---

[1]That means that sheath of joy i.e.। आनन्दमय कोश, Covering of respiration means प्राणमय कोश

[2]Cows come back home in the evening after grazing all day long. The quiet, calm devotees of God realise God, Who is the root cause of the Vedas, and is deep like an ocean

[3]See Yajurveda 3-3. There the interpretation is different.

V

१. आ नो मित्रावरुणा घृतैर्गव्यूतिमुक्षतम् । मध्वा रजाᳵसि सुक्रतू ॥

1. O teacher and preacher, with showers of divine joy, sprinkle the path of our enlightenment. Fill all parts of the world with pleasant conduct! (663)[1]

२. उरुशᳵसा नमोवृधा मह्ना दक्षस्य राजथः । द्राघिष्ठाभिः शुचिव्रता ॥

2. Prāṇa and Apāna, most laudable, growing strong through food, with soul's force, and the masters of strength. With their most developed powers they are the impellers of noble deeds. (664)[2]

३. गृणाना जमदग्निना योनावृतस्य सीदतम् । पातᳵ सोममृतावृधा ॥

3. O Prāṇa and Apāna, the developers of truth, displaying your strength with the aid of a yogi or exalted soul, stick fast to your seat of worship, and acquire all-impelling force! (665)[3]

VI

१. आ याहि सुषुमा हि त इन्द्र सोमं पिबा इमम् । एदं बर्हिः सदो मम ॥

1. O God, let us contact Thee. For Thee, we conceive pure sentiment in our heart. Pray accept it. Purify my heart, Thy worshipper! (666)[4]

२. आ त्वा ब्रह्मयुजा हरी वहतामिन्द्र केशिना । उप ब्रह्माणि नः शृणु ॥

2. O God, may soul and mind, seeking union with Thee, following their mode of action, realize Thee. Accept our Vedic praises! (667)

३. ब्रह्माणस्त्वा युजा वयᳵ सोमपामिन्द्र सोमिनः । सुतावन्तो हवामहे ॥

3. O God, we, tranquil-minded, pure-hearted, Veda-knowing Yogis, invoke through Yoga, Thee, the Recipient of the tranquil-minded! (668)

VII

१. इन्द्राग्नी आ गतᳵ सुतं गीर्भिर्नभो वरेण्यम् । अस्य पातं धियेषिता ॥

1. O teacher and preacher, just as air and Sun protect the whole world, so in this world, with your illuminating discourses and intellect, protect the entire world and the excellent son! (669)[5]

[1]See 220. Interpretation of 663 is different from that of 220.
Sprinkle the path means make us perform noble deeds.
[2]मित्र and वरुण mean Prāṇa Apāna.
[3]Jamdagni is not the name of a Rishi, as interpreted by Sayana. It means a Yogi, the fervour of whose soul is highly exalted.
[4]See the verse 191.
It is the same as 666, but with a different interpretation.
[5]See Yajur 7-31, The text is the same, but interpretation differs.

२. इन्द्राग्नी जरितुः सचा यज्ञो जिगाति चेतनः । अया पातमिमᳵ सुतम् ॥

2. O King and learned Brahman, ye both possess a sentient soul. With that soul-force, in unison with a true worshipper, nourish this created world ! (670)

३. इन्द्रमग्निं कविच्छदा यज्ञस्य जूत्या वृणे । ता सोमस्येह तृम्पताम् ॥

3. I recognise with the internal light of the Venerable soul, the teacher and the preacher, as the companions and guardians of a wise man. They both, in this world, through the height of prosperity, should satisfy themselves and others. (671)[1]

VIII

१. उच्चा ते जातमन्धसो दिवि सद्भूम्या ददे । उग्रᳵ शर्मं महि श्रवः ॥

1. O Soma, the denizen of the earth, enjoys the intense pleasure and great glory, derived from drinking thee found in a happy spot ! (672)[2]

२. स न इन्द्राय यज्यवे वरुणाय मरुद्भ्यः । वरिवोवित् परि स्रव ॥

2. May the Holy God, the Giver unto us of the wealth of foodstuffs, grant the strength of pouring rain to the lightning, the Apāna and airs, that are worthy of performing sacrifice. (673)[3]

३. एना विश्वान्यर्यं आ द्युम्नानि मानुषाणाम् । सिषासन्तो वनामहे ॥

3. O God, we worship Thee, desiring for the acquisition and fair distribution of all these foodstuffs of the people ! (674)[4]

IX

१. पुनानः सोम धारयापो वसानो अर्षसि ।
   आ रत्नधा योनिमृतस्य सीदस्युत्सो देवो हिरण्ययः ॥

1. O soul, residing in our actions, and purifying all, thou manifestest thyself. Thou art the treasure of all charms. The root of truth is thy abode. By nature thou art lustrous and the fountain of divine happiness! (675)[5]

---

[1]I means a learned person. 'They both' refers to teacher and preacher.

[2]See verse 467, which is the same as 672, but with a different interpretation.

Persons residing on the Earth, who drink the Soma juice derive pleasure and glory. Soma juice is derived from creepers which are white like the milk, vide Rigveda 9-10-9, and Rig 9-61-10.

[3]See the verse 592, which is the same as 673, but with a different interpretation.

[4]No man should be allowed to starve. The food-stuffs and grains should be fairly distributed by the State to allay the hunger of all. None should be allowed to hoard agricultural products for black-marketing and making huge profits.

[5]See the verse 511, which is the same as 675, but with a different interpretation, hence free from the charge of repetition.

2. दुहान ऊर्ध्वदिव्यं मधु प्रियं प्रत्न꣱ सधस्थमासदत् ।
आपृच्छच्च धरुणं वाज्यर्षसि नृभिर्धौतो विचक्षण: ॥

2. A wise Yogi derives through self-exertion, the ameliorating, divine, pure, excellent joy, the immemorial companion of the soul. He thereby attains to God, the Mainstay of all, and Knowable by the sages. (676)

X

१. प्र तु द्रव परि कोशं नि षीद नृभि: पुनानो अभि वाजमर्ष ।
अश्वं न त्वा वाजिनं मर्जयन्तोऽच्छा बर्ही रशनाभिर्नयन्ति ॥

1. Oh supreme joy, advance and seat thyself in the heart. Grow strong, purified by the sages. Just as a strong and fast horse is led by the reins, so thou, fast in motion, and derived through knowledge, art taken to the heart, being purified and controlled by them. (677)[1]

२. स्वायुध: पवते देव इन्दुरशस्तिहा वृजना रक्षमाण: ।
पिता देवानां जनिता सुदक्षो विष्टम्भो दिवो धरुण: पृथिव्या: ॥

2. A prosperous King, equipped with arms, the queller of the rebels, the guardian of his forces, the father of his subjects, the nourisher of the learned, full of power, is the supporter of the virtuous, and protector of the State. (678)

३. ऋषिर्विप्र: पुरएता जनानामृभुर्धीर उशना काव्येन ।
स चिद्विवेद निहितं यदासामपीच्या꣱ गुह्यं नाम गोनाम् ॥

3. A Yogi, who is the seer of Truth, wise, the leader of men, shining with true knowledge, unwavering, and the well-wisher of all, preaches through the Vedas, the beautiful internally realisable, secret essence of these Vedic texts. (679)

XI

१. अभि त्वा शूर नोनुमोऽदुग्धा इव धेनव: । ईशानमस्य जगत: स्वर्दृशमीशानमिन्द्र तस्थुष: ॥

1. O Powerful God, the Lord of the animate and inanimate creation and All-knowing, we bow unto Thee with devotion, as unmilked kine bow before their calves ! (680)[2]

२. न त्वावा꣱ अन्यो दिव्यो न पार्थिवो न जातो न जनिष्यते ।
अश्वायन्तो मघवन्निन्द्र वाजिनो गव्यन्तस्त्वा हवामहे ॥

2. O Supreme God, no one divine like Thee has ever been born, nor ever shall be. No one like Thee has ever been born on this Earth nor ever shall be.

[1]Them—the sages, See the verse 523.
[2]See verse 169. It is the same as 682, but with a different interpretation.

We, the aspirants after knowledge and power, longing for the control of our organs of cognition and action, praise Thee ! (681)[1]

XII

१. कया नश्चित्र आ भुवदूती सदावृधः सखा । कया शचिष्ठया वृता ॥

1. O King in what manner wilt Thou become our friend? Through protection wilt thou be our friend. With what conduct wilt thou be the master of extraordinary traits, actions and nature? Through wisdom wilt thou be. Thus wilt thou ever progress ! (682)[2]

२. कस्त्वा सत्यो मदानां मँहिष्ठो मत्सदन्धसः । दृढा चिदारुजे वसु ॥

2. O King, what excellent, pleasant, truly pleasure-giving object, infusest thee with strength to break asunder the fortress of the foe? Know, it is food ! (683)

३. अभी षु णः सखीनामविता जरितृणाम् । शतं भवास्यूतये ॥

3. O God, be Thou the Guardian for one hundred years, for the protection of our friendly learned persons ! (684)

XIII

१. तं वो दस्ममृतीषहं वसोर्मन्दानमन्धसः ।
अभि वत्सं न स्वसरेषु धेनव इन्द्रं गीर्भिनवामहे ॥

1. Just as cows low to their calves in the day-time, so we invoke with praises the King, who is handsome, the subduer of Cupid the Settler of his subjects and the enjoyer of the food of knowledge. (685)[3]

२. द्युक्षँसुदानुं तविषीभिरावृतं गिरिं न पुरुभोजसम् ।
क्षुमन्तं वाजँ शतिनँ सहस्रिणं मक्षू गोमन्तमीमहे ॥

2. O God, we pray unto Thee to grant us soon, a King, who is full of splendour, highly charitable, equipped with armies, a great nourisher like the cloud, the master of foodstuffs, highly powerful, and the master of thousands of cows ! (686)

[1]God preaches to the King, that he should avoid the use of intoxicants and consider food as the best tonic to lend him strength to shatter the fortress of the enemy.
[2]See verse 236. It is the same as 685, but free from the fault of repetition, on account of a different interpretation.
[3]'I' refers to God.
Soma Yajna means the Yajna (sacrifice) in which Soma-oblations are poured. Brihat Sāma is a part of the Sāmaveda.

XIV

१. तरोभिर्वो विदद्वसुमिन्द्रꣳ सबाध ऊतये ।
बृहद्गायन्तः सुतसोमे अध्वरे हुवे भरं न कारिणम् ।

1. O men, I preach unto ye, the priests in Soma Yajna, for the safety of the Yajna, reciting aloud the Brihat Sāma, should praise God, the Bestower of riches, as children praise their affectionate father ! (687)[1]

२. न यं दुध्रा वरन्ते न स्थिरा मुरो मदेषु शिप्रमन्धसः ।
य आदृत्या शशमानाय सुन्वते दाता जरित्र उक्थ्यम् ॥

2. God, Who is unsubdued by the uncontrollable passions of anger and lust, Who is unassailed by idleness, Who is unmoved by the ephemeral, transient sentiments, in His felicity of ignorance-killing light, grants reverentially the knowledge of the Vedas, to the sage who preaches truth to humanity, practises Yoga, and worships Him. (688)

XV

१. स्वादिष्ठया मदिष्ठया पवस्व सोम धारया । इन्द्राय पातवे सुतः ॥

1. O Soma, flow in an extremely sweet and pleasant shower. Thou hast been extracted for the King ! (689)

२. रक्षोहा विश्वचर्षणिरभि योनिमयोह्ते । द्रोणे सधस्थमासदत् ॥

2. God, the Queller of the ignoble, the Seer of the universe, active through His motive force, pervading the world, engulfs this firm atmosphere. (690)

३. वरिवोधातमो भुवो मꣳहिष्ठो वृत्रहन्तमः । पर्षि राधो मघोनाम् ।

3. O God, the Dispeller of ignorance, Thou art the Master of manifold riches, and Most Charitable. Thou givest wealth even to the wealthy! (691)[2]

XVI

१. पवस्व मधुमत्तम इन्द्राय सोम क्रतुवित्तमो मदः । महि द्युक्षतमो मदः ॥

1. O medicinal herb, full of sweetness, bestower of wisdom, giver of joy, worthy of reverence, most exhilarating, expose thyself to the Sun ! (692)[3]

२. यस्य ते पीत्वा वृषभो वृषायतेऽस्य पीत्वा स्वर्विदः ।
स सुप्रकेतो अभ्यक्रमीदिषोऽच्छा वाजं नैतशः ॥

---

[1]See verse 468.
[2]Even rich persons ask for wealth from God to become fully rich, as they consider their wealth meagre and incomplete.
[3]Medicinal plants that are exposed to the light of the Sun, ripen soon, and acquire efficacy and healing properties.

2. O God, realizing Thy felicity, the soul strengthens the organs and uses them rightly. Having drunk deep that divine joy, the giver of happiness and light, the wise soul, overcomes the desires of the mind, as a swift horse does overcome the battle ! (693)

XVII

१. इन्द्रमच्छ सुता इमे वृषणं यन्तु हरयः । श्रुष्टे जातास इन्दवः स्वर्विदः ॥

1. May these extracted, well prepared, pleasant Soma juices with yellow smoke, soon reach the rain-pouring sky. (694)[1]

२. अयं भराय सानसिरिन्द्राय पवते सुतः । सोमो जैत्रस्य चेतति यथा विदे ॥

2. This desire for happiness longed for by all, is derived for the ameliora-tion of the soul. An amiable Yogi knows the soul that subdues anger and lust, as if he has fully visualised it. (695)

३. अस्येदिन्द्रो मदेष्वा ग्राभं गृभ्णाति सानसिम् । वज्रं च वृषणं भरत् समप्सुजित् ॥

3. May the soul, revelling in its streams of joy, spread all around, the power of knowledge, that subdues anger and lust, and is worthy of reverence and acceptance. A Yogi who controls his breaths, dispelling ignorance, seeks the shelter of God, the Showerer of joys. (696)[2]

XVIII

१. पुरोजिती वो अन्धसः सुताय मादयित्नवे ।
अप श्वानꣳ श्नथिष्टन सखायो दीर्घजिह्व्यम् ॥

1. Ye friends, for the protection of the provisions stored in Yajna, which lead to success and afford pleasure, turn aside the long-tongued dog. (697)[3]

२. यो धारया पावकया परिप्रस्यन्दते सुतः । इन्दुरश्वो न कृत्व्यः ॥

2. An accomplished Yogi, is skilful in the performance of actions like a horse. He with his devotion and purifying flow of knowledge, roams about in all directions, preaching truth. (698)[4]

---

[1]See verse 566. It is the same as 694, but with a different interpretation. When oblations of the Soma juice are offered, the yellow smoke produced thereby rises to the sky and brings rain.

[2]It refers to the soul.

He refers to Yogi.

[3]See verse 545. It is the same a 697, but with a different interpretation.

The provisions collected for a Yajna should be preserved from being eaten by long-tongued dogs and other greedy animals.

'Which' refers to provisions.

[4]Just as a horse is skilful in battle, so is a Yogi in performing actions.

३. तं दुरोषमभी नर: सोमं विश्वाच्या धिया । यज्ञाय सन्त्वद्रय: ॥

3. People approach a majestic and amiable Yogi, with universal love and devotion. They being large-hearted like a cloud, should continue performing noble deeds of charity. (699)

XIX

१. अभि प्रियाणि पवते चनोहितो नामानि यह्वो अधि येषु वर्धते ।
   आ सूर्यस्य बृहतो बृहन्नधि रथं विश्वञ्चमरुह द्विचक्षण: ॥

1. The great Sun, pours waters all round, which satisfy the world, and are helpful in growing corn. The Sun stands high in the sky over the waters present in the atmosphere. The Soma, possessing unusual lustre, growing in volume, rises high to the orbit of constantly moving great Sun. (700)[1]

२. ऋतस्य जिह्वा पवते मधु प्रियं वक्ता पतिर्धियो अस्या अदाभ्य: ।
   दधाति पुत्र: पित्रोरपीच्यां३नाम तृतीयमधि रोचनं दिव: ॥

2. The tongue of a truthful Yogi imparts heart-appeasing knowledge. The lord of such an intellect and the speaker of truth is unconquerable by sin. The Yogi, a true son of his parents, the diffuser of the light of knowledge like the Sun, acquires a third glorious position, unknown to his father and mother. (701)[2]

३. अव द्युतान: कलशाँ अचिक्रदन्नृभिर्यमाण: कोश आ हिरण्यये ।
   अभी ऋतस्य दोहना अनूषताधि त्रिपृष्ठ उषसो वि राजसि ॥

3. The soul of a Yogi, in the fullness of its lustre, restrained through breath-control, gradually enters the sheath of supreme felicity. The currents of true knowledge applaud it. On the confluence of three breaths, it shines forth like the morning dawn, in the midst of griefless discernments. (702)[3]

XX

१. यज्ञायज्ञा वो अग्नये गिरागिरा च दक्षसे ।
   प्रप्र वयममृतं जातवेदसं प्रियं मित्रं न शँसिषम् ॥

1. O men, I preach unto Ye, in every sacrifice and Vedic recitation, that I

---

[1] An oblation put in the fire goes upto the sun, from where it comes down in the shape of rain, which produces corns, which produce semen, from which, man is born. See Manu 3—76.

[2] 'The lord' refers to the Yogi, 'Third' may mean a position higher than that acquired by his father and mother, or it may mean a dignified position higher than that acquired by him through birth from his father and mother of which his parents had no knowledge.

[3] Sheath of supreme felicity means आनन्दमय कोश.

Confluence of three breaths means त्रिपुटी.

am Omniscient, Almighty, Eternal, the Revealer of the Vedas, and a Friend unto Ye ! (703)[1]

२. ऊर्जो नपातꣳस हिनायमस्मयुदशिम हृव्यदातये ।
भुवद्वाजेष्वविता भुवद्वृध उत त्राता तनूनाम् ॥

2. God never allows our strength fall. He is ever our well-wisher. We dedicate our soul to Him, Who is the Giver of all valuable objects. He is our Guardian in battles, our Ameliorator and the Preserver of our bodies. (704)

XXI

१. एह्यू षु ब्रवाणि तेऽग्न इत्थेतरा गिरः । एभिर्वंर्धास इन्दुभिः ॥

1. O fire, come. May I utter Vedic and worldly speeches with thy aid. Thou growest through these Yajnas ! (705)[2]

२. यत्र क्व च ते मनो दक्षं दधस उत्तरम् । तत्र योनिं कृणवसे ॥

2. O soul, wherever the mental force wields exalted power in thee; there thou createst thy dwelling place ! (706)[3]

३. न हि ते पूर्तमक्षिपद्भुवन्नेमानां पते । अथा दुवो वनवसे ॥

3. O God, the Lord of us mortals, let not Thy splendour harm our organs. Thou identifiest Thy self with Thy worshipper ! (707)[4]

XXII

१. वयमु त्वामपूर्व्य स्थूरं न कच्चिद्भरन्तोऽवस्यवः । वज्रि चित्रꣳ हवामहे ॥

1. O Chastising, Young King, longing for our protection, we call on thee, matchless, filling thy treasury through the payment of taxes just as one fills a bin with corn ! (708)[5]

२. उप त्वा कर्मन्नूतये स नो युवोग्रश्चक्राम यो धृषत् ।
त्वामिध्यविंतारं ववृमहे सखाय इन्द्र सानसिम् ॥

[1]See verse 35. The text is the same, but the interpretation is different, hence free from the charge of repetition. 'I' refers to God.

[2]'Come' means I may realise thy true nature. All words are uttered and speeches made through the fire in our mouth. मुखादग्निरजायत (Yajur 31—12). The three characteristics of fire are speech, touch and light, vide Mahabharat Shanti parva 184—32. Fire is the devta of speech. See verse 7. It is the same as 705.

[3]The soul of a man of iron determination helps him in achieving his aim.

[4]The lustre of God should help and not harm our organs.

[5]The subjects should fill the treasure of a King by paying taxes, just as a prudent person fills the bin with corn, to be utilised at the time of need. This verse is the same as 408, but with a different interpretation.

2. O God, for protection in all actions, we worship Thee. Thou art Mighty, Splendid, the Subduer of the foes like lust and anger, O God, therefore, we Thy friends, have chosen Thee as our succourer and worthy of adoration ! (709)

XXIII

१. अ्रधा हीन्द्र गिर्वण उप त्वा काम ईमहे ससृग्महे । उदेव ग्मन्त उदभि: ॥

1. O praiseworthy King, we implore Thee, and soon get our desire fulfilled, just as waters mingle with waters ! (710)[1]

२. वार्ण त्वा यव्याभिर्वर्धन्ति शूर ब्रह्माणि । वावृध्वाꣴसं चिदद्रिवो दिवेदिवे ॥

2. O Heroic, Omniscient God, just as rivers swell the ocean, so do Vedic verses magnify Thee, the Almighty, day by day ! (711)

३. युञ्जन्ति हरी इषिरस्य गाथयोरौ रथ उरुयुगे वचोयुजा । इन्द्रवाहा स्वर्विदा ॥

3. Thy Yogis through the praise of the All-urging God, with deep concentration of the soul, control through Yoga, both Prāna and Apāna, which are mastered through the recitation of Om. Both of them, the bestowers of light and happiness serve as two horses of the soul. (712)

Chapter 2

I

१. पान्तमा वो अ्रन्धस इन्द्रमभि प्र गायत । विश्वासाहꣴशतक्रतुं मꣴहिष्ठं चर्षणीनाम् ॥

1. O men, sing the praise of the King, the guardian of our foodstuffs, the subduer of all foes, the doer of hundreds of deeds, the giver of riches to his subjects ! (713)[2]

२. पुरुहूतं पुरुष्टुतं गाथान्याꣳ३ꣴ सनश्रुतम् । इन्द्र इति ब्रवीतन ॥

2. O men know God as Indra, lauded by many, much invoked, knowable through Vedic verses, Renowned of old ! (714)

३. इन्द्र इन्रो महोनां दाता वाजानां नृतु: । महाꣴ अभिज्ञ्वा यमत् ॥

3. God alone is the Giver unto us of mighty powers. He makes us reap the fruit of our actions, is Almighty, All-knowing, and keeps all under His Law. (715)

---

[1] The verse is the same as 406. Just as waters instantaneously mingle with waters, so our desires are at once fulfilled when we express them before the King.

[2] The verse is the same as 155.

II

१. प्र व इन्द्राय मादन॒ हर्यश्वाय गायत । सखाय: सोमपान्ने ॥

1. O Comrades, sing delightfully the praise of the King, who is the guardian of his amiable subjects, and gifted with comprehensive virtues ! (716)[1]

२. श॒सेदुक्थ॒ सुदानव उत द्युक्षं यथा नर: । चक्रमा सत्यराधसे ॥

2. Just as men eulogise a noble charitable person, and acquire wealth, so should we acquire true wealth, by praising God, the rich Giver of that true wealth. (717)[2]

३. त्वं न इन्द्र वाजयुस्त्वं गव्यु: शतक्रतो । त्व॒हिरण्ययुर्वसो ॥

3. O God, Thou grantest us wealth of knowledge. O Lord of boundless might, Thou grantest us light. O Settler, Thou grantest us beautiful, attractive and useful objects like gold ! (718)

III

१. वयमु त्वा तदिदर्था इन्द्र त्वायन्त: सखाय: । कण्वा उक्थेभिर्जरन्ते ॥

1. O King, we thy friends, longing to be associated with thee, and devoted to thee, sing thy praise. Learned persons also praise thee with Vedic verses ! (719)

२. न घेमन्यदा पपन वज्रिन्नपसो नविष्टौ । तवेदु स्तोमेश्चिकेत ॥

2. O God, the Chastiser of the sinners, in the beginning of my action, I praise none except Thee. I derive knowledge through Vedic verses sung in Thy praise ! (720)[3]

३. इच्छन्ति देवा: सुन्वन्तं न स्वप्नाय स्पृहयन्ति । यन्ति प्रमादमतन्द्रा: ॥

3. The sages like an intellectual man of action and not a dreamer. Those free from idleness alone derive supreme enjoyment. (721)[4]

IV

१. इन्द्राय मद्वने सुतं परि ष्टोभन्तु नो गिर: । अर्कमर्चन्तु कारव: ॥

[1] The verse is the same as 156.
[2] True wealth means the wealth of spiritual knowledge.
[3] सप्त संसद: may mean seven postures in which a Yogi sits or seven associated priests at a Yajna. Seven postures are:
1. Padma Āsana, 2. Siddha Āsana, 3. Shirsha Āsana, 4. Matsya Āsana, 5. Mayura Āsana, 6. Dhanur Āsana, 7. Sarvānga Āsana.
Seven priests: 1. Hotā, 2. Adhvaryu, 3. Udgātā, 4. Brahmā, 5. Maitrāvaruṇa, 6. Brahman Achhansi, 7. Achhāvaka.
[4] Three regions: Earth, Space, Sky. It refers to the Yajna, sacrifice.

1. For the King, lover of happiness, loud be our songs about the Soma juice; let poets sing the song of praise. (722)

२. यस्मिन्विश्वा अधि श्रियो रणन्ति सप्त सर्ँसद: । इन्द्रँ सुते हवामहे ॥

2. The Yogis seated in seven Yogic postures, meditate fully on God, in whom all glories rest. We invoke Him when our heart is pure. (723)

३. त्रिकद्रुकेषु चेतनं देवासो यज्ञमत्नत । तमिद्वर्धन्तु नो गिर: ॥

3. The sages expand the Yajna of the soul in three regions. Let our songs aid and prosper it. (724)

V

१. अयं त इन्द्र सोमो निपूतो अधि वर्हिषि । एह्रीमस्य द्रवा पिव ॥

1. O rain bringing force of nature, this purified Soma, used in oblation in the Yajna, is meant for thee. Run hither, come and drink it ! (725)[1]

२. शाचिगो शाचिपूजनायँ रणायँ ते सुत: । आखण्डल प्र हूयसे ॥

2. O mighty soul, adorable, for thy powers, for thy enjoyment, O beautiful soul, has this whole world been created. Thou art invoked, O dispeller of ignorance ! (726)[2]

३. यस्ते श्रृङ्गवृषो णपात् प्रणपात् कुण्डपाय्य: । न्यस्मिन् दध्र आ मन: ॥

3. O God, Thy soul-protecting knowledge, which is realizable through Prānas, does not allow the ignorance-dispelling soul degrade. A Yogi concentrates his mind on it ! (727)[3]

VI

१. आ तू न इन्द्र क्षुमन्तं चित्रं ग्राभँ सं गृभाय । महाहस्ती दक्षिणेन ॥

1. O King, as one with long arms, gather for us with thy right hand, nutritious and manifold wealth ! (728)

२. विद्मा हि त्वा तुविकूर्मिं तुविदेष्णं तुवीमघम् । तुविमात्रमवोभि: ॥

2. O King, we know thee, mighty in thy deeds of mighty bounty, mighty wealth, mighty in knowledge for thy manifold favours ! (729)

---

[1]The verse 725 is the same as 159, but with a different interpretation. The Soma, a medicinal herb used in oblations in a Yajna rises high to the sky and brings rain.

[2]Griffith has not translated Akhandala. He considers the meanings of the words shāchigo and shāchipūjana as uncertain. All these three words are the names of soul.

[3]'It' means the knowledge of God.

Wilson observes, the construction of the verse, is loose and the explanation not very satisfactory.

Grassman places the stanza in his appendix as having no connection with the rest of the original hymn. Sorry both the Commentators take a wrong view. The meaning of the verse is clear as day-light.

3. न हि त्वा शूर देवा न मर्तासो दित्सन्तम् । भीमं न गां वारयन्ते ॥

3. Hero, when thou wouldst give thy gifts, neither the sages nor ordinary mortal men, can restrain thee like a fearful bull. (730)[1]

VII

१. अभि त्वा वृषभा सुते सुत॑ सृजामि पीतये । तृम्पा व्यश्नुही मदम् ॥

1. O rain-pouring Sun, on the Soma being prepared, for thy gratification, I pour its juice in oblations. Sate thee and drink it deep ! (731)[2]

२. मा त्वा मूरा अविष्यवो मोपहस्वान आ दभन् । मा कीं ब्रह्मद्विषं वनः ॥

2. O soul, let not the foolish, licentious persons, or those who mock at thee, beguile thee. Love not the enemy of the Veda ! (732)

३. इह त्वा गोपरीणसं महे मन्दन्तु राधसे । सरो गौरो यथा पिब ॥

3. O soul, surrounded by organs, may Yogis cheer thee to great spiritual knowledge. Just as a white deer drinks from a tank filled with water, so shouldst thou residing in the heart enjoy God's felicity ! (733)

VIII

१. इदं वसो सुतमन्धः पिबा सुपूर्णमुदरम् । अनाभयिन् ररिमा ते ॥

1. O fearless King, the settler of thy subjects, eat thou to thy heart's content, this nicely prepared food, which we offer thee ! (734)[3]

२. नृभिर्धौतः सुतो अश्नैरव्या वारैः परिपूतः । अश्वो न निक्तो नदीषु ॥

2. Spiritual knowledge, purified by learned persons, developed by penetrating intellectual scholars, cleansed through Yogic exercises of the breath, is like a courser bathed in streams. (735)

३. तं ते यवं यथा गोभिः स्वादुमकर्मं श्रीणन्तः । इन्द्र त्वास्मिन्त्सधमादे ॥

3. Just as cooked food made from barley, is sweetened by blending it with cow's milk; so, O soul, do Yogis realise thee, full of knowledge, in a joyful beauty, in this state of deep concentration, practising Yoga with organs of cognition ! (736)[4]

[1]'Hero' means a heroic King.
[2]The Sun receives the Soma in its rarefied form after the performance of Homa. It returns it in the shape of rain. This verse is the same as 161.
[3]The verse is the same as 124, but with a different interpretation.
[4]Deep concentration means Samādhi. 'Organs of cognition' means Jnān Indriyas.

IX

१. इदᳫ ह्यन्वोजसा सुतᳫराधानां पते । पिबा त्वाऽस्य गिर्वण: ॥

1. O King, the lord of riches, worthy of praise drink this Soma juice, prepared with exertion ! (737)

२. यस्ते अनु स्वधामसत् सुते नि यच्छ तन्वम् । स त्वा ममत्तु सोम्य ॥

2. O soul, dedicate thyself to the delight derived after self-concentration. O amiable soul, let the sap of knowledge grant thee extreme happiness ! (738)

३. प्र ते अश्नोतु कुक्ष्यो: प्रेन्द्र ब्रह्मणा शिर: । प्र बाहू शूर राधसा ॥

3. O soul, let spiritual joy enter both thy flanks, enter thy head with the knowledge of God, O heroic soul, let it enter both thine arms with bounty! (739)[1]

X

१. आ त्वेता नि षीदतेन्द्रमभि प्र गायत । सखाय स्तोमवाहस: ॥

1. O priests, eulogising continuously, come sharp, sit down, and recite the Sāma verses in praise of the King ! (740)[2]

२. पुरूतमं पुरूणामीशानं वार्याणाम् । इन्द्रᳫसोमे सचा सुते ॥

2. Laud unitedly, with exultation, God, richest of the rich, Who ruleth over noblest wealth. (741)

३. स घा नो योग आ भुवत्स राये स पुरन्ध्या । गमद्वाजेभिरा स न: ॥

3. May God stand near us in our Yogic practices, for our wealth, and for acquiring manifold wisdom. With different sorts of knowledge may He come nigh to us. (742)

XI

१. योगेयोगे तवस्तरं वाजेवाजे हवामहे । सखाय इन्द्रमूतये ॥

1. In every need, in every fray we call, as friends to succour us, King, the mightiest of all. (743)[3]

---

[1]'Both thy flanks' means contemplation and action. 'Thy head' means the power of meditation. 'Both arms' refers to the strength of the soul to achieve worldly progress. The language is figurative. For a detailed explanation of flanks, head and arms of the soul, see Taitriya Upanishad.
[2]The verse is the same as 164.
[3]The verse is the same as 163.

२. अनु प्रत्नस्यौकसो हुवे तुविप्रर्ति नरम् । यं ते पूर्वं पिता हुवे ॥

2. I remember again and again, God, the Fulfiller of the desires of many, the Bestower of immemorial salvation. Thee whom my sire invoked of old. (744)[1]

३. आ घा गमद्यदि श्रवत्सहस्त्रिणीभिरूतिभिः । वाजेभिरप नो हवम् ॥

3. If God will hear our call, He will come with succour of a thousand kinds, and with riches. (745)

XII

१. इन्द्र सुतेषु सोमेषु क्रतुं पुनीष उक्थ्यम् । विदे वृधस्य दक्षस्य महाँ हि पः ॥

1. O God, Thou purifiest the Yajna, on the preparation of Soma herbs, That yajna is mighty for gaining great strength ! (746)[2]

२. स प्रथमे व्योमनि देवानाँ सदने वृधः । सुपारः सुश्रवस्तमः समप्सुजित् ॥

2. In heaven's first region, in the seat of gods, is the Mightiest God. He makes us overcome all privations, is most Glorious, and the Giver of the fruit of actions. (747)

३. तमु हुवे वाजसातय इन्द्र भराय शुष्मिणम् । भवा नः सुम्ने अन्तमः सखा वृधे ॥

3. I invoke God, Almighty, the Giver of Salvation and strength. He is our most intimate friend in our bliss and prosperity. (748)

XIII

१. एना वो अग्नि नमसोर्जो नपातमा हुवे ।
प्रियं चेतिष्ठमरतिँ स्वध्वरं विश्वस्य दूतममृतम् ॥

1. With this Vedic verse I invoke thee Agni, the son of strength, dear, wisest envoy, skilled in noble sacrifice, immortal, messenger of all. (749)[3]

२. तेअग्जोसय रुषा विश्वभोजसा स दुद्रवत्स्वाहुतः ।
सुब्रह्मा यज्ञः सुशमी वसूनां देवँ राधो जनानाम् ॥

2. God appoints both the luminous Sun and Earth, the protectors of all. He, well praised pervades every where. He is the Creator of all, highly Charitable, most Calm. Worship Him, Worthy of adoration by all living people. (750).

---

[1]Sire means parents, and preceptors.
[2]The verse is the same as 381.
[3]Here 'Agni' means fire. It is called the son of strength, as fire is a very powerful thing.

XIV

१. प्रत्यु अदर्श्यायत्यू३च्छन्ती दुहिता दिवः ।
अपो मही वृणुते चक्षुषा तमो ज्योतिष्कृणोति सुनरी ॥

1. Dawn, the daughter of the Sun, advancing and dispelling darkness, is seen by all. It removes the darkness of the night by its appearance. Goading men, it spreads light. (751)[1]

२. उद्‌स्रिया: सृजते सूर्यः सचा उद्यन्नक्षत्रमचिवत् ।
तवेदुषो व्युषि सूर्यस्य च सं भक्तेन गमेमहि ॥

2. God, the Creator of all, creates lands simultaneously, as the Sun its rays, and manifesting His glory, being Steadfast and Constant like a star, He is full of refulgence.

Oh intellect, the burner of sins, at the time of the manifestation of thee and the luminous soul, may we unite ourselves with the Adorable God ! (752)

XV

१. इमा उ वां दिविष्टय उस्ना हवन्ते अश्विना ।
अयं वामह्वे ऽवसे शचीवसू विशंविश उँ हि गच्छथः ॥

1. O Prāṇa and Apāna, the settlers of all, these seven forces working in the head, also sing Your glory. I, for the protection of my life, call Ye again and again from inside outside and from outside inside. O both powerful breaths, Ye move in each body. (753)[2]

२. युवं चित्रं ददथुर्भोजनं नरा चोदेथा उँ सूनृतावते ।
अर्वाग्रथं उँ समनसा नि यच्छतं पिबत उँ सौम्यं मधु ॥

2. O learned man and woman, Ye bestow wonderful nourishment; and give money to him who recites the Vedas. One-minded, both of Ye, drive your car down to us, and enjoy fine pure air and health ! (754)[3]

XVI

१. अस्य प्रत्नामनु द्युत उँ शुक्रं दुदुह्रे अह्रयः । पयः सहस्रसामृषिम् ॥

1. The Venerable sages, following the ancient Vedic splendour of God, acquire knowledge, which is the bestower of thousands of fruits, immaculate, and expositor of objects beyond the cognizance of senses. (755)[4]

---

[1]The verse is the same as 303, but with a different interpretation.

[2]The verse 753 is the same as 304. 'I' refers to soul.

[3]'Car' means the soul or body. Learned men and women should practice Prāṇāyāma and observe Brahmcharya;
'Sūnrita' means Vedic speech. They both should give right lead to the people.

[4]'Things beyond-senses' are God, soul, Matter. Knowledge alone explains and throws light on these things.

२. अयꣳ सूर्यं इवोपदृगयꣳ सराꣳसि धावति । सप्त प्रवत आ दिवम् ॥

2. Like the Sun, God is the Seer of all. He pervades all worlds. He leads the seven organs towards the domain of light. (756)[1]

३. अयं विश्वानि तिष्ठति पुनानो भुवनोपरि । सोमो देवो न सूर्यः ॥

3. God, purifying all worlds, stands high over them all, just as the lustrous Sun does. (757).

XVII

१. एष प्रत्नेन जन्मना देवो देवेभ्यः सुतः । हरिः पवित्रे अर्षति ॥

1. This luminous soul, manifests itself for the organs, with its eternal strength. Putting them into action, it moves between the purifying Pran and Apān. (758)[2]

२. एष प्रत्नेन मन्मना देवो देवेभ्यस्परि । कविर्विप्रेण वावृधे ॥

2. This Amiable soul, with its immemorial power of reflection, being conscious and wise for the right use of its organs, is strengthened by the All-knowing God. (759)

३. दुहानः प्रत्नमित्पयः पवित्रे परि षिच्यसे । क्रन्दं देवाꣳ अजीजनः ॥

3. O soul, granting the sap of ancient knowledge to all, thou sprinklest thy heart with it. Reciting aloud Om, thou makest the organs resound with it. (760)

XVIII

१. उप शिक्षापतस्थुषो भियसमा धेहि शत्रवे । पवमान विदा रयिम् ॥

1. O God, elevate with Thy teachings, the fallen and the degraded. Terrorise enmity, our spiritual foe; grant us riches. (761)

२. उपो षु जातमप्तुरं गोभिर्भङ्गं परिष्कृतम् । इन्दुं देवा अयासिषुः ॥

2. The forces of nature like air and sun approach with their rays, Soma, well-purified, squeezed with stones, rising in vapour to the watery clouds, and duly prepared. (762)[3]

३. उपास्मै गायता नरः पवमानायेन्दवे । अभि देवाꣳ इयक्षते ॥

---

[1]Seven organs: two eyes, two ears, two nostrils and mouth.
[2]'Them' means organs.
[3]When oblations with well-prepared, purified and squeezed Soma are given, it rises in vapours through the rays of the Sun to watery clouds, and comes back on the earth in the form of rain.

3. O bold persons, expatiate on the nectar of happiness derived by the soul, which preaches self-abnegation to the wonderful organs ! (763)[1]

XIX

१. प्र सोमासो विपश्चितोऽपो नयन्त ऊर्मयः । वनानि महिषा इव ॥

1. Just as powerful conveyances carry eatables from one place to the other, so wise, supreme felicity, with full intensity goads us to actions like waves. (764)[2]

२. अभि द्रोणानि बभ्रवः शुक्रा ऋतस्य धारया । वाजं गोमन्तमक्षरन् ॥

2. Learned persons brown in colour, with red apparel on, shining with the excellence of knowledge and penance, coming to the people, impart knowledge through Vedic Verses. (765)[3]

३. सुता इन्द्राय वायवे वरुणाय मरुद्भ्यः । सोमा अर्षन्तु विष्णवे ॥

3. May all these delightful created objects be available for the learned, and the soul absorbed in All-pervading, Wise, Vigorous God. (766)

XX

१. प्र सोम देववीतये सिन्धुर्न पिप्ये अर्णसा ।
अंशोः पयसा मदिरो न जागृविरच्छा कोशं मधुश्चुतम् ॥

1. O soul, for acquiring the glory of God, thou developest, with knowledge as does ocean with water. May the gladdening, ever-waking, pervading soul, with its inherent pleasure attain to ʻthe sheath of felicity, the developer of the knowledge of the soul ! (767)[4]

२. आ हर्यतो अर्जुनो अत्के अव्यत प्रियः सूनुर्न मर्ज्यः ।
तमीं हिन्वन्त्यपसो यथा रथं नदीष्वा गभस्त्योः ॥

2. The lovely soul, liked by the Prāṇas (breaths) should be kept pure as a son is washed and kept clean. The soul absorbs itself in God, and concentrates the forces of meditation on God, in veins lying between Idā and Pinglā, just as skilful driver carries the car to the battlefield. (768)

XXI

१. प्र सोमासो मदच्युतः श्रवसे नो मघोनाम् । सुता विदथे अक्रमुः ॥

[1]‘Which’ means happiness of the soul.
[2]The verse is the same as 478.
[3]Idā and Pinglā are two well-known tubular vessels (नाड़ी) in the body.
[4]Soma juices, used as libations in a Yajna, bring timely rain, where-with we grow more food and add to our prosperity. The verse is the same 477, but the interpretation is different.

1. The pleasure-giving, duly extracted Somas, Come for prosperity, in the Yajna of us, the performers of Homa. (769)

२. आदीꣳ हꣳसो यथा गणं विश्वस्याबीवशन्मतिम् । ग्रत्यो न गोभिरज्यते ॥

2. Just as the soul controls the flock of breaths, so does God control the minds of all. Just as a horse exhibits his qualities by different gaits, so does God display His power through Vedic verses. (700)

३. आदीꣳ त्रितस्य योषणो हरिꣳ हिन्वन्त्यद्रिभिः । इन्दुमिन्द्राय पीतये ॥

3. For enjoyment of the soul, the seekers after truth, acquire through durable and steady devices, the pleasant and fascinating supreme happiness, present in all the three regions. (771)[1]

XXII

१. ग्रया पवस्व देवयू रेभन् पवित्रं पर्येषि विश्वतः । मधोर्धारा ग्रसृक्षत ॥

1. O Yogi, longing for the learned manifest thyself with this knowledge of thine. Eulogising God, be fully devoted to Him. May then the delightful streams of knowledge flow ! (772)

२. पवते हर्यतो हरिररति ह्वरांसि रंह्या । ग्रभ्यर्षं स्तोतृभ्यो वीरवद्यशः ॥

2. O active soul, thou shinest overcoming rapidly all impediments. O soul grant adequate glory to those, who relate thy qualities ! (773)

३. प्र सुन्वानायान्धसो मर्तो न वष्ट तद्वचः । ग्रप श्वानमराधसं हता मखं न भृगवः ॥

3. O learned persons, don't wait for the asking for Dakshiṇā by a priest who officiates at a sacrifice (Yajna). Give it voluntarily. Don't mar a Yajna by giving no Dakshina. Cast aside those who interfere like a dog in a sacrifice ! (774)[2]

BOOK II*
Chapter I**
I

१. पवस्व वाचो ग्रग्निय: सोम चित्राभिरूतिभिः । ग्रभि विश्वानि काव्या ॥

1. O God, Foremost of all, with Thy wondrous aids, Thou revealest unto us the Vedas, the holy lore of every sort ! (775)

---

[1]Three regions: Earth, Atmosphere, Sky.

[2]The verse is the same as 553. Dakshina means a present or gift to Brahmanas at the completion of a religious rite. such as a sacrifice. A Yajna is incomplete without the Dakshina.

*is Prapāthaka I.

**is Ardh Prapāthaka I.

२. त्वꣳसमुद्रिया अपोऽग्रियो वाच ईरयन् । पवस्व विश्ववर्षणे ॥

2. O Eternal God, the Seer of all, revealing the Vedas, Thou preachest the due performance of ennobling and elevating deeds ! (776)

३. तुभ्येमा भुवना कवे महिम्ने सोम त स्थिरे । तुभ्यं धावन्ति धेनव: ॥

3. O wise God, these worlds stand to show Thy Might. O Tranquil God, the Vedic verses rush to sing Thy glory ! (777)

II

१. पवस्वेन्दो वृषा सुत: कृधी नो यशसो जने । विश्वा अप द्विषो जहि ॥

1. O learned soul, being well equipped, the giver of all joys, display thyself in us. Make us glorious. Remove all our moral weaknesses ! (778)

२. यस्य ते सख्ये वयꣳसासह्याम पृतन्यत: । तवेन्दो द्युम्न उत्तमे ॥

2. In Thy friendship, O God, Most Sublime and Glorious, may we subdue all those who war with us ! (779)

३. या ते भीमान्यायुधा तिग्मानि सन्ति धूर्वणे । रक्षा समस्य नो निद: ॥

3. O God, the dreadful and sharp weapons Thou hast for the destruction of the violent, guard us therewith from all revilers ! (780)

III

१. वृषा सोम द्युमाꣳ असि वृषा देव वृषव्रत: । वृषा धर्माणि दधिषे ॥

1. O soul, thou art strong, bright, and potent. O soul, with potent sway, Thou mighty one, ordainest laws ! (781)[1]

२. वृष्णस्ते वृष्ण्यꣳशवो वृषा वनं वृषा सुत: । स त्वं वृषन् वृषेदसि ॥

2. O Most Powerful God, Thy strength grants us character, wealth, fulfilment of desires and salvation !
Thy service makes us pious. Thy realisation makes us religious. Thou art the showerer of religious sentiments. (782)

३. अश्वो न चक्रदो वृषा सं गा इन्दो समर्वत: । वि नो राये दुरो वृधि ॥

3. O happiness-giving God, like the enjoying soul, lend knowledge to the organs, strengthen our breaths moving fast like a horse. Just as a King makes his cattle prosperous, so shouldst Thou. O All-pervading God, preach the Vedic teachings, and give instruction to the learned. Open the gates of our head for the wealth of knowledge ! (783)[2]

---

[1]The verse is the same as 504, but with a different interpretation.
[2]'Hitherward' means in our mind, the thinking faculty. अन्त:करण.

IV

१. वृषा ह्यसि भानुना द्युमन्तं त्वा हवामहे । पवमान स्वदृशम् ॥

1. O holy soul, thou art competent in fulfilling our aspirations. We call on thee, lustrous with the light of knowledge; as thou showest us the abode of happiness ! (784)

२. यदद्रिः परिषिच्यसे मसृज्यमान आयुभिः । द्रोणे सधस्थमश्नुषे ॥

2. O soul, purified by men, when thou art cleansed again and again through Yogic practices, thou attainest to the Unchangeable Supreme Soul, thy Companion in the body ! (785)

३. आ पवस्व सुवीर्यं मन्दमानः स्वायुध । इहो ष्विन्दवा गहि ॥

3. Do thou, O soul, rejoicing, nobly equipped with the arms of Yamas and Niyamas, pour on us heroic strength. O Soul, come thou hitherward ! (786)

V

१. पवमानस्य ते वयं पवित्रमभ्युन्दतः । सखित्वमा वृणीमहे ॥

1. O God, the Purifier, Thou fillest my heart with love. We seek to win Thy friendly love ! (787)[1]

२. ये ते पवित्रमूर्मयोऽभिक्षरन्ति धारया । तेभिनं: सोम मृडय ॥

2. O God, Thy powers reveal themselves in our heart in the shape of Thy power of sustaining the universe ! With these be gracious unto us. (788)

३. स नः पुनान आ भर रयिं वीरवतीमिषम् । ईशानः सोम विश्वतः ॥

3. O God, Thou art the Lord of all. Purifying us, bring us riches and invigorating food ! (789)

VI

१. अग्निं दूतं वृणीमहे होतारं विश्ववेदसम् । अस्य यज्ञस्य सुक्रतुम् ॥

1. We recognise fire as an envoy, invoker of the forces of nature, the exhibitor of all things, and the skilled performer of this holy rite. (790)[2]

---

[1]'We' refers to worshippers. 'My' refers to a devotee.

[2]The verse is the same as 3. Fire is दूत, an envoy, as it carries the oblations put into it to the sky. It is Hota होता, as it calls air and other forces of nature near it, which due to its warmth are rarefied and ascend upto the atmosphere, being replaced by another air. This process goes on during the performance of the Yajna. Fire is विश्ववेदस् as it displays all things. Nothing can be seen in darkness. We can see things only in light. Fire is the skilled performer of the Yajna. विश्ववेदस् may also mean the possessor of all wealth. Through Yajna we get rain, wherewith crops ripen, and give us foodstuffs, which bring us wealth.

२. अग्निमग्निॐहवीमभि: सदा हवन्त विश्पतिम् । हव्यवाहं पुरुप्रियम् ॥

2. The learned, always remember with praise-songs, God, the Recipient of all eulogies, Beloved of all, the Lord of all Creatures, the Destroyer of sins, Full of Refulgence. (791)

३. अग्ने देवाॐइहा वह जज्ञानो वृक्तबर्हिषे । असि होता न ईडच: ॥

3. O God, manifest in the heart of a Yogi noble qualities. Thou art the Giver of laudable divine traits ! (792)

VII

१. मित्रं वयॐ हवामहे वरुणॐ सोमपीतये । या जाता पूतदक्षसा ॥

1. We control Prāṇa and Apāna, to enjoy the divine felicity accruing from deep concentration (Samādhi). Those both exist endowed with holy strength. (793)[1]

२. ऋतेन यावृतावृधावृतस्य ज्योतिषस्पती । ता मित्रावरुणा हुवे ॥

2. I long for Prāṇa and Apāna, which both, on the strength of Law, uphold our life, and are lords of the shining light of the soul. (794)[2]

३. वरुण: प्राविता भुवन्मित्रो विश्वाभिरूतिभि: । करतां न: सुराधस: ॥

3. Let Apāna be our Chief defence, let Prāṇa guard us with all aids. Both make us rich exceedingly. (795)[3]

VIII

१. इन्द्रमिद्गाथिनो बृहदिन्द्रमर्केभिरर्किण: । इन्द्रं वाणीरनूषत ॥

1. Udgāthās, the singers of the Sāmaveda glorify soul through Brihat Sāma. Hotās, the reciters of the Rigveda. Adhvaryus glorify soul with the verses of the Yajurveda. (796)

२. इन्द्र इद्धर्यो: सचा सम्मिश्ल आ वचोयुजा । इन्द्रो वज्री हिरण्यय: ॥

2. The soul alone keeps together simultaneously knowledge and action, which unite on its behest. It possesses destructive power, brilliance, affection and beauty. (797)

३. इन्द्र वाजेषु नोऽव सहस्रप्रधनेषु च । उग्र उग्राभिरूतिभि: ॥

3. O powerful King, protect us with thy mighty powers, in our intellectual pursuits and thousands of struggles ! (798)

---

[1]The verse is the same as 198 Udgātās, Hotās, Adhvaryus are the reciters of the Vedas.
[2]The verse is the same as 597.
[3]The verse is the same as 598.

४. इन्द्रो दीर्घाय चक्षस आ सूर्य्यँरोह्यद्दिवि । वि गोभिरद्रिमेरयत् ॥

4. God sets up the Sun aloft in heaven, that we may see afar. He with ra s extends the cloud hither and thither. (799)[1]

IX

१. इन्द्रे अग्ना नमो बृहत् सुवृक्तिमेरयामहे । धिया धेना अवस्यवः ॥

1. Let us sing high praises of our prosperous preceptor, and bow before him in veneration. Longing for knowledge, let us recite the Vedic verses with full mental attention. (800)

२. ता हि शश्वन्त ईळत इत्था विप्रास ऊतये । सबाधो वाजसातये ॥

2. The learned, since times immemorial, for self-protection and acquisition of knowledge, laud their excellent preceptors. The learned yoked together sing their praise. (801)

३. ता वां गीर्भिर्विपन्युवः प्रयस्वन्तो हवामहे । मेधसाता सनिष्यवः ॥

3. We learned and intellectual eulogisers, for acquiring knowledge, longing for wealth, praise ye both. (802)[2]

X

१. वृषा पवस्व धारया मरुत्वते च मत्सरः । विश्वा दधान ओजसा ॥

1. Let Soma, infuser of strength, master of various qualities, imparter of happiness, increaser of semen, be available with its flow for the King. (803)[3]

२. तं त्वा धर्तारमोण्यो३: पवमान स्वद्ृशम् । हिन्वे वाजेषु वाजिनम् ॥

2. O God, the Revolver of the universe, the Banisher of afflictions, the Sustainer of the Earth and Sky, the Bestower of Supreme happiness, the Treasure of knowledge and strength, I remember Thee in all expeditions ! (804)

३. अया चित्तो विपानया हरिः पवस्व धारया । युजं वाजेषु चोदय ॥

3. O God, the Remover of all privations, with this flow of divine pleasure, especially worthy of enjoyment, manifest Thyself in the heart, and good a Yogi with multifarious knowledge ! (805)

---

[1]'He' refers to the Sun.

[2]Ye both: Agni and Indra occuring in the previous verse. The words refer to excellent preceptors.

[3]See verse 469.

XI

१. वृषा शोणो अभिकनिक्रदद् गा नदयन्नेषि पृथिवीमुत द्याम् ।
इन्द्रस्येव वग्नुरा श्रृण्व आजौ प्रचोदयन्नर्षसि वाचमेमाम् ॥

1. The All-pervading God, the Bestower of happiness, preaching knowledge to humanity, fillest the Earth and Heaven with His vibrations, just as a cloud fills the earth with water, or an ox imparts semen to a cow, or an Achārya fills a pupil with knowledge. I listen in the heart to the voice of the inner soul. O God, granting knowledge to all souls, Thou preachest the Veda, this Word of Thine to all ! (806)[1]

२. रसाय्य: पयसा पिन्वमान ईरयन्नेषि मधुमन् तमँ शुम् ।
पवमान सन्तनिमेषि कृण्वन्निन्द्राय सोम परिषिच्यमान: ।

2. O All-creating God, full of happiness, satisfying all with knowledge, urging the learned soul, Thou manifestest Thyself. Purifying all souls, meditated upon repeatedly for the amelioration of the soul, strengthening the steady abstraction of the mind, dwell in the heart ! (807)

३. एवा पवस्व मदिरो मदायोद्ग्राभस्य नमयन्वधस्नुम् ।
परि वर्णं भरमाणो रुशन्तं गव्युर्नो अर्षं परि सोम सिक्त: ॥

3. O God, the Embodiment of rapture, the Awakener of delight controlling the mind of the soul, the recipient of true knowledge, do manifest Thyself. Possessing Thy Resplendent, Adorable nature, full of felicity, urging all the organs, manifest Thyself ! (808)

XII

१. त्वामिद्धि हवामहे सातौ वाजस्य कारव: ।
त्वा वृत्रेष्विन्द्र सत्पति नरस्त्वां काष्ठास्वर्वत: ॥

1. O God, the valiant horseman, leading an army, calls on Thee for aid, when besieged by enemies. Men call in all directions on Thee the Protector of the noble. We Thy worshippers call on Thee, for strength to subdue our carnal passions ! (809)[2]

२. स त्वं नश्चित्र वज्रहस्त धृष्णुया मह स्तवानो अद्रिव: ।
गामश्वँ रथ्यमिन्द्र सं किर सत्रा वाजं न जिग्युषे ॥

2. O Wonderful God, the Possessor of the armour of knowledge for dispelling ignorance, Indivisible, the Censurer of all, Almighty, Adorable, just as

---

[1]The thundering and roaring of the clouds and lightning are metaphorically spoken of as God's vibrations.
[2]See verse 234.

Thou bestowest knowledge on him who controls his organs, so grant us nicely the organs of cognition and action, the well-wishers of the chariot of this body ! (810)[1]

XIII

१. अभि प्र व: सुराधसमिन्द्रमर्च यथा विदे ।
यो जरितृभ्यो मघवा पुरूवसु: सहस्रेणेव शिक्षति ॥

1. The rich King, equipped with the wealth of cattle, grants us, his eulogisers, thousand kinds of wealth. Just as we know him, so should the priests praise the opulent King. (811)[2]

२. शतानीकेव प्र जिगाति घृष्णुया हन्ति वृत्राणि दाशुषे ।
गिरेरिव प्र रसा अस्य पिन्विरे दत्राणि पुरुभोजस: ॥

2. Just as a self-controlled hero overcomes and destroys the forces of the enemy, so does God subdue and remove the sin of a self-sacrificing soul. As from a mountain flow the water-brooks, thus flow His gifts Who feedeth many a one. (812)

XIV

१. त्वामिदा ह्यो नरोऽपीप्यन् वज्रिन् भूर्णय: ।
स इन्द्र स्तोमवाहस इह श्रुध्युप स्वसरमा गहि ॥

1. O powerful King, thy devoted praise-singers had appeased thee before. Listen to them, and be master of thy house ! (813)[3]

२. मत्स्वा सुशिप्रिन् हरिवस्तमीमहे त्वया भूषन्ति वेधस: ।
तव श्रवांस्युपमान्युक्थ्य सुतेष्विन्द्र गिर्वण: ॥

2. O God, full of knowledge and action, meet for praise, the learned adorn themselves with Thy traits. Be gracious unto Thy worshippers. O Adorable God, Thy Vedic verses reveal Thy knowledge unto us ! (814)

XV

१. यस्ते मदो वरेण्यस्तेना पवस्वान्धसा । देवावीरघशंसहा ॥

1. O soul, shine forth with thy life-infusing extreme felicity, agreeable to all. Thou art the nourisher of noble sentiments, and the suppressor of sinful propensities ! (815)[4]

[1]'The well wishers' refers to us.
[2]See verse 235.
[3]See verse 302. Thy house means thy body.
[4]See verse 470.

२. जघ्निवृँ त्रममित्रियँ ससिन्वर्जं दिवेदिवे । गोषातिरश्वसा असि ॥

2. O Gracious God, Thou art the Destroyer of the unfriendly sin, and the Bestower of knowledge day by day, Thou grantest strength to the organs of cognition and action ! (816)

३. सम्मिश्लो अरुषो भुवः सुपस्थाभिर्न धेनुभिः । सीद च्छ्येनो न योनिमा ॥

3. O pupil, a seeker after knowledge, just as easily accessible, mild kine yield milk, so dost thou become brilliant, by coming in contact with the preceptor, and being united with Vedic speeches. Then alone does soul, fast like a falcon, rest in God, its home! (817)[1]

XVI

१. अयं पूषा रयिर्भंगः सोमः पुनानो अर्षति । पतिर्विश्वस्य भूमनो व्यख्यद्रोदसी उभे ॥

1. This God's supreme felicity, which comes in its pure form, is invigorating, gracious, and lovely. Being the lord of entire soul, it lends lustre to both the Earth and Heaven. (818)[2]

२. समु प्रिया अनूषत गावो मदाय घृष्वयः । सोमासः कृण्वते पथः पवमानास इन्दवः ॥

2. Fascinating speeches, vying with each other, praise the soul, for the attainment of joy. Purifying the heart, the Yogis adopt measures for the attainment of salvation. (819)

३. य ओजिष्ठस्तमा भर पवमान श्रवाय्यम् । यः पञ्च चर्षणीरभि रयिं येन वनामहे ॥

3. O God, the Purifier of the hearts of all, Thou art most Beautiful and Lustrous, Worthy of being ascertained through the Vedas. Grant us that Supreme joy of Thine, which pervades all the five organs of cognition, and wherewith we acquire the wealth of knowledge ! (820)[3]

XVII

१. वृषा मतीनां पवते विचक्षणः सोमो अह्नां प्रतरीतोषसां दिवः ।
प्राणा सिन्धूनां कलशाँ अचिक्रददिन्द्रस्य हार्द्याविशन्मनीषिभिः ॥

1. Soma, the developer of intellect, highly bright, the furtherer of days, of dawns and of heaven, the filler of streams with water through rain, flows sounding to its receptacles. Being used as an oblation by the wise performers of Homa, it goes up to the sky, entering the heart of the lightning. (82I)[4]

---

[1]'United' means instructed. 'Vedic speeches' means Vedic teachings.
[2]See verse 546.
[3]Griffith has translated Panch Charshni, a five Aryan tribes.
This is irrelevant. The word means five Jnana Indriyas.
[4]See verse 559.

२. मनीषिभि: पवते पूर्व्य: कविनृँभिर्यत: परि कोशाँ असिष्यदत् ।
त्रितस्य नाम जनयन्मधु क्षरन्निन्द्रस्य वायुँ सख्याय वर्धयन् ॥

2. The eternal soul, purified and controlled by the learned persons, establishes its sway over the five Koshās. In all its three stages, displaying its nature, and shedding forth the nectar of knowledge, the soul enhances in a friendly way the strength of breaths. (822)[1]

३. अयं पुनान उषसो अरोचयदयं सिन्धुभ्यो अभवदु लोककृत् ।
अयं त्रि: सप्त दुदुहान आशिरँ सोमो हृदे पवते चारु मत्सर: ॥

3. This Soma, zooing out, makes more pleasant the time of the appearance of knowledge. It makes more lovely the arteries of the body, that convey knowledge. It creates happiness through twenty one channels, fills the heart with joy and flows nicely. (823)[2]

XVIII

१. एवा ह्यसि वीरयुरेवा शूर उत स्थिर: । एवा ते राध्यं मन: ॥

1. O King, thou art verily the friend of the brave. Thou art heroic and steady. Thy heart is praiseworthy ! (824)[3]

२. एवा रातिस्तुविमघ विश्वेभिर्धायि धातृभि: । अधा चिदिन्द्र न: सचा ॥

2. O King, the Lord of wealth, all thy dependents accept thy charity. O King, be thou our supporter ! (825)[4]

३. मो षु ब्रह्मेव तन्द्रयुर्भुवो वाजानां पते । मत्स्वा सुतस्य गोमत: ॥

3. O King, the lord of strength, be never slothful, ever remain alert like the knower of the Vedas. Enjoy thou the pleasure derived through knowledge! (826)

[1]Kosha is in Vedic Philosophy a term for the five vestures (sheath or cases) which successively make the body, enshrining the soul. They are Anna (अन्नमय), Prāṇa (प्राणमय) Manas (मनोमय), Jnāna (ज्ञानमय), Ānand (आनन्दमय).
Three stages refer to the जाग्रत (walking) स्वप्न (Sleeping) सुषुप्ति (Profound sleep) states of the soul. Ludwig interprets Trita as the Celestial preparer of the heavenly Soma for Indra. This is inadmissible as the Vedas are free from historical references.
[2]Soma refers to God's supreme felicity. Twenty one channels: Mind, Ten breaths, Ten organs of cognition ज्ञान and action कर्म. Sayana interprets त्रिसप्त as 21 cows. Griffith interpets the words 'The three times seven' as the seven Celestial rivers, corresponding to the rivers of earth multiplied by three to accord with the threefold division of the heavens. The interpretation is illogical and unappealing.
[3]See verse 232.
[4]The verse may apply to a King as well.

XIX

१. इन्द्रं विश्वा अवीवृधन्त्समुद्रव्यचसं गिरः । रथीतमर्ऽरथीनां वाजानार्ऽसत्पतिं पतिम् ॥

1. All sacred songs have magnified the King, who travels by sea; is the best of all warriors borne on cars, the lord of heroes, lord of strength. (827)

२. सख्ये त इन्द्र वाजिनो मा भेम शवसस्पते । त्वामभि प्र नोनुमो जेतारमपराजितम् ॥

2. The Lord of might, God, may we ne'er, strong in Thy friendship, be afraid ! We glorify with praises Thee, the never Conquered Conqueror. (828)

३. पूर्वीरिन्द्रस्य रातयो न वि दस्यन्त्यूतयः । यदा वाजस्य गोमत स्तोतृभ्यो मर्ऽह्ते मघम् ॥

3. The eternal gifts and saving succour of God never fail, as He gives the wealth of knowledge and strength to His worshippers. (829)

Chapter 2

I

१. एते असृग्रमिन्दवस्तिरः पवित्रमाशवः । विश्वान्यभि सौभगा ॥

1. These rapid exhilarating juices of joy flow in the true, pure heart to bring us all felicities. (830)[1]

२. विघ्नन्तो दुरिता पुरु सूगा तोकाय वाजिनः । तमना कृण्वन्तो अर्वतः ॥

2. The learned, through self-restraint and mental calmness, subjugating various sins, disciplining the breaths through self-exertion, for removing all their afflictions, devise pleasant, convenient walks of life. (831)

३. कृण्वन्तो वरिवो गवेऽभ्यर्षन्ति सुष्टुतिम् । इडामस्मभ्यर्ऽ संयतम् ॥

3. The learned, singing the noble praise of the Omniscient God, pour on us wealth, strengthening food, and nice relative position. (832)

II

१. राजा मेधाभिरीयते पवमानो मनावधि । अन्तरिक्षेण यातवे ॥

1. The flow of joy, with its full lustre, for entering the heart, fills the mind with various sorts of wisdom. (833)

२. आ नः सोम सहो जुवो रूपं न वर्चसे भर । सुष्वाणो देववीतये ॥

2. O soul, for fulfilment of their aim by the learned, grant us toleration, activity and beauty, for being prosperous ! (834)

---

[1]Some commentators are of opinion, this verse refers to the Creation of the universe. It can therefore be thus interpreted. 'These revolving globes, for the sake of bringing all kinds of joy, are created by God, the Everlasting, Most Efficient Cause.

३. आ न इन्दो शातग्विनं गवां पोष॑ स्वइ्व्यम् । वहा भगतिमूतये ॥

3. O God, grant us for our protection, prosperity, which is linked with
manifold forms of knowledge, which strengthens the organs of cognition,
and is easily attainable by the organs of action ! (835)

III

१. तं त्वा नृम्णानि बिभ्रत॑ सधस्थेषु महो दिव: । चारु॑ सुक्रत्ययेमहे ॥

1. O God, the Lord of riches, through noble deeds, do we attain unto Thee,
Who is Almighty, and pervades the various globes in the universe ! (836)

२. संवृत्तधृष्णुमुक्थ्यं महामहिव्रतं मदम् । शतं पुरो रुरक्षणिम् ॥

2. We win God, the Crusher of the enemies of lust and anger, Worthy of
praise, the Doer of mighty deeds, the Gladdener of humanity, the Elevator of
hundreds of human beings to the stage of salvation. (837)

३. व्रतस्त्वा रयिरभ्ययद्राजान॑ सुक्रतो दिव: । सुपर्णो अ्व्यथी भरत् ॥

3. Hence, Thou, the Lord of the universe, the Doer or noble deeds, possessest the strength and glory of the Sun. Being the Master of knowledge and
power, unwearied, Thou sustainest and nourishest the entire universe. (838)[1]

४. अधा हिन्वान इन्द्रियं ज्यायो महित्वमानशे । अभिष्टिकृद्विचर्षणि: ॥

4. God, the Seer and Supervisor of the universe, the Giver of the fruit of
action to all, impelling the bodies coupled with souls, possesses mighty power.
(839)

५. विश्वस्मा इत्स्वदृशे साधारण॑ रजस्तुरम् । गोपामृतस्य विभरत् ॥

5. The soul, migrating from one body to the other like a bird, for visualising all sorts of knowledge, should verily contemplate upon God, the general
Sustainer of all globes, the Revolver of all planets, and the Guardian of truth.
(840)

IV

१. इषे पवस्व धारया मृज्यमानो मनीषिभि: । इन्दो रुचाभि गा इहि ॥

1. O soul, purified by the learned sages, manifest thyself with the flow of
joy, for the attainment of God. O glorious soul, approach the organs with
thy lustre ! (841)[2]

२. पुनानो वरिवस्कृध्यूर्जं जनाय गिर्वण: । हरे सृजान आशिरम् ॥

2. O God praised through songs, Immaculate in nature, creating this mortal
body, bring wealth and vigour to the folk ! (842)

[1]Thou refers to God.
[2]See verse 505.

३. पुनानो देववीतय इन्द्रस्य याहि निष्कृतम् । द्युतानो वाजिभिर्हितः ॥

3. O God, realised by the learned through deep concentration, granting light to the blind, purifying the impure, come to the resting place of the soul, to be acquired by the learned devotees ! (843)[1]

V

१. अग्निनाग्निः समिध्यते कविगृहपतिर्युवा । हव्यवाड् जुह्वास्यः ॥

1. The wise, eternal soul, the lord of its house, the body, the reaper of the fruit of actions, charitable by nature, is illumined by God. (844)[2]

२. यस्त्वामग्ने हविष्पतिर्दूतं देव सपर्यति । तस्य स्म प्राविता भव ॥

2. O Omniscient God, be the sure Guardian of the devotee, the recipient of the fruit of actions, who worships Thee, the Giver ! (845)[3]

३. यो अग्नि देववीतये हविष्माँ आविवासति । तस्मै पावक मृडय ॥

3. Be gracious, brilliant God ! to him, who for noble conduct of life, would fain worship Thee. (846)

VI

१. मित्रँ हुवे पूतदक्षं वरुणं च रिशादसम् । धियं घृताचीँ साधन्ता ॥

1. I recognise the efficacy of the purifying Prāna, and the disease-destroying Apāna, which both contribute to the function of enhancing the beauty and virility of the body. (847)[4]

२. ऋतेन मित्रावरुणावृतावृधावृतस्पृशा । ऋतुं बृहन्तमाशाथे ॥

2. By Truth, O Mitra, Varuna, Truth-strengtheners, who cleave to Truth, have you obtained your lofty power ! (848)[5]

३. कवी नो मित्रावरुणा तुविजाता उरुक्षया । दक्षं दधाते अपसम् ॥

3. Mitra, Varuna, the developers of intellect, born for doing good, vast in dimension, bestow on us strength and activity. (849)

---

[1]Resting place of the soul means the heart.

[2]I have accepted the interpretation of Swami Tulsi Ram, Pt. Jaidev Vidyalankar interprets the verse thus: Just as fire, the carrier of oblations to the atmosphere, possessing a blazing mouth. is illumined by fire, so does a wise youngman receive knowledge from another, and a householder, instruction from another householder.

[3]Giver means God, Who gives to the soul the fruit of actions.

[4]See Yajur 33-57. Maharshi Dayanand has translated the verse differently. Mitra and Varuna are the ingoing and outcoming breaths.

[5]Truth means law, regularity observed by the breaths controlled by a Yogi.

VII

१. इन्द्रेण सꣳ हि दृक्षसे संजग्मानो अबिभ्युषा । मन्दू समानवर्चसा ॥

1. The mind is seen seeing working with the fearless soul. Both of equal splendour bring bliss. (850)

२. आदह स्वधामनु पुनर्गर्भत्वमेरिरे । दधाना नाम यज्ञियम् ॥

2. The soul, roaming in the atmosphere, and after enjoying the bliss of salvation, assuming its sacrificial nature, takes birth again through air. (851)[1]

३. वीडु चिदारुजत्नुभिर्गुहा चिदिन्द्र वह्निभि: । अविन्द उस्त्रिया अनु ॥

3. The soul, thus taking birth, shattering the inmost and impregnable recesses of the heart, with the flames of knowledge, solves its problems, in unison with the five organs of cognition. (852)

VIII

१. ता हुवे ययोरिदं पप्ने विश्वं पुरा कृतम् । इन्द्राग्नी न मर्धत: ॥

1. I invoke both God and soul, praised by all since times immemorial. They are immortal. (853)

२. उग्रा विघनिना मृध इन्द्राग्नी हवामहे । ता नो मृडात ईदृशे ॥

2. We praise God and soul, the destroyers of the terrible, violent, evil tendencies. They gladden us in this struggle of life. (854)

३. हथो वृत्राण्यार्या हथो दासानि सत्पती । हथो विश्वा अप द्विष: ॥

3. They both, the urgers to prosperity, remove all hindrances. The guardians of noble sentiments, they both suppress the marauding mental feelings. They both cast aside all evil tendencies. (855)[2]

IX

१. अभि सोमास आयव: पवन्ते मद्यं मदम् ॥
समुद्रस्याधि विष्टपे मनीषिणो मत्सरासो मदच्युत: ॥

1. The learned people, who have obtained immortal light, full of joy,

---

[1]This verse preaches, that the soul after relinquishing its body, roams in the atmosphere, before it attains to salvation. After enjoying the bliss of final beatitude, it returns and through air, water or food is reborn. Salvation is not eternal, it is for a limited, though long period. As soul is finite, the result of its efforts cannot be infinite; hence soul returns after enjoying the bliss of salvation, and is reborn. This is Vedic doctrine.

[2]They both: God and soul.

preaching happiness all round, create the feeling of felicity, inside the vast ocean of the heart. (856)[1]

२. तरत्समुद्रं पवमान ऊर्मिणा राजा देव ऋतं बृहत् ।
अर्षा मित्रस्य वरुणस्य धर्मणा प्र हिन्वान ऋतं बृहत् ॥

2. A learned Yogi, the purifier of all moral weaknesses, through his wisdom, attains to God, the Embodiment of all true knowledge. Treading the path of virtue, through his excellent character, he realises the Eternal God, the Saviour and Friend unto all. (857)[2]

३. नृभिर्येमाणो हर्यतो विचक्षणो राजा देव: समुद्रच: ॥

3. The lustrous, self-controlled soul, guided by the teachers of Yoga, lovely, far-seeing, absorbs itself in God, vast like an ocean. (858)

X

१. तिस्रो वाच ईरयति प्र वह्निऋतस्य धीति ब्रह्मणो मनीषाम् ।
गावो यन्ति गोपतिं पृच्छमाना: सोमं यन्ति मतयो वावशाना: ॥

1. The soul urges the three faculties, preaches the retention of truth and the wisdom of God. Just as kine run in search after the cowherd, so do the mental faculties, for self-embellishment, search after profound happiness. (859)[3]

२. सोमं गावो धेनवो वावशाना: सोमं विप्रा मतिभि: पृच्छमाना: ।
सोम: सुत ऋच्यते पूयमान: सोमे अर्का स्त्रिष्टुभ: सं नवन्ते ॥

2. The Vedic verses long for God. The learned, with their intellect inquire into God. God, contemplated, purifying the heart, is praised through Vedic songs. The knowers of the Vedas, eulogise God, by thought, word and deed. (860)[4]

३. एवा न: सोम परिषिच्यमान आ पवस्व पूयमान: स्वस्ति ।
इन्द्रमा विश बृहता मदेन वर्धया वाचं जनया पुरन्धिम् ॥

3. O God, realised through profound meditation, Immaculate, Welfare. Wisher manifest Thyself unto us. Come to the soul with great joy and rapture, develop our power of speech, let our wisdom grow ! (861)

---

[1]See verse 518.
[2]He refers to the Yogi.
[3]The three faculties: Intellect, Mahat-Tatva, Ego, Ahankara, and Mind, See verse 525.
[4]त्रिष्टुभ: may also mean with verses in Trishtup metre.

XI

१. यद्याव इन्द्र ते शत꣼ शतं भूमीरुत स्यु: ।
न त्वा वज्रिन्त्सहस्र꣼ सूर्या अनु न जातमष्ट रोदसी ॥

1. O God, even the hundred skies, a hundred earths cannot encompass Thee. O Punisher of the wicked, thousands of heavens and earths, may the whole universe cannot encompass Thee! (862)[1]

२. आ पप्राथ महिना वृष्ण्या वृषन्विश्वा शविष्ठ शवसा ।
अस्मा꣼ अव मघवन् गोमति व्रजे वज्रि चित्राभिरूतिभि: ॥

2. O God, the Showerer of happiness, Almighty, Thou art pervading all objects like the cloud and earth. O Glorious God, the Master of knowledge, in this body full of organs, protect us with wondrous aids ! (863)

XII

१. वयं घ त्वा सुतावन्त आपो न वृक्तबर्हिष: ।
पवित्रस्य प्रस्रवणेषु वृत्रहन् परि स्तोतार आसते ॥

1. O God, the Remover of vice, we, the worshippers, who have purified the mind, and are engaged in sacrifice, do verily contemplate upon Thee in a calm composure, like waters in a cascade ! (864)[2]

२. स्वरन्ति त्वा सुते नरो वसो निरेक उक्थिन: ।
कदा सुतं तृषाण ओक आ गम इन्द्र स्वब्दीव व꣼सग: ॥

2. O God, the Bestower of wealth on the poor, many learned worshippers invoke Thee alone. Just as a thirsty person goes to a place of water; or as a cloud moving nicely rains water, so when wilt Thou shower happiness on this world, Thy son ! (865)[3]

३. कण्वेभिधृ꣐ष्णवा धृषद्वाजं दर्षि सहस्रिणम् ।
पिशङ्गरूपं मघवन्विचर्षणे मक्षू गोमन्तमीमहे ॥

3. O Wealthy, All-seeing, Patient God, Thou grantest to the wise, a thousand kind of foe-subduing power. We constantly pray for charming wealth of knowledge ! (866)

---

[1]God is greater than all earths, heavens and suns. They all are insignificant compared to God. See verse 278.
[2]See verse 261.
Just as waters in a spring flow calmly and quietly, so do the devotees worship God peacefully and silently.
[3]This world is spoken of as the son of God, as it has been created by Him.

XIII

१. तरणिरित्सिषासति वाजं पुरंध्या युजा ।
आ व इन्द्रं पुरुहूतं नमे गिरा नेमिं तष्टेव सुद्रुवम् ॥

1. The Sun, with great skill, rapidly enjoys the Soma oblations. I make Ye, the sacrificers, bow unto God with my speech, just as a carpenter bends the wheel for easy motion. (867)[1]

२. न दुष्टुतिर्द्रविणोदेषु शस्यते न स्रेधन्तं रयिनंशत् ।
सुशक्तिरिन् मघवन् तुभ्यं मावते देष्णं यत्पार्ये दिवि ॥

2. They who bestow great riches love not paltry praise: wealth comes not to the violent churl. All the things worth giving, that exist in the uninterrupted atmosphere, for a man like me, indicate. O God, Thy excellent power. (868).

XIV

१. तिस्रो वाच उदीरते गावो मिमन्ति धेनवः । हरिरेति कनिक्रदत् ॥

1. The three forces urge us, as milch-kine low for their calves. A learned person appears to be preaching knowledge. (869)[2]

२. अभि ब्रह्मीरनूषत यह्वीऋ्तस्य मातरः । मर्जयन्तीर्दिवः शिशुम् ॥

2. Vedic verses, the sacred mothers of great Truth, praise God, Who pervades the atmosphere. (870)[3]

३. रायः समुद्रांश्चतुरोऽस्मभ्य सोम विश्वतः । आ पवस्व सहस्रिणः ॥

3. O God, for our welfare, grant us, from every side, the four seas, filled full with thousandfold riches ! (871)[4]

XV

१. सुतासो मधुमत्तमाः सोमा इन्द्राय मन्दिनः । पवित्रवन्तो अक्षरं देवान्गच्छन्तु वो मदाः ॥

1. Sweet Soma juices, prepared for the joyful soul, being purified spread in all directions. May these pleasant juices beautify our organs. (872)[5]

---

[1]See verse 238.
'I' means a preacher.
[2]Thers forces are (I) Ida, mother-tongue, Saraswati, mother-civilization, Mahi, motherland.
[3]दिविशिशुम् has been translated by Griffith as Soma, the Child of heaven. It means God, Who pervades the heaven and atmosphere.
[4]Four seas: The four sources of progress, i.e., Dharma, Arth, Kama, Moksha. On account of their immensity these sources of progress have been spoken of as seas in the Veda.
[5]Soma juices lend beauty and strength to the organs when they are taken. See verse 547.

२. इन्दुरिन्द्राय पवत इति देवासो अब्रुवन् । वाचस्पतिर्मखस्यते विश्वस्येशान ओजस: ॥

2. God, manifests Himself for the soul, so do the sages declare. God, full of power, the Lord of the Universe, the Revealer of the Vedas, is worthy of praise, (873)

३. सहस्रधार: पवते समुद्रो वाचमीङ्खय: । सोमस्पती रयीणाꣳ सखेन्द्रस्य दिवेदिवे ॥

3. God, the Embodiment of thousand powers, Vast like the ocean, the Revealer of the Vedas, the Lord of the animate and inanimate creation, the Friend of the soul, manifests Himself day by day. (874)

XVI

१. पवित्रं ते विततं ब्रह्मणस्पते प्रभुर्गात्राणि पर्येषि विश्वत: ।
अतप्ततनूर्न तदामो अश्नुते श्रृतास इद्वहन्त: सं तदाशत ॥

1. O Soma, the guardian of the knower of the Vedas, thy purity is spread all round. Full of strength, thou pervadest all the organs of the body. A raw, immature person cannot enjoy thy purity. The mature sacrificers only can enjoy thee ! (875)[1]

२. तपोष्पवित्रं विततं दिवस्पदेर्चन्तो अस्य तन्तवो व्यस्थिरन् ।
अवन्त्यस्य पवितारमाशवो दिव: पृष्ठमधि रोहन्ति तेजसा ॥

2. God, the Warmer and Purifier of all, pervades all luminous objects. The multifarious sacrificial verses which display His attributes, His mighty powers, guard the Sun and Air, and have mounted upto the height of heaven. (876)

३. अरूरुचदुषस: पृश्निरग्रिय उक्षा मिमेति भुवनेषु वाजयु: ।
मायाविनो ममिरे अस्य मायया नृचक्षस: पितरो गर्भमा दधु: ॥

3. The Sun connected with the Dawn shines chiefly. The showerer of rain (sun) pours water on all parts of the world. The wise, strengthened with Soma, transact their business. Rays, the givers of light to men, and their nourishers like mothers, fill their womb with water for the sake of raining. (877)[2]

XVII

१. प्र मꣳहिष्ठाय गायत ऋताग्ने बृहते शुक्रशोचिषे । उपस्तुतासो अग्नये ॥

1. O singers recite verses in praise of the benevolent, sacrificial, mighty blazing fire ! (878)

---

[1] See verse 565. This verse refers to the purity of Soma.
[2] See verse 596. This first 'their' refers to men and second to rays in the last sentence.

२. श्रा व[ँ]सते मघवा वीरवद्यशः समिद्धो द्युम्न्याहुतः ।
कुविन्नो श्रस्य सुमतिर्भवीयस्यच्छा वाजेभिरागमत् ॥

2. The Wealthy, Refulgent, Munificent God, invoked by the sages, bestows invigorating food. May His sharp wisdom amply dawn upon us with various sorts of knowledge. (879)

XVIII

१. तं ते तदं गृणीमसि वृषणं पृक्षु सासहिम् । उ लोककृत्नुमद्रिवो हरिश्रियम् ॥

1. O Unconquerable God, may we praise Thy supreme felicity which is our Nourisher, Helper in struggles, Conqueror of the world, and Worthy of taking under shelter by the learned ! (880)[1]

२. येन ज्योती[ँ]ष्यायवे मनवे च विवेदिथ । मन्दानो श्रस्य बर्हिषो वि राजसि ॥

2. O God, with whatever strength thou bestowest the rays of knowledge on a reflective person who practises Prāṇāyāma ; with the same strength, full of felicity, Thou manifestest Thyself as the support of this mighty Yajna of the universe ! (881)[2]

३. तदद्या चित्त उक्थिनोऽनु ष्टुवन्ति पूर्वथा । वृषपत्नीरपो जया दिवेदिवे ॥

3. O God, the sages sing Thy praise, till this day, as of old, Control thou, the forces of knowledge and action, which rear the God-given faculties, the bestowers of internal ! (882)[3]

XIX

१. श्रुधी हवं तिरश्च्या इन्द्र यस्त्वा सपर्यति । सुवीर्यस्य गोमतो रायस्पूर्धि महा[ँ] श्रसि ॥

1. O King, listen to the call of a petty person like me, who praises thee. Fill him with wealth of kine and valiant offspring ! Great art thou ! (883)[4]

२. यस्त इन्द्र नवीयसीं गिरं मन्द्रामजीजनत् । चिकित्विन्मनसं धियं प्रत्नामृतस्य पिप्युषीम् ॥

2. O God, to him, who uses a beautiful, deep language in Thy praise. Thou

---

[1]See verse 383.

[2]Prāṇāyāma means control of breath. Griffith translates Āyu the son of Purūravas and Urvaśi, and Manu according to Griffith is the Representative Man, the father of the human race. This explanation is unacceptable as there is no history in the Vedas.

It is regretable that in Sayana's commentary published by the Asiatic Society following the German text, the word मनवे has been printed twice by mistake. The same error has been committed by the Vedic Press Ajmer. The metre of the verse is Ushnin the addition of three letters is inadmissible, for then the metre will be changed. The word is not used twice in Sayana's commentary of Muradabad, nor is it repeated is Rigveda 8-15-5. Even in Jivanand's recension the word is not used twice.

[3]Thou refers to a learned person.

[4]See verse 346.

grantest intellect, perennial, full of sacred truth, accompanied by a diserning mind ! (884)

३. तमु ष्टवाम यं गिर इन्द्रमुक्थानि वावृधु: । पुरूण्यस्य पौंऽस्या सिषासन्तो वनामहे ॥

3. Let us worship that God alone, Whom songs and Vedic hymns of praise magnify. We praise Him, longing to expatiate on His many mighty deeds. (885)[1]

BOOK III*

Chapter 1**

I

१. प्र त आश्विनी: पवमान धेनवो दिव्या असृग्रन् पयसा धरीमणि ।
प्रान्तरिक्षात् स्थाविरीस्ते असृक्षत ये त्वा मृजन्त्यृषिषाण वेधस: ॥

1. O Holy God, Thy universal, divine, firm forces, manifest themselves through knowledge in the recipient soul. O God, Thou art worshipped by the sages who being learned, realise Thy pure nature, and contemplate upon Thee, perceiving in their heart the unchanging, steady abstractions of the mind ! (886)

२. उभयत: पवमानस्य रश्मयो ध्रुवस्य सत: परि यन्ति केतव: ।
यदी पवित्रे अधि मृज्यते हरि: सत्ता नि योनौ कलशेषु सीदति ॥

2. The knowledge-bestowing beams of God, are pervading the animate and inanimate creation of the Unchanging Lord. Whenever God is perceived in the mind through discernment, then, being present in the hearts, He residing in all bodies, is found seated in the soul. (887)

३. विश्वा धामानि विश्वचक्ष ऋभ्वस प्रभोष्टे सत: परि यन्ति केतव: ।
व्यानशी पवसे सोम धर्मणा पतिर्विश्वस्य भुवनस्य राजसि ॥

3. O All-seeing, All-creating, Grand, Almighty God. Thy mighty powers are spread over all parts of the universe. Pervading Thou purifiest all with Thy natural powers, and as the whole world's Lord, Thou shinest like a King ! (888)

II

१. पवमानो अ्रजीजनद्दिवश्चित्रं न तन्यतुम् । ज्योतिर्वं श्वानरं बृहत् ॥

---

[1]Mighty deeds refer to the Creation, Sustenanee and Dissolution of the universe by God.
  *is Prapathaka I.
  **is Ardh Prapathaka I.

1. From heaven hath Soma made, as 'twere, the marvellous thunder, and the lofty light of all mankind. (889)[1]

२. पवमान रसस्तव मदो राजन्नदुच्छुनः । वि वारमव्यमर्षति ॥

2. O Refulgent, Holy God, Thy gladdening, auspicious, felicity flows on to the pure soul free from lust and anger ! (890)[2]

३. पवमानस्य ते रसो दक्षो वि राजति द्युमान् । ज्योतिर्विश्वꣳ स्वदृॅशे ॥

3. O God, the Purifier of mind, the flow of Thy felicity, coupled with knowledge, and glow, shines pre-eminently. Thy Light is the bringer of all sorts of happiness ! (891).

III

१. प्र यद् गावो न भुर्णयस्त्वेषा अयासो अक्रमुः । ध्नन्तः कृष्णामप त्वचम् ॥

1. The nourishing, brilliant, impetuous souls roam casting aside the injurious sentiment of simulation, as do the rays. (892)[3]

२. सुवितस्य वनामहेऽति सेतुं दुराय्यम् । साह्याम दस्युमव्रतम् ॥

2. We seek the shelter of God, the Excellent Ruler of the universe, May we thereby, subdue the breaker of law and transgressor of social bond, the uncontrollable and undutiful plunderer. (893)[4]

३. शृण्वे वृष्टेरिव स्वनः पवमानस्य शुष्मिणः । चरन्ति विद्युतो दिवि ॥

3. Just as lightning-flashes move in heaven, so when soul's beauties display themselves in the universe, I hear the proclamation of the Purifying, Mighty God, like cloud's thunder. (894)

४. आ पवस्व महीमिषं गोमदिन्दो हिरण्यवत् । अश्ववत् सोम वीरवत् ॥

4. O Glorious God, grant us abundant food, with store of cattle and of gold, with steeds and heroic sons ! (895)

५. पवस्व विश्वचर्षण आ मही रोदसी पृण । उषाः सूर्यो न रश्मिभिः ॥

5. O All-seeing God, fill full the mighty Heaven and Earth, as the Sun fills the Dawn with his beams. Be Kind unto us ! (896)

६. परि णः शर्मयन्त्या धारया सोम विश्वतः । सरा रसेव विष्टपम् ॥

---

[1]See verse 484. Soma when put into the fire in the form of oblations, rises to the sky, and produces rain accompanied by the thunder and light of lightning.

[2]अदुच्छुनः: literary means free from the internal moral demons of lust and anger.

[3]Just as rays of the sun remove darkness, so do strong souls avoid show and fraud. See verse 491.

[4]Plunderer may also mean lust or anger which degrades the soul.

6. O God, approach us on every side with Thy happiness-bestowing strength, as a river flows to a low-level place ! (897)[1]

IV

१. आशुरर्षं बृहन्मते परि प्रियेण धाम्ना । यत्रा देवा इति ब्रुवन् ॥

1. O Omniscient God, come readily unto us with Thy beloved halo. Thou art there, where reside the sages. This is Thy teaching ! (898)

२. परिष्कृण्वन्ननिष्कृतं जनाय यातयन्निष: । वृष्टिं दिव: परि स्रव ॥

2. O God, consecrating the unconsecrated worshipper, and bringing store of food to man, make Thou the rain descend from heaven ! (899)

३. अयं स यो दिवस्परि रघुयामा पवित्र आ । सिन्धोरूर्मा व्यक्षरत् ॥

3. This is the Soma, which, free from the dirt, reaches heaven diversely in a rarefied form, through the air of the atmosphere. (900)

४. सुत एति पवित्र आ त्विषि दधान ओजसा । विचक्षाणो विरोचयन् ॥

4. The All-Creating God, through His Might, infusing lustre in objects free from dirt, sending forth His light, seeing all objects, is All-Pervading. (901)

५. आविवासन्परावतो अथो अर्वावत: सुत: । इन्द्राय सिच्यते मधु ॥

5. The All-Creating God manifests the distant and nigh worlds. He is served with knowledge for the betterment of soul. (902)

६. समीचीना अनूषत हरिं हिन्वन्त्यद्रिभि: । इन्दुमिन्द्राय पीतये ॥

6. The learned together realise God through strict devices. They praise the joy felt in the heart, for the pleasure of the soul. (903)

V

१. हिन्वन्ति सूरमुस्रय: स्वसारो जामयस्पतिम् । महामिन्दुं महीयुव: ॥

1. Just as active sisters and daughters resort to their guardian, so do the intrepid and agile persons, longing for greatness, eulogise the Worshipful, joyful God, the Creator and Nourisher. (904)

२. पवमान रुचारुचा देव देवेभ्य: सुत: । विश्वा वसून्या विश ॥

2. O Refulgent, Purifying God, worshipped by the sages, grant us, with Thy full power, all sorts of riches ! (905)

[1]Griffith considers Rasa: a mystical river which flows round the world. This interpretation is inadmissible, as there are no historical references in the Vedas.

३. श्रा पवमान सुष्टुति वृष्टि देवेभ्यो दुव: । इषे पवस्व संयतम् ॥

3. O Purifying God, send regularly nice rain in time, for the Yajna of the sages, and for food ! (906)

VI

१. जनस्य गोपा श्रजनिष्ट जागृविरग्नि: सुदक्ष: सुविताय नव्यसे ।
घृतप्रतीको बृहता दिविस्पृशा द्युमद्वि भाति भरतेभ्य: शुचि: ॥

1. A leader, the guardian of the people, free from idleness full of strength, well-known for vitality, pure in heart, is born for fresh prosperity. He with high heaven-touching lustre like the sun, shines splendidly for the learned with his knowledge. (907)[1]

२. त्वामग्ने श्रङ्गिरसो गृहा हितमन्वविन्दञ्छिश्रियाणं वनेवने ।
स जायसे मथ्यमान: सहो महत्त्वामाहु: सहस्रपुत्रमङ्गिर: ॥

2. O Omniscient God, present in each soul, hidden in the inmost recesses of the heart, the learned search for and find Thee in each object. Thou art Great, O Almighty Father, worthy of meditation in the heart again and again, O God, the Embodiment of knowledge, the sages call Thee the Saviour of men from sins through Yoga. (908)[2]

३. यज्ञस्य केतुं प्रथमं पुरोहितर्ग्नि नरस्त्रिषधस्थे समिन्धते ।
इन्द्रेण देवै: सरथ॑ स बर्हिषि सीदन् नि होता यजथाय सुक्रतु: ॥

3. The learned enkindle in His threefold seat God, the Preacher of sacrifice and Foremost Existent. He, the Bestower of all pleasures, Creator of all, manifests Himself in our life's sacrifice in the heart along with soul and organs. (909)[3]

VII

१. श्रयं वां मित्रावरुणा सुत: सोम ऋतावृधा । ममेदिह श्रुत॑हवम् ॥

1. Ye teacher and pupil, advancers of truth, this knowledge is meant for Ye. Hence listen here to my call. (910)[4]

[1]See Yajur 15-27.
[2]See Yajur 15-28.
Griffith translates Angirasas as members of a family of priestly Fathers, regarded as the typical first sacrificers. According to Griffith, Agni, fearing to share the fate of his three elder brothers who had perished in the service of the gods, fled away and hid himself. The gods or the Angirasas discovered him and persuaded him to return to his sacred duties. Angiras: Agni is called the best or oldest of Angirasas, as his aid was necessary for the due performance of sacrifice. This explanation is inadmissible and wide the mark, as there is no history in the Vedas. Angiras mean learned people, and Angiras means God full of knowledge.
[3]Threefold seat may mean Ida, Pingla, Sushumna, the three arteries, or Jagrit, Swapan, Sushupti states of the soul.
[4]Here means in this world. May refers to a King.

२. राजानावनभिद्रुहा ध्रुवे सदस्युत्तमे । सहस्रस्थूण आशाते ॥

2. O Prāna and Apāna, the rulers of this body, free from mutual malice, reside Ye in sublime, eternal, thousand pillared home, the soul. (911)[1]

३. ता सम्राजा घृतासुती आदित्या दानुनस्पती । सचेते अनवह्वरम् ॥

3. Prāna and Apāna, creators of lustrous halo, brilliant like the sun, lords of wealth, sovereign Kings, free from fraud, work together harmoniously. (912)[2]

VIII

१. इन्द्रो दधीचो अस्थभिर्वृत्राण्यप्रतिष्कुतः । जघान नवतीनव ॥

1. O General, just as the firm sun, with its unsteady rays, which reach the sustaining and preserving air, engulfing ninety nine parts of all directions, releases the minute particles of water from the cloud, so shouldst thou destroy numerous irreligious foes ! (913)[3]

२. इच्छन्नश्वस्य यच्छिरः पर्वतेष्वपश्रितम् । तद्विदच्छर्यणावति ॥

2. Longing for its chief characteristic, hidden in inaccessible recesses, the soul finds it in the heart. (914)[4]

३. अत्राह गोरमन्वत नाम त्वष्टुरपीच्यम् । इत्था चन्द्रमसो गृहे ॥

3. All admit, that as there is a part of the light of the sun in the moon, so the light of God is present in pleasant superhuman joys. (915)

IX

१. इयं वामस्य मन्मन इन्द्राग्नी पूर्व्यस्तुतिः । अभ्राद्वृष्टिरिवाजनि ॥

1. O God and soul, this noblest praise of yours comes out of a contemplative learned person, as rain from out of the cloud ! (916)[5]

२. शृणुतं जरितुर्हवमिन्द्राग्नी वनतं गिरः । ईशाना पिप्यतं धियः ॥

[1]Thousand pillared: The soul which possesses a thousand virtues, that serve as it props in its march to final-beatitude.

[2]Ascribing human sentiments to inanimate objects is a poetic way of mentioning their usefulness· Prāna and Apāna are two life breaths in the body.

[3]'Ninety nine' means many. See verse 179. The interpretation given to this verse is taken from Swami Dayananda's commentary on Rig I-84-13.

[4]'Chief Characteristic' means the true nature of the soul i.e. eternity. Griffith translates Śaryanāvān as the name of a lake in Kurukshetra, near the modern Delhi. This interpretation is inadmissible as it involves history, but the Vedas are free from it. The word means heart. The verse may also refer to the teacher and his disciple.

[5]See verse 174.

2. O teacher and disciple, listen to the singer's call, enjoy Vedic verses. Ye mighty lords, improve your intellects ! (917)

३. मा पापत्वाय नो नरेन्द्राग्नी माभिशस्तये । मा नो रीरधतं निदे ॥

3. O Preacher and Teacher, the leaders of humanity, induce us not to sin, violence and slander ! (918)

X

१. पवस्व दक्षसाधनो देवेभ्य: पीतये हरे । मरूद्ध्यो वायवे मद: ॥

1. O Soma, the infuser of strength and joy, mayest thou be acquired for air and other forces of nature ! (919)[1]

२. सं देवैं: शोभते वृषा कविर्योनावधि प्रिय: । पवमानो अ्रदाभ्य: ॥

2. A gladdening, purifying, invincible, lovable learned steadfast Yogi, looks graceful along with other scholars. (920)

३. पवमान धिया हितो३ऽभि योनिं कनिक्रदत् । धर्मणा वायुमारुह: ॥

3. O soul, with the force of meditation, residing in thy basic place, the heart, singing the praise of God, control thy breath with full exertion. (921)

XI

१. तवाहꣳ सोम रारण सख्य इन्दो दिवेदिवे ।
पूरूणि वभ्रो नि चरन्ति मामव परिधीꣳ रति ताꣳ इहि ॥

1. O gladdening King, may I enjoy thy friendship every day. O nourisher, many are the baser sentiments, which pull me down. Help me to overcome these foes of morality ! (922)

२. तवाहं नक्तमुत सोम ते दिवा दुहानो बभ्र ऊधनि ।
घृणा तपन्तमति सूर्य पर: शकुना इव पप्तिम ॥

2. O God, the Sustainer of the universe, I derive joy day and night from Thy treasure of happiness. Just as birds fly in the morning, so may we, meditating upon Thee, Refulgent with Lustre, Higher than the Sun, overcoming the shackles of birth, attain to salvation ! (923)

XII

१. पुनानो अक्रमीदभि विश्वा मृधो विचर्षणि: । शुम्भन्ति विप्रं धीतिभि: ॥

1. Soma, viewed from different points of view, overcomes all inimical forces. Soma, the sharpener of intellect is purified with fingers. (924)[2]

[1]See verse 516.
[2]See verse 488.

२. श्रा योनिमरुणो रुह॒द॒ग्मदिन्द्रो॑ वृषा सुत॑म् । ध्रुवे मद॑सि सीद॑तु ॥

2. The lovely soul, manifests itself in the heart. Soul, the diffuser of joys, bows before God, the Embodiment of happiness. May God always reside in a steady soul. (925)

३. नू नो रयिं महामि॒न्दोऽस्मभ्य॒ꣳ सोम॑ विश्वत॑: । श्रा प॑वस्व सह॒स्रिण॑म् ॥

3. O Joyful God, send us soon great opulence from every side. Pour on us, treasures thousandfold ! (926)

XIII

१. पिबा सोममि॑न्द्र म॒न्दतु॑ त्वा॒ यं ते॑ सुषाव ह॒र्य॑श्वाद्रि॒: । सोतुर्बा॒हुभ्या॒ꣳ सु॒यतो॒ नार्वा॑ ॥

1. O Sun, Lord of rays, this stone presses the Soma with the arms of the presser. Just as a disciplined horse impelled by the hands of a rider takes us to destination, so accept the Soma and be satiated ! (927)[1]

२. यस्ते॒ मदो॑ युज्य॒श्चारुर॑स्ति॒ येन॑ वृ॒त्राणि॑ हर्य॒श्व ह॒ꣳसि । स त्वामि॑न्द्र प्रभू॒वसो॒ ममत्तु ॥

2. O soul, united with organs fleeting like a horse, beautiful is thy pleasure derivable from yoga; on whose strength thou subduest thy mental foes like lust and anger. O soul, residing in all living beings, may that pleasure fill thee with joy ! (928)

३. बोधा सु मे॑ मघवन् वाचमेमां यां ते॒ वसि॑ष्ठो अर्च॑ति प्रश॒स्तिम् ।
इमा ब्रह्म॑ सध॒मादे॑ जुष॒स्व ॥

3. O King, make me understand the language, used by a learned person in eulogy for thee. Meditate in thy heart on these Vedic verses ! (929)[2]

XIV

१. विश्वा॑: पृत॒ना अ॒भिभू॑तरं नर॒: स॒जूस्त॑तक्षु॒रिन्द्रं॑ जज॒नुश्च॑ राज॒से ।
क्र॒त्वे वरे॒ स्थेम॒न्यामु॑री॒मुतो॒ग्रमोजि॑ष्ठं तर॒सं त॑रस्विनम् ॥

1. All men collectively should elect as their King one, who is the subduer of enemies, firm in his seat of power, Killer or foes, fierce, exceedingly strong, stalwart and full of vigour, and equip him with warlike instruments and missiles, for effective administration and philanthropic deeds. (930)

२. नेमिं नम॑न्ति च॒क्षसा॒ मेषं॒ विप्रा॑ अ॒भिस्वरे॑ ।
सु॒दीत॑यो वो श्र॒द्रुहोऽपि॑ क॒र्णे त॑रस्विन: सम॒ृक्व॑भि: ॥

---

[1] When Soma is put in the fire in the form of oblations, it rises to the sun being rarefied, satiates it and brings down rain, See verse 398.

[2] Me: a devoted follower of the King. He wants to know, in what way the learned praise the King, so that he may also do in the same way Vasishtha is not the name of a Rishi, as interpreted by Griffith. It simply means a learned person.

2. The wise, through foresight, in chorus, bow unto God, Who is the Subduer of all, and Bestower of happiness. Ye also, full of brilliance, free from deceit, quick in action, should nicely worship Him with Vedic verses. (931)[1]

३. समु रेभासो ग्रस्वरन्निन्द्र॒ँ सोमस्य पीतये ।
स्व: पतिर्यंदी वृधे धृतव्रतो ह्योजसा समूतिभि: ॥

3. Bards, for enjoying extreme felicity, sing in unison the praise of the soul. It is the Lord of extreme pleasure. When it is filled with iron determination, it advances with its power, and expedients of progress. (932)[2]

XV

१. यो राजा चर्षणीनां याता रथेभिरध्रिगु: । विश्वासां तरुता पृतनानां ज्येष्ठं यो वृत्रहा गृणे ॥

1. I praise the King, who is the sovereign lord of men, who moves with his chariots understrained, is the slayer of foes, and the conqueror of fighting hosts, and mighty in strength. (933)

२. इन्द्रं त॒ँ शुम्भ पेरुह॒न्मन्नवसे यस्य द्विता विधर्तरि ।
हस्तेन वज्र: प्रति धायि दर्शतो महान्देवो न सूर्य: ॥

2. O soul, the master of the organs of senses, invoke the God for thy safety, Who is thy Nourisher, Who is thy Master, and thou His servant, Who sustaineth the armour of knowledge in His hand, Who is handsome, Mighty, the Bestower of all joys, and the Displayer of all sorts of knowledge like the sun ! (934)

XVI

१. परि प्रिया दिव: कविर्वया॒ँसि नप्त्योहित: । स्वानैर्याति कविक्रतु: ॥

1. A quick-witted, wise person, the well-wisher of Heaven and Earth, along with his fellow conductors of the Yajna, acquires pleasant, delightful powers of life. (935)[3]

२. स सूनुर्मातरा शुचिर्जातो जाते ग्ररोचयत् । महान्मही ऋतावृधा ॥

2. God, being the Bestower of joy like a son, is Pure and Mighty. Just as a son makes his venerable parents, the advancers of true knowledge and life, shine, so does God make splendid the Heaven and Earth, the preceptor and disciple, the King and his subjects. (936)

---

[1]Griffith considers this hymn to be obscued and very difficult. I don't find any obscurity and difficulty in it. Ye means learned persons. The sense is clear.
[2]It means the soul.
[3]'Follow conductors' means Adhvaryus. A performer of the Yajna is a well-wisher of the Heaven and Earth, as he purifies them both through Havan. See verse 476.

३. प्रप्र क्षयाय पन्यसे जनाय जुष्टो अद्रुह: । वीत्यर्ष पनिष्टये ॥

3. O Lovable and Guileless God, grant supremacy to a panegyrist for living and success in business ! (937)

XVII

१. त्वꣳ ह्या३ꣳङ्त देव्य पवमान जनिमानि द्युमत्तम: । अमृतत्वाय घोषयन् ॥

1. O Beloved, Pure God, setting forth a flood of divinity, Thou givest a message of immortality to my several births ! (938)[1]

२. येना नवग्वा दध्यङ्ङपोर्णुते येन विप्रास आपिरे ।
देवानाꣳ सुम्ने अमृतस्य चारुणो येन श्रवाꣳस्याशत ॥

2. By Whom, a person newly instructed in Vedic philosophy, becomes learned and diffuses knowledge. Through Whose aid, the sages explore the essence of Vedic hymns, and through Whose support, the wise acquire the seeret's of the knowledge of the beautiful soul, at the places of Yajna of the learned, may Thou O God, be realised by us. (939)[2]

XVIII

१. सोम: पुनान ऊर्मिणाव्यं वारं वि धावति । अग्रे वाच: पवमान: कनिक्रदत् ॥

1. A pure-hearted, tranquil Yogi, through self-amelioration, crosses the lid of ignorance. Purifying himself still more, being initiated in the mysteries of the Vedas, he plunges himself in devotion to God. (940)

२. धीभिर्मृजन्ति वाजिनं वने क्रीडन्तमत्यविम् । अभि त्रिपृष्ठं मतय: समस्वरन् ॥

2. The learned purify the strong soul, sporting in the body, through noble deeds. The reflective sages praise the soul of triple height. (941)[3]

३. असर्जि कलशाꣳ अभि मीढ्वांत्सप्तिनं वाजयु: । पुनानो वाचं जनयन्नसिष्यदत् ॥

3. The joyful soul, lends speed and vigour to the bodies like a swift horse in a battle-field. It glides on lifting its voice of protest, and casting aside all moral impurities. (942)

[1]See verse 583, God preachest that salvation is obtained by the soul after ceaseless efforts in several births.

[2]Whom and Whose refer to God.

Griffith describes Dadhichi to be the son of Atharvan, the priest who first obtained fire and offered prayer and Soma to the Gods. Here he is called a Navagvā. This explanation is beside the mark, as it entails history, whereas the Vedas are free from history

See verse 572.

[3]Triple height may refer to the Jagrat (waking) Swapan (sleeping) and Sushupti (Deep slumber) states of the soul, or mind, tongue, body, where the soul resides, Sāyana has interpreted अत्यविम् as Soma, and त्रिपृष्ठं as three vessels in which Soma is kept, i.e. Droṇakalaśa‘ Ādhavaniya, and Pūtabhṛit, or the firmament, the mountain, and the altar, the different homes of Soma, This interpretation is not plausible,

XIX

१. सोम: पवते जनिता मतीनां जनिता दिवो जनिता पृथिव्या: ।
जनिताग्नेर्जनिता सूर्यस्य जनितेन्द्रस्य जनितोत विष्णो: ॥

1. The soul manifests itself as the Creator of all mental feelings, the Creator of light like the Sun, the Creator of skin extended like the earth, the Creator of fire-like speech, the Creator of sun-like eye, the Creator of Prana, and the Creator of space-like ear. (943)[1]

२. ब्रह्मा देवानां पदवी: कवीनामृषिर्विप्राणां महिषो मृगाणाम् ।
श्येनो गृध्राणाꣳ स्वधितिर्वनानाꣳ सोम: पवित्रमत्येति रेभन् ॥

2. Soul is Brahma amongst the learned, the leader of the sages, the seer of the intellectuals, the Controller of the organs searching for sensuality, falcon amid the vultures, axe of forests. Voicing forth its characteristics, overcoming all impediments, it attains to Immaculate God. (944)[2]

३. प्रावीविपद्वाच ऊर्मि न सिन्धुर्गिर स्तोमान् पवमानो मनीषा: ।
अन्त: पश्यन् वृजनेमावराण्या तिष्ठति वृषभो गोषु जानन् ॥

3. Pure soul, the goader of reflective faculties, like a river stirs the wave of voice, our songs and praises, Through self-introspection, the soul lends strength to the organs, as an ox does to a cow through semination. Knowing well, it subdues the passions unworthy of acceptance. (945)[3]

XX

१. अग्नि वो वृधन्तमध्वराणां पुरूतमम् । अच्छा नप्त्रे सहस्वते ॥

1. Know God to be the sublimest of all, Who is the Helper of your Yajnas, powerful, your Benefactor and Lord of mighty worlds. (946)[4]

२. अयं यथा न आभुवत् त्वष्टा रूपेव तक्ष्या । अस्य क्रत्वा यशस्वत: ॥

2. Just as a carpenter makes nice articles through cutting so does God properly create for us beautiful objects. We too have been created through the might of the same Glorious God. (947)

३. अयं विश्वा अभि श्रियोऽग्निर्देवेषु पत्यते । आ वाजैरुप नो गमत् ॥

3. This God is the Lord Supreme of all glories midst the learned. May He come nigh unto us with strength and knowledge. (948)

[1]See verse 527.
[2]"Falcon amid the vultures' means, the soul is powerful and wide awake amongst the lustful organs, which the soul subdues, as a falcon is powerful amongst the vultures thirsty for the flesh of a carcase.
Axe of forests: Just as an axe lops down the forest trees, so does the soul cut asunder the shackles that prevent it from the attainment of salvation.
[3]Griffith considers the second line of this verse as obscure. I notice no obscurity, The sense is clear.
[4]See verse 21.

XXI

१. इममिन्द्र सुतं पिब ज्येष्ठममर्त्यं मदम् । शुक्रस्य त्वाभ्यक्षरन् धारा ऋतस्य सादने ॥

1. O King, enjoy this divine, excellent, well-established pleasure. Mayest thou acquire the sentiments of truth in the house of a holy man like me ! (949)

२. न किष्ट्वद्रथीतरो हरी यदिन्द्र यच्छसे । न किष्ट्वानु मज्मना न किः स्वश्व आनशे ॥

2. O God, Thou Controllest knowledge and action like two powerful horses to maintain the world. None is stronger than Thee. None hath surpassed Thee in Thy Might. None is more pervading and faster than Thee ! (950)

३. इन्द्राय नूनमर्चतोक्थानि च ब्रवीतन । सुता अमत्सुरिन्दवो ज्येष्ठं नमस्यता सहः ॥

3. O men, verily worship God, recite Vedic verses. Under His shelter all created Yogis derive enjoyment. Pay reverence to His noblest might. (951)

XXII

१. इन्द्र जुषस्व प्र वहा याहि शूर हरिह । पिबा सुतस्य मतिनं मधोश्चकानश्चारुर्मंदाय ॥

1. O soul, enjoy pleasure, drive forward, manifest thyself. Hero!, Controller of the horse-like organs, enjoy happiness thou createst. Fair, like a sage, for the acquisition of delight, ever desire for Divine rapture ! (952)

२. इन्द्र जठरं नव्यं न पृणस्व मधोदिवो न ।
अस्य सुतस्य स्वार्नों प त्वा मदाः सुवाचो अस्थुः ॥

2. O soul, just as Heaven is filled with light, so fill thy belly anew with the juice of Divine rapture. The delights derived from it come unto thee like sweet voiced joy ! (953)[1]

३. इन्द्रस्तुराषाण्मित्रो न जघान वृत्रं यतिनं । बिभेद बलं भृगुर्नं ससाहे शत्रून् मदे सोमस्य ॥

3. Soul is the queller of the sentiments of violence like the Sun. It is the subduer of the passions of lust and anger, like a self-controlled sage. Like a Yogi, the quencher of sins, the soul breaks the citadel of overpowering passions. It supresses the internal foes and remains absorbed in supreme joy. (954)[2]

[1]It refers to divine rapture. Just as a sweet voice brings joy, so divine rapture imparts joy to the soul.
[2]Just as the sun dispels darkness, so the soul shuns violence. Internal foes are lust, anger, avarice, Infatuation and pride. Griffith translates Yati as one of a mystical race of ascetics, connected with the Bhrigus, and said, according to one legend, to have taken part in the creation of the world. Ludwig suggests 'wrestler' as the possible meaning

Chapter 2
I

१. गोवित्पवस्व वसुविद्धिरण्यविद्रेतोधा इन्दो भुवनेष्वर्पित: ।
त्वॱꣳ सुवीरो असि सोम विश्ववित्तं त्वा नर उप गिरेम आसते ॥

1. O Exultant God, Thou art the Bestower of the light of knowledge, the Giver of wealth, glory and muscular strength. Thou pervadest all worlds. O God, Mighty and Omniscient art Thou. All these men worship Thee with song. Manifest Thyself in our heart ! (955)

२. त्वं नृचक्षा असि सोम विश्वत: पवमान वृषभ ता वि धावसि ।
स न: पवस्व वसुमद्धिरण्यवद्वयॱꣳ स्याम भुवनेषु जीवसे ॥

2. O God, Thou beholdest men from every side. O Pure God, the Showerer of joys, Thou art pervading Thy subjects. Pour down upon us wealth in treasure and in gold. May we have strength to live long under different circumstances ! (956)

३. ईशान इमा भुवनानि ईयसे युजान इन्दो हरित: सुपर्ण: ।
तास्ते क्षरन्तु मधुमद् घृतं पयस्तव व्रते सोम तिष्ठन्तु कृष्टय: ॥

3. O Lord of the Universe, O Glorious God, leading on the path of virtue. the active, virtuous, passionate and ignorant soul, Thou controllest all these worlds. May Thy subjects pour forth for Thee feelings of joy filled with love and devotion. O God may Thy subjects abide by Thy decree ! (957)

II

१. पवमानस्य विश्ववित् प्र ते सर्गा असृक्षत । सूर्यस्येव न रश्मय: ॥

1. O Omniscient God, just as sun's rays dispel darkness, so do the Vedic hymns, amanating from Thy Pure self benefit humanity ! (958)

२. केतुं कृण्वं दिवस्परि विश्वा रूपाभ्यर्षसि । समुद्र: सोम पिन्वसे ॥

2. O God, Thou art deep like the ocean. In the atmosphere Thou purifiest different objects of nature, Diffusing knowledge through the Vedas, Thou grantest different forms of riches ! (959)

---

of Yati. Griffith translates Bhrigu as a Rishi regarded as the ancestor of the ancient race of Bhrigus.

Griffith translates Valam as demon of drought, who steals the cows of the Gods, and hides them in a cave, that is, keeps the rain imprisoned. All these interpretations are wide the mark. Yati means a self-controlled sage.

Bhrigu means a Yogi who suppresses sins Valam means forceful passion.

(1,2,3) These three stanzas are not found in the Rigveda. No Rishi's name is mentioned. Griffith calls these three verses as obscure. He has not been able to grasp their significance. I see no obscurity in them.

३. जज्ञानो वाचमिष्यसि पवमान विधर्मणि । क्रन्दं देवो न सूर्यः ॥

3. O God, just as the sun goads men to action in the morning, so dost Thou, shining, everywhere preaching, being present in the heart, in the beginning of the creation reveal the Vedas in the hearts of the Rishis ! (960)

III

१. प्र सोमासो अधन्विषुः पवमानास इन्दवः । श्रीणाना अप्सु वृञ्जते ॥

1. The pure, enlightened, liberated souls, mature in experience and knowledge, roam about midst men. (961)[1]

२. अभि गावो अधन्विषुरापो न प्रवता यतीः । पुनाना इन्द्रमाशत ॥

2. The learned, treading the path of virtue, go on marching forward like the streams of water. Purifying themselves and overcoming all impediments, they attain to God. (962)

३. प्र पवमान धन्वसि सोमेन्द्राय मादनः । नृभिर्यतो वि नीयसे ॥

3. O active, learned pupil, derive knowledge, contributing to the happiness of thy preceptor. May thou humbly receive education under the strict discipline of thy instructors ! (963)

४. इन्दो यदद्रिभिः सुतः पवित्रं परिदीयसे । अरमिन्द्रस्य धाम्ने ॥

4. O devoted disciple, being educated by the teachers whose knowledge is mountain-like solid, thou art being delivered unto God. Be thou fit to take the place of thy teacher! (964)[2]

५. त्वँ सोम नृमादनः पवस्व चर्षणीधृतिः । सस्नियों अनुमाद्यः ॥

5. O pupil, enhancing the pleasure of the teachers, and being considered as a youth of sterling worth by the examiners, spread knowledge, and be a source of joy unto all, after graduation! (965)

६. पवस्व वृत्रहन्तम उक्थेभिरनुमाद्यः । शुचिः पावको अद्भुतः ॥

6. O pupil, the controller of the internal base passions of lust and anger, worthy of adulation through nice words, pure, wonderful purifier, roam about every where and spread knowledge ! (966)

७. शुचिः पावक उच्यते सोमः सुतः स मधुमान् । देवावीरघशँसहा ॥

7. This Brahmchari, the knower of God, pure in thought, word and deed,

---

[1]Highly enlightened, emancipated souls move midst men preaching the eternal truths of the Vedas.

[2]Being delivered to God means, thou art progressing on the path of knowledge and character.

the purifier of others, the observer of noble traits, the slayer of sinners, is called Soma. (967)[1]

IV

१. प्र कविर्देववीतयेऽव्या वारेभिरव्यत । साह्वान्विश्वा अभि स्पृधः ॥

1. The learned Brahmchari, for acquiring knowledge, covers himself with blankets made of sheep's wool, and subdues all sorts of opposition. (968)[2]

२. स हि ष्मा जरितृभ्य आ वाजं गोमन्तमिन्वति । पवमानः सहस्रिणम् ॥

2. The same Brahmchari, travelling far and wide, offers to his preceptors as Guru Dukhshina riches and cattle, the givers of thousandfold comforts. (969)[3]

३. परि विश्वानि चेतसा मृज्यसे पवसे मती । स नः सोम श्रवो विदः ॥

3. O Brahmchari, thou purifiest all with thy knowledge, and graspest all things with thy mind. Grant us the knowledge of the Vedas ! (970)

४. अभ्यर्ष बृहद्यशो मघवद्भ्यो ध्रुवं रयिम् । इषं स्तोतृभ्य आ भर ॥

4. O Celebate Sanātik, acquire lofty glory, receive money from the opulent, give food and cash to the preceptors, the preachers of truth ! (971)[4]

५. त्वं राजेव सुव्रतो गिरः सोमा विवेशिथ । पुनानो वह्ने अद्भुत ॥

5. O Sanatik, O recipient of knowledge. O wonderfully learned Brahmchari, firm in resolve, purifier of all, worthy of praise like a King, go deep into the secrets of the Vedic verses ! (972)

६. स वह्निरप्सु दुष्टरो मृज्यमानो गभस्त्योः । सोमश्चमूषु सीदति ॥

6. The calm, austere Brahmchari, the repository of knowledge, unconquerable amongst men, purified through knowledge and action, takes his seat in the hearts of the people. (973)

७. क्रीडुर्मखो न मंहयुः पवित्रं सोम गच्छसि । दधत् स्तोत्रे सुवीर्यम् ॥

7. O jovial pupil, worthy of admiration like a Yajna, thou stickest to thy noble resolve, and under the guidance of thy teacher, thou acquirest excellent knowledge and strength ! (974)

[1]This Brahmchāri refers to the pupil mentioned in previous verses. A Brahmchāri possessing these characteristics is called a Soma Brahmchāri.

[2]A Brahmchāri should lead a life of penance and not ease.

[3]Guru Dakshiṇa: In Vedic times it was the usual practice, for a pupil, to offer to his teacher, at the time of departure, after completing his studies, whatever he could according to his means. This offering made as a token of gratitude is called Guru Dakshiṇa.

[4]A Snātik is he who has graduated in Vedic lore and theology.

V

१. यवंयवं नो अन्धसा पुष्टंपुष्टं परि स्त्रव । विश्वा च सोम सौभगा ॥

1. O God, pour on us with Thy strength all kinds of corn, each sort of nourishment and all sorts of felicities ! (975)

२. इन्दो यथा तव स्तवो यथा ते जातमन्धसः । नि बर्हिषि प्रिये सदः ॥

2. O Glorious God, the Dispeller of ignorance, as is Thy praise and fame, so dear Lord, come and reside in our heart ! (976)

३. उत नो गोविदश्ववित् पवस्व सोमान्धसा । मक्षूतमेभिरहभिः ॥

3. O learned fellow, the master of the faculties of knowledge and action, the Controller of breaths, come unto us through days that fly most rapidly ! (977)[1]

४. यो जिनाति न जीयते हन्ति शत्रुमभीत्य । स पवस्व सहस्रजित् ॥

4. As one, who conquers, ne'er subdued, attacks and slays the enemy; thus, vanquisher of thousands, come unto us ! (978)[2]

VI

१. यास्ते धारा मधुश्चुतोऽसृग्र मिन्द ऊतये । ताभिः पवित्रमासदः ॥

1. O God, Thy forces, affording knowledge and pleasure, let loose, are meant for protection. Reside with them in a subtle form in the purifying sun! (979)[3]

२. सो अर्षेन्द्राय पीतये तिरो वाराण्यव्यया । सीदन्नृतस्य योनिमा ॥

2. O learned man, cast aside the coverings of the mind, for the satisfaction of the soul. Manifest thyself, realizing God, the Refuge of Truth ! (980)

३. त्वँ सोम परि स्त्रव स्वादिष्ठो अङ्गिरोभ्यः । वरिवोविद्घृतं पयः ॥

3. O God, Thou art the Giver of spiritual joy to the enlightened souls, the Imparter of supreme felicity, grant us excellent divine happiness ! (981)

VII

१. तव श्रियो वर्ष्यस्येव विद्युतोऽग्नेश्चिकित्र उपसामिवेतयः ।
   यदोषधीरभिसृष्टो वनानि च परि स्वयं चिनुषे अन्नमासनि ॥

1. O God, Thy glories are visible, like lightnings from the rainy cloud, like

---

[1]Through days rapidly means as early as possible.
[2]One refers to the King.
[3]Them refers to forces.

the coming rays at Dawn. When Thou prevadest plant and forest trees, Thou crammest by Thyself all objects like food into Thy mouth ! (982)[1]

२. वातोपजूत इषितो वशाँ॑ अनु तृषु यदन्ना वेविषद्वितिष्ठसे ।
    आ ते यतन्ते रथ्यो३यथा पृथक् शर्धाँ॑स्यग्ने अजरस्य धक्षतः ॥

2. O learned man, urged by knowledge, when thou roamest about soon acquiring according to thy desire medicinal herbs and food, undecaying, dispelling the darkness of ignorance like fire, thy powers succeed in different enterprises, as do the arrows of men on chariots fly in different directions ! (983)

३. मेधाकारं विदथस्य प्रसाधनमग्निँ॑ होतारं परिभूतरं मतिम् ।
    त्वामर्भस्य हविषः समानमित् त्वां महो वृणते नान्यं त्वत् ॥

3. O God, the Waker of wisdom, the Highest Source of knowledge, the Leader of all, the Refuge of all, the Displayer of His strength all round, the Controller of thought, for knowledge, great or small, we choose Thee alike, none else but Thee ! (984)

VIII

१. पुरूरुणा चिद्धस्त्यवो नूनं वां वरुण । मित्र वँ॑सि वाँ॑सुमतिम् ॥

1. Ye Mitra and Varuṇa, verily highly great is your protection. Ye both give me good counsel ! (985)[2]

२. ता वाँ॑ सभ्यगद्र्ह्वाणेषमश्याम धाम च । वयं वां मित्रा स्याम ॥

2. Free from malice are Ye both. May we acquire strength and glory through You; and ever remain attached to you. (986)

३. पातं नो मित्रा पायुभिरुत त्रायेथाँ॑ सुत्रात्रा । साह्याम दस्यून् तनूभिः ॥

3. Ye Mitra and Varuṇa, guard us with Your guards, save us with Your devices of safety May we subdue by ourselves the feelings of violence. (987)

IX

१. उत्तिष्ठन्नोजसा सह पीत्वा शिप्रे अवेपयः । सोममिन्द्र चमू सुतम् ॥

1. O soul, realising the force of organs and breaths, like a King of his army at the time of coronation, arising in thy might, thou bringest into motion, knowledge and action, thy jaws! (988)

---

[1]Just as fire consumes all plants and forest trees, and takes them in its grip, so does God keep all objects under His control, as a man takes food in his mouth.
[2]Mitra and Varuṇa are the in-going and out-going breaths, which maintain our body, and lend us sound advice to practise prāṇāyāma and keep ourselves healthy.
    They may also refer to the King and queen, the Speaker of the Assembly and the Commander-in-Chief.

२. अनु त्वा रोदसी उभे स्पर्धमानमददेताम् । इन्द्र यद्दस्युहाभवः ॥

2. O advancing soul, when thou overcomest moral weaknesses, the Prāna and Apāna, in thy wake, derive delight ! (989)

३. वाचमष्टापदीमहं नवस्रक्तिमृतावृधम् । इन्द्रात् परितन्वं ममे ॥

3. I receive from God, the knowledge of the vast, eight-footed Vedic speech, with nine parts, which is the urger of supreme truth. (990)[1]

X

१. इन्द्राग्नी युवामिमे ३ऽभि स्तोमा अनूषत । पिबत ॐ शम्भुवा सुतम् ॥

1. O preceptor and disciple, these words of praise have been uttered for Ye. Ye benefactors, imbibe knowledge ! (991)

२. या वा ॐ सन्ति पुरुस्पृहो नियुतो दाशुषे नरा । इन्द्राग्नी ताभिरा गतम् ॥

2. O teacher and preacher, the leaders of men, come with Your desirable definite beliefs and ideas, which Ye entertain for a charitable person ! (992)

३. ताभिरा गच्छतं नरोपेद ॐ सवन ॐ सुतम् । इन्द्राग्नी सोमपीतये ॥

3. Ye heroes, teacher and preacher, come to this well-prepared Yajna with Your enviable characteristics, for leading us on the path of virtue ! (993)

XI

१. अर्षा सोम द्युमत्तमोऽभि द्रोणानि रोरुवत् । सीदन्योनौ वनेष्वा ॥

1. O most beautiful soul, resting in God, thy Refuge, roam in different worlds and reside in mortal bodies preaching aloud truth ! (994)[2]

२. अप्सा इन्द्राय वायवे वरुणाय मरुद्भ्यः । सोमा अर्षन्तु विष्णवे ॥

2. Let learned persons, the comprehenders of knowledge and action, move about, for the amelioration of soul, for mastering Prāna, Apāna, and other breaths, and for the realisation of the knowledge of God. (995)

[1]Eight footed: Consisting of four Vedas Rig, Yajur, Sām, Atharva, and four Up Vedas, Ājur Veda, medicine, Dhanur Veda, military science, Gāndharva Veda, music, and Arth Veda, political science.
Nine parts: (1) Shiksha, the science of articulation and pronunciation.
(2) Kalpa, rituai (3) Vyākaraṇa, Grammar, (4) Nighanṭu Glossary of Vedic words, (5) Nirukta, Etymological explanation of difficult Vedic words, (6) Chhand, Prosody, (7) Jyotish, Astronomy, (8) Dharam-Shāstra, Code of morality, (9) Mimānsa-Correct interpretation of the rituals of the Veda and the settlement of dubious points in regard to Vedic texts. These nine sciences help in arriving at the right interpretation of the Vedas.
[2]See verse 503.
After death, the soul roams in different worlds before assuming a bodily form. This idea is expressed in the Yajurveda. 39-6.

३. इषं तोकाय नो दधदस्मभ्यⷨ सोम विश्वतः । आ पवस्व सहस्रिणम् ॥

3. O God, bestowing food upon our progeny from every side, pour on us riches thousandfold ! (996)

XII

१. सोम उ ष्वाणः सोतृभिरधि ष्णुभिरवीनाम् ।
अश्वयेव हरिता याति धारया मन्द्रया याति धारया ॥

1. Just as Soma extracted from the stones of the mountains by the priests, goes up in a fast-moving greenish stream of fume from the altar, so is God realised by the devotees, worshipped with deep concentration of mind. (997)[1]

२. अनूपे गोमान् गोभिरक्षाः सोमो दुग्धाभिरक्षाः ।
समुद्रं न संवरणान्यग्मन् मन्दी मदाय तोशते ॥

2. Just as a cowherd takes Kine for grazing to a low marshy place, so do the streams of delight, full of knowledge pure like milk, flow down to the heart. Just as waters flow to the ocean, so do spiritual joys flow to a calm soul. The soul, absorbed in happiness, goes forward for acquiring still greater happiness. (998)

XIII

१. यत्सोम चित्रमुक्थ्य दिव्यं पार्थिवं वसु । तन्नः पुनान आ भर ॥

1. O Purifying God, bring to us the wondrous, laudable, excellent treasure, that exists in earth ! (999)[2]

२. वृषा पुनान आयूⷨषि स्तनयन्नधि बर्हिषि । हरिः सन्योनिमासदः ॥

2. O God, the Bestower of all comforts, preaching truth unto us by Thy presence in the body, purifying the lives of men, alleviating miseries manifest Thyself in the heart ! (1000)

३. युवⷨ हि स्थः स्वःपती इन्द्रश्च सोम गोपती । ईशाना पिप्यतं धियः ॥

3. For Ye twain, God, Soul, are Lords of knowledge, happiness, men and bodily organs; as mighty ones, develop our intellects. (1001)

XIV

१. इन्द्र मदाय वावृधे शवसे वृत्रहा नृभिः ।
तमिन्महत्स्वाजिषूतिमर्भे हवामहे स वाजेषु प्र नोऽविषत् ॥

[1] See verse 515.
[2] See verse 411.

1. A King, the subduer of the turbulent, advances to joy and strength, with the aid of heroes. Him only we invoke for help in battles whether great or small. May he aid us in, our conflicts. (1002)

२. अ्रसि हि वीर सेन्योऽसि भूरि परादि: ।
   अ्रसि दभ्रस्य चिद्वृद्धो यजमानाय शिक्षसि सुन्वते भूरि ते वसु ॥

2. O Valiant King ! thou art the well-wisher of the army, thou art the conqueror of many foes, thou art the strengthener of even the feeble, thou givest thy great wealth to the sacrificer, who advances happiness ! (1003)

३. यदुदीरत आजयो घृष्णवे धीयते धनम् ।
   युङ्क्ष्वा मदच्युता हरी कं हन: कं वसौ दधोऽस्माउ इन्द्र वसौ दध: ॥

3. Glory is achieved by a strong soul, who overcomes all impediments in life's struggle. O soul, when the organs of cognition and action, controlled by thee, act as thy helper, thou removing all obstacles, and distributing riches, bestowest prosperity on us! (1004)[1]

XV

१. स्वादोरित्था विषुवतो मधो: पिबन्ति गौर्य: ।
   या इन्द्रेण सयावरीर्वृष्णा मदन्ति शोभथा वस्वीरनु स्वराज्यम् ॥

1. The rays, which reside in the sun, and help men in their habitation, enjoy the sweet Soma, when offered as an oblation into the fire. They feel satisfied with lightning, the bringer of rain, and look beautiful as they emanate from the Sun. (1005)[2]

२. ता अस्य पृशनायुव: सोमउ श्रीणन्ति पृश्नय: ।
   प्रिया इन्द्रस्य धेनवो वज्रउ हिन्वन्ति सायकं वस्वीरनु स्वराज्यम् ॥

2. These lovely organs, longing for the proximity of the soul, in their search for essence, strengthen knowledge. Thy create asceticism, the killer of desires. The soul-forces reside in it, under its brilliant control. (1006)

३. ता अस्य नमसा सह: सपर्यन्ति प्रचेतस: ।
   व्रतान्यस्य सश्चिरे पुरूणि पूर्वचित्तये वस्वीरनु स्वराज्यम् ॥

3. With veneration, passing wise, the organs honour the soul's forbearance. For acquiring full knowledge, the organs follow many laws for the amelioration of the soul. (1007)

---

[1]See verse 414.
[2]Just as a hawk flies fast and sits down, so Soma through Homa, rises up in the sky, and comes back to the mountain its home in the shape of rain.
See verse 473.

XVI

१. श्रसाव्य ॐ शुर्मंदायाप्सु दक्षो गिरिष्ठा: । श्येनो न योनिमासदत् ॥

1. Strong, mountain-born Soma, hath been pressed in the streams for rapturous joy. Hawk-like it settles in its home. (1008)

२. शुभ्रमन्धो देववातमप्सु धौतं नृभि: सुतम् । स्वदन्ति गाव: पयोभि: ॥

2. The learned taste with food juices, the fair, life infusing, spiritual delight, beloved of sages, purified through contemplation, and realised by the Yogis. (1009)

३. आदीमश्वं न हेतारमशूशुभन्नमृताय । मधो रस ॐ सधमादे ॥

3. Then, just as Kings decorate a horse in the battlefield, so does an active soul, adorn this spiritual joy in his heart, for the acquisition of salvation. (1010)

XVII

१. श्रभि द्युम्नं बृहद्यश इषस्पते दिदीहि देव देवयुम् । वि कोशं मध्यमं युव ॥

1. O Refulgent God, Lord of food, make high and splendid glory shine all round. Unclose the covering of the mind, that longs for the learned ! (1011)[1]

२. श्रा वच्यस्व सुदक्ष चम्वो: सुतो विशां वह्निनं विश्पति: ।
वृष्टि दिव: पवस्व रीतिमपो जिन्वन् गविष्टये धिय: ॥

2. O Mighty God, like a King bearing the burden of administering his subjects, and standing in the midst of two armies, for the good of humanity, sending down waters, pour rain on us from heaven, for ripening our harvest. and develop our intellects ! (1012)[2]

XVIII

१. प्राणा शिशुर्महीना ॐ हिन्वन्नृतस्य दीधितिम् । विश्वा परि प्रिया भुवध द्विता ॥

1. Soma, the child-like supporter of mankind, granting us the lustre of the Yajna, surpasses all nice oblations, and doubly stands on the earth and in the sky. (1013)

[1]Soma stands on the earth, when it is put into the fire, in the form of an oblation. It stands in the sky, when it rises in its rarefied form of smoke. Just as a child, when grown up supports men, so does Soma contribute to the health and vigour of men.

[2]Sāyana has translated Trita as a Rishi. This explanation as inacceptable as there is no history in the Veda. Trita means thought, word and deed.

Some commentators have explained Sapta Dhama as seven metres as Gayatri. Trishtup Anushtup, Brihati, Jagti, Ushnik and Pankti. Pt. Jaidev Vidyalankar translates it as seven breaths besides Prāna, Apāna, Vyāna, Udāna, Samāna, Kurma, Krikla, Dev Dutta, Dhananjaya. Griffith writes, this stanza is almost unintelligible, and its meaning is obscure. Sorry, Griffith has not been able to understand the significance of this stanza.

२. उप त्रितस्य पाष्यो॒३रभक्त यद् गुहा पदम् । यज्ञस्य सप्त धामभिरध प्रियम् ॥

2. When a Yogi, worshipping God through thought, word and deed, gains stability in the inmost recesses of the heart, and feels joy betwixt Prāna and Apāna, adamant like a stone, he realises the pleasing, spiritual felicity in the upper seven breaths of the sacrificing soul. (1014)

३. त्रीणि त्रितस्य धारया पृष्ठेष्वेरयद्रयिम् । मिमीते अस्य योजना वि सुक्रतुः ॥

3. A Yoga practising soul, through the steady abstraction of the mind, realises its three stations. In all these stations the soul displays its brilliant glory. A disciplined Yogi full well knows through Yoga these three stations of the soul. (1015)[1]

XIX

१. पवस्व वाजसातये पवित्रे धारया सुतः । इन्द्राय सोम विष्णवे देवेभ्यो मधुमत्तरः ॥

1. O learned person, urged by steady intellect, for the acquisition of knowledge, constantly shedding happiness, manifest thyself, for spreading the light of soul and God, and for the good of literary persons ! (1016)[2]

२. त्वाꣳ रिहन्ति धीतयो हरि पवित्रे अद्रुहः । वत्सं जातं न मातरः पवमान विधर्मणि ॥

2. O God, just as milch-kine lick the newly born calf, so do the modes of contemplation, in the pure heart, the seat of concentration, relish Thee, the Remover of afflictions ! (1017)

३. त्वं द्यां च महिव्रत पृथिवीं चाति जभ्रिषे । प्रति द्रापिममुञ्चथाः पवमान महित्वना ॥

3. O Lord of mighty actions, Thou transgressest the Heaven and the Earth. O God, with Thy majesty, Thou sustainest the universe ! (1018)

XX

१. इन्दुर्वाजी पवते गोन्योधा इन्द्रे सोमः सह इन्वन्मदाय ।
हन्ति रक्षो बाधते पर्यरातिं वरिवस्कृण्वन् वृजनस्य राजा ॥

1. The Soma juice, possessing the property of trickling, lending vigour to the organs, infusing strength in the heart, flows for joy. It quells malignity, and slays all devilish diseases, Being the source of nice wealth, it is the King of strength. (1019)

[1]Three Stations (1) Brahm Randhra, ब्रह्म रन्ध्र. (2) Ājnā Chakra. आज्ञा चक्र A mystical Circle or diagram. (3) Manipura: The Navel.
OR
(1) मूलाधारः a mystical circle above the organs of generation (2) हृदयः Heart.
(3) भ्रूमध्यः the space between the eyebrows.
A Yogi in Samadhi rivets his soul on these three places according to its will.
[2]See verse 540.

२. अध धारया मध्वा पृचानस्तिरो रोम पवते अद्रिदुग्धः ।
इन्दुरिन्द्रस्य सख्यं जुषाणो देवो देवस्य मत्सरो मदाय ॥

2. Spiritual joy, achieved through stern austerity, united with the steady abstraction of the mind, overcoming all intervening obstacles, manifests, itself. Winning the love of soul, the lustrous joy becomes the source of happiness for the soul. (1020)

३. अभि व्रतानि पवते पुनानो देवो देवान्त्स्वेन रसेन पृश्चन् ।
इन्दुर्धर्माण्यृतुथा वसानो दश क्षिपो अव्यत सानो अव्ये ॥

3. Powerful semen, satisfying the learned with its delightful essence, pure in nature by itself, ennobling all actions, pervades the body. The soul, accomplishing its attributes according to each season, acquires the ten fast moving organs, in the happiness-imbibing heart. (1021)[1]

XXI

१. आ ते अग्न इधीमहि द्युमन्तं देवाजरम् ।
यद्ध स्या ते पनीयसी समिद्दीदयति द्यवीषऽ स्तोतृभ्य आ भर ॥

1. O Omniscient, Refulgent God, for Thy attainment, we kindle our undecaying, immortal, everlasting soul. The highly praiseworthy light of the sun, that shines in heaven, has also emanated from Thee. Grant knowledge and food to those who sing Thy praise ! (1022)[2]

२. आ ते अग्न ऋचा हविः शुक्रस्य ज्योतिषस्पते ।
सुश्चन्द्र दस्म विश्पते हव्यवाट् तुभ्यऽ ह्यत इषऽ स्तोतृभ्य आ भर ॥

2. O Lord of luminous objects, to Thee, the Splendid, we consecrate the soul, like an oblation with the Vedic verse. O Bestower of joy, Remover of impediments, Sustainer of the universe, Lord of all the subjects, grant knowledge and food to those who sing Thy praise ! (1023)

३. आ ओभे सुश्चन्द्र विश्पते दर्वीं श्रीणीष आसनि ।
उतो न उत्पुपूर्या उक्थेषु शवसस्पत इषऽ स्तोतृभ्य आ भर ॥

3. O Omnipotent, Glorious, Lord of men, Thou maturest both knowledge and action under Thy hold. Fulfil our desires in religious acts. Grant knowledge and food to those who sing Thy praise ! (1024)

---

[1]The Yogis who live in perpetual celebacy and abstain from sexual intercourse make their semen grant them peace of mind, toleration, and physical strength in all seasons.
[2]See verse 419.

XXII

१. इन्द्राय साम गायत विप्राय बृहते बृहत् । ब्रह्मकृते विपश्चिते पनस्यवे ॥

1. Sing a great song for the Lofty, Wise God, for Him Who creates food-stuffs through rain, for the Learned God, Who is Worthy of adoration. (1025)[1]

२. त्वमिन्द्राभिभूरसि त्वँ सूर्यमरोचयः । विश्वकर्मा विश्वदेवो महाँ असि ॥

2. O God, Thou art the Conqueror, Thou givest splendour to the Sun, Thou art the Maker of all things, Thou art the God of gods, and art Mighty! (1026)

३. विभ्राजञ्ज्योतिषा स्व३रगच्छो रोचनं दिवः । देवास्त इन्द्र सख्याय येमिरे ॥

3. O God, the Illuminator of the world with Thy light, the Illuminator of Heaven, the Enjoyer of eternal happiness, the learned strive to win Thy friendly love ! (1027)

XXIII

१. असावि सोम इन्द्र ते शविष्ठ धृष्णवा गहि ।
आ त्वा पृणक्त्विन्द्रिँ रजः सूर्यो न रश्मिभिः ॥

1. O mighty King, the Conqueror of foes, come unto us for our protection, we have made thee enjoy the tranquillity of mind. May our mind be united with thee, just as the sun fills the universe with its rays ! (1028)[2]

२. आ तिष्ठ वृत्रहन् रथं युक्ता ते ब्रह्मणा हरी ।
अर्वाचीनँ सु ते मनो ग्रावा कृणोतु वग्नुना ॥

2. O God, the Remover of impediments, ride on this conveyance, the soul, which has been yoked by Divine device, with two horses of the organs of cognition and action. May a worshipper with his praise-song, subordinate his mind to Thee ! (1029)

३. इन्द्रमिद्धरी वहतोऽप्रतिधृष्टशवसम् । ऋषीणाँ सुष्टुतीरुप यज्ञं च मानुषाणाम् ॥

3. Knowledge and action bring the soul, full of resistless power, to the praise-songs of the sages, and God worthy of worship by men. (1030)[3]

---

[1] See verse 388.
[2] See verse 347.
[3] Knowledge and action are two horses of the soul, which take it to God.

BOOK IV
Chapter 1

I

१. ज्योतिर्यंज्ञस्य पवते मधु प्रियं पिता देवानां जनिता विभूवसुः ।
दधाति रत्नꣳ स्वधयोरपीच्यं मदिन्तमो मत्सर इन्द्रियो रसः ॥

1. The Omnipresent God, the Illuminator of the entire universe, Most Excellent, Realizable through Yogic Samadhi (concentration), the Lord of the forces of Nature, the Creator, All-Pervading, subtly residing in soul and matter, Most Joyous, the Best of cheerers, the Well-Wisher of souls, grants us salvation. (1031)

२. अभिक्रन्दन् कलशं वाज्यर्षति पतिर्दिवः शतधारो विचक्षणः ।
हरिर्मित्रस्य सदनेषु सीदति मर्मृं जानोऽविभिः सिन्धुभिर्वृषा ॥

2. The Omnipotent God, the Lord of Heaven, the Master of myriad powers, Far-Seeing, resides with full force in the hearts of living beings. The Remover of all afflictions, lords supreme in the dwelling places of His companion, the soul. God, the Bestower of all joys, is sought for again and again, by the soul through Prāṇāyāma, the breath-force ever moving like an ocean. (1032)[1]

३. अग्रे सिन्धूनां पवमानो अर्षस्यग्रे वाचो अग्रियो गोषु गच्छसि ।
अग्रे वाजस्य भजसे महद् धनꣳ स्वायुधः सोतृभिः सोम सूयसे ॥

3. O pure soul, thou goest before the organs, before speech, and before breaths. As master of knowledge and power, thou acquirest the vast treasure of delight, even before, Prāna. Equipped with manifold powers, thou art realised by the Yogis! (1033)[2]

II

१. असृक्षत प्र वाजिनो गव्या सोमासो अश्वया । शुक्रासो वीरयाशवः ॥

1. Powerful, active, shining souls exert, longing for mastery over speech, control over senses, and having brave sons. (1034)[3]

२. शुम्भमाना ऋतायुभिर्मृं ज्यमाना गभस्त्योः । पवन्ते वारे अव्यये ।

2. The Yogis extolled by seekers after truth, and purified through knowledge and Yoga, roam in Immortal, Fearless God. (1035)[4]

---

[1]'Dwelling places' means hearts.
[2]The true nature of the soul cannot be perceived by our physical organs, words and Prānas. Soul is higher than these and beyond their grasp. Yogis alone can realise it.
[3]See verse 482.
[4]'Thy place' means the heart.

३. ते विश्वा दाशुषे वसु सोमा दिव्यानि पार्थिवा । पवन्तामान्तरिक्ष्या ॥

3. These Yogis pour forth all heavenly, terrestrial and mid-air treasures. on the disciple, who dedicates himself to them. (1036)

III

१. पवस्व देववीरति पवित्रꣳ सोम रꣳह्या । इन्द्रमिन्दो वृषा विश ॥

1. O soul, the urger of breaths and earthly objects, swiftly manifest thyself in the heart. Full of lustre and glory, raining joys, realise thou the nature of God! (1037)

२. श्रा वच्यस्व महि प्सरो वृषेन्दो द्युम्नवत्तम: । श्रा योनि धर्णसि: सद: ॥

2. O soul, the bestower of delights, highly luminous and glorious, display vast knowledge. Armed with fortitude, rest in thy place! (1038)

३. श्रधुक्षत प्रियं मधु धारा सुतस्य वेधस: । अपो वसिष्ट सुक्रतु: ॥

3. The steady abstraction of the mind of a learned Yogi, equipped with Yogic accomplishments, yields spiritual joy. The Yogi devoted to the performance of religious acts, controls all his deeds. (1039)

४. महान्तं त्वा महीरन्वापो श्रर्षन्ति सिन्धव: । यद्गोभिर्वासयिष्यसे ॥

4. O soul, when thou wilt be enwrapped in the rays of knowledge, the great conceptions of action will follow in the wake of Thee, the mighty ! (1040)

५. समुद्रो श्रप्सु मामृजे विष्टम्भो धरुणो दिव: । सोम: पवित्रे श्रस्मयु: ॥

5. The soul, the mine of extreme joy, our shelter, and the prop of light, is purified by actions. It becomes our support, in the heart. (1041)

६. श्रचिक्रदद्वृषा हरिर्महान्मित्रो न दर्शत: । सꣳ सूर्येण दिद्युते ॥,

6. Fair to behold like a friend, the highly attractive soul, endowed with the capacity of bestowing happiness, shines with its power of persuasion. (1042)

७. गिरस्त इन्द ओजसा ममृ ज्यन्ते अपस्युव: । याभिर्मदाय शुम्भसे ॥

7. O soul, through thy might, songs preaching knowledge and action, are beautified. With them we extol thee for rapturous joy ! (1043)[1]

८. तं त्वा मदाय घृष्वय उ लोकक्तनुमीमहे । तव प्रशस्तये महे ॥

8. O God, for acquiring the joy, the soul derives by coming in contact with

[1]Them refers to songs.

Thee, we pray unto Thee, the Maker of the universe, so that Thou mayest have exalted praise ! (1044)

८. गोषा इन्दो नृषा अस्यश्वसा वाजसा उत । आत्मा यज्ञस्य पूर्व्यः ॥

9. O God, Thou art the Giver of knowledge, progeny, enterprise and prosperity. Thou art the Primeval Lord of the universe ! (1045)

१०. अस्मभ्यमिन्दविन्द्रियं मघोः पवस्व धारया । पर्जन्यो वृष्टिमाँ इव ॥

10. O God, pour on us, with Thy Immortal strength, the soul-strengthening elixir, like a cloud that sends rain ! (1046)

IV

१. सना च सोम जेषि च पवमान महि श्रवः । अथा नो वस्यसस्कृधि ॥

1. O Immaculate God, bring us victory, make us win high renown. May Thou make us better than we are ! (1047)

२. सना ज्योतिः सना स्वाइर्विश्वा च सोम सौभगा । अथा नो वस्यसस्कृधि ॥

2. O God, grant us the light of knowledge, happiness and all felicities, Make us better than we are ! (1048)

३. सना दक्षमुत क्रतुमप सोम मृधो जहि । अथा नो वस्यसस्कृधि ॥

3. O God, grant us skilful strength and mental power, drive away our foes. Make us better than we are ! (1049)

४. पवीतारः पुनीतन सोममिन्द्राय पातवे । अथा नो वस्यसस्कृधि ॥

4. O learned realisers of God, create happiness for the enjoyment of the soul, and make us better than we are ! (1050)

५. त्वँ सूर्ये न आ भज तव क्रत्वा तवोतिभिः । अथा नो वस्यसस्कृधि ॥

5. O God, through Thy power of knowledge and powers of protection, make us realise Thee, the All-urger. Make us better than we are ! (1051)

६. तव क्रत्वा तवोतिभिर्ज्योक् पश्येम सूर्यम् । अथा नो वस्यसस्कृधि ॥

6. O God, through Thy, knowledge and aids, may we long look upon Thee, the Diffuser of Light. Make us better than we are! (1052)[1]

७. अभ्यर्ष स्वायुध सोम द्विबर्हसँ रयिम् । अथा नो वस्यसस्कृधि ॥

7. O God, possessing manifold strength, grant us riches which expand through knowledge and action. Make us better than we are! (1053)

[1]'Look upon Thee', means worship Thee.

८. अभ्याइर्षानिपच्युतो वाजिन्त्समत्सु सासहि: । अथा नो वस्यसस्कृधि ॥

8. O powerful, Immortal God, the Queller of sinners, come to our succour in our struggles against passions. Make us better than we are ! (1054)

९. त्वां यज्ञैरवीवृधन् पवमान विधर्मणि । अथा नो वस्यसस्कृधि ॥

9. O Pure God, the sages magnify Thee in the soul, through knowledge, action and penance. Make us better than we are ! (1055)

१०. रयि नश्चित्रमश्विनमिन्दो विश्वायुमा भर । अथा नो वस्यसस्कृधि ॥

10. O God, grant us wondrous, sense-controlling, life-prolonging spiritual force. Make us better than we are ! (1056)

V

१. तरत्स मन्दी धावति धारा सुतस्यान्धस: । तरत्स मन्दी धावति ॥

1. By drinking the life-infusing Soma juice, effused in a flow, a sage full of delight crosses the ocean of life, and marches fast on the path of progress. A sage crossing the ocean of life delightfully, goes fast on the path of progress. (1057)[1]

२. उस्रा वेद वसूनां मर्तस्य देव्यवस: । तरत्स मन्दी धावति ॥

2. The lustrous flow of Soma, the giver of riches, knows how to protect man. The soul of a Yogi full of intense delight, marches fast to God. (1058)

३. ध्वस्रयो: पुरुषन्त्योरा सहस्राणि दद्महे । तरत्स मन्दी धावति ॥

3. May we acquire the thousandfold power of knowledge that banishes affliction, and action that lends strength. With them the soul of a Yogi, full of intense delight marches fast to God. (1059)[2]

४. आ ययोस्त्रिꣳशतं तना सहस्राणि च दद्महे । तरत्स मन्दी धावति ॥

4. On the strength of God and soul, we pass our life for 3,00,000 days and nights, on the same strength the soul of a Yogi, full of intense delight, marches fast to God. (1060)[3]

---

[1]See verse 500. Repetition in the verse of तरत् समन्दी धावति is for the sake of emphasis.

[2]Them refers to the power of knowledge and action. Griffith translates Dhvasra and Purushanti as two kings who conferred great wealth on Taranta and Purumilha, two rishis of the family of Vidadaśva. See p. XXXIII of Max Muller's Rigveda, Vol. V. See Cowell's Note in Wilson's Translation. This explanation is inadmissible, as it smacks of history in the Vedas, whereas they are free from historical references. The word means knowledge and action.

[3]The life of a man can extend to three lakh days and nights, i.e., for more than 800 years,

VI

१. एते सोमा असृक्षत गृणानाः शवसे महे । मदिन्तमस्य धारया ॥

1. Through the firm joyous strength of the Most Gladdening God, may these learned preceptors be born, for acquiring vast knowledge, through the study and preaching of the Vedas. (1061)

२. अभि गव्यानि वीतये नृम्णा पुनानो अर्षसि । सनद्वाजः परि स्रव ॥

2. O God, for spreading light and beauty all round, Thou manifestest Thyself, purifying the hearts of men, worthy of imbibing knowledge. O Bestower of knowledge and strength, grant us knowledge and strength. (1062)

३. उत नो गोमतीरिषो विश्वा अर्ष परिष्टुभः । गृणानो जमदग्निना ॥

3. O God, eulogised by a Yogi, who visualises the soul, fulfil our Vedic desires and prayers. (1063)[1]

VII

१. इमꣳ स्तोममर्हते जातवेदसे रथमिव सं महेमा मनीषया ।
भद्रा हि नः प्रमतिरस्य सꣳसद्वग्ने सख्ये मा रिषामा वयं तव ॥

1. May we sing with our intellect, for the venerable preceptor, this praise song, that bestows happiness like knowledge. In his company may our knowledge contribute to our good. May we never suffer in his friendship. O Guru, we are thine ! (1064)[2]

२. भरामेध्मं कृणवामा हवीꣳषि ते चितयन्तः पर्वणापर्वणा वयम् ।
जीवातवे प्रतरꣳ साधया धियोग्ने सख्ये मा रिषामा वयं तव ॥

2. O God, may we realise Thy glory, may we sacrifice for Thee valuable things. May we gain strength and knowledge at each successive holy time. Nicely fulfil our knowledge and action, [so that we may prolong our lives. May we never suffer in Thy friendship ! (1065)[3]

३. शकेम त्वा समिधꣳ साधया धियस्त्वे देवा हविरदन्त्याहुतम् ।
त्वमादित्याꣳ आ वह तान् हूꣳ३मस्यग्ने सख्ये मा रिषामा वयं तव ॥

3. Refine our intellect, may we be able to serve Thee, O Refulgent God. The learned enjoy what is offered in charity in Thy name. O God, grant us divine virtues, we long for them. Let us not, in Thy friendship, suffer harm ! (1066)

[1]Griffith translates Jamdagni as the name of a Rishi, following Sāyana. This interpretation is unacceptable, as the Vedas are free from historical references. The words means a Yogi who visualises his soul.
[2]See verse 66. This verse can refer to God and soul as well.
[3]The verse may refer to a preceptor, Guru as well.

VIII

१. प्रति वा ॐ सूर उदिते मित्रं गृणीषे वरुणम् । अर्यमण ॐ रिशादसम् ॥

1. On the awakening of the soul, I voluntarily admire judgment and justice, each acting as my guardian, and remover of impediments. (1067)[1]

२. राया हिरण्यया मतिरियमवृकाय शवसे । इयं विप्रा मेधसातये ॥

2. May this fascinating, precious power of discernment, be for the attainment of non-violent strength free from crookedness. May this power of discrimination be for the acquirement of purity. (1068)

३. ते स्याम देव वरुण ते मित्र सूरिभि: सह । इष ॐ स्वश्च धीमहि ॥

3. O Master of sinless nature, O Emblem of fitness and comradeship, may we be Thine with our impulses. May knowledge and supreme joy be our ideal! (1069)[2]

IX

१. भिन्धि विश्वा अप द्विष: परि बाधो जही मृध: । वसु स्पाहँ तदा भर ॥

1. O King suppress all feelings of hatred, wipe out the sentiment of troubling violence, be endowed with enviable spiritual wealth! (1070)[3]

२. यस्य ते विश्वमानुषग्भूरेदत्तस्य वेदति । वसु स्पाहँ तदा भर ॥

2. O God, give us the wealth we long for, which Thou abundantly givest, and the world ever feels for it! (1071)

३. यद्वीडाविन्द्र यत् स्थिरे यत् पर्शाने पराभृतम् । वसु स्पाहँ तदा भर ॥

3. O God, grant us the desirable firmness and prosperity found in a formidable, steady, and contemplative person! (1072)[4]

X

१. यज्ञस्य हि स्थ ऋत्विजा सस्नी वाजेषु कर्मसु । इन्द्राग्नी तस्य बोधतम् ॥

1. O God and Guru (Teacher) Ye both are verily the promoters of the Yajna of life. Ye are well versed in knowledge and action. Keep me awake in this life's struggle! (1073)[5]

---

[1]Griffith translates Mitra and Varuṇa as deities, as does Sâyana. Pt. Jaidev Vidyalankar, Swami Tulsi Ram translate these words as Prāna and Apāna.
[2]Master refers to God.
[3]See verse 134.
[4]See verse 207.
[5]Yajña means struggle.

२. तोशासा रथयावाना वृत्रहणापराजिता । इन्द्राग्नी तस्य बोधतम् ॥

2. O God and Guru, in my life's struggle, Ye are the Removers of obstacles, the contributors to happiness, the Dispellers of ignorance, and invincible. Keep me awake in this life's struggle! (1074)

३. इदं वां मदिरं मध्वधुक्षन्नद्रिभिनॆरः । इन्द्राग्नी तस्य बोधतम् ॥

3. O God and Guru, learned persons, through austere acts of penance, acquire this delightful knowledge of Ye both. Keep me awake in this life's struggle! (1075)

XI

१. इन्द्रायेन्दो मरुत्वते पवस्व मधुमत्तमः । अर्कस्य योनिमासदम् ॥

1. O Soma, full of intense sweetness, go up to the lightning in a cloud filled with air. I sit near the altar of a Yajna! (1076)[1]

२. तं त्वा विप्रा वचोविदः परिष्कृण्वन्ति धर्णसिम् । सं त्वा मृजन्त्यायवः ॥

2. Sages, who know the essence of the Vedas, sing Thy praise, O God, the Sustainer of the Universe. Men realise Thee through Yoga and purify their soul. (1077)

३. रसं ते मित्रो अर्यमा पिबन्तु वरुणः कवे । पवमानस्य मरुतः ॥

3. O sage, may Mitra, Aryama, Varuṇa and other airs in the body, enjoy thy ever-flowing strength! (1078)[2]

XII

१. मृज्यमानः सुहस्त्या समुद्रे वाचमिन्वसि । रयि पिशङ्गं बहुलं पुरुस्पृहं पवमानाभ्यर्षसि ॥

1. O soul, the sagacious destroyer of ignorance, being purified in the ocean-like heart, thou preachest the Vedas. O purifier of the heart from sin, thou acquirest, yellow, abundant, much desired riches! (1079)[3]

२. पुनानो वारे पवमानो अव्यये वृषो अचिक्रदद्वने ।
देवानाꣳ सोम पवमान निष्कृतं गोभिरञ्जानो अर्षसि ॥

2. Purified through the control of breath, O pervading soul, showering happiness, thou spreadest joy in the universe. O pure soul, exhibiting thyself

---

[1]See verse 472. Soma put into the fire as an oblation, being rarefied goes up to the sky to come back in the form of rain. I refers to the performer of a Yajña, who sits near the altar for Performing the Yajña.

[2]Mitra, the air that saves us from death. Aryamā means Saman air. Varuṇa means Apān air. Maruts mean other airs.

[3]Yellow means gold-like. See verse 517.

with the rays of the light of knowledge, thou residest in the heart, the stay and support of the organs! (1080)[1]

XIII

१. एतमु त्यं दश क्षिपो मृजन्ति सिन्धुमातरम् । समादित्येभिरख्यत ॥

1. The ten vital life-breaths verily decorate this soul, which perceives all objects through the organs of cognition. (1081)[2]

२. समिन्द्रेणोत वायुना सुत एति पवित्र आ । सꣳ सूर्यस्य रश्मिभि: ॥

2. The joy derived by the soul through the control of breath fills the heart. It is united with the beams of knowledge. (1082)

३. स नो भगाय वायवे पूष्णे पवस्व मधुमान् । चारुर्मित्रे वरुणे च ॥

3. The Divine and Lovely God manifests Himself for our prosperity, physical vigour, and spiritual strength, as our Friend and Alleviator of afflictions. (1083)

XIV

१. रेवतीनं: सधमाद इन्द्रे सन्तु तुविवाजा: । क्षुमन्तो याभिर्मंदेम ॥

1. With the pleasure of the King, may our subjects be rich and strong. May we, wealthy in food, rejoice with them. (1084)[3]

२. आ घ त्वावान् त्मना युक्त स्तोतृभ्या धृष्णवीयान: । ऋणोरक्षं न चक्र्यो: ॥

2. O soul, the subduer of lust and anger, just as the axle of the wheels of a car, takes it to distant places, so dost thou, concentrated in thyself, taking us, the praisers, to our goal, attain to salvation! (1085)[4]

३. आ. यद् दुव: शतक्रतवा कामं जरितृणाम् । ऋणोरक्षं न शचीभि: ॥

3. Just as the axle with its spokes takes a car to distant places, so dost thou, O soul, the master of hundredfold powers, grant to the praisers, the wealth desired by them! (1086)

[1]Pervading soul, means the soul that pervades the body, unlike God. Who pervades the entire universe.
[2]Ten vital life breaths are Prāna, Apāna Samāna, Udān, Vyāna, Nāga, Kūrma, Krikla, Dev Dutta, Dhananjaya. Organs of cognition are Gyāna Indriyas. The verse may refer to God as well. In that case दशक्षिप: will mean ten directions, and आदित्य will mean the sun.
[3]Them refers to the subjects. Our refers to the officials.
[4]Griffith remarks: The lines in this and the following stanza referring to the axle and the chariot are somewhat obscure and have been variously interpreted. I accept Ludwigs explanation. I see no obscurity in these verses. The sense is clear. The simile of the axle and chariot is quite apposite.

XV

१. सुरूपकृत्नुमूतये सदुघामिव गोदुहे । जुहूमसि द्यविद्यवि ॥

1. We daily invoke for our protection the King, the doer of nice deeds, just as we invoke a cow for him who milks. (1087)

२. उप न: सवना गहि सोमस्य सोमपा: पिब । गोदा इद्रेवतो मद: ॥

2. Come thou near us, O Acharya, the guardian of disciples, for spreading knowledge in the world. Make others as learned as thou art. The bestower of the vision of knowledge alone, pleases the soul, the seeker after desired objects! (1088)[1]

३. अथा ते अन्तमानां विद्याम सुमतीनाम् । मा नो अति ख्य आ गहि ॥

3. O God, may we thus acquire Thy knowledge from the learned sages, who enjoy Thy proximity. Forget us not, come hither-ward to give us shelter! (1089)

XVI

१. उभे यदिन्द्र रोदसी आपप्राथोषा इव । महान्त त्वा महीना ऽ सम्राजं चर्षणीनाम् ॥
देवी जनिभ्यजीजनन्द्रद्रा जनिभ्यजीजनत् ॥

1. Just as the Dawn fills the universe with light, so dost Thou, God, fill the Earth and Heaven with Thy lustre. Thy light, the Creator of the world, exhibits Thee, the Mightiest of the mighty, the Lord of men. Thy blessed light, the Creator of the world manifests Thee. (1090)[2]

२. दीर्घ ऽ ह्यङ्कुशं यथा शक्ति बिभर्षि मन्तुम: । पूर्वेण मघवन् पदा वयामजो यथा यम: ।
देवी जनिभ्यजीजनन्द्रद्रा जनिभ्यजीजनत् ॥

2. O Omniscient God, just as Thou bearest the far-fetching goad of knowledge. Thou possessest the power of its right application as well. O Glorious God, as Thou Unborn, the Controller of the universe, with Thy immemorial knowledge lordest over Matter, hence this gifted Matter, the Creator of the universe creates this world. This beneficent matter creates this world! (1091)[3]

३. अव स्म दुह्णायतो मर्तस्य तनुहि स्थिरम् ।
अधस्पदं तमीं कृधि यो अस्मा ऽ अभिदासति ।
देवी जनिभ्यजीजनन्द्रद्रा जनिभ्यजीजनत् ॥

---

[1] Achārya means the guru or preceptor. Bestower of the vision of knowledge means the preceptor. The verse may apply to God as well.

[2] See verse 379. Repetition of the words is meant for emphasis.

[3] The repetition in the last line is for the sake of emphasis. God is the most efficient, and Matter the physical cause of the universe. Griffith, Sāyana and some other commentators have translated अज: as goat, but the word may mean God as well, Who is free from the pangs of birth.

3. O God, relax that mortal's stubborn strength whose heart is bent on wickedness. Trample him down beneath Thy feet, who wants to enslave us. The gifted mother, Matter manifests Thy glory. The gracious Matter, the mother of all objects, manifests Thy glory ! (1092)[1]

XVII

१. परि स्वानो गिरिष्ठाः पवित्रे सोमो अक्षरत् । मदेषु सर्वधा असि ॥

1. O supreme bliss, perceivable through tongue, when achieved, thou beginnest to flow in the heart. O God, through Thy power of joy, Thou keepest all absorbed in joys ! (1093)[2]

२. त्वं विप्रस्त्वं कविर्मधु प्र जातमन्धसः । मदेषु सर्वधा असि ॥

2. O God, Thou art Wise and Developer of intellect, Grant us semen born of food. Thou keepest all absorbed in joys ! (1094)

३. त्वे विश्वे सजोषसो देवासः पीतिमाशत । मदेषु सर्वधा असि ॥

3. O God, all learned lovers of Thine, enjoy the juice of Thy felicity. Thou keepest all absorbed in joys ! (1095)

XVIII

१. स सुन्वे यो वसूनां यो रायामानेता य इडानाम् । सोमो यः सुक्षितीनाम् ॥

1. God, Who is the Bestower of riches, milch-kine, foods and houses wherein dwell our handsome children, is realised by the worshippers. (1096)[3]

२. यस्य त इन्द्रः पिबाद्यस्य मरुतो यस्य वार्यमणा भगः ।
आ येन मित्रावरुणा करामह एन्द्रमवसे महे ।

2. O God, the soul drinks of Thy felicity, all learned persons derive happiness from Thee, our powers of discernment and worldly enjoyment depend upon Thee. On Thy strength we set in motion the Prāna and Apāna. On Thy strength we visualise the soul. Thou art our Refuge and Giver of happiness ! (1097)

XIX

१. तं वः सखायो मदाय पुनानमभि गायत । शिशुं न हव्यैः स्वदयन्त गूर्तिभिः ॥

1. Friends, sing the praise of the chief Prāna, which removes impurities. Just as a child is appeased by offering him sweets and nice play things, so

[1]'Beneath Thy feet' means through Thy strength and power. The word feet has been used figuratively as God has got no feet.
[2]See verse 475.
[3]See verse 582.

should the soul be controlled through noble ideas and spiritual knowledge !
(1098)[1]

२. सं वत्स इव मातृभिरिन्दुर्हिन्वानो ग्रज्यते । देवावीर्मंदो मतिभि: परिष्कृत: ॥

2. Just as a calf, nourished by the cows, grows strong, so is a learned disciple, coached by the able preceptors, endowed with knowledge and noble virtues. He, the companion of the learned, the diffuser of joy, is decorated by contemplative men of learning. (1099)[2]

३. ग्रयं दक्षाय साधनोऽयСे शर्धाय वीतये । ग्रयं देवेभ्यो मधुमत्तर: सुत: ॥

3. A learned person is the accomplisher of mighty deeds, a striver after the acquisition of knowledge and glory. He is equipped with extreme sweetness for the welfare of scholars. (1100)

XX

१. सोमा: पवन्त इन्दवोऽस्मभ्यं गातुवित्तमा: । मित्रा: स्वाना ग्ररेपस: स्वाध्य: स्वविद: ॥

1. May the brilliant sages, the treaders on the right path, friendly, self reliant, sinless, reflective, full of knowledge, come unto us. (1101)

२. ते पूतासो विपश्चित: सोमासो दध्याशिर: । सूरासो न दर्शतासो जिगत्नवो ध्रुवा घृते ॥

2. May Aditya Brahmcharis, pure in heart, advanced in intellect, affable in nature, mature in contemplation, marchers on the path of progress towards God, visit us. (1102)

३. सुष्वाणासो व्यद्रिभिश्चिताना गोरधि त्वचि । इषमस्मभ्यमभित: समस्वरन् वसुविद: ॥

3. Receiving instruction under the guardianship of a noble teacher, and acquiring multifarious knowledge from the learned, may the masters of the knowledge of self, teach us moral law from every side. (1103)

XXI

१. ग्रया पवा पवस्वेना वसूनि माँश्चत्व इन्दो सरसि प्र धन्व ।
ब्रध्नश्चिद्यस्य वातो न जूति पुरुमेधाश्चित्तकवे नरं धात् ॥

1. O sentiment of happiness, with this purifying flow of thine, goad the Prānas; and flow in the fascinating heart. The soul itself feels thy rapidity as one feels the swift motion of the air. A Yogi, the lord of manifold intellectual powers, imbibes thee for taking the soul to its final goal! (1104)[3]

२. उत न एना पवया पवस्वाधि श्रुते श्रवाय्यस्य तीर्थे ।
षष्टिँसहस्रा नेगुतो वसूनि वृक्षं न पक्वं धूनवद्रणाय ॥

---

[1]See verse 548.
[2]Āditya Brahmchāris are those learned persons who observe celibacy for 48 years.
[1]See verse 541. Thee refers to the elixir of happiness.

2. O God, preach unto us more of this purifying knowledge, imparted by Thee, the Lord of the universe, in the Veda, our holy refuge. Just as an aspirant after fruit shakes a tree full of ripe fruits, and gets down many of them, so dost Thou, the Preserver of the innermost knowledge, grant for the pleasure of the soul, thousands of the gems of knowledge ! (1105)[1]

३. महीमे अस्य वृष नाम शूषे माऽश्चत्वे वा पृशने वा वधत्रे ।
  अस्वापयन् निगुतः स्नेहयच्चापामित्राँ अपाचितो अचेतः ॥

3. The two big tasks the soul has to perform in the heart, are the spread of happiness, and the suppression of evil conceptions. They are pleasant and nice, concern all and save all from misery. Sending to sleep lust and anger, the hidden foes, and exterminating them, O soul, drive away these foes of morality, drive away the ignorant and heartless persons ! (1106)[2]

XXII

१. अग्ने त्वं नो अन्तम उत त्राता शिवो भुवो वरूथ्यः ।

1. O God, through Omnipresence Thou art nearest to us, Worthy of worship, Thou art our Protector and Well-wisher ! (1107)[3]

२. वसुरग्निर्वंसुश्रवा अच्छा नक्षि द्युमत्तमो रयिं दाः ॥

2. O Omnipresent God, the source of spiritual knowledge, Most Resplendent, come, give us wealth of knowledge ! (1108)

३. तं त्वा शोचिष्ठ दीदिवः सुम्नाय नूनमीमहे सखिभ्यः ॥

3. To Thee, O Most Bright, O Radiant God, verily do we pray for happiness for our friends ! (1109)

XXIII

१. इमा नु कं भुवना सीषधेमेन्द्रश्च विश्वे च देवाः ।

1. May our soul and organs of senses, and all these existing worlds, contribute to our happiness. (1110)

२. यज्ञं च नस्तन्वं च प्रजां चादित्यैरिन्द्रः सह सीषधातु ॥

2. May God, bring to fruition our soul, our bodies, and our offspring, through learned persons. (1111)

[1]The Veda has been spoken of as a holy refuge. Just as spiritually advanced persons preach morality and truth to the pilgrims who visit them, so do the Vedas teach us religion when we approach them in a spirit of reverence considering them as holy scriptures. The words षष्टिं सहस्रा: may mean sixty thousand or 1060. I have translated them as thousands.
[2]'They' refers to tasks.
[3]See verse 448.

३. आदित्यैरिन्द्रः सगणो मरुद्भिरसमभ्यं भेषजा करत् ॥

3. May soul, with its powers of reflection, organs, and other potentialities, work as medicine to heal us. (1112)

XXIV

१. प्र वोऽर्चोप ॥ प्र व इन्द्राय वृत्रहन्तमाय विप्राय गाथं गायत यं जुजोषते ॥

२. अर्चन्त्यकं मरुतः स्वर्का आ स्तोभति श्रुतो युवा स इन्द्रः ॥

३. उप प्रक्षे मधुमति क्षियन्तः पुष्येम रयिं धीमहे त इन्द्र ॥

Praise and worship God nicely. (1113, 1114, 1115)[1]

Chapter 2

I

१. प्र काव्यमुशनेव ब्रुवाणो देवो देवानां जनिमा विवक्ति ।
महिव्रतः शुचिबन्धुः पावकः पदा वराहो अभ्येति रेभन् ॥

1. A wise, learned person, contributing to the happiness of mankind, and preaching the essence of Vedic knowledge fully explains the secret of the creation of all the objects of nature. The master of grand action and knowledge, the friend of the pious, the purifier of all, the utterer of excellent speech, preaching knowledge, attains to the happy stages of life. (1116)[2]

२. प्र हँसासस्तृपला वग्नुमच्छामादस्तं वृषगणा अयासुः ।
अङ्घोषिणं पवमानँ सखायो दुर्मषं वाणं प्र वदन्ति साकम् ॥

2. Yogis, the discriminators between truth and untruth, like swans, the discriminators between milk and water, controlling lust and anger, keeping in view the voice of conscience, practising deep concentration (Samadhi), through spiritual force and knowledge, possess a venerable soul. These friends of God, train the pure, irresistible soul, residing in the body. (1117)

३. स योजत उरुगायस्य जूतिं वृथा क्रीडन्तं मिमते न गावः ।
परीणसं कृणुते तिग्मश्रृङ्गो दिवा हरिर्ददृशे नक्तमृज्रः ॥

3. A Yogi realises through Samadhi the glory of God, the Possessor of grand virtues. Ordinary mortals have no knowledge of Him, Who easily creates, sustains and dissolves the universe. He (Yogi), the alleviator of all miseries, endowed with blazing halo, sheds diverse lustre like the sun, and

---

[1]Sāyana considers it as one verse, Other Commentators consider it to be the limbs, of three verses 'प्र च इन्द्राय' (446) अर्चन्त्यकं (445), उप प्रक्षे मधुम—(444). The combination of three verses into one is meant to show the song, named as 'Udvanshputra.'
[2]See verse 524.

full of light, travelling on the straight path of virtue, shines day and night. (1118)

४. प्र स्वानासो रथा इवार्वन्तो न अवस्यव: । सोमासो राये अक्रमु: ॥

4. Like cars that thunder on their way, like a fast horse, the pure, learned persons, longing for wealth, knowledge and prosperity, march forward for the attainment of supreme bliss. (1119)

५. हिन्वानासो रथा इव दधन्विरे गभस्त्यो: । भरास: कारिणामिव ॥

5. Like chariots that are urged to speed, like warriors fighting in a battle, they, progressing onward, achieve their goal through knowledge and action. (1120)[1]

६. राजानो न प्रशस्तिभि: सोमासो गोभिरञ्जते । यज्ञो न सप्त धातृभि: ॥

6. Just as Kings are graced with eulogies, and the sacrifice (Yajna) is graced with seven priests, so do the learned adorn the soul with the beams of knowledge (1121)

७. परि स्वानास इन्दवो मदाय बर्हणा गिरा । मधो अर्षन्ति धारया ।

7. The learned Yogis, realising God, through [mighty Vedic speech, and endowed with the force of spiritual joy, go forward for the attainment of divine happiness. (1122)[2]

८. आपानासो विवस्वतो जिन्वन्त उषसो भगम् । सूरा अण्वं वि तन्वते ॥

8. The Yogis who control the outgoing breath, attain to the ignorance banishing vigour of the soul. The Yogis lustrous like the sun, visualise the subtle secret of the soul. (1123)

९. अप द्वारा मतीनां प्रत्ना ऋण्वन्ति कारव: । वृष्णा हरस आयव: ॥

9. The aged, disciplined performers of Yogic practices, who have realised the true nature of the gladdening soul, open the doors of meditation and cogitation. (1124)

१०. समीचीनास आशत होतार: सप्तजानय: । पदमेकस्य पिप्रत: ॥

10. The truthful people acting as seven priests, sit in a Yajna, fulfilling the task of the sacrificer. (1125)[3]

११. नाभा नाभिं न आ ददे चक्षुषा सूर्यं दृशे । कवेरपत्यमा दुहे ॥

[1]They refers to pure, learned persons mentioned in the previous verse.
[2]See verse 485.
[3]Sacrificer is he who performs the Yajna. Seven priests are (1) Hota, होता (2) Maitrā-varuṇa मैत्रावरुण: (3) Brāhman-Āchhansi ब्राह्मणाच्छंसी (4) Pota पोता (5) Neshṭha नेष्ठा (6) Achhāvaka अच्छावाक: (7) Agnidhra आग्नीध्र: ।

11. May we preserve the soul in our mind, so that we may visualise God Brilliant like the sun. May we enjoy the bliss of God, Who always saves a sage from degradation. (1126)[1]

१२. अभि प्रियं दिवस्पदमध्वर्युभिर्गुहा हितम् । सूरः पश्यति चक्षसा ॥

12. An expert Yogi, beholds with divine eye, the true nature of the dear, lustrous soul, hidden in the inmost recesses of the heart, coupled with the subtle forces of the organs of senses. (1127)[2]

II

१. असृग्रमिन्दव: पथा धर्मन्नृतस्य सुश्रिय: । विदाना अस्य योजना ॥

1. The Yogis endowed with spiritual wealth and mental quietness, taking shelter in God, the Lord of true knowledge, and treading on the path of virtue, feel highly satisfied enjoying the union of this soul with God through Yoga. (1128)

२. प्र धारा मधो अग्रियो महीरपो वि गाहते । हविर्हविःषु वन्द्य: ॥

2. Higher than all desired objects, is the soul fit for praise. Like oceans it swims across meditation, mental abstractions, actions and judgments, and attains to the chief forces of immortality. (1129)

३. प्र युजा वाचो अग्रियो वृषो अचिक्रदद्वने । सद्माभि सत्यो अध्वर: ॥

3. The noble soul alone utters decent words for God. The soul of a Yogi, who practises truth and non-violence, perceives God, his last Refuge. (1130)[3]

४. परि यत्काव्या कविनृं'म्णा पुनानो अर्षति । स्ववर्जी सिषासति ॥

4. When a wise and learned person, purging the hearts of men, acquires the the knowledge of Vedic verses, then through his superior knowledge, he cherishes the joy of final beatitude. (1131)[4]

---

[1]Pischel interprets it as 'Soma unites our navel with the Gods in heaven.' Wilson interprets the verse as, 'I take into my navel the navel of the sacrifice.' Ludwig interprets it as 'He (Soma) as Kinsman has brought us a Kinsman (Surya). These explanations are wide of the mark. नाभि means soul in the verse and not a navel.

[2]Griffith describes this verse to be very obscure. I see no obscurity in the verse. The significance is clear like day light. Griffith has adopted Benfey's explanation. He takes it as meaning that the sun looks towards the place where the Soma lies while it is pressed. Sāyana seems to interpret this verse as meaning that Indra views the Soma with affection even after it has been drunk by the priests. Both the interpretations don't appeal to me. They don't look so logical and rational.

[3]His refers to a Yogi. Griffith writes. 'The stanza is very difficult, and I am unable to offer a satisfactory translation. He has translated 'Vana' as wood, and Sāyana as water. The word in the verse means God.

[4]Final beatitude means salvation.

५. पवमानो अभि स्पृधो विशो राजेव सीदति । यदीमृण्वन्ति वेधस: ॥

5. When the Yogis goad this soul, the lustrous soul, quelling all opposing forces, sits enthroned as a King, who overpowers the warring subjects. (1132)

६. अव्या वारे परि प्रियो हरिर्वनेषु सीदति । रेभो वनुष्यते मती ॥

6. Dearest soul, the queller of afflictions, crossing mental coverings, dwells in our bodies. The praise worthy soul is realised through reflection. (1133)

७. स वायुमिन्द्रमश्विना साकं मदेन गच्छति । रणा यो अस्य धर्मणा ॥

7. A Yogi, who revels in the steady abstraction of the soul, controls the forces of breath, and mind, and the organs of action and cognition. (1134)

८. आ मित्रे वरुणे भगे मधो: पवन्त ऊर्मय: । विदाना अस्य शक्मभि: ॥

8. The currents of this pleasant soul, move in Prāna, Apāna and Samana, and a Yogi nicely acquires knowledge through the forces of this soul. (1135)

९. अस्मभ्यꣳ रोदसी रयिं मध्वो वाजस्य सातये । श्रवो वसूनि सञ्जितम् ॥

9. O Ye Heaven and Earth, to make us win knowledge and happiness, grant us control over riches, renown and cattle ! (1136)

१०. आ ते दक्षं मयोभुवं वह्निमद्या वृणीमहे । पान्तमा पुरुस्पृहम् ॥

10. O soul, we always realise thy force, the giver of peace, riches, protection, and desired by all. (1137)[1]

११. आ मन्द्रमा वरेण्यमा विप्रमा मनीषिणम् । पान्तमा पुरुस्पृहम् ॥

11. O God, we realise Thee, as Excellent, Wise, the Urger of the hearts of all, our Guardian, and the Idol of all ! (1138)

१२. आ रयिमा सुचेतुनमा सुक्रतो तनूष्वा । पान्तमा पुरुस्पृहम् ॥

12. O God, the Embodiment of knowledge and action. the Goader of all, we accept Thee for ourselves, as Wealth, fair Intelligence, our Gaurdian and Worthy of love by all ! (1139)

III

१. मूर्धानं दिवो अरति पृथिव्या वैश्वानरमृत आ जातमग्निम् । कविꣳ सम्राजमतिथिं जनानामासन्न: पात्रं जनयन्त देवा: ॥

1. The learned priests, kindle in our sacrifice, fire, that goes up from the earth to the sky, contributes to the welfare of mankind, is created in the beginning

---

[1]See verse 498, अद्य means today literally, i.e., every day.

of the universe, is beautiful in appearance, burns brightly, ever moves fast, protects men, and is the mouth of the forces of nature. (1140)[1]

२. त्वां विश्वे अमृत जायमान॑ शिशुं न देवा अभि सं नवन्ते ।
तव क्रतुभिरमृतत्वमायन् वैश्वानर यत्पित्रोरदीदे: ॥

2. O Immortal God, just as people like, love and praise a newly born child, so do all learned persons praise Thee, Who is All-pervading, and Who manifests Himself in all places through His strength. O pervader in the hearts of all men, the learned Yogis attain to salvation by following the laws of action and knowledge preached by Thee. Thy majestic lustre is perceived in the Sushumma artery! (1141)[2]

३. नाभि यज्ञाना॑ सदन॑ रयीणां महामाहावमभि सं नवन्त ।
वैश्वानर॑ रथ्यमध्वराणां यज्ञस्य केतुं जनयन्त देवा: ॥

3. The learned praise God, the solitary Refuge for worship, Comradeship, love and charity, the House of riches, the Almighty, and the Ocean of life. They describe Him as the Impeller of all noble acts of non-violence, the Leader of all, and the Commander of the soul. (1142)

IV

१. प्र वो मित्राय गायत वरुणाय विपा गिरा । महिक्षत्रावृतं बृहत् ॥

1. Sing forth the praise of a learned person and a preacher, with your inspired song. They both are highly powerful and preach lofty spiritual truth. (1143)[3]

२. सम्राजा या घृतयोनी मित्रश्चोभा वरुणश्च । देवा देवेषु प्रशस्ता ॥

2. Both Prāna and Apāna are the originators of loveliness, brilliancy and beauty. They themselves shed lustre. Of all the organs, they are fit for praise the givers of happiness. (1144)

३. ता न: शक्त' पार्थिवस्य महो रायो दिव्यस्य । महि वां क्षत्रं देवेषु ॥

3. Ye are competent to grant us great terrestrial and celestial wealth. Great is the strength of Ye both amongst the organs of senses. (1145)[4]

---

[1]Fire is the mouth of the forces of nature, as air, water, light all enjoy it and stand in need of it. See verse 67.
[2]Sushumna: A particular artery of the human body, said to lie between Idā and Pinglā two of the vessels of the body. When a Yogi concentrates his attention on the Sushumna artery, he feels the spiritual force and majestic lustre of God.
[3]Mitra and Varuna may also mean Prāna and Apāna, the ingoing and outgoing breaths.
[4]Ye refers to Mitra and Varuna, i.e., teacher and preacher.

V

१. इन्द्रा याहि चित्रभानो सुता इमे त्वायव: । अण्वीभिस्तना पूतास: ॥

1. O God, marvellously bright, take us under Thy protection. All these objects of the world long for Thee. Thou art Worthy of acceptance, Pure and Vast as Thou art, through the threads of subtle knowledge ! (1146)

२. इन्द्रा याहि धियेषितो विप्रजूत: सुतावत: । उप ब्रह्माणि वाघत: ॥

2. O God, Realisable through intellect, Knowable by the learned, Endowed with knowledge, accept the eulogies offered through Vedic verses by the knowers of the significance of the Vedas. (1147)

३. इन्द्रा याहि तूतुजान उप ब्रह्माणि हरिव: । सुतं दधिष्व नश्चन: ॥

3. O learned person, lord of the organs of senses, quick in action, thou attainest to the Vedic praises in this created world. Pray accept our eulogies ! (1148)

VI

१. तमीडिष्व यो अर्चिषा वना विश्वा परिष्वजत् । कृष्णा कृणोति जिह्वया ॥

1. O worshipper, supplicate that Agni (God) Who encompasses all enjoyable objects, and with His glow renders all free from sin ! (1149)

२. य इद्ध आविवासति सुम्नमिन्द्रस्य मर्त्य: । द्युम्नाय सुतरा अप: ॥

2. A highly intellectual mortal, who unfurls knowledge that gladdens the soul, finds an easy way over the shackles of Karma, to splendid knowledge. (1150)

३. ता नो वाजवतीरिष आशून् पिपृतमर्वत: । एन्द्रमग्निं च वोढवे ॥

3. Give us, Ye twain, the organs of cognition and action, where with we may be able to realise easily the soul and God in our heart. (1151)[1]

VII

१. प्रो अयासीदिन्दुरिन्द्रस्य निष्कृतꣳ सखा सख्युनं प्र मिनाति सङ्गिरम् ।
मर्यं इव युवतिभि: समर्षति सोम: कलशे शतयामना पथा ॥

1. The soul, through its purity, attains to the light of God. As a friend, the soul never violates the behest of God, its friend. Just as a young man looks graceful, walking in the company of young maids, so does soul appear beautiful, when it approaches God through hundred paths of virtue. (1152)[2]

[1]Ye twain: Prāṇa and Apāna.
[2]See verse 557.

२. प्र वो धियो मन्द्रयुवो विपन्युवः पनस्युवः संवरणेष्वक्रमुः ।
हरिं क्रीडन्तमभ्यनूषत स्तुभोऽभि धेनवः पयसेदशिश्रयुः ॥

2. O learned persons, your intellects, concentrated on the joyous God, long-ing for praise, lauding Him, display themselves in the assembly halls of the learned. The learned eulogise Him, Who Creates and dissolves the universe. The Vedic verses dwell in Him with all their knowledge ! (1153)

३. आ नः सोम संयतं पिप्युषीमिषमिन्दो पवस्व पवमान ऊर्मिणा ।
या नो दोह्ते त्रिरह्नसश्चतुषी क्षुमद्वाजवन्मधुमत्सुवीर्यम् ॥

3. O Glorious, All-pervading God, grant us the well-organised and ever-growing prosperity, which shall yield us ceaselessly thrice a day, glory, know-ledge, happiness and strength! (1154)[1]

VIII

१. न किष्टं कर्मणा नशद्यश्चकार सदावृधम् । इन्द्रं न यज्ञैर्विश्वगूर्तमृभ्वसमधृष्टं धृष्णुमोजसा ॥

1. He, who worships through Yoga, God, the constant Benefactor of His devotees, praised of all, Almighty, Unconquerable, the Subduer of all through His unlimited power, remains untouched by the onslaught of an enemy like lust. (1155)[2]

२. अषाढमुग्रं पृतनासु सासहिं यस्मिन्महीरुरुज्रयः !
सं धेनवो जायमाने अनोनवुर्द्यावः क्षामीरनोनवुः ॥

2. I praise the ruler, the powerful conqueror, invincible in war, at whose appearance the highly wealthy person bows, the learned and ordinary persons of the world also lean before him in reverence. (1156)

IX

१. सखाय आ नि षीदत पुनानाय प्र गायत । शिशुं न यज्ञैः परि भूषत श्रिये ॥

1. Sit down, O friends, and sing aloud to him who purifies himself. Deck him for glory, like a child, with acts of sacrifice. (1157)[3]

२. समी वत्सं न मातृभिः सृजता गयसाधनम् । देवाव्यां३ मदमभि द्विशवसम् ॥

2. Just as a calf is associated with the kine to drink milk, so should a pupil, seeker after knowledge, be associated with learned teachers. Instruct fully the disciple, who controls his breaths, is the master of loveliness and physical strength, full of joy, and possesses both knowledge and action. (1158)[4]

---

[1]Thrice a day: in the morning, at noon and in the evening.
[2]See verse 243.
[3]Him refers to a virtuous learned person.
See verse 568.
[4]In the text printed in the Vedic Press Ajmere प्र is unnecessarily printed after अभि by mistake.

३. पुनाता दक्षसाधनं यथा शर्धाय वीतये । यथा मित्राय वरुणाय शन्तमम् ॥

3. Preserve semen, the augmentor of physical strength, in such a way, that it may contribute to the growth of the body and our beauty, and make Prāna and Apāna, the sources of life, more propitious and benefic. (1159)

X

१. प्र वाज्यक्षाः सहस्रधारस्तिरः पवित्रं वि वारमव्ययम् ॥

1. A learned person, endowed with a thousand excellent forces, nicely, directly realises the firm purifying soul, the alleviator of miseries. (1160)

२. स वाज्यक्षाः सहस्ररेता अद्रिमृंजानो गोभिः श्रीणानः ॥

2. The strong soul of a Yogi, endowed with a thousand merits, purified through noble acts and intellect, ripened through beams of knowledge, manifests itself in the heart. (1161)

३. प्र सोम याहीन्द्रस्य कुक्षा नृभिर्यमानो अद्रिभिः सुतः ॥

3. O soul, disciplined by the learned through God's profound meditation, controlled through ceaseless austerities, enter thou the inmost recesses of the heart! (1162)

XI

१. ये सोमासः परावति ये अर्वावति सुन्विरे । ये वादः शर्यणावति ॥

२. य आर्जीकेषु कृत्वसु ये मध्ये पस्त्यानाम् । ये वा जनेषु पञ्चसु ॥

३. ते नो वृष्टि दिवस्परि पवन्तामा सुवीर्यम् । स्वाना देवास इन्दवः ॥

1,2,3. The learned persons found in distant and adjacent countries, in inaccessible deserts or even plains, in the midst of domestic people in the houses built by them, or amongst five classes of men should shower on us for our welfare their sound instructions, and grant us fine strength, as the learned alone, who are endowed with knowledge and divine qualities are known as Indus. (1163, 1164, 1165)[1]

XII

१. आ ते वत्सा मनो यमत् परमाच्चित् सधस्थात् । अग्ने त्वां कामये गिरा ॥

1. O physical fire, I long for thee with speech; as the speaking fire of mind extends through thee, from thy loftiest dwelling-place, the heart ! (1166)[2]

---

[1]Five classes of men: Brāhmanas, Kshatriyas, Vaishyas, Shūdras, and Nishādas. Learned persons are found amongst all these classes.

इन्दु Indu means a man full of learning and piety.

[2]With the aid of fire, the mental flash spreads throughout the body from the heart, and enables everyone to speak. There is a close connection between speech and fire. The word वत्स used in the verse does not refer to the Rishi named vatsa. It means a speaker. See verse 8.

२. पुरुत्रा हि सदृङ्ङसि दिशो विश्वा अनु प्रभु: । समत्सु त्वा हवामहे ॥

2. O God, Thou art alike towards all Thy subjects. Thou art Lord through all the regions. We invoke Thee for aid in battles and on difficult occasions ! (1167)[1]

३. समत्स्वग्निमवसे वाजयन्तो हवामहे । वाजेषु चित्रराधसम् ॥

3. In our fight against moral weaknesses, for the acquisition and enhancement of knowledge, strength and food-stuffs, longing for wisdom and prosperity, we invoke for our protection, God, the Giver of wondrous gifts. (1168)

XIII

१. त्वं न इन्द्रा भर ओजो नृम्णँ शतक्रतो विचर्षणे । आ वीरं पृतनासहम् ॥

1. O King, the doer of manifold deeds, the knower of the secret of the subjects through spies, give us strength and wealth. Give us a hero conquering in war ! (1169)[2]

२. त्वँ हि न: पिता वसो त्वं माता शतक्रतो बभूविथ । अथा ते सुम्नमीमहे ॥

2. O All-pervading God, the Doer of hundreds of deeds, Thou hast ever been a mother and a sire unto us. So now, for bliss we pray to Thee ! (1170)

३. त्वाँ शुष्मिन् पुरुहूत वाजयन्तमुप ब्रुवे सहस्कृत । स नो रास्व सुवीर्यम् ॥

3. To Thee, Strong, Much-invoked, the Origin of all powerful objects, the Giver of knowledge and strength, do I pray. Grant Thou us heroic power ! (1171)[3]

XIV

१. यदिन्द्र चित्र म इह नास्ति त्वादातमद्रिव: । राधस्तन्नो विदद्वस उभयाहस्त्या भर ॥

1. O King, the Chastiser of the sinners, treasure-finder, wondrous, what wealth thou hast not given me in this world, bring to us that bounty filling, full both thy hands ! (1172)

२. यन्मन्यसे वरेण्यमिन्द्र द्युक्षं तदा भर । विद्याम तस्य ते वयमकूपारस्य दावन: ॥

2. O God, give us the wealth and food, which Thou deemest as precious. May we receive the charity of Thine, a boundless Giver of gifts ! (1173)

---

[1]In battles: In our struggle against immoral forces like lust and anger.
[2]See verse 345.
[3]God grants His knowledge of the Vedas to the learned, to be imparted alike to all without distinction of caste, colour or creed. God's knowledge is meant for mankind, and not for the chosen few.

३. यत्ते दिक्षु प्रराध्यं मनो श्रस्ति श्रुतं बृहत् । तेन दृढा चिदद्रिव श्रा वाजं दर्षि सातये ॥

3. O Omniscent God, Thy adorable, vast, acceptable knowledge is spread in all regions. With this Thou bestowest on us Thy perfect knowledge, to be imparted alike to mankind ! (1174)

BOOK V

Chapter 1

I

१. शिशुं जज्ञानꣳ हर्यतं मृजन्ति शुम्भन्ति विप्रं मरुतो गणेन ।
कविर्गीर्भि: काव्येन कवि: सन्त्सोम: पवित्रमत्येति रेभन् ॥

1. The learned, with their flock of breaths, brighten and decorate the soul, the seeker after knowledge, lovely, and endowed with learning and action. A wise person, with verses of God's poetry, the Vedas, the instructor of mankind, having attained salvation, contemplating upon God, the purifier of the fallen, crosses the bondage of Karma. (1175)[1]

२. ऋषिमना य ऋषिकृत् स्वर्षा: सहस्रनीथ: पदवी: कवीनाम् ।
तृतीयं धाम महिष: सिषासन्त्सोमो विराजमनु राजति ष्टुप् ॥

2. He is a great man, who is Rishi-minded, Rishi-maker, the seer of the secrets of things, the eulogiser of God in a thousand ways, and the bestower of knowledge to the intellectual. The soul longing for emancipation, attaining to the third stage of salvation, singing the praise of God, acquires bliss through His grace. (1176)

३. चमूषच्छ्येन: शकुनो विभृत्वा गोविन्दुर्द्रप्स श्रायुधानि बिभ्रत् ।
अपामूर्मिꣳ सचमान: समुद्रं तुरीयं धाम महिषो विवक्ति ॥

3. Residing full well in all the organs of senses, the active soul, marching on the path of salvation, full of force, free to move in all spheres, the seeker after God, master of passions, wielding manifold powers, full of majesty, contemplating upon God, the Refuge of all like an ocean, the Urger of all the worlds, achieves the bliss of salvation. (1177)

II

१. एते सोमा श्रभि प्रियमिन्द्रस्य काममक्षरन् । वर्धन्तो श्रस्य वीर्यम् ॥

1. These learned persons of affable nature, expatiating upon the might of God, manifest His dear desire of creation, sustenance and philanthropy. (1178)

---

[1]Flock of breaths: Prāṇa, Apāna, Vyāna, Udāna, Samāna, Nāg, Kūrma, Krikal, Dev Dutta, Dhananjya.

The instructor of mankind refers to a wise person.

२. पुनानासश्चमूषदो गच्छन्तो वायुमश्विना । ते नो धत्त सुवीर्यम् ॥

2. The pure Prāṇa and Apāna, dwelling in the organs of senses, marching towards the soul, achieve glory and force on the strength of internal soul alone. (1179)

३. इन्द्रस्य सोम राधसे पुनानो हार्दि चोदय । देवानां योनिमासदम् ॥

3. O pure Yogi, for the contemplation of God, develop in your heart, the power of reflection, the main seat and origin of all the organs of senses! (1180)

४. मृजन्ति त्वा दश क्षिपो हिन्वन्ति सप्त धीतयः । अनु विप्रा अमादिषुः ॥

4. O Yogi, the ten limbs purify thee, the seven thoughts contribute to thy joy. The sages rejoice, following in thy wake! (1181)[1]

५. देवेभ्यस्त्वा मदाय कꣳ सृजानमति मेष्यः । सं गोभिर्वासयामसि ॥

5. O joyous soul, for the rapture of the learned, through the control of breath, we expatiate upon thy felicity with Vedic Verses! (1182)

६. पुनानः कलशेष्वा वस्त्राण्यरुषो हरिः । परि गव्यान्यव्यत ॥

6. Purified in the recesses of the heart, the beautiful soul, our saviour from miseries, puts on the clothes of the knowledge of the Vedas. (1183)[2]

७. मघोन आ पवस्व नो जहि विश्वा अप द्विषः । इन्दो सखायमा विश ॥

7. O soul, enrich us with knowledge. Drive away all feelings of enmity. Go unto God, thy Friend! (1184)

८. नृचक्षसं त्वा वयमिन्द्रपीतꣳ स्वविदम् । भक्षीमहि प्रजामिषम् ॥

[1] Ten limbs may refer to five Yamas and five Niyamas, or ten attributes of religion (1) Dhriti, Fortitude, (2) Kshmā, Forgiveness, (3) Dama, Self Command, (4) Asteya, Non-theft, (5) Shauch, Purity, (6) Indriya Nigraha, control over senses, (7) Dhīr, Calmness, (8) Vidyā, Learning, (9) Satya, Truth, (10) Akrodha, Freedom from anger.

Niyamas are (1) Shauch, Purity, (2) Santosh, contentment, (3) Tapa, Austerity, (4) Swadhayāya, Study, (5) Ishwar Praṇidhāna, Resignation to the will of God.

Yamas are (1) Ahinsā, Non-voilence, (2) Satya, Truth, (3) Asteya, Freedom from theft. (4) Brahmacharya, Celibacy, (5) Aprigraha, Renunciation.

Ten limbs may also refer to ten Prāṇas.

(1) Prāṇa, (2) Apāna, (3) Vyāna, (4) Udāna, (5) Samāna, (6) Nāga, (7) Kūrma, (8) Krikla, (9) Dev Dutta, (10) Dhanañjya.

Seven thoughts may refer to seven concentrations of the mind on different parts of the body, or seven breath forces in the seven apertures in the head, i.e.

two eyes, two ears, two nostrils and the mouth.

[2] An enlightened and pure soul equips itself with the knowledge of the Vedic verses, which act as its clothes. Just as clothes protect us against heat and cold, so do the Vedic teachings save the soul from the passions of lust, anger, avarice, infatuation and pride.

8. O soul, may we serve thee, the enjoyer of the bliss of emancipation, satisfied with the favour of God, the Seer of mankind with the same eye. May we gain progeny, strength, food and knowledge! (1185)

९. वृष्टि दिव: परि स्रव द्युम्नं पृथिव्या अधि । सहो न: सोम पृत्सु धा: ॥

9. O God, rain happiness on the Earth, as a cloud sends water from the sky. Give us spirit and forbearance in life's struggles! (1186)

III

१. सोम: पुनानो अर्षति सहस्रधारो अत्यवि: । वायोरिन्द्रस्य निष्कृतम् ॥

1. The purifying soul, endowed with manifold merits, attains to the supreme dignity, having crossed the covering of breath. (1187)[1]

२. पवमानमवस्यवो विप्रमभि प्र गायत । सुष्वाणं देववीतये ॥

2. Sing forth, Ye men who long for help, for the attainment of God, to the soul, the purifer of all, the bestower of knowledge and happiness on all, and urger of all. (1188)

३. पवन्ते वाजसातये सोमा: सहस्रपाजस: । गृणाना देववीतये ॥

3. The learned, equipped with thousand spiritual powers, for the acquisition of knowledge, and the attainment of God, purify themselves, singing His praise. (1189)

४. उत नो वाजसातये पवस्व बृहतीरिष: । द्युमदिन्दो सुवीर्यम् ॥

4. O God, grant us mighty powers for acquiring knowledge. O God, give us excellent strength endowed with divine attributes ! (1190)

५. अत्या हियाना न हेतृभिरसृग्रं वाजसातये । वि वारमव्यमाशव: ॥

5. Learned persons, marching fast on the path of knowledge, exerting hard to acquire learning and happiness through different methods cross the covering of matter. (1191)

६. ते न: सहस्रिणं रयिं पवन्तामा सुवीर्यम् । स्वाना देवास इन्दव: ॥

6. May they, the learned Yogis, practising Yoga, give us wealth in thousands and heroic power. (1192)

७. वाश्रा अर्षन्तीन्दवोऽभि वत्सं न मातर: । दधन्विरे गभस्त्यो: ॥

7. The learned preachers go unto God, like milch-kine lowing to their calves. They make themselves firm and steady through the arms of knowledge and action. (1193)

---

[1]"Having crossed-breath' means after controlling the breath.

८. जुष्ट इन्द्राय मत्सर: पवमान: कनिक्रदत् । विश्वा ग्रप द्विषो जहि ॥

8. O pure Yogi, the lover of God, full of joy, preaching alike to mankind, thou drivest away all feelings of hatred ! (1194)

९. ग्रपघ्नन्तो ग्रराव्ण: पवमाना: स्वदृ॑श: । योनावृतस्य सीदत ॥

9. Ye, purifiers of the world by leading a religious life, Ye seers of salvation, suppressing the feelings of miserliness, seat yourselves in God, the Chief Refuge of true knowledge ! (1195)

IV

१. सोमा ग्रसृग्रमिन्दव: सुता ऋतस्य धारया । इन्द्राय मधुमत्तमा: ॥

1. Endowed with divine knowledge, goaded by the stream of true knowledge, the gladdeners of all, the learned persons, equipped with fine traits, are born for the worship of God. (1196)

२. ग्रभि विप्रा ग्रनूषत गावो वत्सं न धेनव: । इन्द्र॑ सोमस्य पीतये ॥

2. Sages invoke God for drinking the juice of knowledge, as milchkine low to their calves. (1197)

३. मदच्युत् क्षेति सादने सिन्धोरूर्मा विपश्चित् । सोमो गौरी ग्रधि श्रित: ॥

3. A wise person, the gleaner of knowledge and action, the distiller of rapture, having full faith in the teachings of the Vedas, dwells in God, the Ocean of knowledge, his last Refuge and Guide to spiritual advancement. (1198)[1]

४. दिवो नाभा विचक्षणोऽव्या वारे महीयते । सोमो य: सुक्रतु: कवि: ॥

4. A highly intellectual and wise person, the seer of Truth, achieves great power through God, Who encompasses Matter, and controls the Heaven. (1199)

५. य: सोम: कलशेष्वा अन्त: पवित्र ग्राहित: । तमिन्दु: परि षस्वजे ॥

5. In close embracement the soul holds God, Who pervades the bodies and resides in a pure soul. (1200)[2]

६. प्र वाचमिन्दुरिष्यति समुद्रस्याधि विष्टपि । जिन्वन् कोशं मधुश्चुतम् ॥

6. A learned person, enjoying the supreme glow of God, the Ocean of joy, achieving the sheath of supreme happiness, receives the exalted knowledge of Vedic speech, worthy of veneration. (1201)

---

[1]'Gauri Adhi Shrita' has been translated as 'Resting on the wild cow's hide' by Benfey, whom Griffith has followed. Pt. Jaidev Vidyalankara translates it as 'Having full faith on the teachings of the Vedas' which is more rational and convincing.

[2]In this verse Soma means God. Indu means the soul. Ludwig suggests that Indu may be the Moon, upon whose phases the time of important liturgical ceremonies depends. This interpretation is not so logical and rational.

७. नित्यस्तोत्रो वनस्पतिर्धेनामन्तः सबर्दुघाम् । हिन्वानो मानुषा युजा ॥

7. A learned person, the lord of eulogies, worthy of praise, enhances mental force, that yields supreme bliss in the hearts of persons who practise Yoga. (1202)

८. आ पवमान धारया रयिꣳ सहस्रवर्चसम् । अस्मे इन्दो स्वाभुवम् ॥

8. O All-pervading, Glorious God, give us wealth bright with a thousand splendours, and endowed with fine power! (1203)

९. अभि प्रिया दिवः कविर्विप्रः स धारया सुतः । सोमो हिन्वे परावति ॥

9. A lovely, learned fellow, attached to God, the last stage of protection, full of wisdom, with his mental abstraction of the mind, flies to the excellent heights of knowledge, lustrous like the sun. (1204)

V

१. उत्ते शुष्मास ईरत सिन्धोरूर्मेरिव स्वनः । वाणस्य चोदया पविम् ॥

1. Just as a river's waves roar aloud, so let thy powers manifest themselves. Impel thou the power of the body. (1205)[1]

२. प्रसवे त उदीरते तिस्रो वाचो मखस्युवः । यदव्य एषि सानवि ॥

2. On Thy realisation, upward rise three voices of Thy worshipper, when Thou manifestest Thyself in the heart elevated through mental abstraction. (1206)[2]

३. अव्या वारेः परि प्रियꣳ हरिꣳ हिन्वन्त्यद्रिभिः । पवमानं मधुश्चुतम् ॥

3. Learned persons realise through Yogic practices, abstraction and deep meditation, God, Dear, the Alleviator of miseries, Purifying and the Distiller of divine bliss. (1207)

४. आ पवस्व मदिन्तम पवित्रं धारया कवे । अर्कस्य योनिमासदम् ॥

4. O most joyous and wise soul, for attaining to the exalted stage of God, go thou unto the Purifier of the sinners, with thy fortitude! (1208)

५. स पवस्व मदिन्तम गोभिरञ्जानो अक्तुभिः । एन्द्रस्य जठरं विश ॥

5. O soul, the best giver of delight, anointed with wise acts and Vedic teachings, exert thou hard, and revel in God! (1209)

VI

१. अया वीती परि स्रव यस्त इन्दो मदेष्वा । अवाहन्नवतीर्नव ॥

---

[1] 'Thy and Thou' refer to the soul.
[2] 'Thy and Thou' refer to God. Three voices refer to Rig, Sama and Yajur, pertaining to knowledge, meditation and action.

1. O God, shower blessing through universal pervasion, whereby the soul enjoying the delights granted by Thee, overcomes eight hundred and ten sins ! (1210)[1]

२. पुर: सद्य इत्थाधिये दिवोदासाय शंबरम् । अध त्यं तुर्वशं यदुम् ॥

2. O God, Thou annihilatest lust and anger, the foes of happiness, for a living emancipated soul, endowed with true knowledge and virtuous actions ! (1211)[2]

३. परि णो अश्वमश्वविद्गोमदिन्दो हिरण्यवत् । क्षरा सहस्रिणीरिष: ॥

3. O soul, controlling the mind, endowed with action, knowledge, and supremacy, fulfil thousands of our desires ! (1212)

VII

१. अपघ्नन् पवते मृधोऽप सोमो अराव्ण: । गच्छन्निन्द्रस्य निष्कृतम् ॥

1. God, rising in the pure heart of the soul, chasing all sources of misery, manifests Himself. (1213)

२. महो नो राय आ भर पवमान जही मृध: । रास्वेन्दो वीरवद्यश: ॥

2. O God, fill us with great riches, and destroy our foes. O Glorious God, grant us fame with manly sons ! (1214)

३. न त्वा शतं च न ह्रुतो राधो दित्सन्तमा मिनन् । यत्पुनानो मखस्यसे ॥

3. O God, a hundred obstacles have ne'er checked Thee when fain to give Thy boons, being Pure, Thou wishest to give us wealth ! (1215)

VIII

१. अया पवस्व धारया यया सूर्यमरोचय: । हिन्वानो मानुषीरप: ॥

1. O learned person, with whatever strength a man urges the breaths, or makes known his learned preceptor, the urger of all like the sun, with the same strength illuminate thyself every where ! (1216)

---

[1]See verse 495.
See verse 179 for the detailed explanation of 810 sins.
[2]Griffith following Sāyana translates Śambara as one of the demons who withhold the rain; and Yadu and Turvasa, as ancient heroes, eponymi of two of the Five Tribes frequently mentioned in the Rigveda; and Divodasa, called also Atithigva, as a pious and liberal, prince protected and favoured by Indra. This interpretation is unacceptable as it savours of history in the Vedas, which are absolutely free from historical references. Divodasa means a living emancipated soul, i.e., जीवन्मुक्त Yadu means lust. Turvasha mean anger. Shambra means the dissipator of happiness. It is a pity Griffith and Sāyana have miserably failed in grasping the real significance of the verse.
The words अव अहन् are imported from the previous verse.

२. अयुक्त सूर एतशं पवमानो मनावधि । अन्तरिक्षेण यातवे ॥

2. A learned person, the purifier of the soul, mentally treading on the path of salvation, unites with God, through Yoga Samādhi, his mind fast in motion like a horse. (1217)

३. उत त्या हरितो रथे सूरो अयुक्त यातवे । इन्दुरिन्द्र इति ब्रुवन् ॥

3. A learned Yogi also, going fast towards God, unites through Yoga those fleeting breaths, with God, saying, 'God is Glorious'. (1218)

IX

१. अग्नि वो देवमग्निभिः सजोषा यजिष्ठं दूतमध्वरे कृणुध्वम् ।
यो मर्त्येषु निध्रुविऋतावा तपुर्मूर्धा घृतान्नः पावकः ॥

1. O learned persons, free from partisanship towards other wise men, in your non-violent religious dealings, appoint him as your messenger, who is learned, renowned, virtuous, firm and patient among mankind, truthful, austere, forbearing, leader of men, taker of non-stimulating diet like clarified butter, and ennobling ! (1219)[1]

२. प्रोथदश्वो न यवसेऽविष्यन् यदा महः संवरणाद्व्यस्थात् ।
आदस्य वातो अनु वाति शोचिरध स्म ते व्रजनं कृष्णमस्ति ॥

2. Just as a steed neighing eagerly goes to the grass, just so when a Brahmachari comes out of the house of his preceptor to enter the domestic life after finishing his studies, and thereafter his breath follows his dignity, then, alone, O learned person, does thy conduct in life, attract mankind towards thee. (1220)[2]

३. उदस्य ते नवजातस्य वृष्णोऽग्ने चरन्त्यजरा इधानाः ।
अच्छा द्यामरुषो धूम एषि सं दूतो अग्न ईयसे हि देवान् ॥

3. O learned new graduate, thy kindled flames of dignity, showering knowledge, rise upward. O lovely young scholar, striking terror in the hearts of the opponents, thou gainest knowledge, O learned fellow, thou approachest the learned persons as their teacher and messenger of learning ! (1221)[3]

X

१. तमिन्द्रं वाजयामसि महे वृत्राय हन्तवे । स वृषा वृषभो भुवत् ॥

[1]See verse 493.

[2]After entering the Grihastha Āshrama, if a man follows the path of virtue and righteousness, he sets an example for others and persuades them to follow in his wake.

[3]नवजातस्य means a young man, who has just finished his studies, and been declared a graduate स्नातक, i.e., who has just come out of the womb of the goddess of learning.

1. We develop intellect, for overcoming the formidable forces of ignorance, the foe of learning. The divine intellect rains happiness on us, with its flow of knowledge. (1222)[1]

२. इन्द्र: स दामने कृत श्रोजिष्ठ: स बले हित: । द्युम्नी श्लोकी स सोम्य: ॥

2. That intellect is competent to subdue all sorts of crookedness, is mightiest, is attached to acts of enterprise, is the enjoyer of supreme bliss, is glorious and praiseworthy. (1223)

३. गिरा वज्रो न सम्भृत: सबलो श्रनपच्युत: । ववक्ष उग्रो श्रस्तृत: ॥

3. That powerful intellect, never failing in its duty, strong, invincible, solid like a weapon, sharpened by Vedic study, sustains the universe. (1224)

XI

१. श्रध्वर्यो अद्रिभि: सुत ॐ सोमं पवित्र श्रा नय । पुनाहीन्द्राय पातवे ॥

1. O Yogi, establish in the heart, the knowledge acquired through yogic practices; make thou it pure for the soul to drink ! (1225)[2]

२. तव त्य इन्दो श्रन्धसो देवा मधोव्यशित । पवमानस्य मरुत: ॥

2. O God, the self-abnegating learned persons, enjoy Thy purifying, divine bliss! (1226)

३. दिव: पीयूषमुत्तम ॐ सोममिन्द्राय वज्रिणे । सुनोता मधुमत्तमम् ॥

3. O learned persons, pour out for the soul, armed with knowledge and asceticism, the sweetest, gladdening nectar of God's bliss! (1227)

XII

१. धर्ता दिव: पवते कृत्व्यो रसो दक्षो देवानामनुमाद्यो नृभि: ।
हरि: सृजानो श्रत्यो न सत्वभिर्वृथा पाजा ॐ सि कृणुषे नदीष्वा ॥

1. On flows the juice of joy, sustainer of the heavens, the strength of the learned, hailed by men with shouts of joy. When that charming, pain-assuaging joy is matured, it voluntarily fills the organs of senses with different sorts of strength. (1228)

२. शूरो न धत्त श्रायुधा गभस्त्यो: स्व ३: सिषासन् रथिरा गविष्टिषु ।
इन्द्रस्य शुष्ममीरयन्नपस्युभिरिन्दुर्हिन्वानो अज्यते मनीषिभि: ॥

2. Just as a hero takes his weapons in his hands, so should a Yogi control his breaths for acquiring God. Like a heroic charioteer, a Yogi following the

[1]To drink means to enjoy, relish.
[2]See verse 558.

teachings of the Vedas, longing for happiness, stimulating his soul's might, with the aid of learned Karmyogis (men of action), urged by learning for his Yogic practices, and filled with glory, should kindle himself with knowledge. (1229)

३. इन्द्रस्य सोम पवमान ऊर्मिणा तविष्यमाणो जठरेष्वा विश ।
प्र न: पिन्व विद्युदभ्रेव रोदसी धिया नो वाजाᳲ उप माहि शश्वत: ॥

3. O seeker after salvation, O purifier of the heart, with thy great strength, enter thou the worlds created by God, with thy rising knowledge. Just as lightning fills the clouds with water, so shouldst thou perfect our Prāṇa and Apāna; mete out exhaustless powers for us with thy wisdom. (1230)

XIII

१. यदिन्द्र प्रागपागुदङ्न्यग्वा हूयसे नृभि: । सिमा पुरू नृषूतो अस्यानवेऽसि प्रशर्ध तुर्वशे ॥

1. O God, Thou art extolled by men in the East, West, North and South. Thou art worshipped like a King, by all men, living beings, and Yogis who control their organs of senses. (1231)[1]

२. यद्वा रुमे रुशमे श्यावके कृप इन्द्र मादयसे सचा ।
कण्वासस्त्वा स्तोमेभिर्ब्रह्मवाहस इन्द्रा यच्छन्त्या गहि ॥

2. O God, though Thou shinest alike on a beautiful place, or on a depraved, an enterprising, or an affluent person; yet the wise preachers of the Vedas, who seek after Thee, attain unto Thee with hymns of praise. (1232)[2]

XIV

१. उभयᳲ शृणवच्च न इन्द्रो अर्वागिदं वच: ।
सत्राच्या मघवान्त्सोमपीतये धिया शविष्ठ आ गमत् ॥

1. May God listen to both this word of ours uttered in praise and supplication. May the Almighty and Glorious God, come unto us with His true wisdom to acknowledge the lovely and charming feeling of our heart. (1233)

२. तᳲ हि स्वराजं वृषभं तमोजसा धिषणे निष्टतक्षतु: ।
उतोपमानां प्रथमो नि षीदसि सोमकामᳲ हि ते मन: ॥

2. O Refulgent God, the Giver of happiness, the denizens of the Earth and Sky seek after Thee, with their spiritual power. Verily Thy knowledge longs for the lovely feeling of our heart. Thou art the Foremost and Subtlest amongst the forces of Nature, and art present every where, being All-Pervading ! (1234)

---

[1]See verse 279.
[2]Griffith translates Ruma, Ruśama, Śyāwaka, and Kripa as princes favoured by Indra. This explanation is inadmissible as the Vedas are free from historical references.

XV

१. पवस्व देव आयुषगिन्द्रं गच्छतु ते मदः । वायुमा रोह धर्मणा ॥

1. O Soul, manifest thyself May thy flow of joy constantly reach a learned person. May thou with thy power of holding control the breath ! (1235)[1]

२. पवमान नि तोशसे रयिं सोम श्रवाय्यम् । इन्दो समुद्रमा विश ॥

2. O holy learned person, thou, the Creator of fame and glory, bestowest spiritual wealth. May thou go to God, Vast like the ocean. (1236)

३. अपघ्नन् पवसे मृघः [ऋतुवित्सोम मत्सरः । नुदस्वादेवयुं जनम्] ॥

3. O learned person, full of joy, the master of knowledge and noble acts, thou chasing mutual wrangles and feuds establishest purity. Drive thou the godless folk afar. (1237)

XVI

१. अभी नो वाजसातमं रयिमर्ष शतस्पृहम् । इन्दो सहस्रभर्णसं तुविद्युम्नं विभासहम् ॥

1. O God, grant us wealth, the giver of strength, desired by hundreds, the nourisher of thousands, full of glory, the eclipser of the splendour of the mighty foe ! (1238)[2]

२. वयं ते अस्य राधसो वसोर्वंसो पुरुस्पृहः । नि नेदिष्ठतमा इषः स्याम सुम्ने ते अध्रिगो ॥

2. O Constant, Almighty Father, the Bestower of residence to all, may we Thy devotees live for long, nearest unto Thee in the bliss of salvation. May we also live nearest unto the worldly wealth and foodstuffs, desired by many men, and the source of existence! (1239)[3]

३. परि स्य स्वानो अक्षरदिन्दुरव्ये मदच्युतः ।
धारा य ऊर्ध्वो अध्वरे भ्राजा न याति गव्ययः ॥

3. Just as the semen, residing in the organs of senses with its lustre, in Yogic practices, with its steadiness goes to the upper parts, similarly the same semen, coursing through the subtle arteries, trickling happiness, with its beauty, manifests itself in the sheath of the Prāṇas. (1240)[4]

---

[1]See verse 483.
[2]See verse 549.
[3]Both worldly prosperity and the happiness of salvation should be the aim of our life. We should not ignore any of these two ideals. Those who neglect this world in their search after God, cannot attain true happiness, and fall short of the Vedic ideal. The vedas preach the temporal prosperity along with the spiritual.
[4]This verse preaches the beauty, lustre and significance of semen, which every one should preserve, and strengthen his soul and body therewith.

XVII

१. पवस्व सोम महान्त्समुद्र: पिता देवानां विश्वाभि धाम ॥

1. O Tranquil God, Thou art a Mighty ocean, in Whom reside all beings. Thou art the Father of all the forces of Nature. Purify all dwelling places! (1241)[1]

२. शुक्र: पवस्व देवेभ्य: सोम दिवे पृथिव्यें शं च प्रजाभ्य: ॥

2. O God, Thou art Pure. Be Blissful to the forces of Nature, Heaven and Earth, and living beings! (1242)

३. दिवो धर्तासि शुक्र: पीयूष: सत्ये विधर्मन् वाजी पवस्व ॥

3. O Pacific God, Lovely, Divine, Omnipotent and Sustainer of the Sun etc., art Thou. Purify us in the world of multifarious duties ; beyond the reach of Present, Past and Future!(1243)

XVIII

१. प्रेष्ठं वो अतिथि^ॐ स्तुषे मित्रमिव प्रियम् । अग्ने रथं न वेद्यम् ॥

1. O men, for your welfare, I describe fire, dear as a friend, most respectable as a guest, fit to be burnt in an altar, and messenger of gods like a chariot! (1244)[2]

२. कविमिव प्रश^ॐस्यं यं देवास इति द्विता । नि मर्त्येष्वादधु: ॥

2. The learned establish in mortal men, in two different aspects, Him Praiseworthy like a sages. (1245)[3]

३. त्वं यविष्ठ दाशुषो नृ:^ॐ पाहि श्रृणुही गिर: । रक्षा तोकमुत त्मना ॥

3. O Omnipotent God, do Thou protect the men who are charitably disposed, hear their say, preserve even the tiniest creature! (1246)

XIX

१. एन्द्र नो गधि प्रिय सत्राजिदगोह्य । गिरिनं विश्वत: पृथु: पतिर्दिव: ॥

[1] See verse 429.
[2] See verse 5.
I refers to God. Gods: the forces of nature like air, water, light etc. Fire sets in motion the air and other physical objects. Just as a guest अतिथि does not stay in one place alone, but keeps moving, so fire by nature is ever moving. Fire is our friend as it serves us in various ways.
[3] The wise look upon the soul in two aspects, i.e., God and soul. One of them i.e., God is the Pervader and Seer, while the other, i.e., soul, is the doer of acts, and the reaper of their fruits. Some commentators have interpreted Dwit, as heaven and earth, organs of action and cognition, and the गार्हपत्य and आहवनीय aspects of fire.

1. O Lightning, dear unto us, the Conqueror of all clouds, apparent and hence unhidden, expanded on all sides like a cloud, thou pervadest all directions! (1247)[1]

२. अभि हि सत्य सोमपा उभे बभूथ रोदसी । इन्द्रासि सुन्वतो वृध: पतिर्दिव: ॥

2. O Truthful and Supreme God, Thou art the Creator and Dissolver of the universe. Thou art Mightier than both the worlds. Thou art the Strengthener and Lord of the created heaven! (1248)[2]

३. त्वꣳ हि शश्वतीनामिन्द्र धर्ता पुरामसि । हन्ता दस्योर्मनोर्वृध: पतिर्दिव: ॥

3. O God, Thou art the Grantor of salvation to eternal souls, the Slayer of ignorance, the Advancer of a contemplative learned soul, and the Lord of Yogis shining like the Sun! (1249)

XX

१. पुरां भिन्दुर्युवा कविरमितौजा अजायत । इन्द्रो विश्वस्य कर्मणो धर्ता वज्री पुरुष्टुत: ॥

1. Lightning appears as the renderer of forts, young, the thunderer, unmeasured in strength, the sustainer of all acts, armed with power, and highly spoken of in the Vedas. (1250)[3]

२. त्वं वलस्य गोमतोऽपावरद्रिवो बिलम् । त्वां देवा अबिभ्युषस्तुज्यमानास आविषु: ॥

2. O immortal soul, thou equipped with the organs of senses, dost depart breaking open the body, the shelter of breaths. All gods, free from fear under thy protection, imbibing strength from thee, come pressing to thy side ! (1251)[4]

३. इन्द्रमीशानमोजसाभि स्तोमैरनूषत । सहस्रं यस्य रातय उत वा सन्ति भूयसी: ॥

3. Glorify with Vedic hymns of praise, God, Who reigneth by His might, Whose bounteous gifts are thousands, ye, even more. (1252)

Chapter 2

I

१. अक्रान्त्समुद्र: प्रथमे विधर्मन् जनयन् प्रजा भुवनस्य गोपा: ।
वृषा पवित्रे अधि सानो अव्ये बृहत्सोमो वावृधे स्वानो अद्रि: ॥

---

[1]See verse 393.
[2]Both the worlds: Heaven and Earth.
[3]See verse 359.

[4]The soul at the time of its departure, bursts open the body and goes out. Gods refer to fire, air, water etc., the five devas. Griffith interprets Vala, as the brother of Vritra, or Vritra himself, who stole the cows of the Gods and hid them in a cave. There is no history in the Vedas, hence this interpretation is inadmissible. Vala means breath.

1. In a chaste, solitary mountainous region, realised and derived through contemplation, the divine joy of the soul waxes profusely like a cloud. God, the Guardian of the Earth, in Whom are revolving different worlds, creating creatures of the universe, overpowers all in the vast sky, and fulfils all desires. (1253)[1]

२. मत्सि वायुमिष्टये राधसे नो मत्सि मित्रावरुणा पूयमान: ।
मत्सि शर्धो मारुतं मत्सि देवान्मत्सि द्यावापृथिवी देव सोम ॥

2. O Refulgent God, Thou infusest life in the air, Thou makest us happy for the achievement of our goal, and for worship. O Pure God, Thou movest in motion the sun and the cloud through Thy strength, Thou makest the powerful wind blow joyfully, Thou makest all the forces of nature work gladly in obedience to Thy Law. Thou makest the learned and the ignorant rejoice ! (1254)

३. महत्तत्सोमो महिषश्चकारापां यद्गर्भोऽवृणीत देवान् ।
अदधादिन्द्रे पवमान श्रोजोऽजनयत्सूर्यं ज्योतिरिन्दु: ॥

3. The mighty soul, performs this grand deed, that keeping our actions under its control, it protects all the organs of senses. The Immaculate God lends strength to the soul, and gives light to the Sun. (1255)

II

१. एष देवो अमर्त्य: पर्णवीरिव दीयते । अभि द्रोणान्यासदम् ॥

1. This brilliant, immortal soul, flies fast like a bird to the bodies to reside in them. (1256)

२. एष विप्रैरभिष्टुतोऽपो देवो वि गाहते । दधद्रत्नानि दाशुषे ॥

2. Praised by the sages, this brilliant soul, dives deep into knowledge and action, and bestows rich gifts upon a self-abnegating worshipper. (1257)

३. एष विश्वानि वार्या शूरो यन्निव सत्वभि: । पवमान: सिषासति ॥

3. This soul, purifying the body, leads us with its spiritual forces like a warrior, and grants all pleasures. (1258)[2]

४. एष देवो रथर्यति पवमानो दिशस्यति । आविष्कृणोति वग्वनुम् ॥

4. This brilliant soul, purifying the heart, resides in the body, as if it were a chariot. It preaches unto us, and lets its voice of knowledge be heard by all. (1259)

५. एष देवो विपन्युभि: पवमान ऋतायुभि: । हरिर्वाजाय मृज्यते ॥

[1]See verse 529.
[2]See verse 542.

5. This lustrous pure soul, the alleviator of afflictions, is adorned for acquiring spiritual strength, by the preachers of, and seekers after truth. (1260)

६. एष देवो विपा कृतोऽति ह्वराँसि धावति । पवमानो अदाभ्य: ॥

6. This pure soul, the bestower of joy, mastered through knowledge, immortal in nature, overcomes all sinful desires. (1261)

७. एष दिवं वि धावति तिरो रजाँसि धारया । पवमान: कनिक्रदत् ॥

7. This pure soul, through its fortitude and firmness, overcoming all acts of moral passions, singing the praise of God, attains to salvation. (1262)

८. एष दिवं व्यासरत्तिरो रजाँस्यस्तृत: । पवमान: स्वध्वर: ॥

8. This pure soul, unharassed by desires, performing virtuous deeds, casting aside the impediments arising out of passion, attains to salvation. (1263)

९. एष प्रत्नेन जन्मना देवो देवेभ्य: सुत: । हरि: पवित्रे अर्षति ॥

9. This brilliant soul, steady in its path of rectitude, the annihilator of all sufferings, for the welfare of the learned, taking a noble birth as the result of past actions, unifies itself with God. (1264)[1]

१०. एष उ स्य पुरुव्रतो जज्ञानो जनयन्निष: । धारया पवते सुत: ॥

10. The same soul, the performer of manifold noble acts, after entering the body, being the author of various acts, equipped with knowledge, treads on the right path through its steadiness. (1265)

III

१. एष धिया यात्यण्व्या शूरो रथेभिराशुभि: । गच्छन्निन्द्रस्य निष्कृतम् ॥

1. Just as a warrior goes in rapid cars, so does this Yogi, with fine, quick intellect, going to the exalted divine stage of God, acquire supreme bliss. (1266)

२. एष पुरु धियायते बृहते देवतातये । यत्रामृतास आशत ॥

2. This soul, performing various virtuous deeds, practises Yoga, for the realisation of God, in Whom other emancipated souls, enjoy the bliss of salvation. (1267)

३. एतं मृजन्ति मर्ज्यमुप द्रोणेष्वायव: । प्रचक्राणं महीरिष: ॥

3. The learned, longing for longevity, beautify in their hearts, this soul, worthy to be beautified, and the cherisher of multifarious desires. (1268)

[1]See verse 758.

४. एष हितो वि नीयतेऽन्तः शुन्ध्यावता पथा । यदी तुञ्जन्ति भूर्णयः ॥

4. When learned persons exert, controlling their breaths through Prānāyāma this soul hidden inside, is realised through consecrated path. (1269)[1]

५. एष रुक्मिभिरीयते वाजी शुभ्रेभिरꣳशुभिः । पतिः सिन्धूनां भवन् ॥

5. Just as the ocean is full of brilliant, pure waters, so is this powerful soul known as the compendium of knowledge. (1270)

६. एष शृङ्गाणि दोधुवच्छिशीते यूथ्यो३ वृषा । नृम्णा दधान ओजसा ॥

6. Just as a bull, roaming in a herd of cows, waves and whets his horns, so does a learned person, with his power of leading men, acquiring riches, attain to the heights of knowledge. (1271)

७. एष वसूनि पिब्दनः परुषा ययिवाꣳ अति । अव शादेषु गच्छति ॥

7. A learned person, urging the breaths, and crossing each stage of advance-ment, enters severe austerities. (1272)

८. एतमु त्यं दश क्षिपो हरिꣳ हिन्वन्ति यातवे । स्वायुधं मदिन्तमम् ॥

8. The ten breaths, urge for elevation, this soul, well-armed, the best giver of delight and the alleviator of miseries. (1273)

IV

१. एष उ स्य वृषा रथोऽव्या वारेभिरव्यत । गच्छन् वाजꣳ सहस्रिणम् ॥

1. An aspirant after emancipation raining happiness, ever active, acquiring knowledge, the giver of a thousand joys, treads on the path of salvation, through excellent accomplishments of mental power. (1274)

२. एतं त्रितस्य योषणो हरिꣳ हिन्वन्त्यद्रिभिः । इन्दुमिन्द्राय पीतये ॥

2. The organs of an ascetic, longing to be freed from threefold pains, enhance through different expedients, the strength of his soul, the alleviator of sufferings. They desire the soul to enjoy the bliss of God. (1275)[2]

३. एष स्य मानुषीष्वा श्येनो न विक्षु सीदति । गच्छं जारो न योषितम् ॥

3. A Yogi like a falcon quickly settles down amid the families of men, just as a husband goes eagerly to his beloved wife. (1276).

४. एष स्य मद्यो रसोऽव चष्टे दिवः शिशुः । य इन्दुर्वारमाविशत् ॥

4. The soul, that enters the lovely path of salvation, full of exhilaration and

---

[1]Consecrated path means Yoga.
[2]Threefold: Spiritual, Physical, Elemental. They refers to the organs.

joy, sits in the lap of God, liké a child in that of the mother, and surveys all worlds. (1277)

५॰ एष स्य पीतये सुतो हरिरर्षति धर्णसि: । क्रन्दन् योनिमभि प्रियम् ॥

5. This soul, longing for salvation, the leader of all the organs of senses, the lord of all breaths, ready to drink the juice of happiness, goes to God, its beloved Refuge. (1278)

६॰ एतं त्यं हरितो दश मर्मृं ज्यन्ते अपस्युव: । याभिर्मंदाय शुम्भते ॥

6. The ten organs of senses, ever intent upon work, purify the soul, where-with, longing for salvation, it equips itself for acquiring the supreme bliss of God. (1279)

V

१. एष वाजी हितो नृभिर्विश्वविन् मनसस्पति: । ग्रव्यं वारं वि धावति ॥

1. This Powerful, Omniscient God, the Lord of the minds of all, realised by the ascetics, transgresses the utmost limit of the soul. (1280)

२. एष पवित्रे अक्षरत् सोमो देवेभ्य: सुत: । विश्वा धामान्याविशन् ॥

2. This God manifests Himself to the wise, learned persons, and is realised in various beautiful forms. He pervades all places. (1281)

३. एष देव: शुभायतेऽधि योनावमर्त्य: । वृत्रहा देववीतम: ॥

3. This Glorious, Immortal God, is the Dispeller of all the coverings of ignorance, and the Absorber of all divine objects. He shines in Matter in its primordial state. (1282)

४. एष वृषा कनिक्रद् दशभिर्जामिमिभिर्यत: । अभि द्रोणानि धावति ॥

4. This God, the fulfiller of all desired joys, revealing the Vedas, held by ten sisters, the directions, pervades all the worlds. (1283)

५. एष सूर्यमरोचयत् पवमानो ग्रधि द्यवि । पवित्रे मत्सरो मद: ॥

5. This All-pervading God, lends lustre to the Sun in heaven and grants joy and happiness to the pure soul. (1284)

६. एष सूर्येण हासते संवसानो विवस्वता । पतिर्वाचो ग्रदाभ्य: ॥

6. This Omnipotent God, overshadowing the entire universe with the lustrous Sun is verily full of splendour, as the Unconquerable Lord of Vedic speech. (1285)

VI

१. एष कविरभिष्टुतः पवित्रे अधि तोशते । पुनानो धन्नप द्विषः ॥

1. This Omniscient God, casting aside persons full of hatred, this Purifier of all, and Uplifter of the down-trodden, applauded by all, lends contentment to a pure heart. (1286)

२. एष इन्द्राय वायवे स्वर्जित् परि षिच्यते । पवित्रे दक्षसाधनः ॥

2. This God, the Giver of strength, the Lord of the joys of salvation, for the subtle soul, is contemplated in the heart. (1287)[1]

३. एष नृभिर्वि नीयते दिवो मूर्धा वृषा सुतः । सोमो वनेषु विश्ववित् ॥

3. This Omniscient God, the Head of Heaven, the Bestower of joys, Worthy of worship, is remembered by men in their bodies. (1288)

४. एष गव्युरचिक्रदत् पवमानो हिरण्ययुः । इन्दुः सत्राजिदस्तृतः ॥

4. This Glorious God, the Purifier of all, pervading all luminous heavenly bodies, still Conquering, never Overcome, the Well-Wisher of all, preaches to humanity through the Vedas. (1289)

५. एष शुष्म्यसिष्यददन्तरिक्षे वृषा हरिः । पुनान इन्दुरिन्द्रमा ॥

5. The Glorious God, the Alleviator of all sufferings, the Bestower of all joys, Omnipotent, purifying the soul, reigneth supreme in the heart. (1290)

६. एष शुष्म्यदाभ्यः सोमः पुनानो अर्षति । देवावीरघशꣳसहा ॥

6. This Invincible God, the Protector of the godly, the Slayer of the sinful, the Purifier of all, is Omnipresent. (1291)

VII

१. स सुतः पीतये वृषा सोमः पवित्र अर्षति । विघ्नन्रक्षाꣳसि देवयुः ॥

1. That Consummate God, The Bringer of delights, the Fulfiller of the desires of the learned, pervades the heart for filling it with joy. (1292)

२. स पवित्रे विचक्षणो हरिरर्षति धर्णसिः । अभि योनिं कनिक्रदत् ॥

2. That God, the Alleviator of sufferings, the Seer of all, the Sustainer of the universe, preaching the Vedas to the world, reigneth supreme in the heart. (1293)

३. स वाजी रोचनं दिवः पवमानो वि धावति । रक्षोहा वारमव्ययम् ॥

---

[1]Yoni योनि means the world, the cause and birth place of the animate and inanimate creation.

3. That God, Powerful, the Illuminator of the Sun, the Purifier of all, the Slayer of sins, manifesteth Himself in the recesses of the heart. (1294)

४. स त्रितस्याधि सानवि पवमानो अरोचयत् । जामिभिः सूर्यं सह ॥

4. The All-purifying God, refines with allied function the intellect in the head of an ascetic longing for release from threefold sufferings. (1295)[1]

५. स वृत्रहा वृषा सुतो वरिवोविददाभ्यः । सोमो वाजमिवासरत् ॥

5. The soul, the banisher of ignorance, the bestower of happiness, the bringer of prosperity and invincible, goes eagerly towards God as a warrior to the battle-field. (1296)

६. स देवः कविनेषितोऽभि द्रोणानि धावति । इन्दुरिन्द्राय मंहयन् ॥

6. The lustrous, joyful soul, urged by God, worshipping Him, revels in the treasures of knowledge. (1297)

VIII

१. यः पावमानीरध्येत्यृषिभिः संभृतं रसम् । सर्वं स पूतमश्नाति स्वदितं मातरिश्वना ॥

1. He, who studies the ennobling Vedic verses, the essence of which is expounded by the saints, (Rishis), tastes the pure knowledge, relished by the mind. (1298)

२. पावमानीर्यो अध्येत्यृषिभिः संभृतं रसम् । तस्मै सरस्वती दुहे क्षीरं सर्पिमंधूदकम् ॥

2. For him, Who studies the ennobling Vedic verses, the essence of which is expounded by the Rishis (Seers), the Vedic speech pours forth spiritual knowledge, pure like milk, spiritual light, thick like the clarified butter, joy sweet like the honey, and mental tranquillity, cold like water. (1299)

३. पावमानीः स्वस्त्ययनीः सुदुघा हि घृतश्चुतः ।
ऋषिभिः संभृतो रसो ब्राह्मणेष्वमृतं हितम् ॥

3. The purifying Vedic verses pertaining to Soma, are the bestower of eternal happiness, the bearers of nice fruit, and the givers of knowledge. They are the essence of the Vedas realised by the Rishis, and eternal knowledge stored in the knowers of the Vedas. (1300)

४. पावमानीर्दधन्तु न इमं लोकमथो अमुम् । कामान्त्समर्धयन्तु नो देवीर्देवैः समाहृताः ॥

---

[1] Griffith intercepts Trita as a Rishi. This explanation is unsound as there is no history in the Vedas. The word means an ascetic looking for release from threefold sufferings, i.e., (1) आध्यात्मिक, spiritual, (2) आधिदैविक, elemental, (3) आधिभौतिक, physical.

4. So may the divine, purifying Soma hymns bestow on us this world and the next. May they preached by the learned gratify our hearts' desires. (1301)[1]

५. येन देवा: पवित्रेणात्मानं पुनते सदा । तेन सहस्रधारेण पावमानी: पुनन्तु न: ॥

5. The purifying source, wherewith the learned Yogis ever purify themselves, with that, in thousand currents, may the Soma verses of the Vedas purify us. (1302)[2]

६. पावमानी: स्वस्त्ययनीस्ताभिर्गच्छति नान्दनम् ।
पुण्याँश्च भक्षान्भक्षयत्यमृतत्वं च गच्छति ॥

6. The purifying Soma verses bring final beatitude. By their study the soul attains to supreme bliss. In that state enjoying solemn delights it attains to immortality. (1303)

IX

१. अगन्म महा नमसा यविष्ठं यो दीदाय समिद्ध: स्वे दुरोणे ।
चित्रभानुँ रोदसी अन्तरुर्वी स्वाहुतं विश्वत: प्रत्यञ्चम् ॥

1. May we with great reverence approach God, Who shines forth, well-kindled in this vast universe, is All-pervading, controls all between the expanded Heaven and Earth, is Almighty, and Worthy of adoration. (1304)

२. स मह्ना विश्वा दुरितानि साह्वानग्नि ष्टवे दम आ जातवेदा: ।
स नो रक्षिषद् दुरितादवद्यादस्मान् गृणत उत नो मघोन: ॥

2. Through His great might, overcoming all sins, praised in the heart is the Omniscient God. May He preserve us from despicable, sinful behaviour, both of us, who land Him and are wealthy in knowledge. (1305)

३. त्वं वरुण उत मित्रो अग्ने त्वां वर्धन्ति मतिभिर्वसिष्ठा: ।
त्वे वसु सुषणनानि सन्तु यूयं पात स्वस्तिभि: सदा न: ॥

3. O God, Thou art Varuṇa and Mitra. Learned persons and seekers after salvation exalt Thee with their forces of contemplation. Through Thee, may knowledge and wealth be the givers of excellent happiness. Do ye preserve us evermore with blessings! (1306)[3]

X

१. महाँ इन्द्रो य ओजसा पर्जन्यो वृष्टिमाँ इव । स्तोमैर्वत्सस्य वावृधे ॥

Soma verses mean the verses pertaining to God and soul.
[2]The purifying source means Yoga.
[3]God is Varuna as He saves us from sins. He is Mitra as He is the friend of all, and saves us from the pangs of death. Ye refers to learned persons.

1. Like a cloud rich in rain, God is great in His power. He is glorified with the Vedic hymns sung by a Vedic scholar. (1307)[1]

२. कण्वा इन्द्रं यदक्रत स्तोमैर्यज्ञस्य साधनम् । जामि ब्रुवत आयुधा ॥

2. When the learned singers of praise pronounce God as an instrument for accomplishing the Yajna (sacrifice) of life, they declare all other weapons needless. (1308)

३. प्रजामृतस्य पिप्रतः प्र यज्ज्जुरन्त वह्नयः । विप्रा ऋतस्य वाहसा ॥

3. When brilliant learned persons realize the spiritual power of the soul, as its magnifiers they do it with the strength of knowledge and truth. (1309)

XI

१. पवमानस्य जिघ्नतो हरेश्चन्द्रा प्रसृक्षत । जीरा अजिरशोचिषः ॥

1. On flow the gladdening, woe-killing eternal gleams of the soul, pure in nature, the banisher of all sufferings, the destroyer of all the coatings of ignorance. (1310)

२. पवमानो रथीतमः शुभ्रेभिः शुभ्रशस्तमः । हरिश्चन्द्रो मरुद्गणः ॥

2. The pure soul is the best rider of the chariot-like body, most beautiful with its lovely rays of knowledge, the best annihilator of sufferings, and the leader of the forces of breath. (1311)

३. पवमान व्यश्नुहि रश्मिभिर्वाजसातमः । दधत्स्तोत्रे सुवीर्यम् ॥

3. O pure soul, the giver of strength, granting wealth and heroism to a learned person, penetrate the whole world with thy streams of knowledge ! (1312)

XII

१. परीतो षिञ्चता सुतꣽ सोमो य उत्तमꣽ हविः ।
दधन्वाꣽ यो नर्यो अपस्वाꣳन्तरा सुषाव सोममद्रिभिः ॥

1. The semen is the best life-infusing support, the friend of man, the lender of strength and perseverance to the organs of senses. It is created through complete devices of celibacy. O learned persons, let it flow upward to the head from beneath. (1313)

२. नूनं पुनानोऽविभिः परि स्त्रवादब्धः सुरभिन्तरः ।
सुते चित्वाप्सु मदामो अन्धसा श्रीणन्तो गोभिरुत्तरम् ॥

---

[1]Learned persons should try to become ऊर्ध्वरेतः i.e., live in perpetual celibacy.

2. O invincible, more odorous semen, purified through breathing exercises, flow in the whole of the body. On thy production in the body, ripening thee with food and milk, we take delight in performing physical and mental feats. (1314)

३. परि स्वानश्चक्षसे देवमादन: ऋतुरिन्दुर्विचक्षण: ॥

3. A Brahmchari, the preserver of semen, the seer of different sorts of knowledge, the performer of noble deeds, the bringer of joy to the learned, being accomplished, becomes the cynosure of all. (1315)[1]

XIII

१. असावि सोमो अरुषो वृषा हरी राजेव दस्मो अभि गा अचिक्रदत् ।
पुनानो वारमत्येष्यव्ययं श्येनो न योनिं घृतवन्तमासदत् ॥

1. A learned person is born, to shed lustre, bestow happiness and lead others. Just as a handsome King issues proclamations to his subjects, so does a learned teacher teach the Vedas to his pupils. Purifying himself and crossing the covering of breaths, he swiftly goes to the Refulgent God, his real Refuge, as a hawk goes rapidly to his nest. (1316)[2]

२. पर्जन्य: पिता महिषस्य पर्णिनो नाभा पृथिव्या गिरिषु क्षयं दधे ।
स्वसार आपो अभि गा उदासरन्तं ग्रावभिर्वंसते वीते अध्वरे ॥

2. The Guardian of the learned, mighty soul is God. The bestower of joys like a cloud, the soul makes its home in the hearts of the learned, in different earthly relations. The functions of knowledge spontaneously proceed to the organs of senses. The soul dwells with the learned in its effort to acquire brilliant knowledge. (1317)[3]

३. कविर्वेधस्या पर्येषि माहिनमत्यो न मृष्टो अभि वाजमर्षसि ।
अपसेधन् दुरिता सोम नो मृड घृता वसान: परि यासि निर्णिजम् ॥

3. O soul, wise as thou art, with superb intellect, thou marchest on to God. Just as a groomed steed goes fast to the battle-field, so dost thou, with knowledge as thy goal, proceed on the path of salvation, for the acquisition of God. O learned soul, be gracious unto us, driving off our evil desires. Clad in the lustre of knowledge, attain to thy pure self! (1318)

XIV

१. श्रायन्त इव सूर्यं विश्वेदिन्द्रस्य भक्षत ।
वसूनि जातो जनिमान्योजसा प्रति भागं न दीधिम: ॥

---

[1]Brahmchari: One who takes the vow of celibacy.
[2]See verse 562. A learned person crosses the प्राणमय Kosha, and goes to ज्ञानमय Kosha to reach God.
[3]God is spoken of as पर्जन्य: as He grants joys, just as a cloud sends water.

1. All riches that have been and will be created, with their full potency, belong to God, just as a son enjoys the wealth inherited from his father according to his share, so do we enjoy what God hath given us, just as the rays created by the Sun receive light from the Sun. (1319)[1]

२. अर्षिरराति वसुदामुप स्तुहि भद्रा इन्द्रस्य रातयः ।
यो अस्य कामं विधतो न रोषति मनो दानाय चोदयन् ॥

2. O man, praise God, Who is Immaculate, Charitable, and the Giver of riches. Propitious are the gifts that God gives. He goads Himself to spread His knowledge, and satisfies the wish of His devotee ! (1320)

XV

१. यत इन्द्र भयामहे ततो नो अभयं कृधि ।
मघवन् छग्धि तव तन्न ऊतये वि द्विषो वि मृधो जहि ॥

1. O King, make us fearless from that whereof we are afraid. O wealthy King, thou art competent for our protection, thy devotees. Drive away foes and win battles ! (1321)[2]

२. त्वं हि राधसस्पते राधसो महः क्षयस्यासि विधर्ता ।
तं त्वा वयं मघवन्निन्द्र गिर्वणः सुतावन्तो हवामहे ॥

2. O God, Thou art verily the Lord of prosperity, Thou art the supporter of ample bounty and the universe. O Glorious, Praiseworthy God, we learned persons call on Thee ! (1322)

XVI

१. त्वं सोमासि धारयुमन्द्र ओजिष्ठो अध्वरे । पवस्व मंहयद्रयिः ॥

1. O God, Thou art the Lord of Vedic speech, the Embodiment of joy, Mighty, and the Giver of prosperity. Shine in my heart ! (1323)

२. त्वं सुतो मदिन्तमो दधन्वान्मत्सरिन्तमः । इन्दुः सत्राजिदस्तृतः ॥

2. O God, contemplated in the heart, Thou art most delightful, the Supporter of the Yajna, the Best of gladdeners, and Refulgent. Thou art still Conquering, never Subdued ! (1324)

३. त्वं सुष्वाणो अद्रिभिरभ्यर्ष कनिक्रदत् । द्युमन्तं शुष्ममा भर ॥

3. O God, realised through austere penances, Thou, the preacher of knowledge, come unto us. Grant us brightly glorious strength of knowledge ! (1325)

[1]See verse 267.
[2]See verse 274.

XVII

१. पवस्व देववीतय इन्दो धाराभिरोजसा । श्रा कलशं मधुमान्त्सोम नः सदः ॥

1. O God, come unto the learned for their union with Thee. O God, full of joy, reside in our heart, with Thy infinite power and streams of divinity! (1326)[1]

२. तव द्रप्सा उदप्रुत इन्द्रं मदाय वावृधुः । त्वां देवासो श्रमृताय कं पपुः ॥

2. O God, Thy rapid flowing streams of delight exalt the soul. The Yogis unite themselves for immortality with Thee, the Embodiment of happiness! (1327)[2]

३. श्रा नः सुतास इन्दवः पुनाना धावता रयिम् । वृष्टिद्यावो रीत्यापः स्वविदः ॥

3. O learned persons, who penetrate deep into the soul, accomplishing and purifying yourselves, as procurers of joys, showerers of knowledge, bestowers of comforts, move towards the beautiful soul and fill it with joy and tran- quillity ! (1328)

XVIII

१. परि त्यꣳ हर्यतꣳ हरिं बभ्रुं पुनन्ति वारेण ।
यो देवान्विश्वाꣳ इत्परि मदेन सह गच्छति ॥

1. The learned purify through their heart, the soul, beloved by all, the shunner of sins, and lustrous. The soul fills all the organs of senses with joy. (1329)

२. द्रियं पञ्च स्वयशसꣳ सखायो श्रद्रिसꣳहतम् । प्रियमिन्द्रस्य काम्यं प्रस्नापयन्त ऊर्मयः ॥

2. Know the soul, whom, bright with native splendour, indivisible like a rock, loved by God, all-loving, the ten companions, with upward motion, bathe in joys. (1330)

३. इन्द्राय सोम पातवे वृत्रघ्ने परि षिच्यसे । नरे च दक्षिणावते वीराय सदनासदे ॥

3. O power, thou art scattered for the soul, thy fosterer, the annihilator of ignorance, the lord of activity, the permanent dweller in the body, the master of strength, and the leader of all ! (1331)

XIX

१. पवस्व सोम महे दक्षायाश्वो न निक्तो वाजी धनाय ।

[1]See verse 552.
[2]'Ten companions' means breaths having upward motion, i.e·, ऊर्ध्वंगति. Ten com- panions may also refer to ten organs of senses, five Jnāna Indriyas and five Karma Indriyas, i.e., organs of cognition and organs of action.

1. O God, Thou art Pure, and Mighty like the lightning, purify our actions for the acquisition of great power and wealth ! (1332)[1]

२. प्र ते सोतारो रसं मदाय पुनन्ति सोमं महे द्युम्नाय ॥

2. The Yogis make the juice of supreme bliss flow for the attainment of joy and great dignity. (1333)

३. शिशुं जज्ञानꣳ हरिं मृजन्ति पवित्रे सोमं देवेभ्य इन्दुम् ।

3. The Yogis, manifestly realise in the contemplation of God, supreme bliss, that resides in the body, alleviates sufferings, develops consciousness, and is full of lustre. (1334)

XX

१. उपो षु जातमप्तुरं गोभिर्भंगं परिष्कृतम् । इन्दुं देवा अयासिषुः ॥

1. The learned attain to the soul, possessing fine qualities, full of actions and knowledge, adorned with the beams of learning, and the crusher of foes. (1335)[2]

२. तमिद्वर्धन्तु नो गिरो वत्सꣳ सꣳशिश्वरीरिव । य इन्द्रस्य हृदꣳसनिः ॥

2. Just as mothers nourish the child with their milk, so may our learned discourses exalt God, Who resides inside the soul. (1336)

३. अर्षा नः सोम शं गवे धुक्षस्व पिप्युषीमिषम् । वर्धा समुद्रमुक्थ्य ॥

3. O God, grant peaceful calm to our speech, grant us invigorating will-power. O Praiseworthy God, exalt our soul unfathomable like the ocean ! (1337)

XXI

१. आ घा ये अग्निमिन्धते स्तृणन्ति बर्हिरानुषक् । येषामिन्द्रो युवा सखा ॥

1. Learned persons, whose bright intellect is ever young and friendly, kindle their fire of iron determination, and always keep their hearts ready for welcoming spiritual forces. (1338)[3]

२. बृहन्निदिध्म एषां भूरि शस्तं पृथुः स्वरः । येषामिन्द्रो युवा सखा ॥

2. Great is their glory, much their laud, deep is their force of breath, whose friend is God ever Young. (1339)

---

[1]See verse 430.
[2]See verse 487.
[3]See verse 133.

३. अयुद्ध इद्युधा वृत꣱ शूर आजति सत्वभिः । येषामिन्द्रो युवा सखा ॥

3. Unquelled in fight the hero leads his army with the warrior chiefs, whose friend is God, ever Young. (1340)

XXII

१. य एक इद्विदयते वसु मर्ताय दाशुषे । ईशानो अप्रतिष्कुत इन्द्रो अङ्ग ॥

1. O pupil, God alone, Who is Unconquerable and Almighty, bestoweth glory on a Yogi, who is self-abnegating and charitable. (1341)[1]

२. यश्चिद्धि त्वा बहुभ्य आ सुतावा꣱ आविवासति । उग्रं तत् पत्यते शव इन्द्रो अङ्ग ॥

2. O man, whoever amongst the multitude, manifestly realises God, him does He grant tremendous power ! (1342)

३. कदा मर्तमराघसं पदा क्षुम्पमिव स्फुरत् । कदा नः शुश्रवद् गिर इन्द्रो अङ्ग ॥

3. O man, God tramples like the tiny weed with His might, whenever He likes, the atheist, who has no word of praise for Him. He listens to our song of praise, whenever He likes ! (1343)[2]

XXIII

१. गायन्ति त्वा गायत्रिणोऽर्चन्त्यर्कमर्किणः । ब्रह्माणस्त्वा शतक्रत उद्व꣱शमिव येमिरे ॥

1. O King, the doer of hundreds of deeds, the Udagatas praise thee, the Hotas eulogise thee, worthy of reverence, the Adhivaryus and Brahmas exalt thee just as jugglers lift aloft a pole to show their skill ! (1344)[3]

२. यत्सानोः सान्वारुहो भूर्यस्पष्ट कर्त्वम् । तदिन्द्रो अर्थं चेतति यूथेन वृष्णिरेजति ॥

2. When a Yogi reaches the highest pinnacle of mental development, he exerts for the accomplishment of the aim, God, at that stage he knows his resolve, and his soul, the showerer of happiness, and advances like a general with his troop. (1345)

३. युङ्क्ष्वा हि केशिना हरी वृषणा कक्ष्यप्रा । अथा न इन्द्र सोमपा गिरामुपश्रुति चर ॥

3. O soul, the enjoyer of happiness, listen to the sound of our praisesongs. Harness in the chariot of thy destination, the two horses of knowledge and action, that will bring thee happiness and take thee to thy goal! (1346)[4]

---

[1] See verse 389.

[2] Just as a tiny weed is trampled under foot without any effort, so does God destroy an atheist.

[3] See verse 342.

[4] Chariot means body. Destination means salvation.

BOOK VI

Chapter 1

I

१. सुषमिद्धो न आ वह देवाꣴ अग्ने हविष्मते । होत: पावक यक्षि च ॥

1. O Refulgent God, duly kindled in our heart, make us come in contact with the learned persons. O Bestower of all objects, O Purifier of the hearts of all, Thou verily lovest a learned person! (1347)

२. मधुमन्तं तनूनपाद्यज्ञं देवेषु न: । कवे । अद्या कृणुह्यतये ॥

2. O sage, the saviour of the body from decay, accomplish the sweetest Yajna of our life, for our protection, through the learned persons! (1348)[1]

३. नराशꣴसमिह प्रियमस्मिन्यज्ञ उप ह्वये । मधुजिह्वꣴ हविष्कृतम् ॥

3. In this world, in this Yajna of life, I invoke God, praised by the learned, Most Lovely, the sweet-tongued Preacher of the Vedas, and the Perfector of divine knowledge. (1349)

४. अग्ने सुखतमे रथे देवाꣴ ईडित आ वह । असि होता मनुर्हित: ।

4. O God, entreated through Samādhi, fill divine virtues in this most pleasant body. Thou art realisable through deep concentration, and art the Bestower of joys! (1350)

II

१. यदद्य सूर उदितेऽनागा मित्रो अर्यमा । सुवाति सविता भग: ॥

1. On the development of the soul, may God, Worthy of worship, Free from sin, Friendly, Just, the Creator of the universe, bestow happiness on us, (1351)

२. सुप्रावीरस्तु स क्षय: प्र नु यामन्त्सुदानव: । ये नो अꣴहोऽतिपिप्रति ॥

2. They, who are free from sin, preach excellent sermons. May this shelter of theirs prove a source of protection for us. (1352)

३. उत स्वराजो अदितिरदब्धस्य व्रतस्य ये । महो राजान ईशते ॥

3. Those persons of spotless character, who shine through their soulforce, by observing inviolate vow, become fit to rule over others through their supremacy. (1353)

---

[1]Achāraya Shākpūni interprets तनूनपात् as fire.

III

१. उ त्वा मदन्तु सोमाः क्रृणुष्व राधो अद्रिवः । अव ब्रह्माद्विषो जहि ॥

1. O soul, let knowledge and glory gladden thee. Acquire the wealth of knowledge. Drive off the enemies of Vedic teachings! (1354)[1]

२. पदा पणीनराधसो नि बाधस्व महाꣳअसि । न हि त्वा कश्च न प्रति ॥

2. O God, crush with Thy might, the niggard, and those foolish persons who spend not their money on the performance of Yajnas. Mighty art Thou. There is not one to equal Thee! (1355)[2]

३. त्वमीशिषे सुतानामिन्द्र त्वमसुतानाम् । त्वꣳ राजा जनानाम् ॥

3. O God, Thou art the Lord of the born, and the unborn, the learned, and the ignorant. Thou art the sovereign of the people! (1356)

IV

१. आ जागृविर्विप्र ऋतं मतीनाꣳ सोमः पुनानो असदच्चमूषु ।
सपन्ति यं मिथुनासो निकामा अध्वर्यवो रथिरासः सुहस्ताः ॥

1. A vigilant learned person, possessing mental quietness and self control, preaching the essence of the true knowledge of cogitable Vedic verses, manifests himself amongst the people. To him resort the married couples with manifold desires, and in their fine conveyances the learned priests skilled in the performance of noble deeds. (1357)

२. स पुनान उप सूरे दधान आभे अप्रा रोदसी वी ष आवः ।
प्रिया चिद्यस्य प्रियसास ऊती सतो धनं कारिणे न प्र यꣳसत् ॥

2. The learned person, purifying himself, and concentrating on God through profound religious meditation, fills both the literate and the illiterate with the glow of learning, and discloses various sorts of knowledge. The pure and noble desires of a learned person are meant to guard us against fears and obstacles. May he grant us the excellent wealth of spiritual knowledge, as to a servant. (1358)

३. स वर्धिता वर्धनः पूयमानः सोमो मीढ्वाꣳ अभि नो ज्योतिषावित् ।
यत्र नः पूर्वे पितरः पदज्ञाः स्वर्विदो अभि गा अद्रिमिष्णन् ॥

3. May a learned person, the strengthener, and remover of the doubts of all, highly pure, the showerer of joy and comforts with the light of his spiritual knowledge, take us to the place, where our seers of old, the knowers of God, the enjoyers of the happiness of salvation, the realisers of the significance of Vedic verses, had willingly gone to the Indivisible God. (1359)

[1]See verse 194.
[2]The learned person refers to the person mentioned in the previous verse. The word रोदसी may also mean Prāna and Apāna, this world and the next world, heaven and earth.

V

१. मा चिदन्यद्वि शौंसत सखायो मा रिषण्यत ।
इन्द्रमित् स्तोता वृषणौं सचा सुते मुहुरुक्था च शौंसत ॥

1. Glorify naught besides soul, O friends, so shall no sorrow trouble ye. On the divulgence of knowledge, sing unitedly the praise of the excellent soul, by reciting Vedic verses again and again ! (1360)[1]

२. अवक्रक्षिणं वृषभं यथा जुवं गां न चर्षणीसहम् ।
विद्वेषणौं संवननमुभयङ्करं मौंहिष्ठमुभयाविनम् ॥

2. O learned persons, sing the praise of God alone, Who attracts all towards Himself, is active like a bull, the Tolerator of the offences of mankind like the Earth, Free from hatred, the Refuge of the noble, the Protector and Destroyer of men, Most Charitable, and Munificent to the literate and the illiterate ! (1361)

VI

१. उदु त्ये मधुमत्तमा गिरः स्तोमास ईरते ।
सत्राजितो धनसा अक्षितोतयो वाजयन्तो रथा इव ॥

1. Just as chariots, running in battlefields, affording protection, conquering foes, bring us wealth, so do these Vedic hymns full of knowledge and delight, rise unto God, out of the hearts of the devoted scholars. (1362)[2]

२. कण्वा इव भृगवः सूर्या इव विश्वमिद्धीतमाशत ।
इन्द्रौं स्तोमेभिमंहयन्त आयवः प्रियमेधासो अस्वरन् ॥

2. The austere, learned persons, like the rays of the sun, enjoy the whole world through the force of knowledge and meditation. Persons, who are lovers of refined intellect, recite Vedic verses, worshipping God with songs of praise. (1363)

VII

१. पर्यू षु प्र धन्व वाजसातये परि वृत्राणि सक्षणिः । द्विषस्तरध्या ऋणया न ईरसे ॥

1. O Calm, Forbearing God, the Remover of our debts, certainly rain fine happiness all around. Thou art competent to subdue our inimical foes of morality! (1364)[3]

---

[1]See verse 242.
[2]See verse 251.
[3]See verse 428.

२. अजीजनो हि पवमान सूर्यं विधारे शश्मना पयः । गोजीरया रंहमाणः पुरन्ध्या ॥

2. O God, Ever Active, the Motivator of all through Thy power of sustaining the universe, Thou dost beget the sun to support water in the atmosphere through his rays ! (1365)

३. अनु हि त्वा सुत꣠ सोम मदामसि [महे समर्यं राज्ये । वाजा꣠ अभि पवमान प्र गाहसे]॥

3. O King, we feel comfort and delight in living under thy control and administration run by excellent, celibate officials. O excellent ruler, thou movest about unmindful of foes ! (1366)[1]

VIII

१. परि प्र धन्व [इन्द्राय सोम स्वादुर्मित्राय पूष्णे भगाय] ॥

1. O Calm, extremely Sweet God, bestow happiness on the person, who is friendly, life-infusing and dignified ! (1367)[2]

२. एवामृताय महे क्षयाय स शुक्रो अर्षं दिव्यः पीयूषः ॥

2. O God, Thou art Divine, and the Strengthener of all. For granting us salvation and procuring shelter, Thou Immaculate God, shower knowledge and joy on us ! (1368)

३. इन्द्रस्ते सोम सुतस्य पेयात् क्रत्वे दक्षाय विश्वे च देवाः ॥

3. O God, let soul and all learned persons drink Thy juice of happiness for wisdom and strength! (1369)

IX

१. सूर्यस्येव रश्मयो द्रावयित्नवो मत्सरासः प्रसुतः साकमीरते ।
तन्तुं ततं परि सर्गासि आशवो नेन्द्रादृते पवते धाम किं चन ॥

1. Like the beams of the sun, all these fast moving, nicely created, self-revolving, active worlds, simultaneously revolve around their respective orbits taking shelter under the Vast God. Power and glory emanate from no other souce but God. (1370)[3]

२. उपो मतिः पृच्यते सिच्यते मधु मन्द्राजनी चोदते अन्तरासनि ।
पवमानः सन्तनिः सुन्वतामिव मधुमान् द्रप्सः परि वारमर्षति ॥

[1]See verse 432.
[2]See verse 427.

[3]तन्तु is used here for God, Who is the beginningless Creator, Sustainer and Dissolver of the thread of the universe. Benfey, Grassman, and Stevenson, following Sāyana, take the word literally as meaning the net of the filter.

2. When intellect is concentrated on God, the juice of joy flows in the heart. The stream of intense delight is thus felt in the head. The lustrous essence of joy, spreading around, shedding knowledge and happiness, appears in the middle of the eyebrows. (1371)

३. उक्षा मिमेति प्रति यन्ति धेनवो देवस्य देवीरुप यन्ति निष्कृतम् । अत्यक्रमीदर्जुनं वारमव्ययमत्कं न निक्तं परि सोमो अव्यत ॥

3. Just as the cows come nigh to the bellowing bull, so do divine forces approach the pure nature of the soul. The all-impelling power, competent to watch the decay and growth of the body, crossing the covering of physical vigour, attains to a pure stage where it protects us like an armour. (1372)[1]

X

१. अग्नि नरो दीधितिभिररण्योर्हस्तच्युतं जनयत प्रशस्तम् । दूरेदृशं गृहपतिमथर्व्युम् ॥

1. Highly intellectual persons, like fire produced with the strength of hands, by rubbing the fire-sticks with fingers, realise God, Self-Existent, Faultless, Far-seeing, the Protector of His subjects like a lord of the house, All-Pervading. (1373)[2]

२. तमग्निमस्ते वसवो न्यृण्वन्त्सुप्रतिचक्षमवसे कुतश्चित् । दक्षाय्यो यो दम आस नित्य: ॥

2. Learned persons, for all round protection, search in the heart, through Yogic concentration for that fascinating soul, that is expert in imparting strength, eternal, and resides in its house, the body. (1374)

३. प्रेद्धो अग्ने दीदिहि पुरो नोऽजस्रया सूर्म्या यविष्ठ । त्वाꣲ शश्वन्त उप यन्ति वाजा: ॥

3. Shine Thou before us with constant flame of knowledge, O God, Most youthful and Enkindled through Yogic practices. Austere learned persons, since times immemorial, attain unto Thee ! (1375)

XI

१. आयं गौः पृश्निरक्रमीदसदन्मातरं पुर: । पितरं च प्रयन्त्स्व: ॥

1. The All-Pervading, Omnipresent God, verily manifesteth Himself. He is directly realised by the learned, and graciously perceived by a saviour of humanity. (1376)[3]

२. अन्तश्चरति रोचनास्य प्राणादपानती । व्यख्यन्महिषो दिवम् ॥

2. The loving lighto God, animates in the body, facilitating inhalation

---

[1] All-impelling power means intellect.
[2] See verse 72.
[3] See verse 630.

and exhalation. The Mighty God illuminateth the Sun. (1377)[1]

३. त्रि॒ꣳशद्धाम॒ वि रा॑जति॒ वाक्प॑तङ्गाय धीयते । प्रति॒ वस्तो॒रह॒ द्युभिः ॥

3. God shines in the heart with His lustres, throughout the thirty parts of the day. The Vedas should be recited by every one, for the acquisition of God. (1378)[2]

Chapter 2

I

१. उप॒प्रय॒न्तो अध्व॒रं म॒न्त्रं वो॑चेमा॒ग्नये । आ॒रे अ॒स्मे च॑ शृ॒ण्वते ॥

1. Leading a life of non-violence and self-abnegation, let us chant Vedic verses in praise of God, Who hears us even from afar. (1379)

२. यः स्नी॒हि॒ती॒षु पूर्व्यः॑ सं॒जग्मा॑नासु कृ॒ष्टिषु॑ । अ॒रक्ष॒द्दाशु॑षे ग॒यम् ॥

2. Let him, who is just, unprejudiced, disinterested and venerable amongst the loving, social, learned people, preserve the life and wealth of charitable, self-sacrificing persons. (1380)

३. स नो॑ वेदो अ॒मात्य॒मग्नी॑ रक्षतु॒ शन्त॑मः । उ॒तास्मा॒न् पात्व॒ꣳहसः॑ ॥

3. May that Most Blissful God guard our wealth and family, and save us from sin. (1381)

४. उ॒त ब्रु॒वन्तु॒ जन्त॑व उद॒ग्निर्वृ॑त्र॒हाज॑नि । ध॒न॒ञ्ज॒यो रणे॑रणे ॥

4. Yea, let men say, Agni is born, who dispels ignorance and darkness, and winneth wealth in every battle. (1382)[3]

II

१. अग्ने॑ यु॒ङ्क्ष्वा हि ये तवाश्वा॑सो देव सा॒धवः॑ । अरं॒ वह॑न्त्या॒शवः॑ ॥

1. O soul, verily yoke to action the learned persons, who are expert in knowledge and deeds, soon understand thy subtle problems, and derive adequate knowledge! (1383)[4]

२. अच्छा॑ नो या॒ह्या वह॒ अभि प्रया॒ꣳसि॑ वी॒तये॑ । आ दे॒वान्त्सोम॑पीतये ॥

2. O God, reveal Thyself fully unto us. Grant knowledge to the learned, for enjoying happiness, and realizing truth! (1384)

---

[1]See verse 631.
[2]See verse 632.
[3]Agni means the King or Acharya. A preceptor wins every intellectual debate or fight as a King wins a battle.
[4]See verse 25.

३. उदग्ने भारत द्युमदजस्रेण दविद्युतत् । शोचा वि भाह्याजर ॥

3. O Sustainer of the universe, O Deathless God, Ever Radiant manifest Thyself with constant lustrous glory, and nicely illumine the whole world! (1385)

III

१. प्र सुन्वानायान्धसो मर्तो न वष्ट तद्वच: । अप श्वानमराधसं हता मखं न भृगव: ॥

1. Ordinary mortals cannot understand God's Revelation, meant mainly for a Yogi, who banishes ignorance and darkness and enhances the pleasure of life. Just as learned persons burning sin with the fire of knowledge, obviate the necessity of ceremonials, so should they suppress the mind, that does not worship God, and is avaricious like dogs after the fruit of action. (1386)[1]

२. आ जामिरत्के अव्यत भुजे न पुत्र आेण्यो: । सरज्जारो न योषणां वरो न योनिमासदम् ॥

2. A pure-hearted worshipper full of bliss, reaches the soul, his refuge, for the attainment of a steady station; just as a son goes to the lap of his father or mother, or a lover to his dame, or a bridegroom to the house of his bride. (1387)

३. स वीरो दक्षसाधनो वि यस्तस्तम्भ रोदसी । हरि: पवित्रे अव्यत वेधा न योनिमासदम् ॥

3. That brave man, who controls his breaths, Prāṇa and Apāna and organs of senses, being highly intellectual and wise, wanders about in the Purest God, for the attainment of salvation, just as a learned domestic person goes to his house. (1388)

IV

१. अभ्रातृव्यो अना त्वमनापिरिन्द्र जनुषा सनादसि । युधेदापित्वमिच्छसे ॥

1. O King, since thy birth, though thou art foeless, independent, without a leader, all alone, depending on no relative, yet thou longest for friendship in a battle! (1389)[2]

२. न की रेवन्तं सख्याय विन्दसे पीयन्ति ते सुराश्व: ।
यदा कृणोषि नदनुं समूहस्यादित्पितेव हूयसे ॥

2. O God, Thou findest not the wealthy men to be thy friend; as they who are flushed with the wine of wealth destroy even their well-wishers. When Thou makest a preacher of virtue Thy friend, and leadest him on the path of progress then Thou art invoked by him as a Father! (1390)

[1]See verse 553 and 774.
[2]See verse 399.

V

१. आ त्वा सहस्रमा शतं युक्ता रथे हिरण्यये ।
ब्रह्मयुजो हरय इन्द्र केशिनो वहन्तु सोमपीतये ॥

1. O divine mind, may hundreds and thousands of powers of meditation
and knowledge, lead thee on for enjoying the supreme bliss of God! (1391)[1]

२. आ त्वा रथे हिरण्यये हरी मयूरशेप्या ।
शितिपृष्ठा वहतां मध्वो अन्धसो विवक्षणस्य पीतये ॥

2. O soul, in this decaying body, may thy two bays of peacock tails and
white backs, convey thee to quaff the most praiseworthy and sweet essence
of the force of life ! (1392)[2]

३. पिबा त्वाऽऽस्य गिर्वणः सुतस्य पूर्वपा इव ।
परिष्कृतस्य रसिन इयमासुतिश्चारुर्मदाय पत्यते ॥

3. O soul, lover of the song, drink thou this juice of supreme bliss, derived through Samādhi, as one used to, drinks it soon. This savoury sap of
God's joy, refined through Yoga and Pranāyam is good and meet to gladden
thee ! (1393)

VI

१. आ सोता परि षिञ्चताइव न स्तोममन्तुर रजस्तुरम् । वनप्रक्षमुदप्रुतम् ॥

1. Just as a swift horse is adorned, so should the soul, the bringer of knowledge and action, and driver of ignorance, the integrator with God. Our
goal, satiated with knowledge, be perfected, and poured out in each and every
limb of the body. (1394)[3]

२. सहस्रधारं वृषभं पयोदुहं प्रियं देवाय जन्मने ।
ऋतेन य ऋतजातो विवावृधे राजा देव ऋतं बृहत् ॥

2. Visualise in the soul, God, the highest Goal, the Friend of all, the
Grantor of invigorating happiness, the Showerer of joy, the Master of myriad
powers. The soul, the lord of all the organs of senses in the body, refined
through penance, develops through knowledge. It is divine, true in essence,
and mighty. (1395)

VII

१. अग्निवृत्राणि जङ्घनद् द्रविणस्युर्विपन्यया । समिद्धः शुक्र आहुतः ॥

---

[1]See verse 245.
[2]Two bays mean Prāṇa and Apāna, which are beautiful like the tail of a peacock and
absolutely pure.
[3]See verse 580.

1. May fire, kindled through Vedic verses, bright, served with oblations, willing to grow stronger, remove all physical ailments. (1396)[1]

२. गर्भे मातुः पितुः पिता विदिद्युतानो व्रक्षरे । सीदन्नृतस्य योनिमा ॥

2. God, the Father of fathers, shining inside the everlasting soul, banishes all ignorance by revealing the Vedas, the source of true knowledge. (1397)

३. ब्रह्म प्रजावदा भर जातवेदो विचर्षणे । अग्ने यद्दीदयद्दिवि ॥

3. O God, the Knower of all created objects in the universe, the Seer of all, grant us knowledge along with progeny that is valued by the learned! (1398)

VIII

१. अस्य प्रेषा हेमना पूयमानो देवो देवेभिः समपृक्त रसम् ।
सुतः पवित्रं पर्येति रेभन्मितेव सद्य पशुमन्ति होता ॥

1. In obedience to the precious behest of the Veda, the purified and refined soul roams about in the world, preaching truth. God, with all the forces of nature showers pure happiness on the soul, just as an enumerator of cattle or a milk-man goes to the cattle-shed. (1399)[2]

२. भद्रा वस्त्रा समन्याऽवसानो महान् कविनिवचनानि शंसन् ।
आ वच्यस्व चम्वोः पूयमानो विचक्षणो जागृविर्देववीतौ ॥

2. O Yogi, robed in fair raiment meet to wear in combat, pronouncing invocations as a mighty sage, distinguishing between virtue and vice, truth and untruth, pure in heart, free from sloth, move amongst the learned and the ignorant, treading on the path of acquisition of God! (1400)

३. समु प्रियो मृज्यते सानो व्रव्ये यशस्तरो यशसां क्षैतो अस्मे ।
अभि स्वर धन्वा पूयमानो यूयं पात स्वस्तिभिः सदा नः ॥

3. Nobler than the noble, born on this earth, skilled in Prānāyām and top-most penance, dear, the Yogi is adorned with noble virtues for us. Lofty in thy purity, as an ascetic, inculcate in us noble teachings, O Yogi. O learned persons, preserve us evermore with your propitious instructions! (1401)

IX

१. एतो न्विन्द्रँ स्तवाम शुद्धँ शुद्धेन साम्ना । शुद्धैरुक्थैर्वावृध्वाँसँ शुद्धैराशीर्वान्ममत्तु ॥

1. Come now and let us glorify the mighty, pure King, with pure Sāma

---

[1]See verse 4.
[2]See verse 526.

hymns, and pure Vedic verses. May he be delighted with pure songs of praise. (1402)[1]

२. इन्द्र शुद्धो न आ गहि शुद्धः शुद्धाभिरूतिभिः । शुद्धो रयिं नि धारय शुद्धो ममद्धि सोम्य ॥

2. O God, come Thou pure to us. Thou art pure with Thy pure powers. O Pure God, send Thou riches to us, O Divine, Pure God, make us always happy! (1403)

३. इन्द्र शुद्धा हि नो रयिᳲ शुद्धो रत्नानि दाशुषे । शुद्धो वृत्राणि जिघ्नसे शुद्धो वाजᳲ सिषाससि ॥

3. O God, Pure, vouchsafe us wealth, and, Pure God, enrich the virtuous soul, Pure God, Thou strikest the sinners dead, and grantest Thou pure God, knowledge, wealth and strength to all ! (1404)

X

१. अग्ने स्तोमं मनामहे सिद्धमद्य दिविस्पृशः । देवस्य द्रविणस्यवः ॥

1. Eager for wealth we meditate today upon the eternal word of God, Who touches the Heaven through the Sun. (1405)[2]

२. अग्निर्जुषत नो गिरो होता यो मानुषेष्वा । स यक्षद्दैव्यं जनम् ॥

2. God, Who is the Creator and Dissolver of the Universe, Who resides in the hearts of all contemplative persons, listens to our praise-songs. He alone bestoweth joy on the divine emancipated soul. (1406)

३. त्वमग्ने सप्रथा असि जुष्टो होता वरेण्यः । त्वया यज्ञं वि तन्वते ॥

3. Thou, God, art spread widely forth, Lovable, Charitable and Excellent, through Thee men make the sacrifice complete. (1407)

XI

१. अभि त्रिपृष्ठं वृषणं वयोधामङ्गोषिणमववशंत वाणीः । वना वसानो वरुणो न सिन्धुर्वि रत्नधा दयते वार्याणि ॥

1. Vedic verses, reveal their secret essence to the soul, that resides in each part of the body, is the retainer of the force of breaths, the showerer of happiness and knowledge, the controller of speech, mind and body. Residing in all sentient beings, revered by all, it gives us all sorts of desired riches, like an ocean full of treasure. (1408)[3]

---

[1]See verse 350. Sayana has in vain tried to import history in the Verse, Indra killed the demons, felt remorseful and guilty, and requested the Rishis to purify him. This interpretation is illogical and unacceptable.

[2]Eternal word means the Veda.

[3]See verse 528. Just as an ocean gives gold to the divers so does soul give us spiritual wealth.

२. शूरग्राम: सर्ववीर: सहावान् जेता पवस्व सनिता धनानि ॥
तिग्मायुध: क्षिप्रधन्वा समत्स्वषाढ: साह्वान् पृतनासु शत्रून् ॥

2. O soul, thou art the lord of all organs, the greatest warrior forbearing,
the conqueror, the giver of riches, the master of sharpened arms, fastest of all,
unvanquished in battles, the vanquisher of foemen in fights, manifest thyself!
(1409)[1]

३. उरुगव्यूतिरभयानि कृणवन्त्समीचीने आ पवस्व पुरन्धी ।
अप: सिषासन्नुषस: स्वाऽ३र्गः सं चिक्रदो महो अस्मभ्यं वाजान् ॥

3. O soul, the lord of wide dominion, spreading fearlessness all around,
purify in their fulness, the Prāṇa and Apāna, the bearers of the fortress of
this body. Duly discriminating between action and knowledge, preach unto
us, for imparting great spiritual truths, the joy-infusing Vedic verses ! (1410)

XII

१. त्वमिन्द्र यशा अस्यृजीषी शवसस्पति: ।
त्वं वृत्राणि हꣳस्यप्रतीन्येक इत् पूर्वनुत्तश्चर्षणीधृति: ॥

1. O soul, thou art glorious, prosperous, the lord of strength, and the
supporter of men. Thou alone, ungoaded, overpowerest many resistless foes
like lust and anger! (1411)[2]

२. तमु त्वा नूनमसुर प्रचेतसꣳ राधो भागमिवेमहे ।
महीव कृत्ति: शरणा त इन्द्र प्र ते सुम्ना नो अश्नुवन् ॥

2. O God, we verily pray unto Thee, most Wise, craving Thy bounty as
our share, as a son to his father. Thy glory is really a great shelter. May Thy
favours reach unto us! (1412)

XIII

१. यजिष्ठं त्वा ववृमहे देवं देवत्रा होतारममर्त्यम् । अस्य यज्ञस्य सुक्रतुम् ॥

1. O God, we worship Thee, the Best of all sacrificers, Adorable even by
the learned, the Executor of all sacrifices, Immortal, the best Performer of
this Yajna of the universe! (1413)[3]

२. अपां नपातꣳ सुभगꣳ सुदीदितिमग्निमु श्रेष्ठशोचिषम् ।
स नो मित्रस्य वरुणस्य सो अपामा सुम्नं यक्षते दिवि ॥

---

[1]Sharpened arms means effective devices and schemes to achieve success.
[2]See verse 248.
[3]See verse 112. The creation, sustenance and dissolution of the universe is a kind of
Yajna performed by God.

2. I praise the soul, that allows not the spirit of action decay, is full of glory, endowed with halo, and most excellent. It makes us realise in a state of emancipation, the joy of the achievement of God, Who is the friend of all, and the Alleviator of all sufferings. (1414)

XIV

१. यमग्ने पृत्सु मर्त्यमवा वाजेषु यं जुना: । स यन्ता शश्वतीरिष: ॥

1. O God, the mortal man, whom Thou protectest in the fight, and urgest to knowledge and noble deeds, becomes the lord of eternal wealth. (1415)[1]

२. न किरस्य सहन्त्य पर्येता कयस्य चित् । वाजो अस्ति श्रवाय्य: ॥

2. O God, the Remover of all obstacles, none can vanquish Thy devotee. Very glorious is his strength ! (1416)

३. स वाजं विश्वचर्षणिरर्वद्भिरस्तु तरुता । विप्रेभिरस्तु सनिता ॥

3. May God, the Seer of mankind, make us victorious in the struggle of life through the forces of action. May He grant us extreme glory through expanded mental functions. (1417)

XV

१. साकमुक्षो मर्जयन्त स्वसारो दश धीरस्य धीतयो धनुत्री: ।
हरि: पर्यंद्रवज्जा: सूर्यस्य द्रोणं ननक्षे अत्यो न वाजी ॥

1. The quickly moving fingers cleanse the Soma. The ten fingers press the Soma liked by the sages. The gold-hued Soma, goes to different directions, the progeny of the Sun. It flows fastly to the vat, like a fleet courser. (1418)

२. सं मातृभिनं शिशुर्वावशानो वृषा दधन्वे पुरुवारो अद्रि: ।
मर्यो न योषामभि निष्कृतं यन्तं गच्छते कलश उस्रियाभि: ॥

2. The soul, longing for the sages, giving vent to ambitions removing manifold obstacles, is sustained by the organs of action, just as mothers suckle the child, or a young man goes to his wife, or as Soma going to its refined place, the vat, unites with the rays of the Sun. (1419)[2]

३. उत प्र पिप्य ऊधरघ्न्याया इन्दुर्धाराभि: सचते सुमेधा: ।
मूर्धानं गाव: पयसा चमूष्वभि श्रीणन्ति वसुभिनं निक्तं: ॥

3. When the joy of soul fills the top of mental force, when a highly intelligent Yogi full of knowledge and penance, realises the true nature of the

---

[1]When Soma juice is offered as an oblation, being rarefied it goes to different directions. See verse 538.
[2]Organs of action mean Karma-Indriyās.

soul through Yogic practices, then the accumulated forces of the subtle organs, stationed in their respective spheres, with their individual emotion, cover the soul, as mothers cover their children with washed clothes. (1420)

XVI

१. पिबा सुतस्य रसिनो मत्स्वा न इन्द्र गोमत: ।
आपिर्नो बोधि सधमाद्ये वृधे३ऽस्मार्ऐ भवन्तु ते धिय: ॥

1. O God, accept the sweet, devoted heart of a sacrificer. Be kind to us. Thou art All-pervading. Grant us knowledge. Let Thy favours of wisdom guard us for our progress in Yoga ! (1421)[1]

२. भूयाम ते सुमतौ वाजिनो वयं मा न स्तरभिमातये ।
अस्माञ्चित्राभिरवतादभिष्टिभिरा न: सुम्नेषु यामय ॥

2. O God, following in the wake of Thy Vedic teachings, may we still be strong. Cast us not into the net of violent ideas. Guard and succour us with manifold protections, and establish us in pleasures ! (1422)

XVII

१. तिरस्में सप्त धेनवो दुदुह्रिरे सत्यामाशिरं परमे व्योमनि ।
चत्वार्यन्या भुवनानि निर्णिजे चारूणि चक्रे यदृतैरवर्धत ॥

1. The seven milch kine, yield in three stages the milk of truth to a seeker after supreme felicity in his onward march to the pinnacle of progress. As he progresses through different kinds of knowledge, so, for the purification of the fruit of his knowledge, he gradually develops the other four beautiful sheaths. (1423)[2]

२ स भक्षमाणो अमृतस्य चारुण उभे द्यावा काव्येना वि शश्रथे ।
तेजिष्ठा अपो मऐहना परि व्यत यदी देवस्य श्रवसा सदो विदु: ॥

2. When learned persons know from the Guru through his instruction, the real nature of the heart, the seat of God, a pure seeker amongst them enjoying the excellent sense of immortality, with the force of his knowledge, attains to both God and soul, and through the intensity of his penance, full of glory, controls his breaths. (1424)[3]

[1]See verse 239.
[2]Seven milch kine are two eyes, two ears, two nostrils and the mouth. Three stages are, Jagrit, Swapan, Sashupti. Other four sheaths are प्राणमय, मनोमय, ज्ञानमय, आनन्दमय, besides the अन्नमयकोश. See verse 560.
[3]In Rigveda the word भिक्षमाण; is used, but in Samaveda, it is भक्षमाण:. Sayana has translated the word by mistake as भिक्षमाण:, which is not found in the text.

३. ते अस्य सन्तु केतवोऽमृत्यवोऽदाभ्यासो जनुषी उभे अनु ।
येभिनृंऽम्णा च देव्या च पुनत आदिद्राजानं मनना अगृभ्णत ॥

3. Immortal and inviolate superhuman powers are created in a Yogi both in this world and the next; on the strength of which, he roams in different regions which ordinary mortals and learned persons long for. After the attainment of superhuman power, mental, reflective resolves alone sustain the kingly soul. (1425)

XVIII

१. अभि वायुं वीत्यर्षा गृणानो३ऽभि मित्रावरुणा पूयमानः ।
अभी नरं धीजवनꣳ रथेष्ठामभीन्द्रं वृषणं वज्रबाहुम् ॥

1. O praiseworthy learned person, urge the breath to pervade the whole body, urge also the Prāṇa and Apāna, cleansing them seated as a driver in the chariot-like body, actuated by reflection and resolve, urge the mind, the leader of the host of organs. With the weapon of knowledge in thy hand, realise the showerer of joys ! (1426)

२. अभि वस्त्रा सुवसनान्यर्षाभि धेनूः सुदुघाः पूयमानः ।
अभि चन्द्रा भर्तवे नो हिरण्याभ्यश्वान् रथिनो देव सोम ॥

2. O learned person, ever anxious for progress, master the five sheaths, the excellent coverings for the soul; control thou the Sushumna like arteries, the excellent yielders of joy. Grant us, for the satisfaction of the soul, the gladdening glory of knowledge, O Yogi, the seer of knowledge, send us celibate learned persons, who have got control over the chariots of their bodies ! (1427)[1]

३. अभी नो अर्ष दिव्या वसून्यभि विश्वा पार्थिवा पूयमानः ।
अभि येन द्रविणमश्नवामाभ्यार्षेयं जमदग्निवन्न: ॥

3. O learned person, grant us celestial riches, with a pure mind, preach unto us of all things on the Earth. Grant us strength wherewith we may gain knowledge, wealth and food. Instruct us, like God, in Vedic knowledge, obtainable through the Rishis! (1428)[2]

---

[1]Five sheaths mean the five koshas as explained before.
Sushumna : A particular artery of the human body, said to lie between इडा (Idā) and पिंगला (Pinglā) two of the vessels of the body.

[2]Griffith has translated the word Jamadagni, like Sāyana as a Rishi. There is no history in the Vedas, hence this interpretation is unacceptable. Pt. Jaidev Vidyalankara translates the word as God, Who controls all luminous and fiery objects like the sun. Swami Tulsi Ram translates the word as 'eye' on the authority of Shata path, ''चक्षुर्वै-जमदग्निऋषि'' Shatapath 8-1-2-5. God reveals the Vedas in the beginning of the world through the four Rishis, Agni, Vāyu, Āditya, Angara.

XIX

१. यज्जायथा अपूर्व्य मघवन् वृत्रहत्याय । तत्पृथिवीमप्रथयस्तदस्तभ्ना उतो दिवम् ॥

1. O Eternal God, when Thou, for removal of the darkness of dissolution, createst the universe, Thou spreadest out the spacious Earth, and upholdest the Heaven! (1429)[1]

२. तत्ते यज्ञो अजायत तदर्कं उत हस्कृति: । तद्विश्वमभिभूरसि यज्जातं यच्च जन्त्वम् ॥

2. Then was the sacrifice produced by God, then was the Sun created, and simultaneously the day. O God, Thou art the efficient cause of the creation of all that now is and yet shall be born! (1430)[2]

३. आमासु पक्वमेरय आ सूर्यं रोह्यो दिवि ।
धर्मं न सामं तपता सुवृक्तिभिर्जुष्टं गिर्वणसे बृहत् ॥

3. O God, Thou makest the immature objects mature, hence dost Thou make the sun rise in heaven. O learned persons, just as ye perform the Pravargya ceremony with Sāma hymns, so should ye recite the Brihat Sama in intellectual discussions, in praise of God sung in Vedic verses! (1431)[3]

XX

१. मत्स्यपायि ते मह: पात्रस्येव हरिवो मत्सरा मद: । वृषा ते वृष्ण इन्दुर्वाजी सहस्रसातम: ॥

1. Just as exhilarating water or milk placed in a receptacle is quaffed, so, O God, the Master of ignorance banishing forces, is enjoyed Thy mighty strength, that gives satiety and joy. O God, the Giver of all joys and powers, Thy mighty glory, the bestower of myriad delights, is the showerer of all pleasures! (1432)

२. आ नस्ते गन्तु मत्सरो वृषा मदो वरेण्य: । सहावाँ इन्द्र सानसि: पृतनाषाडमर्त्य: ॥

2. O God, may we gain Thy exhilarating knowledge. Thou art the Bestower of joys, the Giver of satisfaction, Adorable, Self-Confident, Worthy of Service, the Ruler of all subjects and Immortal. (1433)

३. त्वं हि शूर: सनिता चोदयो मनुषो रथम् । सहावान् दस्युमव्रतमोष: पात्रं न शोचिषा ॥

3. God, Thou urgest men to action, Thou art the best Giver, Thou urgest that verse, the chariot of the meditative soul. Thou through Thy mighty

---

[1]God creates, sustains and disiolves the universe. After the expiry of the period of dissolution which lasts for 43,2,00,00,000 years, He brings cosmos out of chaos, and creates anew the Earth and Heaven etc. This cycle of creation and dissolution is beginningless and endless.

[2]Sacrifice includes air, atmosphere, time, directions and mind.

[3]Pravargya: A ceremony preliminary to the Soma sacrifice (Yajna).

Brihat Sāma is a part of the Sāmaveda.

strength burnest an ignoble, unprincipled man, as fire does a vessel through its heat ! (1434)

Chapter 3

I

१. पवस्व वृष्टिमा सु नोऽपामूर्मिं दिवस्परि । अयक्ष्मा बृहतीरिष: ॥

1. O God, pour down the rain upon us, pour a wave of water from the sky, and plenteous store of food free from pulmonary consumption ! (1435)[1]

२. तया पवस्व धारया यया गाव इहागमन् । जन्यास उप नो गृहम् ॥

2. O God, urge us with that steady abstraction of the mind, whereby the rays of knowledge may come to our heart, and all the objects conducive to the welfare of man be present in our home ! (1436)

३. घृतं पवस्व धारया यज्ञेषु देववीतम: । अस्मभ्यं वृष्टिमा पव ॥

3. O God, with Thy power of sustenance and nourishment, grant us knowledge, dearest to the sages. Shower on us mental joys ! (1437)

४. स न उर्जे व्य३ऽययं पवित्रं धारया । देवास: शृणवन् हि कम् ॥

4. O God, to give us vigour with Thy power of sustenance and nourishment, come fast to our soul and heart. The learned listen to Thy joyful instruction ! (1438)

५. पवमानो असिष्यदद्रक्षाँऽस्यपज ्जनत् । प्रत्नवद्रोचयन् ्च: ॥

5. When the pure, divine joy of the soul flows onward, flashing out splendour as of old, it extirpates all sins, evil desires and ignoble resolves. (1439)

II

१. प्रत्यस्मै पिपीषते विश्वानि विदुषे भर । अरङ्गमाय जग्मयेऽपश्चादध्वने नर: ॥

1. O men, give all necessary things to this recluse, who is learned, longing for spiritual delight, the master of the ocean of knowledge, spiritually advanced, never retraces his steps in the journey of life, as he renders service unto you in return! (1440)

२. एमेनं प्रत्येतन सोमेभि: सोमपातमम् । अमत्रेभिऋँजीषिण मिन्द्रँ ऊ सुतेभिरिन्दुभि: ॥

2. O learned persons, go nigh to God, this store-house of knowledge, through the aid of sages. Realise through the sermons of renowned scholars, God, the Exhibitor of the path of rectitude! (1441)[2]

[1]See verse 352.
[2]'Gleaned' refers to knowledge.

३. यदी सुतेभिरिन्दुभि: सोमेभि: प्रतिभूषथ । वेदा विश्वस्य मेधिरो धृषत्तन्तमिदेषते ॥

3. O learned persons, when Ye worship God through accomplished, intellectual sages, He, the Controller of all, being Wise, knows everything, and fulfils each desire of yours! (1442)

४. अस्माअस्मा इदन्धसोऽध्वर्यो प्र भरा सुतम् ।
कुवित्समस्य जेन्यस्य शर्धतोऽभिशस्तेरवस्वरत् ॥

4. O learned sacrificer, consign to God alone, the joy derived from life, as He saves us several times from all subduable, presumptuous foes like lust and anger! (1443)[1]

III

१. बभ्रवे नॄ स्वतवसेऽरुणाय दिविस्पृशे । सोमाय गाथमर्चत ॥

1. O learned persons, sing the praise of God, the Sustainer and Nourisher of all, Independent in might. Glorious, and Omnipresent! (1444)

२. हस्तच्युतेभिरद्रिभि: सुतं सोमं पुनीतन । मधावा धावता मधु ॥

2. O learned persons, advance knowledge, through devices skilful like the hands; gleaned by well-charactered scholars, adamant like a mountain, and realise in your soul, the elixir of spiritual knowledge! (1445)

३. नमसेदुप सीदत दध्नेदभि श्रीणीतन । इन्दुमिन्द्रे दधातन ॥

3. O learned persons, worship God with humble homage, strengthen Him internally with contemplation and concentration. Fix the soul on God! (1446)

४. अमित्रहा विचर्षणि: पवस्व सोम शं गवे । देवेभ्यो अनुकामकृत् ॥

4. O God, Foe-Queller, the Seer, fulfilling the desires of the learned, pour forth tranquillity on the soul! (1447)

५. इन्द्राय सोम पातवे मदाय परि षिच्यसे । मनश्चिन्मनसस्पति: ॥

5. O God, Thou art realised for the gratification and enjoyment of the soul, as Thou art Heart-knower, and Sovereign of the heart! (1448)

६. पवमान सुवीर्यं रयिं सोम रिरीहि ण: । इन्दविन्द्रेण नो युजा ॥

6. O God, grant us riches and heroic strength. O Yogi, give us strength through God, our Ally ! (1449)

---

[1]Foe-Queller: The subduer of inimical passions.

IV

१. उद्बेभि श्रुतामघं वृषभं नर्यापसम् । अ्रस्तारमेषि सूर्यं ॥

1. O God, Thou alone exaltest the ruler, who is renowned for his glory, the fulfiller of the desires of his subjects, who works for the welfare of mankind, and casts away foes! (1450)[1]

२. नव यो नवति पुरो बिभेद बाह्वोजसा । अ्रहिं च वृत्रहावधीत् ॥
३. स न इन्द्रः शिवः सखाश्वावद्गोमद्यवमत् । उरुधारेव दोहते ॥

2, 3. God. Who through the force of His arms, finishes the ninety nine years of this body-like castle, and kills the serpent of passion that over-shadows the soul, the dispeller of the demon of ignorance, as our Benefactor and Friend, send us riches in horses, kine and corn, like a full-streaming cow. (1451, 1452)[2]

V

१. विभ्राड् बृहत्पिबतु सोम्यं मध्वायुर्दधद्यज्ञपतावविह्र तम् ॥
वातजूतो यो अ्रभिरक्षति त्मना प्रजाः पिपर्ति बहुधा वि राजति ॥

1. May an illumined Yogi, passing his crookedless, pure, and ever active life in the service of God, drink the juice of the immortal joy derived through the urging of God. The Yogi, urged by the control of breath, guards himself, strengthens his organs, and shines in various ways. (1453)[3]

२. विभ्राड् बृहत्सुभृतं वाजसातमं धर्मं दिवो धरणे सत्यमर्पितम् ।
अ्रमित्रहा वृत्रहा दस्युहन्तमं ज्योतिर्जज्ञे अ्रसुरहा सपत्नहा ॥

2. The lustrous, mighty force of intellect, well-fostered, the bestower of the strength of knowledge, is stabilized in its true aspect, under the asylum of concentration and the light of learning. Soul, the subduer of unfriendly passions like lust and anger, the dispeller of the demon of ignorance, the killer of the demon of vice, the queller of satanic tendencies, enkindles this intellectual light, that vanquishes all violent propensities. (1454)

३. इद ँ श्रेष्ठं ज्योतिषां ज्योतिरुत्तमं विश्वजिद्धनजिदुच्यते बृहत् ।
विश्वभ्राड् भ्राजो महि सूर्यं दृश उरु पप्रथे सह श्रोजो अच्युतम् ॥

3. This light, the best of lights, supreme, is spoken of as all conquering, winner of riches. All-illuminating, radiant, mighty as the soul is to see, it spreadeth wide unshaken forbearance and strength. (1455)[4]

---

[1]See verse 125.
[2]The various devices of knowledge and action are figuratively the arms of God. He ends our long life of ninety-nine years. See verse 179, where detailed explanation of the words नवनवती is given.
[3]See verse 628. The verse may apply to a Brahmchāri, God and Sun as well.
[4]'This light' means the light of intellect.

VI

१. इन्द्र क्रतुं न आ भर पिता पुत्रेभ्यो यथा ।
शिक्षा णो अस्मिन् पुरुहूत यामनि जीवा ज्योतिरशीमहि ॥

1. O Yogi, give us wisdom, as a father gives wealth and knowledge to his son. O much-invoked Yogi, instruct us in this path of spiritual progress, so that we souls may receive thy light! (1456)[1]

२. मा नो अज्ञाता वृजना दुराध्यो३माशिवासोऽव क्रमुः ।
त्वया वयं प्रवतः शश्वतीरपोऽति शूर तरामसि ॥

2. O God, may not unknown sins, or malevolent, unhallowed foes over-power us. O Heroic God, may we through Thy assistance, accomplish all enterprises without let or hindrance! (1457)[2]

VII

१. अद्याद्या श्वःश्व इन्द्र त्रास्व परे च नः ।
विश्वा च नो जरितॄन्त्सत्पते अहा दिवा नक्तं च रक्षिषः ॥

1. Protect us, O God, each today, each morrow, and each following day. Lord of the virtuous, Thou preservest us, Thy singers, through all the days, both by day and night! (1458)

२. प्रभङ्गी शूरो मघवा तुवीमघः सम्मिश्लो वीर्याय कम् ।
उभा ते बाहू वृष्णा शतक्रतो नि या वज्रं मिमिक्षतुः ॥

2. O God, the Doer of myriad actions, both Thy arms, are the fulfillers of desires. They wield the weapon of immense strength for punishing the ignoble. Thou art the Dissolver of the universe at the time of dissolution, the Conqueror, Charitable, passing Rich, All-Pervading and Lord of the people! (1459)

VIII

१. जनीयन्तो न्वग्रवः पुत्रीयन्तः सुदानवः । सरस्वन्तꣳ हवामहे ॥

1. We progressing, bounteous people, longing for wives, and yearning for sons, daily call upon the Omniscient God. (1460)[3]

---

[1]See verse 259.
[2]Both arms of God are knowledge and action.
[3]In the opinion of Satyavrat Samashrami, this stanza does not contain one verse alone, the next verse also forms a part of it. Vivarnkār also holds the same view. Sāyan Achārya differs from this view. Vedic Yantrālya of Ajmere, Swami Tulsi Ram, and Pt. Jaidev Vidyalankara agree with Sāyana.

IX

१. उत नः प्रिया प्रियासु सप्त स्वसा सुजुष्टा । सरस्वती स्तोम्या भूत् ॥

1. Yea, the Vedic speech, most dear amid dear things, seven sistered, enjoyed by the ancient sages, deserves our praise. (1461)[1]

X

१. तत्सवितुर्वरेण्यं भर्गो देवस्य धीमहि । धियो यो नः प्रचोदयात् ॥

1. Let us attain to the adorable glory of that Divine God, the Creator of the universe. May He direct our understandings aright. (1462)[2]

XI

१. सोमानां स्वरणं कृणुहि ब्रह्मणस्पते । कक्षीवन्तं य औशिजः ॥

1. O God, make me, the son of a learned person, expert in manufacturing medicines, like a skilled artisan! (1463)[3]

XII

१. अग्न आयूंषि पवसे आ सुवोर्जमिषं च नः । आरे बाधस्व दुच्छुनाम् ॥

1. O God, Thou pourest life, send down upon us food and vigorous strength. Drive Thou evil courses of conduct far away ! (1464)

XIII

१. ता नः शक्तं पार्थिवस्य महो रायो दिव्यस्य । महि वा क्षत्रं देवेषु ॥

1. May they help us to great earthly and heavenly wealth. Great is their sway over other organs of senses. (1465)[4]

---

[1]Seven sistered : The Vedic speech has got seven sisters, the organs, which convey knowledge, two eyes, two ears, two nostrils, and tongue, Some commentators refer to seven metres like Gāyatri, Trishtup, Jagati, Brihati, Anushtup, Ushnik, Pankti.

Griffith refers to seven rivers in this verse, namely, Indus, Vitasta, Asikni, Parushni, Vipāshā, Sutudri, Saraswati. This explanation is unacceptable as the Vedas are free from historical references. Saraswati does not mean a river, but Vedic speech, couched in seven metres.

[2]This verse is the Gāyatri par excellence, the most celebrated verse of the Vedas which forms part of the daily devotion of the Aryas. This verse occurs thrice in the Yajurveda, twice in the Rigveda, and once in the Sāmaveda. The well-known Vedic Scholar Satyavrat Samashrami believes that this verse along with the next two verses, all three constitute one Sūkta, whereas Sāyana and some other commentators differ from him.

[3]See verse 139.

[4]'They' refers to Mitra and Varuṇa, i.e , Prāna and Apāna.

२. ऋतमृतेन सपन्तेषिरं दक्षमाशाते । अद्रुहा देवो वर्धेते ॥

2. Learning truthful knowledge from the Vedas, both the teacher and the pupil, devoid of guile, acquire desired vigorous might and wax strong. (1466)[1]

३. वृष्टिद्यावा रीत्यापेषस्पती दानुमत्या: । बृहन्तं गर्तमाशाते ॥

3. The Guru and the pupil, the sources of raining happiness and knowledge, the achievers of their aim through learning, Charitable in nature, masters of invigorating food, remain engaged in this chariot of the world. (1467)

XIV

१. युञ्जन्ति ब्रध्नमरुषं चरन्तं परि तस्थुष: । रोचन्ते रोचना दिवि ॥

1. The learned Yogis, who through Yogic Samadhi (deep meditation) attain to God, Who pervades all moving and stationary objects, and is the Friend of all, shine in their full splendour in their state of emancipation. (1468)[2]

२. युञ्जन्त्यस्य काम्या हरी विपक्षसा रथे । शोणा धृष्णू नृवाहसा ॥

2. They, who, in this body, the chariot of the soul, harness the Prāṇa and Apāna, the bearers of their leader, the soul, charming, active, sustainers of the body in diverse ways, ever-moving and steadfast, achieve glory. (1469)[3]

३. केतुं कृण्वन्नकेतवे पेशो मर्या अपेशसे । समुषद्भिरजायथा: ॥

3. O mortals, just as the Sun with its fiery rays grants consciousness in the morning to the persons sleeping at night, and lends light at dawn to the objects engulfed in darkness at night, so is the soul, lending knowledge to the ignorant and riches to indigent, reborn, reaping the fruits of its actions! (1470)

XV

१. अयꣳ सोम इन्द्र तुभ्यꣳ सुन्वे तुभ्यं पवते त्वमस्य पाहि ।
त्वꣳ ह यं चकृषे त्वं ववृष इन्दुं मदाय युज्याय सोमम् ॥

1. O God, this calm Yogi, is born for Thee, and exerts for Thy acquisition, Whom Thou createst and grantest strength, him, endowed with glory, austerity, tranquillity and self-command. Thou guardest against calamities for salvation and Thy proximity! (1471)

[1]Mitra and Varuṇa refer to the preceptor and the disciple.
[2]This verse has been translated in various ways by different commentators. Another plausible rendering of the verse is given below : The artisans who properly use the Sun, fire and air, attain to supremacy and derive happiness. Maharishi Dayānand has interpreted the verse in three ways, in his commentary on the Rigveda 1-6-1.
[3]The adjectives charming, active etc., refer to they.

२. स ई꣢ रथो न भूरिषाड꣫योजि मह꣢: पुरूणि꣢ सातये꣢ वसूनि꣢ ।
श्रादीं꣫ विश्वा꣢ नहु꣫ष्याणि꣢ जाता꣫ स्वर्षाता꣢ वन ऊ꣯र्ध्वा꣯ नवन्त ॥

2. When the calm Yogi, firm like a branchless trunk, being highly forbearing, harnesses his organs to Yoga for acquiring dignity, then in this task of acquiring desired supreme bliss, he voluntarily wins all excellent objects worthy of attainment by men. (1472)

३. शुष्मी꣢ शर्धो꣫ न मारु꣢तं पव꣫स्वानभिशस्ता꣢ दिव्या꣢ यथा꣢ विट् ।
श्रापो꣢ न म꣯क्षू सुम꣫तिर्भवा꣢ न꣢: सह꣫स्राप्स꣢: पृत꣫नाषाण्꣢ न य꣫ज्ञ: ॥

3. O Yogi, thou hast power like the strength of breaths, thou bringest the body in motion, and art unblamable like the host of beautiful breaths. Thou are mentally like fast-moving waters. Thousand-fashioned, like a victorious commander in a battle, thou art the sacrificer (Yajmāna) in this sacrifice of the body. Be gracious unto us! (1473)

XVI

१. त्वम꣢ग्ने यज्ञाना꣢ होता꣢ विश्वेषा꣢ हित꣢: । देवे꣢भिर्मानु꣢षे꣫ जने꣢ ॥

1. O path-pointer, our organs of cognition and action, take as our leader, thee, our urger to all noble actions! (1474)[1]

२. स नो꣢ मन्द्राभि꣢रध्व꣫रे जि꣫ह्वाभि꣢र्यज꣢ मह꣢: । श्रा देवान्꣢ वक्षि꣫ यक्षि꣢ च ॥

2. O God, with Thy sweet sounding instructions, with Thy Omnipotence, Thou regulatest the universe in non-violence. Thou takest the learned under Thy shelter and leadest them on the path of progress, and fulfillest all their desires! (1475)[2]

३. वेत्था꣢ हि वेधो꣢ श्रध्व꣫न: पथ꣢श्च꣫ देवा꣢ञ्जसा । श्रग्ने꣢ यज्ञे꣢षु꣫ सुक्रतो꣢ ॥

3. O God, Thou art the Doer of many deeds, Refulgent, and Creator of the universe. In all human enterprises Thou knowest the big and small devices! (1476)

XVII

१. होता꣢ देवो꣢ श्रमर्त्यः꣢ पुर꣫स्तादे꣢ति꣫ मायया꣢ । विद꣢थानि꣫ प्रचो꣢दयन् ॥

1. The Immortal, Effulgent God, the Accomplisher of the sacrifice of life,

[1]Path-pointer means a learned leader who shows to the people the path of right conduct. See verse 2.

[2]The verse is applicable to fire as well. In that case the tongues of fire will refer to the seven flames named (1) Kāli, (2) Karali, (3) Manojavā (4) Sulohitā, (5) Sudhumra varṇā, (6) Sphulingini, (7) Vishvarūpa. Satyavrat Samashrami adds in his commentary Lilā as the 8th tongue of the fire.

urging knowable noble deeds and spiritual truths in the heart, is directly realised through intellect! (1477)

२. बाजी वाजेषु धीयतेऽध्वरेषु प्र णीयते । विप्रो यज्ञस्य साधन: ॥

2. A strong, learned person is entrusted with gigantic tasks. He is specially deputed for the performance of non-violent deeds. A learned person is the accomplisher of all deeds requiring charity, sacrifice, austerity, study and unity. (1478)

३. धिया चक्रे वरेण्यो भूतानां गर्भमा दधे । दक्षस्य पितरं तना ॥

3. An excellent learned person, should work with the force of his intellect and capacity for work. He alone keeps all material objects under his sway. The sons of God look upon him as their father. (1479)

XVIII

१. आ सुते सिञ्चत श्रियꣳ रोदस्योरभिश्रियम् । रसा दधीत वृषभम् ॥

1. Establish in the mind, the strength that resides in Prāṇa and Apāna, and thereby gladden the soul. (1480)[1]

२. ते जानत स्वमोक्यांꣳ सं वत्सासो न मातृभि: । मिथो नसन्त जामिभि: ॥

2. The Prāṇas remain attached to their parent organs, as calves to their mothers, who give them birth. They consider the organs as their home, and identify themselves with them. (1481)[2]

३. उप स्रक्वेषु बप्सत: कृण्वते धरुणं दिवि । इन्द्रे अग्ना नम: स्व: ॥

3. The learned accept, through the light of knowledge as their resort, God, Who brings dissolution in all places of creation. They worship Him, the Annihilator of sins, in their soul with vigour and gusto. (1482)[3]

XIX

१. तदिदास भुवनेषु ज्येष्ठं यतो जज्ञ उग्रस्त्वेषनृम्ण: ।
सद्यो जज्ञानो नि रिणाति शत्रूननु यं विश्वे मदन्त्यूमा: ॥

1. In all the worlds God was the Best and Highest, whence sprang the mighty man, of splendid valour. Soon after his birth, he smites his foemen; in whom all who lend him aid are joyful. (1483)

---

[1] Sāyaṇa translates the verse, saying, mix the cow's milk with that of goat, and boil them well. Sorry this interpretation does not appeal to me.

[2] They refer to Prāṇas. Them refers to organs.

[3] Doubted : When they get a wife or a son.
Trebled : When they get a son or a grandson.

२. वावृधान: शवसा भूर्योजा: शत्रुर्दासाय भियसं दधाति ।
   अव्यनच्च व्यनच्च सस्निं सं ते नवन्त प्रभृता मदेषु ॥

2. God, growing mighty in His strength, of ample vigour, the Queller of
obstacles, strikes terror in the heart of the sinner. He purifies the animate
and the inanimate world. O God, all those breathing and breathless objects,
full of joy, sing Thy praise! (1484)

३. त्वे ऋतुमपि वृञ्जन्ति विश्वे द्विर्यदेते त्रिर्भवन्त्यूमा: ।
   स्वादो: स्वादीय: स्वादुना सृजा समद: सु मधु मधुनाभि योधी: ॥

3. All these human beings concentrate on Thee, O God, their mental vigour, when they are doubled and trebled. Blend the bodily pleasure with the
sweeter pleasure of God's bliss. Blend that extremely sweet bliss of God with
the sweet pleasure of salvation ! (1485)

<h1 style="text-align:center">XX</h1>

१. त्रिकद्रुकेषु महिषो यवाशिरं तुविशुष्मस्तृम्पत्सोममपिबद्विष्णुना सुतं यथावशम् ।
   स ई ममाद महि कर्म कर्त्तवे महामुरु꣢ꣳ सेन꣢ꣳ सश्चद्देवो देव꣢ꣳ सत्य इन्दु: सत्यमिन्द्रम् ॥

1. The highly venerable and strong soul enjoys according to its capacity,
the knowledge and pleasure (efficacious like the Soma juice mixed with barley) created by the Omnipresent God in the three parts of the world. The
same soul always remains full of joy for attaining mighty achievements. The
learned soul attains to God, the Almighty, Vast, and the Lord of innumerable powers. The ture lustrous soul achieves this True Refulgent God. (1486)[1]

२. साकं जात: ऋतुना साकमोजसा ववक्षिथ साकं वृद्धो वीर्यें: सासहिमृ꣢ꣳ धो विचर्षणि: ।
   दाता राध स्तुवते काम्यं वसु प्रचेतन सेन꣢ꣳ सश्चद्देवो देव꣢ꣳ सत्य इन्दु: सत्यमिन्द्रम् ॥

2. O Omniscient God, with Thy coexistent wisdom and strength, Thou sustainest the universe. Thou art Mighty with Thy manifold powers. Thou subduest all foes. Thou art the Seer of the whole world. Thou art the Giver of
lovely wealth to him, who worships and praises Thee. The true lustrous soul
achieves this True, Refulgent God. (1487)

३. अध त्विषीमा꣢ꣳ अभ्योजसा कृवि युधाभवदा रोदसी अपृणदस्य मज्मना प्र वावृधे ।
   अधत्तान्यं जठरे प्रेमरिच्यत प्र चेतय सेन꣢ꣳ सश्चद्देवो देव꣢ꣳ सत्य इन्दु: सत्यमिन्द्रम् ॥

3. Alter thus visualizing God, the lustrous soul, with its might and intense
struggle, shatters its five sheaths, fills the earth and heaven, and waxes strong
with its majesty. God takes the soul under His shelter, and makes it specially

---

[1]See verse 457. Swāmi Dayānanda has translated कद्रुकेषु as लोकेषु in his commentary
on the Rigveda. Three parts of the world refer to the Earth, the Atmosphere and the
Sun.

strong and full of knowledge. The learned Yogic soul achieves this True, Refulgent God. (1488)

BOOK VII

Chapter 1

I

१. अभि प्र गोपतिं गिरेन्द्रमर्चं यथा विदे । सूनुं ꣱ सत्यस्य सत्पतिम् ॥

1. O man, sing with thy speech, the praise of the King, as thou knowest him, the lord of the earth, the son of justice, and the protector of the virtuous ! (1489)[1]

२. आ हरयः ससृज्रिरेऽरुषीरघि बर्हिषि । यत्राभि संनवामहे ॥

2. In the mind are rising fast, resplendent waves of thought, wherein we bow before God. (1490)

३. इन्द्राय गाव आशिरं दुदुह्रे वज्रिणे मधु । यत्सीमुपह्वरे विदत् ॥

3. The energetic rays of knowledge create supreme felicity for the dynamic soul, which it cherishes internally. (1491)[2]

II

१. आ नो विश्वासु हव्यमिन्द्रꣳ समत्सु भूषत ।
उप ब्रह्माणि सवनानि वृत्रहन् परमज्या ऋचीषम ॥

1. O learned persons, on all occasions of joy, adorn God, Worthy of our praise. O Remover of obstacles, Greatest Conqueror, Worthy of reflection through Vedic hymns, remain near us on occasions of our sacrifices and Vedic studies ! (1492)[3]

२. त्वं दाता प्रथमो राधसामस्यसि सत्य ईशानकृत् ।
तुविद्युम्नस्य युज्या वृणीमहे पुत्रस्य शवसो महः ॥

2. O God, Thou art the Primordial Bestower of all riches and knowledge. Thou art the Giver of true strength and supremacy. May we claim through Samadhi, the alliance of God, Almighty, the Guardian of the people against calamities, the Supreme, and the Lord of wealth ! (1493)

---

[1]'Just as thou knowest him' means as he deserves. Don't praise him for the sake of flattery.
Son of justice : Embodiment of justice. See verse 168.
[2]Which refers to felicity.
[3]See verse 269.

III

१. प्रत्नं पीयूषं पूर्व्यं यदुक्थ्यं महो गाहादिव आ निरधुक्षत ।
इन्द्रमभि जायमानꣳ समस्वरन् ॥

1. When learned persons visualise through deep and most prominent part of the head, the primeval immemorial, praiseworthy, divine joy of God, they nicely sing His praise, Who manifests Himself unto them. (1494)

२. आदीं के चित् पश्यमानास आप्यं वसुरुचो दिव्या अभ्यनूषत ।
दिवो न वारꣳ सविता व्यूर्णुते ॥

2. When the darkness of the soul is removed by God like the Sun, then only, some intellectually superior persons, the implementers of the soul, praise God, visualising Him as their attainable Friend. (1495)[1]

३. अध यदिमे पवमान रोदसी इमा च विश्वा भुवनाभि मज्मना ।
यूथे न निष्ठा वृषभो वि राजसि ॥

3. Just as a bull is supreme among the herd of cows, so dost Thou, O God, shine when Thou takest in Thy might this Earth and Heaven and all existence ! (1496)

IV

१. इममू षु त्वमस्माकꣳ सनि गायत्रं नव्याꣳसम् । अग्ने देवेषु प्र वोच: ॥

1. O fire, carry effectively to the elements this oblation, and our praise-worthy recitation of Vedic verses ! (1497)[2]

२. विभक्तासि चित्रभानो सिन्धोरूर्मा उपाक आ । सद्यो दाशुषे क्षरसि ॥

2. O God, the Lord of manifold suns, just as small canals are dug out of a big river, so, out of Thy ocean of superhuman power, dost Thou distribute might, and make joy flow for Thy devotee ! (1498)

३. आ नो भज परमेष्वा वाजेषु मध्यमेषु । शिक्षा वस्वो अन्तमस्य ॥

3. O God, give us a share of celestial, atmospheric, and terrestrial wealth ! (1499)[3]

---

[1]Like the sun : Just as the sun at dawn removes the darkness of the earth, so does God remove the darkness of the soul, when it goes into Samādhi.

[2]See verse 28.

[3]Celestial wealth; the light of the sun.

Atmospheric wealth means rain. Terrestrial wealth means worldly riches and prosperity.

V

१. अहमिद्धि पितुष्परि मेधामृतस्य जग्रह । अह॑ँ सूर्य॑ इवाजनि ॥

1. Verily have I acquired Vedic intelligence from my Father, and have hence become illustrious like the Sun. (1500)[1]

२. अहं प्रत्नेन जन्मना गिरः शुम्भामि कण्ववत् । येनेन्द्रः शुष्ममिद्दधे ॥

2. After the ancient manner, I, like a wise person adorn my Vedic speech, whereby the soul gains power. (1501)[2]

३. ये त्वामिन्द्र न तुष्टुवृऋषयो ये च तुष्टुवुः । ममेद् वर्धस्व सुष्टुतः ॥

3. O God, the athiests do not praise Thee. The Rishis praise Thee. Make me advance indeed, when praised by myself ! (1502)

VI

१. अग्ने विश्वेभिरग्निभिर्जोषि ब्रह्मा सहस्कृत । ये देवत्रा य आयुषु तेभिर्नो महया गिरः ॥

1. O Wise God, Attainable through spiritual strength, penance, celibacy and Samadhi, Thou preachest to mankind, the knowledge of the Vedas through all learned Yogis. Preach unto us the Vedic instructions, through men of knowledge and action ! (1503)

२. प्र स विश्वेभिरग्निभिरग्निः स यस्य वाजिनः । तनये तोके अस्मदा सम्यङ्वाजैः परीवृतः ॥

2. God, the Embodiment of knowledge and action, Who is valued by all the sages, is the Supreme Light. May He, nicely honoured universally, the Lord of the forces of knowledge and action, be worshipped by our sons and grandsons. (1504)

३. त्वं नो अग्ने अग्निभिर्ब्रह्मा यज्ञं च वर्धय । त्वं नो देवतातये रायो दानाय चोदय ॥

3. O God, advance our knowledge and noble deeds, through learned persons. Urge us to serve the sages and give wealth in charity ! (1505)

VII

१. त्वे सोम प्रथमा वृक्तबर्हिषो महे वाजाय श्रवसे धियं दधुः । स त्वं नो वीर वीर्याय चोदय ॥

1. O God, the emancipated souls of the first order, are they, who concentrate their mind on Thee, the Repository of knowledge and glory. O Omnipotent God, urge us also to acquire heroic power ! (1506)[3]

[1]See Verse 152.
[2]'I' refers to soul. Griffith in the wake of Sāyana translates कण्व (Kanva) as the name of a Rishi. The word means a wise person. As the Vedas are free from historical references, Griffith's explanation is unacceptable.
[3]See verse 386. Bounteous gifts : The lightning dries the Soma juice and sends it back in the shape of the gift of rain.

२. अभ्यभि हि श्रवसा ततर्दिथोत्सं न कं चिज्जनपानमक्षितम् ।
शर्याभिर्नं भरमाणो गभस्त्यो: ॥

2. Just as a skilled artisan with the fingers of his hands forcibly digs a perennial source of water to fill a vast reservoir, so dost thou, O learned person, with the force of knowledge and Yogic practices, dive deep into God, the Limitless Ocean and Perfect Source of joy ! (1507)

३. अजीजनो अमृत मर्त्याय कमृतस्य धर्मन्नमृतस्य चारुण: । सदासरो वाजमच्छा सनिष्यदत् ॥

3. O learned person, thou createst deathless joy for the soul, and spreading knowledge and strength in the religious path preached by the immortal, excellent Veda, thou always nicely manifestest thyself ! (1508)

VIII

१. एन्दुमिन्द्राय सिञ्चत पिबाति सोम्यं मधु । प्र राधाँसि चोदयते महित्वना ॥

1. O priests, perform Homa with the juice of Soma, for the lightning, which dries the Soma juice and through its majesty sends forth its bounteous gifts ! (1509)

२. उपो हरीणां पति राध: पृञ्चन्तमब्रवम् । नूनँ श्रुधि स्तुवतो अश्वस्य ॥

2. I, seeking the shelter of God, say unto Him, the Giver of wisdom and the Guardian of the learned, listen certainly to the soul who sings Thy praise. (1510)

३. न ह्या३ऽङ्ग पुरा च न जज्ञे वीरतरस्त्वत् । न की राया नैवथा न भन्दना ॥

3. O God, never was any hero born before Thee mightier than Thou. None certainly is like Thee in riches, protection and praise ! (1511)

IX

१. नदं व ओदतीनां नदं योयुवतीनाम् । पति वो अघ्न्यानां धेनूनामिषुध्यसि ॥

1. O men, seek the shelter of God, the Lord of imperishable, eternal Vedic verses, the yielders of knowledge, the preachers of action, the instructors of spiritual wisdom ! (1512)

X

१. देवो वो द्रविणोदा: पूर्णां विवष्ट्वासिचम् ।
उद्वा सिञ्चध्वमुप वा पृणध्वमादिद्वो देव ओहते ॥

1. O men, fire, the giver of wealth and strength, desires your full oblation. Pour out the oblation in full, fill it again. Then will fire speedily give Ye the desired fruit. (1513)

२. तꣳ होतारमध्वरस्य प्रचेतसं वह्निं देवा अकृण्वत ।
दधाति रत्नं विधते सुवीर्यमग्निर्जनाय दाशुषे ॥

2. God gives to a charitable person and the worshipper excellent knowledge
and wealth. The learned deem the passing Wise God, the Accomplisher of the
non-violent Yajna of knowledge, and the Consummator of all enterprises.
(1514)[1]

XI

१. अदर्शि गातुवित्तमो यस्मिन् व्रतान्यादधुः ।
उपो षु जातमार्यस्य वर्धनमग्निं नक्षन्तु नो गिरः ॥

1. The fire is kindled, in which the knowers of scientific laws place all their
researches. May we sing the praise of the well-kindled fire, which contributes
to the advancement of an Arya sacrificer and an artisan. (1515)[2]

२. यस्मादेजन्त कृष्टयश्चकृत्यानि कृण्वतः । सहस्रसां मेधसातताविव त्मनाग्नि धीभिर्नेमस्यत ॥

2. Men are afraid of God, the Giver of thousands, and the Administrator
of the universe. For the acquisition of knowledge and the advancement of
intellect, worship Him through soul, with the aid of Yogic practices. (1516)

३. प्र देवोदासो अग्नि[र्देव इन्द्रो न मज्मना ।]
[अनु मातरं पृथिवीं वि वावृते तस्थौ नाकस्य शर्मणि] ॥

3. The light produced in heaven with full splendour, like the blazing Sun,
with its might, overshadows the Earth, the mother of all beings, and stands
in high-heaven's dwelling place. (1517)[3]

XII

१. अग्न आयूंषि पवस [आ सुवोर्जमिषं च नः ।] [आरे बाधस्व दुच्छुनाम्] ॥

1. O God, Thou pourest life, send down upon us food and vigorous
strength, drive Thou evil feelings far away ! (1518)[4]

२. अग्निऋषिः पवमानः पाञ्चजन्यः पुरोहितः । तमीमहे महागयम् ॥

2. God is the Revealer of all the verses, the Purifier of all, the Lover of all

---

[1]Griffith following Sāyana has translated Aśva as a Rishi. The word means active soul
that reaps the fruit of its actions. The Vedas are free from history, hence I reject Griffith's interpretation.
[2]See Verse 47. All scientific progress and researches are carried out through properly
handling and understanding the use of fire. Aeroplanes, Hydrogen bombs, Rockets.
Sputniks are the result of the right use of fire or electricity.
[3]See verse 51.
[4]See verse 627.

five sorts of men, Present in the universe before its creation. To Him we pray Whose knowledge is great. (1519)[1]

३. अग्ने पवस्व स्वपा अस्मे वर्चः सुवीर्यम् । दधद्रयि मयि पोषम् ॥

3. Skilled in Thy task, O God, grant us splendour and heroic strength. Grant me wealth that nourishes ! (1520)[2]

XIII

१. अग्ने पावक रोचिषा मन्द्रया देव जिह्वया । आ देवान् वक्षि यक्षि च ॥

1. O Purifying, Refulgent God, with Thy splendour and pleasant urging, Thou goadest and determinest the learned ! (1521)

२. तं त्वा घृतस्नवीमहे चित्रभानो स्वर्दृशम् । देवाँ आ वीतये वह ॥

2. O Lustrous God, the Urger of all luminous objects, we pray unto Thee, the Displayer of the path of salvation. Bring Thou hither the sages for imparting knowledge ! (1522)

३. वीतिहोत्रं त्वा कवे द्युमन्तँ समिधीमहि । अग्ने बृहन्तमध्वरे ॥

3. O Omnipresent, Luminous God, in a non-violent deed, we kindle Thee, Present in all sacrifices (Yajnas), Full of light, the Almighty ! (1523)

XIV

१. अवा नो अग्न ऊतिभिर्गायत्रस्य प्रभर्मणि । विश्वासु धीषु वन्द्य ॥

1. O Adorable God, protect us in all actions with Thy aids, for nourishing the body! (1524)

२. आ नो अग्ने रयिं भर सत्रासाहं वरेण्यम् । विश्वासु पृत्सु दुष्टरम् ।

2. O God, grant us the wealth of patience, that overcomes poverty, is worthy of our choice and invincible in all struggles! (1525)

३. आ नो अग्ने सुचेतुना रयिं विश्वायुपोषसम् । मार्डीकं धेहि जीवसे ॥

3. Grant us, O God, for completing our Yajna of life, wealth coupled with knowledge, that supports all living men, and gives us freedom from disease! (1526)[3]

---

[1]Five sorts of men : (1) Brāhman, (2) Kshatriya, (3) Vaisha, (4) Shūdra, (5) Nishāda.
[2]See Yajur 8-38.
[3]Use for us: Preach unto us knowledge whereby we may be able to shun sins.

XV

१. अग्निꣳ हिन्वन्तु नो धिय: सप्तिमाशुमिवाजिषु । तेन जेष्म धनंधनम् ॥

1. Let our forces of knowledge and action, urge the soul, as a fleet horse is urged by warriors in battles, whereby we may win immense wealth. (1527)

२. यया गा आकरामहै सेनयाग्ने तवोत्या । तां नो हिन्व मघत्तये ॥

2. O God, send us for the gain of wealth! Thy vast protection and knowledge whereby we gain control over our organs of senses. (1528)

३. आग्ने स्थूरꣳ रयिं भर पृथुं गोमन्तमश्विनम् । अङ्धि खं वर्तया पविम् ॥

3. O God, bring us secure, vast wealth in horses and in kine; send us happiness, use for us the sin-killing weapon of knowledge! (1529)

४. अग्ने नक्षत्रमजरमा सूर्यꣳ रोहयो दिवि । दधज्ज्योतिर्जनेभ्य: ॥

4. O God, Thou hast made the ever-moving, eternal Sun, for giving the boon of light to men! (1530)

५. अग्ने केतुर्विशामसि प्रेष्ठ: श्रेष्ठ उपस्थसत् । बोधा स्तोत्रे वयो दधत् ॥

5. O God, Thou art the Giver of knowledge to mankind, Best, Dearest, seated in the heart. Thou givest learning, food. and life to the worshipper! (1531)

XVI

१. अग्निर्मूर्धा दिव: ककुत्पति: पृथिव्या अयम् । अपाꣳ रेताꣳसि जिन्वति ॥

1. This fire is head and height of heaven, and nourisher of the denizens of the Earth. It carries waters to the mid-atmosphere. (1532)[1]

२. ईशिषे वार्यस्य हि दात्रस्याग्ने स्व: पति: । स्तोता स्यां तव शर्मणि ॥

2. Yea, God, as Lord of supreme bliss, Thou rulest over choicest gifts; may I, Thy worshipper, find shelter in Thee. (1533)

३. उदग्ने शुचयस्तव शुक्रा भ्राजन्त ईरते । तव ज्योतीꣳष्यर्चय: ॥

3. O God, Thy pure, blazing, resplendent splendours magnify Thy powers ! (1534)

---

[1]Fire nourishes men through mechanical contrivances, factories and mills, where electricity is used. Fire in the shape of sun's rays takes water from the Ocean to the atmosphere.

Chapter 2

I

१. कस्ते जामिर्जनानामग्ने को दाश्वध्वर: । को ह कस्मिन्नसि श्रित: ॥

1. O God! who is Thy kin amongst men? Who honours Thee with non-violent sacrifice? Who art Thou? Where dost Thou rest? (1535)[1]

२. त्वं जामिर्जनानामग्ने मित्रो असि प्रिय: । सखा सखिभ्य ईड्च: ॥

2. O God, Thou art [thy Kinsman of mankind, their well-beloved Friend art Thou. A Friend whom friends may supplicate! (1536)

३. यजा नो मित्रावरुणा यजा देवाँ ऋतं बृहत् । अग्ने यक्षि स्वं दमम् ॥

3. O God, grant strength and knowledge to our teacher and preacher, grant immense true knowledge to the sages. Thou grantest us Thy supreme bliss! (1537)

II

१. ईडेन्यो नमस्यस्तिरस्तमाँसि दर्शत: । समग्निरिध्यते वृषा ॥

1. Just as fire, dispels darkness when it burns, so is God, the Dispeller of the darknesses of ignorance and the Displayer of the paths of virtue, meet to be worshipped and implored. God, the Showerer of all joys, is realised in the heart through knowledge. (1538)

२. वृषो अग्नि: समिध्यतेऽश्वो न देववाहन: । तँ हविष्मन्त ईडते ॥

2. God, the Giver of all joys, the Setter in motion of all planets, is kindled in the heart through Yogic practices, like the horse of a warrior desiring for victory in a battle. The worshippers pray unto Him. (1539)

३. वृषणं त्वा वयं वृषन्वृषण: समिधीमहि । अग्ने दीद्यतं बृहत् ॥

3. O Bestower of joys and knowledge, we Yogis, tender-hearted through devotion, kindle in our heart, Thee, the Omnipotent, the Giver of light to the universe, the Almighty God! (1540)

III

१. उत्ते बृहन्तो अर्चय: समिधानस्य दीदिव: । अग्ने शुक्रास ईरते ॥

1. O refulgent fire, thy mighty, bright flames, when thou art enkindled, rise on high! (1541)[2]

---

[1]None is the Kin of God. The true, exact nature of God is not known to men, except what is revealed by Him in the Vedas.

[2]See verse 36. The four Vedas, the repository of the knowledge of God, have been mentioned in the first as well as the second part of the Sāmaveda, so that one who studies only one part may have knowledge of the revelation of God.

२. उप त्वा जुह्वो३ मम घृताचीर्यन्तु हर्यंत । अग्ने हव्या जुषस्व नः ॥

2. O Beloved God, may the feelings of my heart, full of love and devotion go nigh unto Thee. May Thou accept our offerings! (1542)

३. मन्द्रॐ होतारमृत्विजं चित्रभानुं विभावसुम् । अग्निमीड़े स उ श्रवत् ॥

3. I pray to God, the Embodiment of joy, the Administrator of the universe, Adorable by the sages, wonderously splendid, Rich in light, He listens to all prayers. (1543)

IV

१. पाहि नो अग्न एकया पाह्य३त द्वितीयया ।
पाहि गीर्भिस्तिसृभिरूर्जां पते पाहि चतसृभिर्वसो ॥

1. O God, protect us with one Veda (Rig), Protect us by the second Veda (Yajur). Protect us by the three Vedas (Rig, Yajur, Sāma), Guard us O All-Pervading Lord of power, by the four Vedas (Rig, Yajur, Sāma and Atharva)! (1544)

२. पाहि विश्वस्माद्रक्षसो अरावण: प्र स्म वाजेषु नोऽव ।
त्वामिद्धि नेदिष्ठं देवतातय आपि नक्षामहे वृधे ॥

2. O God, protect us from all feelings of violence and miserliness. Succour and save us in life's struggles. We seek the shelter of Thee, the nearest Friend of all, for our weal and that of the learned! (1545)

V

१. इनो राजन्नरति: समिद्धो रौद्रो दक्षाय सुषुमॐ अदर्शि ।
चिकिद्धि भाति भासा बृहतासिक्नीमेति रुशतीमपाजन् ॥

1. Refulgent God, Thou art the Lord of all, All Pervading, with lofty splendour, Thou art the Chastiser of the sinners. Thou manifestest Thyself as the Giver of joy to the soul. Omniscient God, with full lustre of knowledge, Thou shinest every where. Thou convertest the brilliant Dawn of creation into the dark Night of Dissolution! (1546)[1]

२. कृष्णां यदेनीमभि वर्पसाभूज्जनयन्यन्योषां बृहत: पितुर्जाम् ।
ऊर्ध्वं भानुं सूर्यस्य स्तभायन् दिवो वसुभिररतिर्वि भाति ॥

2. When the sole God, through His might, overpowers the fleeting wheel of time, that brings about the dissolution of the universe, and converts the

---

[1]God creates the universe and then dissolves it into chaos. From chaos He evolves Cosmos and Vice-versa. This process is going on since eternity. The Creation and Dissolution of the universe are spoken of as Dawn and Night.

power of dissolution into that of Creation by God the Great; He shines pre-
eminently fixing the lustrous Sun in Heaven, along with other habitable worlds
in the universe. (1547)[1]

३. भद्रो भद्रया सचमान आगात्स्वसारं जारो अभ्येति पश्चात् ॥
सुप्रकेतैर्द्युभिरग्निर्निवितिष्ठन् रुशद्भिर्वर्णैरभि रामस्थात् ॥

3. The Adorable God, the Well-Wisher of all, manifests Himself along
with Matter, the giver of joy to mankind. God, the bringer of dissolution of
the universe, again completely pervades Matter convertible into Creation. The
Refulgent God, with His excellent, intelligent laws, diversely pervading Matter, creates this charming world, with its fascinating beauties. (1548)[2]

VI

१. कया ते अग्ने अङ्गिर ऊर्जो नपादुपस्तुतिम् । वराय देव मन्यवे ॥

1. With what words should we praise Thee, O God, Omnipresent, the Embodiment of strength, Worthy of adoration and meditation! (1549)

२. दाशेम कस्य मनसा यज्ञस्य सहसो यहो । कदु वोच इदं नमः ॥

2. O God! realizable through Yoga and humility, what soul should we
dedicate to Thee with devotion? When should I utter this reverent word?
(1550)[3]

३. अधा त्वꣳ हि नस्करो विश्वा अस्मभ्यꣳ सुक्षिती: । वाजद्रविणसो गिरः ॥

3. O God, so then dost Thou prepare for us all happy habitations, and
reveal for us the Vedas, the augmenters of knowledge! (1551)

VII

१. अग्न आ याह्यग्निभिर्होतारं त्वा वृणीमहे ।
आ त्वामनक्तु प्रयता हविष्मती यजिष्ठं बर्हिरासदे ॥

1. O God, let us realise Thee with Thy lustres. We accept Thee, as the

---

[1]The sole God: God is one, and one alone not more than one, say two, three, four etc.
God creates the universe and then dissolves it. He again creates and dissolves it. This
process continues from eternity and will continue for ever. The world created lasts for
4320000000 years called the Brahma day. The material world is then dissolved. The
matter in its chaotic state lasts for the same period, called the Brahma Night. This process is eternal, without a beginning or end.

[2]Pt. Jawala Prasad wrongly brings in Rama in the verse. The word रामम् does not
refer to Rama Chandra who was not born, when the Vedas were revealed. There is no
history in the Vedas, as they are the word of God and revealed in the beginning of the
world. The word means the charming world.

[3]We have already dedicated the soul to Thee. There is nothing more to be dedicated. I
remember and praise thee at all times, hence there is no specific time when I should pray
unto God.

Giver of joys. May we, with refined intellect recognise, in the inmost recesses of the heart, Thee, most Adorable! (1552)

२. अच्छा हि त्वा सहसः सूनो अङ्गिरः सुचश्चरन्त्यध्वरे ।
ऊर्जो नपातं घृतकेशमीमहेऽग्निं यज्ञेषु पूर्व्यम् ॥

2. O Refulgent God, attainable through penance, for Thy realisation, (just as ladies move in the sacrifice (Yajna) so do breaths move in the non-violent Yajna of life. In all acts of charity and public welfare, we pray unto God, Most Exalted and Immemorial, the Guardian of the soul with His strength, replete with flames of knowledge! (1553)[1]

VIII

१. अच्छा नः शीरशोचिषं गिरो यन्तु दर्शतम् । अच्छा यज्ञासो नमसा पुरूवसुं पुरुप्रशस्तमूतये ॥

1. Let our songs go for protection to God, Beauteous and Bright like fire, very Rich, much lauded. Let our souls with devotion and veneration, realise Him well. (1554)

२. अग्निꣲ सूनुꣲ सहसो जातवेदसं दानाय वार्याणाम् ।
द्विता यो भूदमृतो मर्त्येष्वा होता मन्द्रतमो विशि ॥

2. For the grant of all desirable objects, realise the Omniscient God, Attainable through Yogic force. Immortal, He has got two aspects, as the Giver of life to the mortals, and supreme bliss to His subjects. (1555)

IX

१. अदाभ्यः पुरएता विशामग्निर्मानुषीणाम् । तूर्णी रथः सदा नवः ॥

1. Soul is invincible. It goes ahead of mortal men in the Yajna of life. It is ever new, and like a fast conveyance is a quick and convenient vehicle for the journey of life. (1556)[2]

२. अभि प्रयाꣲसि वाहसा दाश्वाꣲ अश्नोति मर्त्यः । क्षयं पावकशोचिषः ॥

2. A mortal worshipper, with the help of his soul, enjoys all eatables. He realises God, the store-house of purifying power. (1557)[3]

३. साह्वान्विश्वा अभियुजः क्रतुर्देवानाममृक्तः । अग्निस्तुविश्रवस्तमः ॥

3. God is the Conqueror of all invading immoral forces, the Instructor of divine virtues, the Embodiment of diverse sorts of knowledge. (1558)

---

[1]A man attains to salvation and acquires worldly comforts through his soul.
[2]See verse 111.
[3]See Yajur 15-40.

X

१. भद्रो नो ग्रग्निराहुतो भद्रा राति: सुभग भद्रो ग्रध्वर: । भद्रा ऊत प्रशस्तय: ॥

1. May fire duly satiated with oblations give us happiness. O Wealth-producing fire, may our charity, non-violent deeds, and eulogies bring us happiness ! (1559)[1]

२. भद्रं मन: कृणुष्व वृत्रतूर्ये येना समत्सु सासहि: ।
अव स्थिरा तनुहि भूरि शार्धतां वनेमा ते ग्रभिष्टये ॥

2. O God, for the removal of opposing foes, grant us the determination of mind, wherewith success is achieved in fights. Bring down the mighty powers of the enemies. We seek Thy shelter for the attainment of our goal ! (1560)

XI

१. अग्ने वाजस्य गोमत ईशान: सहसो यहो । अस्मे देहि जातवेदो महि श्रव: ॥

1. O fire, thou expandest our intellect with thy light. Thou art the lord of kine and foodstuffs. Thou art the son of strength. Grant us great wealth ! (1561)

२. स इधानो वसुष्कविरग्निरीडेन्यो गिरा । रेवदस्मभ्यं पुर्वणीक दीदिहि ॥

2. O Lustrous, Omnipresent, Wise God, Thou art worthy of adoration through Vedic verses. O Omnipotent God, manifest Thyself in the soul ! (1562)[2]

३. क्षपो राजन्नुत त्मनाग्ने वस्तोरुतोषस: । स तिग्मजम्भ रक्षसो दह प्रति ॥

3. O Refulgent, Wise God, with Thy strength, cast aside all evil thoughts. O Dispeller of darkness with light, burn down our Satanic sentiments ! (1563)[3]

XII

१. विशोविशो वो ग्रतिथि वाजयन्त: पुरुप्रियम् । ग्रग्नि वो दुर्यं वच स्तुषे शूषस्य मन्मभि: ॥

1. O men, desirous for foodstuffs, for Ye, I extol with Vedic verses, fire, the benefactor of Ye all, ever moving like a guest, and the abode of happiness ! (1564)[4]

---

[1]Through Yajna, rain produces grass for the cattle and foodstuffs for men. Fire is the son of strength, as it is produced by rubbing together with great strength the two pieces of wood. See verse 99. The proper use of electricity brings us wealth.
[2]See Yajur 15-36.
[3]See Yajur 15-37.
[4]See verse 87.

२. यं जनासो हविष्मन्तो मित्रं न सर्पिरासुतिम् । प्रशꣴसन्ति प्रशस्तिभिः ॥

2. Self-abnegating devotees glorify with songs of praise, like a friend, God, Who is the Urger of the light of knowledge. (1565)

३. पर्याꣴसं जातवेदसं यो देवतात्युद्धता । हव्यान्यैरयद्दिवि ॥

3. Praise the Laudable Omniscient God, Who goads in the atmosphere, the lofty heavenly bodies like the Sun etc. (1566)

XIII

१. समिद्धमग्नि समिधा गिरा गृणे शुचि पावकं पुरो अध्वरे ध्रुवम् ।
विप्रꣴ होतारं पुरुवारमद्रुहं कविꣴ सुम्नैरीमहे जातवेदसम् ॥

1. In intellectual eloquence I praise God, Refulgent, Pure, Purifier, Primordial in the universe, Eternal. May we implore with profound meditations, the Wise, Charitable, Protecting, Guileless, Omnipresent, and Omniscient God. (1567)

२. त्वां दूतमग्ने अमृतं युगेयुगे हव्यवाहं दधिरे पायुमीडचम् ।
देवासश्च मर्तासश्च जागृवि विभुं विश्पतिं नमसा नि षेदिरे ।

2. O God, the learned have in each age accepted as their object of worship, Thee, Eternal, the Receiver of eulogies, the Sustainer of the universe, and Worthy of adoration. The sages and ordinary mortals, full of devotion and humility sit at the feet of Thee, Ever-Waking, Ubiquitous, and the Lord of mankind! (1568)

३. विभूषन्नग्न उभयाꣴ अनु व्रता दूतो देवानाꣴ रजसी समीयसे ।
यत्ते धीतिꣴ सुमतिमावृणीमहेऽध स्म नस्त्रिवरूथः शिवो भव ॥

3. O God, adorning both the emancipated and confined souls with Thy superhuman power, in all acts of benevolence, manifesting Thyself to seekers after salvation, Thou pervadest the Earth and Heaven. We lay claim to Thy regard and gracious care. May Thou as the Creator, Sustainer, and Dissolver of the universe be kind unto us! (1569)

XIV

१. उप त्वा जामयो गिरो देदिशतीर्हविष्कृतः । वायोरनीके अस्थिरन् ॥

1. O fire, the highly generous hymns of a sacrificer, like a virtuous woman, reach thee in the air! (1570)[1]

[1]See verse 13. Words uttered at one place are carried through air to another place. It is the space that supports words, and air carries them from one place to the other like Telephone.

२. यस्य त्रिधात्ववृतं बहिस्तस्थावसन्दिनम् । आपश्चिन्नि दधा पदम् ॥

2. This three-fold, visible, grand moving universe rests in God. In Him do all worlds find their shelter. (1571)

३. पदं देवस्य मीढुषोऽनाधृष्टाभिरूतिभि: । भद्रा सूर्य इवोपदृक् ॥

3. The Supreme nature of the Lustrous God, the Fulfiller of all ambitions, is full of incomparable joys. His realisation is a source of bliss like the Sun. (1572)

Chapter 3

I

१. अभि त्वा पूर्वपीतय इन्द्र स्तोमेभिरायव: ।
समीचीनास ऋभव: समस्वरन् रुद्रा गृणन्त पूर्व्यम् ॥

1. O God, the wise, eulogistic, noble persons, for their entire satisfaction, praise Thee, the Perfect, and sing Thy glory with Vedic songs ! (1573)[1]

२. अस्येदिन्द्रो वावृधे वृष्णयᵒ शवो मदे सुतस्य विष्णवि ।
अद्या तमस्य महिमानमायवोऽनु ष्टुवन्ति पूर्वथा ॥

2. God develops the happiness-bestowing strength, for the full bodily enjoyment of the soul. Living men today, even as of old, sing forth their praise to His Majesty. (1574)[2]

II

१. प्र वामर्चन्त्युब्रिथनो नीथाविदो जरितार: । इन्द्राग्नी इष आ वृणे ॥

1. O God and soul, Knowers of the path of God, learned eulogisers, and knowers of the Vedas hymn Ye both well. I too choose Ye to bring me spiritual power ! (1575)

[1]See verse 256.

[2]One mighty deed means Yoga Samadhi. Ninety means the innumerable previous births the soul had before attaining to salvation through Yoga, Ninety can also be thus explained. There are six seasons, ten Prānas, ten Organs, Manas, Budhi, Chitta, Ahankār (constituting the Anta-Karan) (अन्त: करण). These thirty with reference to three gunas सत्व, रजस्, तमस्) become ninety. Pt. Jaidev Vidyalankar explains these ninety forts like this: There are ten organs. Taking into consideration their differences with respect to Satva, Rajas and Tamas make them thirty, which become ninety with reference to three Koshas (sheaths) अन्नमय, प्राणमय, मनोमय. Griffith explains ninety forts as the countless strongholds of the barbarians or non-Aryan inhabitants of the country. This explanation is untenable as it smacks of history in the Vedas which are free from it.

२. इन्द्राग्नी नवर्ति पुरो दासपत्नीरधूनुतम् । साकमेकेन कर्मणा ॥

2. O God and soul, Ye shake down, together, with one mighty deed, the ninety forts held by violent passions ! (1576)

३. इन्द्राग्नी अपसस्पर्युप प्र यन्ति धीतयः । ऋतस्य पथ्या३ अनु ॥

3. O God and soul, meditative learned persons, following in the wake of the teachings of divine knowledge, reach Ye, through disinterested acts! (1577)

४. इन्द्राग्नी तविषाणि वाꣲ सधस्थानि प्रयाꣲसि च । युवोरप्तूर्यꣲ हितम् ॥

4. O God and soul, Your powers and knowledge work in concord. Ye both possess the urge to action ! (1578)

III

१. शग्ध्यू३ षु शचीपत इन्द्र विश्वाभिरूतिभिः ।
भगं न हि त्वा यशसं वसुविदमनु शूर चरामसि ॥

1. O God, the Lord of infinite strength, the Dispenser of the fruits of actions we pray unto Thee to grant us glorious renown with all Thy powers of protection. May we verily follow Thee, the Giver of the wealth of knowledge ! (1579)[1]

२. पौरो अश्वस्य पुरुकृद्गवामस्युत्सो देव हिरण्ययः ।
न किंहि दानं परि मर्धिषत् त्वे यद्यद्यामि तदा भर ॥

2. O God, Thou art the Increaser of our horse-like power of action, and the Multiplier of our kine-like power of organs of knowledge. Thou art full of refulgence, and deep like the well. None can impair Thy gift. Bring me whatever thing I ask for ! (1580)

IV

१. त्वꣲ ह्येहि चेरवे विदा भगं वसुत्तये । उद्वावृषस्व मघवन् गविष्टय उदिन्द्राश्वमिष्टये ॥

1. O soul, come to thy devotee. Realise the Adorable God, for the control of organs. O Omnipotent God, grant us happiness to enable the organs to achieve their goal. Grant strength for the good of the horse-like soul ! (1581)[2]

२. त्वं पुरू सहस्राणि शतानि च यूथा दानाय मंहसे ।
आ पुरन्दरं चकृम विप्रवचस इन्द्रं गायन्तोऽवसे ॥

2. O God, Thou bestowest many hundred and thousand kinds of riches on a charitable person. We learned persons, the expositors of different sciences,

[1] See verse 253.
[2] See verse 240. Soul has been compared to a horse, as it is active, alert and fast like a horse.

for the sake of acquiring knowledge, eulogising God, accept Him as the Dismantler of the citadel of lust ! (1582)[1]

V

१. यो विश्वा दयते वसु होता मन्द्रो जनानाम् ।
मघोनं पात्रा प्रथमान्यस्मै प्र स्तोमा यन्त्वग्नये ॥

1. Let primeval Vedic songs be recited, like vessels filled with honey, in praise of fire, wherewith Homa is performed, which gives happiness to mankind and brings wealth to men. (1583)[2]

२. अश्वं न गीर्भी रथ्यं सुदानवो मर्मृ ज्यन्ते येवयवः ।
उभे तोके तनये दस्म विश्पते परि राधो मघोनाम् ॥

2. O Beautiful God, the Lord of men, Thy votaries and devotees, who dedicate themselves to Thee, with Thy eulogies, purify the soul, the carrier of the conveyance of body like a horse. Thou bestowest wisdom on the children grandchildren of learned persons ! (1584)

VI

१. इमं मे वरुण श्रुधी हवमद्या च मृडय । त्वामवस्युरा चके ॥

1. O God, the Destroyer of sins, hear this my call, and show, Thy gracious love today; desiring help I pray unto Thee ! (1585)

VII

१. कया त्वं न ऊत्याभि प्र मन्दसे वृषन् । कया स्तोतृभ्य आ भर ॥

1. O God, the Showerer of joys, with what wonderful aid dost Thou delight us. How beautifully dost Thou bring riches to those who worship Thee ! (1586)

VIII

१. इन्द्रमिद्देवतातय इन्द्रं प्रयत्यध्वरे । इन्द्रं समीके वनिनो हवामह इन्द्रं धनस्य सातये ॥

1. For development of the strength of organs, in the beginning, at the end of each enterprise, and for the acquisition of the wealth of knowledge, we, the worshippers invoke God alone for help. (1587)

---

[1]'Riches' refers to wealth in the shape of kine and cattle.
[2]See verse 44. Fire in the shape of electricity adds to our comfort, happiness and wealth. Vedic songs are as sweet as honey.

२. इन्द्रो मह्ना रोदसी पप्रथच्छव इन्द्र: सूर्यमरोचयत् ।
इन्द्रे ह विश्वा भुवनानि येमिर इन्द्रे स्वानास इन्दव: ॥

2. With the glory of His power hath God spread out Heaven and Earth. God hath granted light to the Sun. In Him do all creatures reside. In Him do emancipated souls revel. (1588)

IX

१. विश्वकर्मन् हविषा वावृधान: स्वयं यजस्व तन्वाꣳ स्वा हि ते ।
मुह्यन्त्वन्ये अभितो जनास इहास्माकं मघवा सूरिरस्तु ॥

1. O soul, the doer of all deeds, developing thyself with knowledge, thou art performing the Yoga-Yajna through the control of breaths, in this body, the fruit of thy actions. Other ignorant souls, who do not know thy significance are infatuated. God alone is our Instructor for the accomplishment of this Yoga-Yajna ! (1589)[1]

X

१. अया रुचा हरिण्या पुनानो विश्वा द्वेषाꣳसि तरति सयुग्वभि: सूरो न सयुग्वभि: ।
धारा पृष्ठस्य रोचते पुनानो अरुषो हरि: ।
विश्वा यद्रूपा परियास्यृक्वभि: सप्तास्येभिरृꣳक्वभि: ॥

1. O man, just as the Sun, with this sap-attracting lustre of his coupled with rays, removes all kinds of darkness, so does a pure soul, remove all sinful feelings of hatred, with the forces of his intellect. Just as the Sun, with his stream of light falling on the earth, shines, and engulfs all visible objects with his seven coloured beams, so does a pure soul become famous in the universe with praises, the people bestow on it ! (1590)

२. प्राचीमनु प्रदिशं याति चेकितत्सꣳ रश्मिभिर्यतते दर्शतो रथो देव्यो दर्शतो रथ: ।
अगमन्नुक्थानि पौꣳस्येन्द्रं जैत्राय हर्षयन् ।
वज्रश्च यद्भुवथो अनपच्युता समत्स्वनपच्युता ॥

2. When God and soul, on occasions of Samādhi, like a steady King and minister, remain unmoved by foes like passion and anger, then a learned Yogi attains to the light of a path worth contemplating and knowing. The beautiful divine soul of a Yogi, then marches forth on the path of salvation, and for his success in this path of salvation, the Yogi gladdening and magnifying the soul, recites life-infusing praise-songs, and achieves the thunderbolt of final beatitude. (1591)[2]

---

[1]See verse 463.

[2]Samādhi means deep concentration. Final beatitude means salvation, which is that kind of thunderbolt that removes all sins and impediments.

३. त्वꣳ ह त्यत्पणीनां विदो वसु सं मातृभिर्मंजेयसि स्व आ दम ऋतस्य धीतिभिर्दमे ।
गरावतो न साम नयत्रां रणन्ति धीतयः ।
त्रिधातुभिररुषीभिर्वंयो दधे रोचमानो वयो दधे ॥

3. O Yogi, thou knowest the life-infusing spiritual knowledge of the learned panegyrists, which thou adornest further in thy soul, that controls the mind and the organs; by means of discernments imbibing true knowledge.

That God is sweet and fascinating like the Sāma song heard from a distance in Whom the Yogis take shelter and rejoice.

The Yogi preserves life and breaths with triple lustrous elements, and shining like the Sun attains to longevity and strength. (1592)[1]

XI

१. उत नो गोर्षणि धियमꣳवसां वाजसामुत । नृवत्कृणुह्यूतये ॥

1. O God, grant for our protection the intellect that impels our organs of cognition and action, that brings us knowledge, glory and progeny ! (1593)

XII

१. शशमानस्य वा नरः स्वेदस्य सत्यशवसः । विदा कामस्य वेनतः ॥

1. O most powerful learned persons, fulfil the ambition of a Yogi, who is calm, and perspires through Prānāyāma (exercise of breath) ! (1594)

XIII

१. उप नः सूनवो गिरः शृण्वन्त्वमृतस्य ये । सुमृडीका भवन्तु नः ॥

1. May the sons of the Immortal God listen to our songs of praise, and be exceeding kind to us. (1595)[2]

XIV

१. प्र वां महि द्यवी अभ्युपस्तुति भरामहे । शुची उप प्रशस्तये ॥

1. O teacher and pupil, pure like heaven and earth, to glorify Ye both, we bring our lofty song of praise ! (1596)

२. पुनाने तन्वा मिथः स्वेन दक्षेण राजथः । ऊह्याथे सनादृतम् ॥

2. O teacher and pupil, Ye shine, sanctifying each other with your body and spiritual strength. Ye always imbibe truth ! (1597)[3]

---

[1]Which refers to knowledge. Triple elements may mean, सत्त्व (truth), रजस् (passion), तमस् (darkness) or mind, speech and body, or वात (wind) पित्त (bile) कफ़ (phlegm). Griffith considers this verse as very difficult and its translation conjectural.

[2]'Sons of the Immortal God' means learned persons.

[3]The verse may apply to God and soul as well.

३. मही मित्रस्य साधथस्तरन्ती पिप्रती ऋतम् । परि यज्ञं नि षेदथु: ॥

3. Promoting and perfecting knowledge, mighty teacher and pupil, Ye worship God, the Friend, and sit in solitude after performing the Yajna of self-study and mutual spread of knowledge. (1598)[1]

XV

१. अयमु ते समतसि कपोत इव गर्भधिम् । वचस्तच्चिन्न ब्रोहसे ॥

1. Just as a pigeon goes to his pregnant mate, so does a faithful subject go to the King, who listens to this prayer of ours. (1599)[2]

२. स्तोत्रं राधानां पते गिर्वाहो वीर यस्य ते । विभूतिरस्तु सूनृता ॥

2. O Lord of various sorts of knowledge, O Omnipotent God, O Preacher through Vedic hymns, Thy teachings are true. Thy Vedic speech is an authority for excellence! (1600)

३. ऊर्ध्वस्तिष्ठा न ऊतयेऽस्मिन् वाजे शतक्रतो । समन्येषु ब्रवावहै ॥

3. Lord of a hundred powers, in this life's struggle against lust and anger, may Thou aid us for our protection. In all other struggles may we follow Thy Vedic injunctions. (1601)

XVI

१. गाव उप वदावटे मही यज्ञस्य रप्सुदा । उभा कर्णा हिरण्यया ॥

1. O Vedic hymns, be Ye recited near the sacrificial place. May it resound with Vedic recitation. May both the ears of the listeners be purified! (1602)[3]

२. अभ्यारमिदद्रयो निषिक्तं पुष्करे मधु । अ्रवटस्य विसर्जने ॥

2. Venerable sages, at the time of relinquishing the body, visualise divine pleasure of knowledge that resides in the soul. (1603)

३. सिञ्चन्ति नमसावटमुच्चाचक्रं परिज्मानम् । नीचीनबारमक्षितम् ॥

3. Learned sages, keep fit with food, the body, possessing eminent circles of breaths, ever aging, uninjured, and equipped with nine feeble gates of organs. (1604)[4]

---

[1]'Mutual spread of knowledge' means that the teacher adds to the knowledge of the pupil and vice versa.
[2]See verse 183.
[3]It refers to sacrificial place. See verse 117.
[4]Nine gates: Two eyes, two ears, two nostrils, mouth, anus, penis.

XVII

१. मा भेम मा श्रमिष्मोग्रस्य सख्ये तव । महत्ते वृष्णो अभिचक्ष्यं कृतं पश्येम तुर्वशं यदुम् ॥

1. In the friendship of the Almighty God, we should have no fear and feel no exhaustion. This world created by Him, is the bestower of happiness, beautiful and grand. May we find that lust stricken soul free from passions. (1605)[1]

२. सव्यामनु स्फिग्यं वावसे वृषा न दानो अस्य रोषति ।
मध्वा सम्पृक्ताः सारघेण धेनवस्तूयमेहि द्रवा पिब ॥

2. O man, God approveth of your friendly and favourable attitude. His charity does not injure man. Drinkable Soma blended with the honey of the bee is ready. Quickly come hither, hasten, and drink it. (1606)

XVIII

१. इमा उ त्वा पूरुवसो गिरो वर्धन्तु या मम ।
पावकवर्णाः शुचयो विपश्चितोऽभि स्तोमैरनूषत ॥

1. O God, the Lord of great wealth, may my songs of praise unto Thee multiply. May the pure learned persons, lustrous like fire, who praise Thee with holy hymns also develop! (1607)[2]

२. अयं ॐ सहस्रमृषिभिः सहस्कृतः समुद्र इव पप्रथे ।
सत्यः सो अस्य महिमा गृणे शवो यज्ञेषु विप्रराज्ये ॥

2. This God, Whom thousands of Rishis resort to for spiritual power, is infinite like an ocean. True is His greatness. I admire His power on occasions of sacrifices (Yajnas) and for the spread of the light of knowledge. (1608)

XIX

१. यस्यायं विश्व आर्यो दासः शेवधिपा अरिः ।
तिरश्चिदर्ये रुशमे पवीरवि तुभ्येत् सो अज्यते रयिः ॥

1. All Aryas are the devotees of God, the guardians and recipients of His knowledge of the Vedas. In God, the Lord, the Leader, the Master of speech is that knowledge hidden. God manifests the Vedic wealth to thee, the devotee. (1609)[3]

---

[1]Griffith following Sāyana translates: Turvasha and Yadu as two tribes. This explanation is untenable as there is no historical reference in the Vedas. Turvasha means lust-stricken soul. Yadu means free from passion.

[2]See verse 250.

[3]Griffith translates Rushma and Pavirn as names of two princes of a tribe. This explanation is unacceptable as it savours of history in the Veda which are free from it. Both the words refer to God as 'Leader and Master of speech.'

२. तुरण्यवो मधुमन्तं घृतश्चुतं विप्रासो अर्कमानृचुः ।
अस्मे रयिः पप्रथे वृष्ण्यꣳ शवोऽस्मे स्वानास इन्दवः ॥

2. Experienced and skilled learned persons worship God, the Bestower of happiness, and pray for the increase of our riches, heroic strength and impelling semen. (1610)

XX

१. गोमन्न इन्दो अश्ववत् सुतः सुदक्ष धनिव । शुचिं च वर्णमधि गोषु धारय ॥

1. O Almighty God, contemplated in the heart, grant us kine and steeds. Lend beautiful appearance to our cattle! (1611)[1]

२. स नो हरीणां पत इन्दो देवप्सरस्तमः । सखेव सख्ये नर्यो रुचे भव ॥

2. O Divine God, the Lord of souls, Most Splendid, the Friend of mankind, lend us lustre, as does friend to a friend! (1612)

३. सनेमि त्वमस्मदा अदेवं कं चिदत्रिणम् । साह्वाꣳ इन्दो परि बाधो अप द्युम् ॥

3. O God, extend Thy ancient friendship unto us. Drive far away from us each godless and voracious foe-like passion. O God remove the lustful shackles of the body, and overcome the persons, whose deeds and thoughts are not one and the same! (1613)

XXI

१. अञ्जते व्यञ्जते समञ्जते क्रतुꣳ रिहन्ति मध्वाभ्यञ्जते ।
सिन्धोरुच्छ्वासे पतयन्तमुक्षणꣳ हिरण्यपावाः पशुमप्सु गृभ्णते ॥

1. The learned, ennobling priests, expand, manifest and supervise the Yajna, and find the grown up Soma in waters. They smear it with honey, and taste it as it waves full of juice in an elevated place. (1614)[2]

२. विपश्चिते पवमानाय गायत मही न धारात्यन्धो अर्षति ।
अहिर्न जूर्णामति सर्पति त्वचमत्यो न क्रीडन्नसरद्वृषा हरिः ॥

2. O learned persons, sing the praise of the soul that treads the path of salvation and knows God, the embodied soul, like a mighty stream of water cuts asunder the bonds of the body and goes out of it. Just as a serpent casts aside the decayed coil and goes away, so does the active soul playing in bodies, like a horse flies from one region to the other! (1615)

[1] See verse 574.
[2] See verse 564.

३. अग्रेगो राजाप्यस्तविष्यते विमानो ब्रह्मां भूवनेष्वर्पितः ।
हरिघृं तस्नुः सुदृशीको अर्णवो ज्योतीरथः पवते राय ओक्यः ॥

3. The soul is the leader of the organs. It is lustrous, excellent in action and knowledge, the shaper of its splendours as the moon is of days. It is established in the Prāṇas. The dynamic soul bathing in knowledge, the realiser of the true Reality, full of knowledge, refulgent, the master of mighty wealth roams about in its fitness to achieve God. (1616)[1]

BOOK VIII

Chapter 1

I

१. विश्वेभिरग्ने अग्निभिरिमं यज्ञमिदं वचः । चनो धाः सहसो यहो ॥

1. O God, attainable through exertion, accept this prayer of ours offered in the company of all learned persons, and this recitation of the Vedas, and grant us perfect knowledge! (1617)

२. यच्चिद्धि शश्वता तना देवंदेवं यजामहे । त्वे इद्धूयते हविः ॥

2. O God, though we worship Varuṇa, Indra etc. through eternal soul, but that worship is meant for Thee! (1618)[2]

३. प्रियो नो अस्तु विश्पतिर्होता मन्द्रो वरेण्यः । प्रियाः स्वग्नयो वयम् ॥

3. May God, the Nourisher of His subjects, the Bestower, the Pleasure-Giver, Worthy of attainment be our friend. May we, full of spiritual fire, be dear to him. (1619)

II

१. इन्द्रं वो विश्वतस्परि हवामहे जनेभ्यः । अस्माकमस्तु केवलः ॥

1. O learned persons, for your good, we worship God, Highest of all, May the Matchless God be our Helper! (1620)

२. स नो वृषन्नमु चरꣳ सत्रादावन्नपा वृधि । अस्मभ्यमप्रतिष्कुतः ॥

2. O God, bestowing all objects simultaneously and showering Happiness, Thou, Infallible, remove this bondage of the body! (1621)[3]

३. वृषा यूथेव वꣳसगः कृष्टीरियर्त्योजसा । ईशानो अप्रतिष्कुतः ॥

---

[1]Prāṇas: Breaths, Roams about: The soul takes birth and rebirth till it succeeds in its goal in achieving salvation.
[2]Varuṇa, Indra are the names of God.
[3]'Remove this bondage' means grant us salvation.

3. Just as a strong bull goes to the herd of kine, so does Unconquerable, Matchless God, bestow knowledge through His magnanimity on men. (1622)

III

१. त्वं नश्चित्र ऊत्या वसो राधाᵕसि चोदय ।
अस्य रायस्त्वमग्ने रथीरसि विदा गाधं तुचे तु नः ॥

1. O fire, one of the eight Vasus, along with our protection, give us riches. Thou art the wonderful leader of this wealth acquired in a battle. Grant safety to our progeny! (1623)[1]

२. पर्षि तोकं तनयं पतृृᳬभिष्ट्वमदब्धैरप्रयुत्वभिः ।
अग्ने हेडाᵕसि दैव्या युयोधि नोᳵदेवानि ह्वराᵕसि च ॥

2. Prosper our son and grandson with Thy protecting, inviolate, never negligent powers. Keep far from us, O God, all celestial wrath, and wickedness of godless men ! (1624)

IV

१. किमित्ते विष्णो परिचक्षि नाम प्र यद्ववक्षे शिपिविष्टो अस्मि ।
मा वर्पो अस्मदप गूह एतद्यदन्यरूपः समिथे बभूय ॥

1. O All-pervading God, when Thou describest Thyself as All-pervading, with what words can I speak of Thy nature. Hide not from us this Form, nor keep it secret, since Thou dost wear another shape in our Samādhi! (1625)[2]

२. प्र तत्ते अद्य शिपिविष्ट ह्व्यमर्यः शᵕसामि वयुनानि विद्वान् ।
तं त्वा गृणामि तवसमतव्यान् क्षयन्तमस्य रजसः पराके ॥

2. O All-pervading God, I, a skilled devotee, knowing Thy acts of the creation, sustenance and dissolution of the universe, ever praise Thee, worthy of invocation. Yea, I, poor and weak, praise Thee, the Mighty, Who dwellest in the realm beyond this region! (1626)

२. वषट् ते विष्णवास आ कृणोमि तन्मे जुषस्व शिपिविष्ट हव्यम् ।
वर्धन्तु त्वा सुष्टुतयो गिरो मे यूयं पात स्वस्तिभिः सदा नः ॥

3. O God, I accept Thee with my mouth, as the Fulfiller of all ambitions. O All-pervading God, accept this offering of mine, May these my songs of eulogy exalt Thee. Do Ye, learned persons preserve us evermore with blessings ! (1627)

---

[1]See verse 41. Through the use of fire-arms and deadly war-like weapons is a battle won. Hence fire is the leader, the procurer of wealth in a battle.

[2]This form means the refulgent, lustrous shape of God we see in Nature. Griffith, not being able to understand the verse fully describes it as unintelligible.

V

१. वायो शुक्रो श्रयामि ते मध्वो अग्रं दिविष्टिषु । आ याहि सोमपीतये स्पाहों देव नियुत्वता ॥

1. O soul, purifying myself through the renunciation of sins, may I, a seeker after truth, in my ambitions for good traits receive from thee, excellent sweet reward. O adorable soul, come for the enjoyment of divine pleasure, yoked as thou art with the strength of Yoga ! (1628)

२. इन्द्रश्च वायवेषां सोमानां पीतिमर्हथः । युवाꣴ हि यन्तीन्दवो निम्नमापो न सध्र्यक् ॥

2. O Prāṇa and soul, Ye both are competent to enjoy the juice of divine pleasure. Yogis go unto Ye, as waters go together to a vale! (1629)[1]

३. वायविन्द्रश्च शुष्मिणा सरथꣴ शवसस्पती । नियुत्वन्ता न ऊतय आ यातꣴ सोमपीतये ॥

3. O learned person and glorious soul, Ye both are the lords of strength. Coupled with horse-like fast mind, come Ye to our succour, for enjoying spiritual pleasure ! (1630)

VI

१. अध क्षपा परिष्कृतो वाजाꣴ अभि प्र गाहसे ।
यदी विवस्वतो धियो हरिꣴ हिन्वन्ति यातवे ॥

1. When the mental attitudes of a Yogi are urged to lean towards God, then, O soul, adorned with the force of mind, that dispels darkness and ignorance, thou absorbest thyself in mighty adventures! (1631)

२. तमस्य मर्जयामसि मदो य इन्द्रपातमः । यं गाव आसभिर्दधुः पुरा नूनं च सूरयः ॥

2. We cleanse this gladdening essence of the soul, the juice which the soul chiefly drinks; that which the learned scholars of the Vedas took into their mouths of old, and take it now. (1632)[2]

३. तं गाथया पुराण्या पुनानमभ्यनूषत । उतो कृपन्त धीतयो देवानां नाम बिभ्रतीः ॥

3. Sages sing the praise of the Purifying and Pure God, with Vedic verses. Vedic songs, which bear the names of different forces of nature like Air, Fire and Sun supplicate Him. (1633)

VII

१. अश्वं न त्वा वारवन्तं वन्दध्या अग्निं नमोभिः । सम्राजन्तमध्वराणाम् ॥

1. With homage, O Fire, I reverentially kindle thee, the lord of mighty deeds, like a long-tailed steed! (1634)[3]

---

[1]God is realizable not in this apparent world, but in the realm of salvation.

[2]Learned knowers of the Vedas have tasted the joy of the soul in ancient times, and taste it even now.

[3]Just as a horse wards off flies and mosquitoes with the hair of his long tail, so does fire kindled in a Yajna remove poisonous insects in the air around it. See verse 17.

२. स घा न: सूनु: शवसा पृथुप्रगामा सुशेव: । मीढ्वाँ अस्माकं बभूयात् ॥

2. May the All-pervading God, Who goads the universe with His strength, be worthy of adoration by us. May He shower all joys on us. (1635)

३. स नो दूराच्चासाच्च नि मर्त्यादघायो: । पाहि सदमिद्विश्वायु: ॥

3. O God, the Bestower of full age to all men, protect our body, house and honour from a sinful man, be he far or near ! (1636)

VIII

१. त्वमिन्द्र प्रतूर्तिष्वभि विश्वा असि स्पृध: । अशस्तिहा जनिता वृत्रतूरसि त्वं तूर्यं तरुष्यत: ॥

1. O God, in our struggles against lust, Thou art the Vanquisher of all hostile feelings. Thou art our Father, the Subduer of sin, the Dispeller of infamy, and the Suppressor of the violent! (1637)[1]

२. अनु ते शुष्मं तुरयन्तमीयतु: क्षोणी शिशुं न मातरा ।
विश्वास्ते स्पृध: श्नथयन्त मन्यवे वृत्रं यदिन्द्र तूर्वसि ॥

2. O soul, the earth and heaven cling close to thy victorious might, as sire and mother to their child. When thou attackest the darkness of ignorance, internal foes like lust and anger shrink and faint at thy wrath! (1638)

IX

१. यज्ञ इन्द्रमवर्धयद् यद्भूमिं व्यवर्तयत् । चक्राण ओपशं दिवि ॥

1. The Yajna, expanding itself in the atmosphere, enhances the power of the Sun, the bringer of rain, and nourishes the Earth. (1639)[2]

२. व्य१न्तरिक्षमतिरन्मदे सोमस्य रोचना । इन्द्रो यदभिनद् वलम् ॥

2. When the soul cleaves to the engulfing covering of lust and anger, in ecstasy of its knowledge and strength, it lends vigour to the brilliant mind. (1640)

३. उद्गा आजदङ्गिरोभ्य आविष्कृण्वन् गुहा सती: । अर्वाञ्चं नुनुदे वलम् ॥

3. God, revealing the hidden Vedic verses, makes them reach the learned sages and suppresses all beastly feelings through their knowledge. (1641)[3]

---

[1]See verse 311.
[2]The Yajna brings rain and nourishes the earth through it. See verse 121.
[3]Griffith translates Vala as the demon who stole the cows of the Gods and hid them in a cave. This explanation savours of history and is hence untenable. The word means the dark covering of ignorance.

X

१. त्यमु व: सत्रासाहं विश्ववासु गीर्ष्वायितम् । आ च्यावयस्यूतये ॥

1. Invoke for succour this King of yours, who conquers all through truth, and is drawn to all our songs. (1642)[1]

२. युध्मं सन्तमनर्वाणं सोमपामनपच्युतम् । नरमवार्यक्रतुम् ॥

2. O learned person, remember for thy protection, God, the Subjugator of internal foes like lust, anger, avarice, infatuation, pride and jealousy; Eternal, Unchangeable, the Enjoyer of the pleasure of knowledge, Unfalterable, the Leader, and Immortal! (1643)

३. शिक्षा ण इन्द्र राय आ पुरु विद्वाँ ऋचीषम । अवा न: षार्ये धने ॥

3. O God, attainable through supplication, Thou art Omniscient, grant us various sorts of riches. Help us in the attainment of salvation, the sublimest wealth! (1644)

XI

१. तव त्यदिन्द्रियं बृहत्तव दक्षमुत क्रतुम् । वज्रं शिशाति धिषणा वरेण्यम् ॥

1. O God, our intellect visualises that lofty power and might, of Thine, Thy strength and Thy intelligence, and Thy adorable instrument of salvation that cuts asunder the bondage of the body! (1645)[2]

२. तव द्यौरिन्द्र पौंस्यं पृथिवी वर्धति श्रव: । त्वामाप: पर्वतासश्च हिन्विरे ॥

2. O God, the Heaven augments Thy force, and the Earth enhances Thy renown. The rivers and mountains sing Thy glory! (1646)

३. त्वां विष्णुर्बृहन्क्षयो मित्रो गृणाति वरुण: । त्वां शर्धो मदत्यनु मारुतम् ॥

3. O God, the atmosphere, the migthy place of residence, water and fire extol Thee. In Thee air's force feels great delight! (1647)

XII

१. नमस्ते अग्न ओजसे गृणन्ति देव कृष्टय: । अमैरमित्रमर्दय ॥

1. O fire, we offer thee oblation of corn. Energetic people sing thy praise for strength. Subdue the sinful foe with diseases! (1648)

[1]See verse 170.

[2]Fire refers to the Yajna. The Yajna is a source of strength for him who performs it. He who does not perform the Yajna falls a prey to various sorts of diseases. See verse 11.

२. कुवित्सु नो गविष्टयेऽग्ने संवेषिषो रयिम् । उरुक्रदुरु णस्क्रधि ॥

2. O God, grant us spiritual wealth for the fulfilment of our soul's goal. O Great God, make us great! (1649)

३. मा नो अग्ने महाधने परा वर्गभारभृद्यथा । संवर्गं सं रयि जय ॥

3. Just as a labourer does not cast aside his load in the middle, so, O God, abandon us not in our struggle for the attainment of salvation, pray, win us the wealth of emancipation! (1650)

XIII

१. समस्य मन्यवे विशो विश्वा नमन्त कृष्टय: । समुद्रायेव सिन्धव: ॥

1. All men and subjects bow before the dignity of the King, as rivers bow themselves to the sea. (1651)[1]

२. वि चिद्वृत्रस्य दोधत: शिरो बिभेद वृष्णिना । वज्रेण शतपर्वणा ॥

2. God, with His hundred-fold powers, and His thunderbolt of knowledge, the Showerer of joys, cuts ignorance from its very root. (1652)

३. ओजस्तदस्य तित्विष उमे यत्समवर्तयत् । इन्द्रश्चर्मेव रोदसी ॥

3. At that time is the power of God displayed when He brings together the worlds of Heaven and Earth, like a skin. (1653)[2]

XIV

१. सुमन्मा वस्वी रन्ती सूनरी ॥

1. Mental faculty is guide to the chariot of the body, the fulfiller of all ambitions, the bringer of riches, and advancer of knowledge. (1654)

२. सरूप वृषन्ना गहीमौ भद्रौ धुर्याविभि । ताविमा उप सर्पत: ॥

2. O beauteous, excellent soul, manifest thyself. This suspicious pair of Prāṇa and Apāna verily sustains the body and moves in it! (1655)

३. नीव शीर्षाणि मृद्वं मध्य आपस्य तिष्ठति । श्रृङ्गेभिर्दशभिर्दिशन् ॥

3. O learned persons, the soul resides in the body, acquiring knowledge and doing noble deeds with the aid of ten organs. Control these turbulent organs! (1656)[3]

---

[1]See verse 137.

[2]Just as a cobbler flattens and contracts a piece of skin with his skill to suit his purpose, so does God create and dissolve Heaven and Earth with His skill in accordance with His eternal Law of the creation and dissolution of the universe, a scene which exhibits His Mighty power.

[3]Ten organs: Five organs of action i.e., Karma Indriyas and five of cognition i.e., Jnāna Indriyas. The word ten may also refer to ten vital airs or life-breaths, which should be controlled for acquiring spiritual happiness. They are named as Prāṇa, Apāna, Vyāna, Udāna, Smāna, Nāga, Kūrma, Krikla, Devadatta, Dhananjaya.

Chapter 2

I

१. पन्यंपन्यमित् सोतार आ धावत मद्याय । सोमं वीराय शूराय ॥

1. O priests, procure excellent Soma for the joyful, heroic and brave King! (1657)[1]

२. एह हरी ब्रह्मयुजा शग्मा वक्षत: सखायम् । इन्द्रं गीर्भिर्गिर्वणसम् ॥

2. Both Prāṇa and Apāna in the body, take to God through prayers, the soul, worthy of being united with God through Samādhi, full of power, and enjoyer of Vedic songs. (1658)

३. पाता वृत्रहा सुतमा घा गमन्नारे अस्मत् । नि यमते शतमूति: ॥

3. The soul, the remover of impediments, the enjoyer of supreme felicity stays not far away from us. Equipped with a hundred powers, it keeps us under control. (1659)

II

१. आ त्वा विशन्त्विन्दव: समुद्रमिव सिन्धव: । न त्वामिन्द्राति रिच्यते ॥

1. The fleeting organs enter the soul as the rivers flow into the sea. O soul, naught is higher than thee! (1660)[2]

२. विव्यन्थ महिना वृषन्भक्षँ सोमस्य जागृवे । य इन्द्र जठरेषु ते ॥

2. O Vigilant God, the Bestower of joys, Thou pervadest the tiniest part of the universe, which takes shelter in Thee! (1661)

३. अरं त इन्द्र कुक्षये सोमो भवतु वृत्रहन् । अरं धामभ्य इन्दव: ॥

3. O God, the Queller of sin, this world resting in Thy womb, is enough to testify to Thy greatness. Many similar worlds are enough to demonstrate Thy preserving powers! (1662)

III

१. जराबोध तद्विविड्ढि विशोविशे यज्ञियाय । स्तोमँ रुद्राय दृशीकम् ॥

1. O fire, kindled with the recitation of thy traits, we sing beautiful laudation for thee, for accomplishing the sacrifice (Yajna) and burning brightly! (1663)[3]

---

[1]See verse 123.
[2]No earthly thing is higher than the soul. God alone is higher, but He is not earthly. See verse 197.
[3]See verse 115.

२. स नो महाꣳ अनिमानो धूमकेतु: पुरुश्चन्द्र: । धिये वाजाय हिन्वतु ॥

2. May this our God, Great, Limitless, All-knowing, excellently Bright, urge us to holy thought and strength! (1664)

३. स रेवाꣳ इव विश्पतिर्दैव्य: केतु: श्रृणोतु न: । उक्थैरग्निबृँहद्भानु: ॥

3. Like some rich lords of men, may He, God, Refulgent, Divine, Commander of the universe, Sustainer of His subjects, listen to our Vedic prayers. (1665)

IV

१. तद्वो गाय सुते सचा पुरुहूताय सत्वने । शं यद् गवे न शाकिने ॥

1. O eulogisers, sing together the praise of the King, who is extolled by many, powerful, the destroyer of foes, and the giver of joy like the Earth! (1666)

२. न घा वसुर्नि यमते दानं वाजस्य गोमत: । यत् सीमुप श्रवद्गिर: ॥

2. The All-pervading God withholdeth not His bounteous gift of Vedic lore, when He hath listened to our songs. (1667)

३. कुवित्सस्य प्र हि व्रजं गोमन्तं दस्युहा गमत् । शचीभिरप नो वरत् ॥

3. Soul, the destroyer of ignorance, verily assumes many a time, the body, the seat of the organs of cognition and vital airs. The same soul, through the instruments of knowledge and noble deeds, casts aside the bondage of the body and attains to final beatitude. (1668)

V

१. इदं विष्णुर्वि चक्रमे त्रेधा नि दधे पदम् । समूढमस्य पाꣳसुले ॥

1. The All-pervading God created this universe, and established His power of pervasion in three places. The whole universe rests in His power of pervasion in three places. The whole universe rests in His power of sustaining all the worlds. (1669)[1]

२. त्रीणि पदा वि चक्रमे विष्णुर्गोपा अदाभ्य: । अतो धर्माणि धारयन् ॥

2. The Eternal, Immortal God, the Sustainer of all the moving worlds, retaining all the worlds, is creating and conducting the whole universe with His threefold power. (1670)[2]

---

[1]Three places: The Earth, Atmosphere and Sky.

Sāyana interprets this verse to establish the incarnation of Vāmana. Yāska does not interpret it thus. As God is incorporeal, hence this explanation is inadmissible. See verse 222.

[2]'Threefold power' refers to God's powers of creation, sustenance and dissolution of the universe.

३. विष्णो: कर्माणि पश्यत यतो व्रतानि पस्पशे । इन्द्रस्य युज्य: सखा ॥

3. Look Ye on God's wondrous works whereby the soul acquires all sorts of knowledge. God is the permanent friend of the soul. (1671)[1]

४. तद्विष्णो: परमं पदꣳ सदा पश्यन्ति सूरय: । दिवीव चक्षुराततम् ॥

4. The learned always behold the loftiest knowledge of God, which is extended over the Earth and Heaven like the Sun that shows all objects. (1672)

५. तद्विप्रासो विपन्यवो जागृवाꣳस: समिन्धते । विष्णोर्यत्परमं पदम् ॥

5. This most sublime knowledge of God, the sages, ever-vigilant, lovers of holy song, kindle in their hearts. (1673)

६. ग्रतो देवा ग्रवन्तु नो यतो विष्णुविचक्रमे । पृथिव्या ग्रधि सानवि ॥

6. Just as the All-pervading God creates and sustains the universe, so should the forces of nature and learned persons take us to the highest stage of salvation on the earth. (1674)

VI

१. मो षु त्वा वाघतश्च नारे ग्रस्मन्नि रीरमन् ।
ग्राराताद्धा सधमादं न आ गहीह वा सन्नुप श्रुधि ॥

1. O God, let not learned priests praise Thee far away from us, (rather they should sing Thy praise sitting near us). Being All-pervading, Thou art verily near us, Come unto our Yajna, Residing in our heart listen to our prayer! (1675)[2]

२. इमे हि ते ब्रह्मकृत: सुते सचा मधौ न मक्ष ग्रासते ।
इन्द्रे कामं जरितारो वसूयवो रथे न पादमा दधु: ॥

2. O God, just as a fly sits on honey, so do the Vedic scholars sit near Thee for procuring the joy of salvation. Just as warriors eager for wealth and conquest set their foot upon a car, so do the learned persons hankering after the realisation of soul, make their desire rest on Thee! (1676)

VII

१. अस्तावि मन्म पूर्व्यं ब्रह्मेन्द्राय वोचत । पूर्वीॠꣳतस्य बृहतीरनूषत स्तोतुर्मेधा ग्रसृक्षत ॥

1. God alone is worthy of worship. Recite in praise of God, the immemorial Vedic song, fit for reflection. Study the ancient Brihati verses of the

---

[1]See Yajur 6-5.
[2]See verse 284.

Vedic lore. Thus does a learned person acquire different sorts of knowledge. (1677)[1]

२. समिन्द्रो रायो बृहतीरधृनुत सं क्षोणी समु सूर्यम् ।
सᴓ शुक्रासः शुचयः सं गवाशिरः सोमा इन्द्रममन्दिषुः ॥

2. God hath granted us mighty stores of wealth. He hath set in motion many planets in the atmosphere as well as the Sun. Celibate, lovely, pure, sinless Yogis, taking the shelter of Vedic knowledge, and controlling their organs, appease God. (1678)

VIII

१. इन्द्राय सोम पातवे वृत्रघ्ने परि षिच्यसे । नरे च दक्षिणावते वीराय सदनासदे ॥

1. O Soma, thou art poured for the heroic worshipper, seated in the altar, the giver of guerdon to the priests, and the queller of foes. so that he may drink thee! (1679)

२. तᴓ सखायः पुरूरुचं वयं यूयं च सूरयः । अश्याम वाजगन्ध्यᴓ सनेम वाजपस्त्यम् ॥

2. O learned friends, may Ye and we, attain to and realise God, All-Illu-minating, Almighty, and Fragrant with knowledge! (1680)

३. परि त्यᴓ हर्यतᴓ हरिं [बभ्रुं पुनन्ति वारेण ।
यो देवान्विश्वाᴓ इत् परि मदेन सह गच्छति] ॥

3. Him with the fleece they purify, brown, golden-hued, beloved of all, which with exhilarating juice flows forth to all the forces of nature. (1681)[2]

IX

१. कस्तमिन्द्र त्वा वस [वा मर्त्यो दधर्षति ।
श्रद्धा हि ते मघवन् पार्ये दिवि वाजी वाजं सिषासति] ॥

1. O God, the Abode of all, who can be disrespectful unto Thee? O God, Thy shelter lies in salvation attainable after overcoming the vicissitudes of life. O Omniscient God, Thou naturally longest to spread knowledge in the universe! (1682)[3]

२. मघोनः स्म वृत्रहत्येषु चोदय ये ददति प्रिया वसु ।
तव प्रणीती हर्यश्व सूरिभिर्विश्वा तरेम दुरिता ॥

---

[1] See verse 1331.
[2] See verse 552. Him refers to Soma, which being put into the fire in the shape of an oblation, being rarefied reaches air, water, sun etc.
[3] See verse 280.
See verse 385.

2. O God, good for the removal of the darkness of ignorance, the learned persons, who give their dear treasures in charity in obedience to the laws preached by Thee in the Vedas. May we with the help of the sages overcome all sins! (1683)

X

१. एदु मधोर्मंदिन्तरꣲ सिꣳस्वाध्वर्यो अ्रन्धसः । एवा हि वीर स्तवते सदावृधः ॥

1. O non-violent leader, the Almighty, Ever Grand God alone is worthy of worship. Acquire through Him the highly satiating, fascinating and pleasant food! (1684)

२. इन्द्र स्थातर्हरीणां न किष्टे पूर्व्यस्तुतिम् । उदानꣳश शवसा न भन्दना ॥

2. O God, the Establisher of the revolving planets like the Sun, Moon etc., none can acquire through power or goodness, Thy qualities sung by the ancient sages! (1685)

३. तं वो वाजानां पतिमहूमहि श्रवस्यवः । अ्रप्रायुभिर्यज्ञेभिर्वावृधेन्यम् ॥

3. We, seeking glory, invoke this God of yours, the Lord of wealth, Grand in His immortal deeds of the creation, sustenance and dissolution of the universe. (1686)[1]

XI

१. तं गूर्द्धया स्वर्णरं देवासो देवमरति दधन्विरे । देवत्रा हव्यमूहिषे ॥

1. Extol God, Whom the learned Yogis achieve; Who is All-pervading, Lord of joy, and the Bestower of the fruit of actions in our beautiful bodies. (1687)[2]

२. विभूतरातिं विप्र चित्रशोचिषमग्निमीडिष्व यन्तुरम् ।
अ्रस्य मेधस्य सोम्यस्य सोभरे प्रेमध्वराय पूर्व्यम् ॥

2. O pupil, the excellent gleaner of, and seeker after knowledge, worship the primordial Teacher, God, Immortal, the Bestower of immense knowledge, the Embodiment of knowledge and penance, this Giver of the joy of knowledge, the Determinant of pure acts of sacrifice! (1688)

XII

१. आ सोम स्वानो अ्द्रिभिस्तिरो वाराण्यव्यया ।
जनो न पुरि चम्वोर्विशद्धरिः सदो वनेषु दधिषे ॥

1. O soul, realized through Yogic practices, crossing the coverings of ignorance, thou enterest both the parts of the head, like a hero, who enters

---

[1] 'God of yours' means God of mankind. Yours refers to the whole of humanity.
[2] See verse 513. Both the parts mean the right and left parts.

a city conquering forts, overcoming all the impediments of nescience, thou takest thy seat in the inmost recesses of the heart! (1689)[1]

२. स मामृजे तिरो अ्रण्वानि मेध्यो मीढ्वान्त्सप्तिनं वाजयु: ।
अनुमाद्य: पवमानो मनीषिभि: सोमो विप्रेभिऋ्चे क्वभि: ॥

2. The soul of a Yogi, like the racing horse, longing for knowledge and spiritual force, achieving the subtle truths of the intellect, showering all sorts of happiness, purifies itself. His tranquil, disciplined and purified soul, becomes worthy of praise by the sages and learned scholars of the Vedas. (1690)[2]

XIII

१. वयमेनमिदा ह्योऽपीपेमेह वज्रिणम् । तस्मा उ अ्द्य सवने सुतं भरा नूनं भूषत श्रुते ॥

1. We have in the past been making this soul, the wielder of the armour of knowledge, drink to its fill. Today also, in this Vedic Yajna of worship, let us bring knowledge and joy for the soul, and enhance its beauty. (1691)[3]

२. वृकश्चिदस्य वारण उरामथिरा वयुनेषु भूषति ।
सेमं न स्तोमं जुजुषाण आ गहीन्द्र प्र चित्रया धिया ॥

2. Even a tormenting dacoit or a thief becomes subservient to the dictates of God. May the Almighty Father graciously accept this our praise, and come forth to us with wondrous wisdom. (1692)

XIV

१. इन्द्राग्नी रोचना दिव: परि वाजेषु भूषथ: । तद्वां चेति प्र वीर्यम् ॥

1. O Sun and Lightning, in your deeds of might, Ye deck heaven's lucid realms. Famed is that strength of yours! (1693)

२. इन्द्राग्नी अपसस्पर्ग [युप प्र यन्ति धीतय: । ऋतस्य पथ्या३ अनु] ॥

2. O God and soul, the instructors of the path of rectitude, following in your wake, our forces of deliberation abandon selfish acts! (1694)

३. इन्द्राग्नी तविषाणि वां [सधस्थानि प्रयांसि च । युवोरप्तूर्यं हितम्] ॥

3. O God and soul, your forces work harmoniously, and lead us on, Ye both goad us to action! (1695)

---

[1]See verse 272.
[2]See verse 1577.
[3]See verse 297. Who can see means none can see or know. The rays of the sun are invisible. The sun breaks the clouds and makes them pour down rain.

XV

१. क ईं वेद सुते सचा [पिबन्तं कद्वयो दधे ।
अयं यः पुरो विभिनत्योजसा मन्दानः शिप्रचन्धसः] ॥

1. Who can see the Sun, enjoying the Soma juice along with gods like air etc. Who knows how long will he do so. This Sun, fast in motion, being satisfied with the Soma juice, breaks down the forts of the clouds? (1696)

२. दाना मृगो न वारणः पुरुत्रा चरथं दधे ।
न किष्ट्वा नि यमदा सुते गमो महाँश्चरस्योजसा ॥

2. As a wild elephant rushes on, this way and that way mad with heat, and none restrains him, so dost thou, O soul, with thy protecting powers roam throughout the worlds. None can restrain thee in this created world. O mighty soul, thou movest freely in the universe with thy power. May thou pervade our heart! (1697)

३. य उग्रः सन्ननिष्टृतः स्थिरो रणाय संस्कृतः ।
यदि स्तोतुर्मघवा श्रृणवद्ध्वं नेन्द्रो योषत्या गमत् ॥

3. The Almignty Father, Immortal, Invincible, Eternal, is competent to pervade the whole universe. When the Omniscient God listens to His praiser's call, He will not stand aloof, but come. (1698)

XVI

१. पवमाना असृक्षत सोमाः शुक्रास इन्दवः । अभि विश्वानि काव्या ॥

1. The pure, noble, calm Yogis visualise all the Vedic verses. (1699)[1]

२. पवमानां दिवस्पर्यन्तरिक्षादसृक्षत । पृथिव्या अधि सानवि ॥

2. The pure, active, learned persons diffuse knowledge on the elevated places of earth, in the atmosphere and luminous planets. (1700)[2]

३. पवमानास आशवः शुभ्रा असृग्रमिन्दवः । घ्नन्तो विश्वा अप द्विषः ॥

3. Noble, active, elevating learned persons, accomplish their task, extirpating all feelings of hatred. (1701)

XVII

१. तोशा वृत्रहणा हुवे सजित्वानापराजिता । इन्द्राग्नि वाजसातमा ॥

1. God and soul I invoke, slayers of mental foes, extinguishers of ignorance, joint victors, unsubdued, and bestowers of strength. (1702)

[1]Visualise: understand the significance and purport of.
[2]See verse 575.

२. प्र वामर्चन्त्युक्थिनो [नीथाविदो जरितार: । इन्द्राग्नी इष श्रा वृणे] ॥

2. O God and soul, singers skilled in Sāma melody, hymn Ye, bringing lauds. I choose Ye both to bring me strength! (1703)

३. इन्द्राग्नी नवति पुरो [दासपत्नीरधूनुतम् । साकमेकेन कर्मणा] ॥

3. O God and soul, Ye cast aside together, with one mighty deed of Yogic deep meditation, the ninety forts held by turbulent passions! (1704)[1]

XVIII

१. उप त्वा रण्वसन्दृशं प्रयस्वन्त: सहस्कृत । अग्ने ससृज्महे गिर: ॥

1. O God, attainable through exertion and meditation, may we, the seekers after knowledge and salvation, recite Vedic verses to approach Thee, Charming and Handsome! (1705)

२. उप च्छायामिव घृणेरगन्म शर्म ते वयम् । अग्ने हिरण्यसन्दृश: ॥

2. O God, Who glitterest like gold, to Thee for shelter may we come, as to the shade from burning heat! (1706)

३. य उग्र इव शर्यहा तिग्मश्रृङ्गो न वँसग: । अग्ने पुरो हरोजिथ ॥

3. Mighty as a warrior, who slays with shafts, or like a bull with sharpened horns, O God, Thou breakest the bondage of the body with Thy shaft of knowledge, and makest the soul attain to final beatitude! (1707)

XIX

१. ऋतावानं वैश्वानरमृतस्य ज्योतिषस्पतिम् । अजस्रं घर्ममीमहे ॥

1. O God, full of lustre, Embodiment of true knowledge, the Friend of mankind, the Lord of all luminous worlds, Eternal, we worship Thee! (1708)

२. य इदं प्रतिपप्रथे यज्ञस्य स्वरुत्तिरन् । ऋतूनुत्सृजते वशी ॥

2. God, Who grants salvation to the soul, and creates this universe, being the Supreme Controller manifests the seasons. (1709)

३. अग्नि: प्रियेषु धामसु कामो भूतस्य भव्यस्य । सम्राडेको विराजति ॥

3. God is the primeval cause of what has been created in the past, and what shall be created in the future. He shines forth as a unique, Sovereign Lord in the most beloved worlds. (1710)

---

[1]See verse 1576. Ninety may refer to innumerable bodies the soul occupied in previous births. For a detailed explanation of the word ninety, see the foot-note to verse 1576.

Chapter 3

I

१. अग्निः प्रत्नेन जन्मना शुम्भानस्तन्व३ऀ स्वाम् । कविर्विप्रेण वावृधे ॥

1. The intellectual soul, through its actions in the past life, beautifying its body, and being wise, exalts itself in communion with God. (1711)[1]

२. ऊर्जो नपातमा हुवेऽग्निं पावकशोचिषम् । अस्मिन् यज्ञे स्वध्वरे ॥

2. I dedicate to this Immortal God, the soul, which does not allow our strength decay, whose glow is bright and pure. (1712)

३. स नो मित्रमहस्त्वमग्ने शुक्रेण शोचिषा । देवैरा सत्सि बर्हिषि ॥

3. O soul, full of lustre in the company of God, thy Friend, with thy pure splendour, thou residest in my heart with thy divine virtues! (1713)

II

१. उत्ते शुष्मासो अस्थू रक्षो भिन्दन्तो अद्रिवः । नुदस्व याः परिस्पृधः ॥

1. O God, worthy of reverence, Thy powers reign supreme, eliminating obstacles. Thou humiliatest the atheists who entertain rivalry unto Thee! (1714)

२. अया निजध्निरोजसा रथसङ्गे धने हिते । स्तवा अबिभ्युषा हृदा ॥

2. O God, with Thy manifest power, Thou removest impediments. On achieving Thy delightful company and obtaining worldly wealth, with fearless heart I sing Thy praise! (1715)

३. अस्य व्रतानि नाधृषे पवमानस्य दूढ्या । रुज यस्त्वा पृतन्यति ॥

3. None evil-minded can assail the holy laws of this pure God. Crush him, O God, who fain would disobey Thy laws. (1716)

४. तऀ हिन्वन्ति मदच्युतऀ हरिं नदीषु वाजिनम् । इन्दुमिन्द्राय मत्सरम् ॥

4. Men worship for the welfare of the soul, God, the Augmentor of rapture, the Eliminator of afflictions, and the Bestower of supreme felicity. (1717)

III

१. आ मन्द्रैरिन्द्र हरिभिर्याहि मयूररोमभिः ।
मा त्वा के चिन्नि येमुरिन्न पाशिनोऽति धन्वेव ताऀ इहि ॥

1. Come, O Sun, with delightful rays, like the multicoloured peacock's plumes. None can check thy course. Thou overcomest the forces of darkness, as a fowler captures the bird, or an archer subdues the foe! (1718)

[1]See verse 246.

२. वृत्रखादो वलं रुज: पुरां दर्मो अपामज: ।
   स्थाता रथस्य हर्योरभिस्वर इन्द्रो दृढा चिदारुज: ॥

2. God, the Dispeller of nescience, the Annihilator of the covering of darkness, the Splitter of the citadels of five sheaths, the Lord of the chariot of the
universe, the Urger to actions, the Impeller of the organs of action and cognition, shatters even things that stand most firm. (1719)[1]

३. गम्भीराꣳ उदधीꣳरिव क्रतुं पुष्यसि गा इव ।
   प्र सुगोपा यवसं घेनवो यथा ह्रदं कुल्या इवाशत ॥

3. O God, just as thousands of pools of water feed the deep oceans, so dost
Thou nourish the soul with many excellences of life. Just as a good herdsman
nicely feeds his cows, so dost Thou grant food to the souls. Just as the milch-
cows go to their fodder, so do the souls go unto Thee. Just as streams flow
into the vast sea, so do the souls absorb themselves in Thee! (1720)

IV

१. यथा गौरो अपा कृतं तृष्यन्नेत्यवेरिणम् ।
   आपित्वे न: प्रपित्वे तूयमा गहि कण्वेषु सु सचा पिब ॥

1. Just as a licentious person, afflicted with the thirst for lust goes to lovely
sensual objects, so shouldest thou, O soul, acquiring the friendship of us, the
devotees of God, awake quickly, and enjoy with us divine felicity! (1721)[2]

२. मन्दन्तु त्वा मघवन्निन्द्रेन्दवो राधोदेयाय सुन्वते ।
   आमुष्या सोममपिबश्चमू सुतं ज्येष्ठं तद्दधिषे सह: ॥

2. O wise and glorious soul, may the experiences of knowledge and deep
concentration (Samādhi) gladden thee. In order to make a Yogi acquire supernatural power, having silently obtained the joy born through the control of
Prāṇa and Apāna, thou enjoyest God's bliss. Thou preservest within thee, the
Supernatural, Great, Almighty Father! (1722)

V

१. त्वमङ्ग प्र शंसिषो देव: शविष्ठ मर्त्यम् ।
   न त्वदन्यो मघवन्नस्ति मडितेन्द्र ब्रवीमि ते वच: ॥

1. O dear soul, brilliant, most learned, thou beautifiest this mortal frame.
O glorious soul, there is no other comforter except thee. I praise thee ! (1723)[3]

[1]Five sheaths: the five cases which successively make the body, enshrining the soul.
[2]See verse 252.
[3]See verse 247.

२. मा ते राधाॐसि मा त ऊतयो वसोऽस्मान् कदा चना दभन् ।
विश्वा च न उपमिमीहि मानुष वसूनि चर्षणिभ्य आ ॥

2. O All-pervading God, let not Thy bounteous gifts, let not Thy saving helps fail us at any time. Thou lover of mankind, grant us mortals all riches ! (1724)

VI

१. प्रति ष्या सूनरी जनी व्युच्छन्ती परि स्वसु: । दिवो अदर्शि दुहिता ॥

1. This lady, Dawn, the daughter of Sun, an excellent path shower, is seen by all, at the end of night, her sister. (1725)[1]

२. अश्वेव चित्रारुषी माता गवामृतावरी । सखा भूदश्विनोरुषा: ॥

2. The Dawn is brilliant like the lightning, red in colour, the mother of rays, the well-wisher of all, and the companion of the Prāṇa and Apāna. (1726)[2]

३. उत सखास्यश्विनोरुत माता गवामसि । उतोषो वस्व ईशिषे ॥

3. O intellect, thou art the friend of the Prāṇa and Apāna, the mother of the beams of knowledge, and the ruler of wealth! (1727)

VII

१. एषो उषा अपूर्व्या व्युच्छति प्रिया दिव: । स्तुषे वामश्विना बृहत् ॥

1. O intellect, the vanquisher of sin, never experienced by a Yogi before, thou art loved by the soul. O teacher and disciple, I extol your praise! (1728)[3]

२. या दक्षा सिन्धुमातरा मनोतरा रयीणाम् । धिया देवा वसुविदा ॥

2. Both the gods are, the suppressors of lust, wrath and sickness, the nice conductors of the veins of blood in the body, the urgers of knowledge and action through mental force, and the vehicles of knowledge for the soul through prayer. (1729)[4]

३. वच्यन्ते वां ककुहासो जूर्णायामधि विष्टपि । यद्वाॐरथो विभिष्पतात् ॥

3. O Aswins, when the soul, your chariot, along with a host of breaths, reaches the final stage of salvation, then are you nice characteristics eulogised! (1730)[5]

---

[1]Pt. Jaidev Vidyalankar has translated this verse as applicable also to a Yogi, his knowledge and emancipation of his soul.

[2]Mother of rays: Rays of the Sun follow the Dawn. She is therefore spoken of as their mother. Companion of: Aswins are the Prāṇa and Apāna, whose friend is the Dawn, as early in the morning the control of the Prāṇa and Apāna is exercised through Yoga.

[3]Aswins may also mean the Prāṇa and Apāna, the Sun and the Moon. See verse 178.

[4]Both the gods: Prāṇa and Apāna.

[5]Aswins: Prāṇa and Apāna.

VIII

१. उषस्तच्चित्रमा भरास्मभ्यं वाजिनीवति । येन तोकं च तनयं च धामहे ॥

1. O bright intellect, full of learning, grant us that attainable knowledge, wherewith we may support our sons and grandsons! (1731)[1]

२. उषो अद्येह गोमत्यश्वावति विभावरि । रेवदस्मे व्युच्छ सूनृतावति ॥

2. O force of mind, the extinguisher of internal sins, thou art here this day, the illuminator of knowledge, the goader to action, the diffuser of light, and the revealer of truth. Let our refulgent soul shine before us! (1732)

३. युङ्क्ष्वा हि वाजिनीवत्यश्वा ꣺ अद्यारुणा ꣺ उष: । अथा नो विश्वा सौभगान्या वह ॥

3. O intellect, the bringer of the wealth of knowledge, yoke the disease-ridden breaths to this car of the body today. Then bring us all delight and felicities! (1733)[2]

IX

१. अश्विना वर्तिरस्मदा गोमद्दस्रा हिरण्यवत् । अर्वाग्रथं ꣺ समनसा नि यच्छतम् ॥

1. O Prāṇa and Apāna, Ye both are the killers of diseases. Aided by the force of our mind, with full sway, control this nice changing chariot of the body, equipped with soul and organs! (1734)[3]

२. एह देवा मयोभुवा दस्रा हिरण्यवर्त्तनी । उषर्बुधो वहन्तु सोमपीतये ॥

2. The wise Yogis, making the soul in this body their impeller and refuge, the rectifiers of sin, the generators of health and happiness, should control the Prāṇa and Apāna for drinking the elixir of God's supreme joy. (1735)[4]

३. यावित्था श्लोकमा दिवो ज्योतिर्जनाय चक्रथु: । आ न ऊर्जं वहतमश्विना युवम् ॥

3. Ye, who thus bring down praiseworthy discernment for a Yogi from the brain, do Ye, O Aświns, bring strength unto us! (1736)

X

१. अग्नि तं मन्ये यो वसुरस्तं यं यन्ति धेनव: ।
अस्तमर्वन्त आशवोऽस्तं नित्यासो वाजिन इष ꣺ स्तोतृभ्य आ भर ॥

1. I consider him to be a King, whom the learned constantly resort to, as

---

[1]Pt. Jaidev Vidyalankar has translated तोकं as mind and तनयं as body.

[2]'Aświns' means Prāṇa and Apāna or sky and earth, or day and night, or sun and moon, vide Nirukta 12-1.

[3]See verse 425. 'I' means a learned man.

[4]See Yajur 15-43.

the milch-kine go to their shed, and the fleet-foot coursers to their stable. O King, fill with prosperity those, who sing thy praise! (1737)

२. अग्निर्हि वाजिनं विशे ददाति विश्वचर्षणिः ।
अग्नी राये स्वाभुवꣷ सु प्रीतो याति वार्यमिषꣷ स्तोतृभ्य आ भर ॥

2. Verily, for the good of humanity, does God give us learned persons. The All-seeing God pervades each and every limb. He filled with intense love, approaches for their welfare, mankind, dependent upon Him, and grants to the lovers of the Vedas, the knowledge worthy of acceptance. (1738)

३. सो अग्निर्यो वसुगृ꣡णे सं यमायन्ति धेनवः ।
समर्वन्तो रघुद्रुवः सं सुजाताः सूरय इषꣷ स्तोतृभ्य आ भर ॥

3. God is He, Who creates and pervades the universe, in Whose shelter the learned go, as kine to their shed, Whom the seekers after knowledge resort to, as swift-footed horses to their stable, Whose refuge, the great religious leaders of mankind seek. May He grant knowledge to the learned worshippers. (1739)

XI

१. महे नो अद्य बोधयोषो राये दिवित्मती ।
यथा चिन्नो अबोधयः सत्यश्रवसि वाय्ये सुजाते अश्वसूनृते ॥

1. O intellect, bright as the Dawn, full of lustre, awaken us today to acquire spiritual wealth. O supplier of excellent knowledge to the soul, O arranger of the uninterrupted organs in a thread, O intellect, beautiful in appearance, diffuse knowledge in our resolute soul, in every possible way! (1740)[1]

२. या सुनीथे शौचद्रथे व्यौच्छो दुहितर्दिवः ।
सा व्युच्छ सहीयसि सत्यश्रवसि वाय्ये सुजाते अश्वसूनृते ॥

2. O Dawn-like intellect, the recipient of the joy of soul, an impeller like the sun, just as thou hast been dispelling the covering of ignorance from the pure emancipated soul, so do thou, O intellect, the retainer of true knowledge in the soul, cast aside the sheath of nescience from a tolerant, strong, beautiful, learned soul, the constant weaver of actions! (1741)[2]

३. सा नो अद्याभरद्वसुर्व्युच्छा दुहितर्दिवः ।
यो व्यौच्छः सहीयसि सत्यश्रवसि वाय्ये सुजाते अश्वसूनृते ॥

3. O intellect, the relisher of the joy of soul, the filler of the joy of soul, the filler of soul and vital airs with knowledge, just as thou removest the

---

[1] See verse 421.

[2] Weaver means architect. Just as a weaver spins the thread so does soul fashion its acts.

covering of ignorance from the patient, austere, learned, constant, excellent and beautiful soul, so do thou, the replenisher of soul with true knowledge, remove today ignorance from us as well! (1742)[1]

XII

१. प्रति प्रियतम⊙ रथं वृषणं वसुवाहनम् ।
स्तोता वामश्विनावृषि स्तोमेभिर्भूषति प्रति माध्वी मम श्रुत⊙हवम् ॥

1. O sweet-tempered denizens of the Earth and Sky, the laudatory Vedic teaching adorns Your desire fullfiling wealth-procuring, lovely, and beautiful course of conduct with praiseworthy songs. Listen to My instruction! (1743)[2]

२. अत्यायातमश्विना तिरो विश्वा अह⊙सना ।
दस्ना हिरण्यवर्तनी सुषुम्णा सिन्धुवाहसा माध्वी मम श्रुत⊙हवम् ॥

2. O Prāṇa and Apāna, the removers of disorder of the humours of the body, subservient to soul, the *bringers* of nice happiness, the urgers of blood in the active veins, sweet and charming, immemorial, come overcoming all impediments. May I subdue all inimical passions. Listen to my behest! (1744)[3]

३. आ नो रत्नानि बिभ्रतावश्विना गच्छतं युवम् ।
रुद्रा हिरण्यवर्तनी जुषाणा वाजिनीवसू माध्वी मम श्रुत⊙हवम् ॥

3. O Aświns, possessing the organs, come unto us. Ye both, which make us weep at the time of leaving the body, ride on the chariot of the soul, dwell in mental faculty full of knowledge and strength, are charming, and constant companions of this sacrifice (Yajna) of life, remain under my control! (1745)[4]

XIII

१. अबोध्यग्निः समिधा जनानां प्रति धेनुमिवायतीमुषासम् ।
यह्वा इव प्र वयामुज्जिहाना: प्र भानव: सस्रते नाकमच्छ ॥

1. Fire is kindled by the people with fuel to meet the Dawn, just as a milk-cow yields milk in the morning. Just as elderly birds, leaving their newly born babies in the nests, fly high into the air, so do the rays of light emanating from the altar rise high up into the atmosphere. (1746)[5]

---

[1]Griffith imports history in the verse. He considers Satyaśravas to be the son of Sunitha who was the son of Vaya, who was the son of Suchadratha. These words are not historical names. They indicates the different virtues of the soul.
[2]My refers to God. See verse 418.
[3]I and my refer to the soul.
[4]Aświns: Prāṇa and Apāna. Us means worshippers. My refers to soul.
[5]Agnihotra should be performed in the morning, just as cows are milked at dawn.

२. अ्रबोधि होता यजथाय देवानूध्वाँ अ्रग्नि: सुमना: प्रातरस्थात् ।
समिद्धस्य रुशददर्शि पाजो महान् देवस्तमसो निरमोचि ॥

2. The Self-Refulgent God, the Creator and Dissolvent of the universe,
Omniscient, appears for imparting knowledge to the learned. He, the Highest
of all, pervades places like the sun rising in the morning. The radiant might
of the Luminous God is made apparent. The Almighty Father releases all
from the darkness of death. (1747)[1]

३. यदीं गणस्य रशनामजीग: शुचिरङ्क्ते शुचिभिर्गोभिरग्नि: ।
आद्दक्षिणा युज्यते वाजयन्त्युत्तानामूध्वोँ अ्रधयज्जुहूभि: ॥

3. When God holds within His sway the mental and guiding forces of the
animate and inanimate world, and manifests all sorts of knowledge through
pure Vedic hymns, He then yokes His All-controlling force to the mighty
deeds of the world. The exalted God, through His acts of the creation and
dissolution of the universe is the Lord of that wide-spread power of His.
(1748)

XIV

१. इद॑ँ श्रेष्ठं ज्योतिषां ज्योतिरागाच्चित्र: प्रकेतो अ्रजनिष्ट विभ्वा ।
यथा प्रसूता सवितु: सवायेंवा रात्र्युषसे योनिमारैक् ॥

1. Just as Dawn is the precursor of the Sun, and Night makes room for
the Dawn, so intellect, the light, fairest amid all lights, wondrous and intelligent, is the precursor of the knowledge of God. (1749)

२. रुशद्वत्सा रुशती श्वेत्यागादारैग् कृष्णा सदनान्यस्या: ।
समानबन्धू अ्रमृते अनूची द्यावा वर्ण चरत अ्रामिनाने ॥

2. The lustrous Dawn, with its calf, the brilliant Sun, is come. The dark
night vacates her dwelling for her (dawn). They both are a Kin, immortal,
indescribable, and destroying the colour of each other, they move in the atmosphere. (1750)[2]

३. समानो अध्वा स्वस्रोरनन्तस्तमन्यान्या चरतो देवशिष्टे ।
न मेथते न तस्थतु: सुमेके नक्तोषासा समनसा विरूपे ॥

3. Common, unending is the sisters' pathway : taught by the Sun alterna-

---

[1]God alone grants salvation to men.
[2]Sun is spoken of as the calf of the Dawn as he follows the Dawn, as a calf follows the
cow.
They both: The Dawn and Night. In the morning the Dawn destroys the dark colour
of the night and shines brilliantly. In the evening the bright colour of the day is changed
into the night's dark colour. Both are allied to each other.

tely they travel. Fair-formed, of different hues and yet, one-minded, Night and Dawn clash not, neither do they tarry. (1751)[1]

XV

१. आ भात्यग्निरुषसामनीकमुद्विप्राणां देवया वाचो श्रस्थुः ।
श्रर्वाञ्चा नून रथ्येह यातं पीपिवार्सामश्विना घर्ममच्छ ॥

1. The Sun, the bright face of the Dawns, is shining : the recitation of Vedic verses by the devotees of God is conducted. O Aświns, (knowledge and action) borne on your chariot of the body, come here before us, and make us acquire dignity and power ! (1752)[2]

२. न संस्कृतं प्र मिमीतो गमिष्ठान्ति नूनमश्विनोपस्तुतेह ।
दिवाभिपित्वेऽवसागमिष्ठा प्रत्यवर्ति दाशुषे शम्भविष्ठा ॥

2. In this spiritual sacrifice, O Aświns, the forces of knowledge and determination, verily Ye destroy not the refined bliss of God, near at hand. On the dawn of the light of learning, Ye assert yourselves with full force, and conduce to the betterment of the self-abnegating soul ! (1753)

३. उता यात संगवे प्रातरह्नो मध्यन्दिन उदिता सूर्यस्य ।
दिवा नक्तमवसा शन्तमेन नेदानीं पीतिरश्विना ततान ॥

3. O Prāna, and Apāna, come at early morning, at noon of day, and when the Sun is setting, by day, at night, with most auspicious favour. At these times, other organs do not perform their functions ! (1754)[3]

XVI

१. एता उ त्या उषसः केतुमक्रत पूर्वे श्रर्धे रजसो भानुमञ्जते ।
निष्कृण्वाना श्रायुधानीव धृष्णवः प्रति गावोऽरुषीर्यन्ति मातरः ॥

1. These Dawns have raised their banner in the eastern half of the atmosphere, and make the sun shine. Just as heroes prepare their weapons for the fray, so do these lustrous Dawns, the mothers of Sun, use the rays as their instructments to fight against darkness, their foe. (1755)[4]

---

[1]Sisters: Night and Dawn. Of different hues: Night is dark and Dawn is bright. One-minded: Both serve mankind with the sole aim of doing them good. They tarry not : They never stop but continue travelling from the beginning of the world till its end.

[2]It is a beautiful description of the performance of Havan in the morning. Here means the Yajna (sacrifice).

[3]In the morning, evening and at noon, the Yogis enjoy the bliss of God, through Prānāyama.

[4]When the sun shines in the eastern hemisphere, there is darkness in the other Western hemisphere.

२. उदपप्तन्नरुणा भानवो वृथा स्वायुजो अरुषीर्गा अयुक्षत ।
अक्रन्न् ूषासो वयुनानि पूर्वशा रुशन्तं भानुमरुषीरशिश्रयुः ॥

2. Spontaneously do the ruddy beams of Dawn shoot up, They harness the luminous rays, like bulls easy to be yoked. The Dawns create all sorts of knowledge as in former times. The red hued, brilliant beams at Dawn, finally merge themselves in refulgent Sun. (1756)[1]

३. अर्चन्ति नारीरपसो न विष्टिभिः समानेन योजनेना परावतः ।
इषं वहन्तीः सुकृते सुदानवे विश्वेदह यजमानाय सुन्वते ॥

3. For a noble-minded, liberal, contented worshipper, supplying all sorts of provisions, these dawns acting as a leader for spreading knowledge, extend light to the farthest west with their beams, as warriors with their weapons spread over all places. (1757)[2]

XVII

१. अबोध्यग्निर्ज्मं उदेति सूर्यो व्यु ३षाश्चन्द्रा महावो अर्चिषा ।
आयूक्षातामश्विना यातवे रथं प्रासावीद्देवः सविता जगत्पृथक् ॥

1. Just as fire is kindled on the Earth at the time of Agni-Hotar, or as it rises in the shape of Sun, or just as the gladdening Dawn, in its spacious form, removes darkness with its light, so is the fire of knowledge kindled in diverse forms in a spiritual sacrifice (Yajna). O Aświns (Knowledge and determination) yoke yourselves to the chariot of the mind for your spiritual journey; wherewith the All-creating God gives us the knowledge of the world in sundry ways ! (1758)

२. यदुञ्जाथे वृषणमश्विना रथं घृतेन नो मधुना क्षत्रमुक्षतम् ।
अस्माकं ब्रह्म पृतनासु जिन्वतं वयं धना शूरसाता भजेमहि ॥

2. O Aświns, (Prāna and Apāna) when Ye concentrate on God through Yoga, the soul, the showerer of joy, Ye then fill our soul with blazing beauty, and create true consciousness in our organs, and we through soul's knowledge, acquire diverse sorts of wonderful learning ! (1759)

३. अर्वाङ् त्रिचक्रो मधुवाहनो रथो जीराश्वो अश्विनोरयातु सुष्टुतः ।
त्रिबन्धुरो मघवा विश्वसौभगः शं न आ वक्षद् द्विपदे चतुष्पदे ॥

3. The three wheeled chariot of Prāna and Apāna, yoked with Om, and immemorial, immortal soul, highly praised in the Vedas, moves manifestly.

---

[1]Dawns create all sorts of knowledge: It is at the time of Dawn, when perfect silence prevails in nature, that Yogis contemplate upon God, mathematicians, philosophers, scientists, and politicians solve all intricate problems.

[2]Pt. Jaidev Vidyalankar has given in his commentary the spiritual interpretation of this hymn, but I have given the apparent interpretation pertaining to the Dawn for the exquisite beauty with which it has been depicted.

May the learned and concentrated soul, the giver of prosperity to mankind, with its three charioteers, bring weal to our bipeds and quadrupeds. (1760)[1]

XVIII

१. प्र ते धारा श्रसश्चतो दिवो न यन्ति वृष्टय: । श्रच्छा वाज ँ सहस्त्रिणम् ॥

1. O soul, thy unattached forces of steady abstraction, coupled with a thousand kinds of knowledge, reach unto God, as showers of rain from heaven reach the earth ! (1761)

२. श्रभि प्रियाणि काव्या विश्वा चक्षाणो अर्षति । हरिस्तुञ्जान श्रायुधा ॥

2. The soul, beholding all well-beloved sacred lore of the Vedas, rending away all shackles, after emancipation roams in all places. (1762)

३. स ममृ ँजान आयुभिरिभो राजेव सुव्रत: । श्येनो न व ँ सु षीदति ॥

3. The soul, purified through Yoga, by aged, learned, and austere persons, being fearless like a King or a falcon, roams in the world as it wills, doing noble deeds. (1763)

४. स नो विश्वा दिवो वसूतो पृथिव्या श्रधि । पुनान इन्दवा भर ॥

4. So bring Thou hitherward to us, O Glorious God, all purified treasures of Heaven and Earth ! (1764)

BOOK IX

Chapter 1

I

१. प्रास्य धारा श्रक्षरन् वृष्ण: सुतस्यौजस: । देवा ँ अनु प्रभूषत: ॥

1. Onward flow the streams of the power of this soul, the impeller of all, the showerer of joy, and the lord of organs. (1765)

२. सप्तिं मृजन्ति वेधसो गृणन्त: कारवो गिरा । ज्योतिर्जंज्ञानमुक्थ्यम् ॥

2. Learned persons, the performers of noble deeds, praising with their speech, the excellent emanating light of knowledge, purify their soul, equipped with seven forces. (1766)[2]

---

[1]There-wheeled: Jāgrat (Waking), Swapan (sleeping) and Sushupti (Intense sleep) stages of the soul. Three charioteers of the soul are Iḍā, Pinglā and Sushumnā Veins, or Satva, Rajas, Tamas conditions of the soul, or three humours, Vāta वात (Wind), Pitta पित्त (Bile), Kaph कफ (Phlegm).

[2]Seven forces: Two eyes, two ears, two nostrils and mouth.

३. सुषहा सोम तानि ते पुनानाय प्रभूवसो । वर्धा समुद्रमुक्थ्य ॥

3. O Omnipresent God, sung in the Vedas, Thy halos realisable in Yoga Samādhis, destroy all opposing forces of evil. Fill full the sea of joy ! (1767)

II

१. एष ब्रह्मा य ऋत्विय इन्द्रो नाम श्रुतो गृणे ॥

1. I praise cloud known as the god of rain, which develops through Yajna in different seasons. (1768)[1]

२. त्वामिच्छवसस्पते यन्ति गिरो न संयत: ॥

2. O Almighty God, all Vedic songs of praise, like the words of a Yogi practising deep religious meditation, go to Thee alone! (1769)

३. वि स्तुतयो यथा पथा [इन्द्र त्वद् यन्तु रातय:] ॥

3. O King, just as from the main channel, streamlets flow in different direction, so do multifarious bounties flow from thee to thy devotees! (1770)[2]

III

१. आ त्वा रथं यथोतये [सुम्नाय वर्तयामसि । तुविकूर्मिमृतीषहमिन्द्रं शविष्ठ सत्पतिम्] ॥

1. O Yogi, the doer of many deeds, the subduer of the impious, the master of spiritual force, the nourisher of the noble, we approach thee for protection and comfort, just as we approach a car! (1771)[3]

२. तुविशुष्म तुविक्रतो शचीवो विश्वया मते । आ पप्राथ महित्वना ॥

2. Infinite in power and knowledge, eloquent Preacher, exceedingly Wise, O God, Thou art Omnipresent with Thy vast-spread Majesty! (1772)[4]

३. यस्य ते महिना मह: परि ज्मायन्तमीयतु: । हस्ता वज्रं हिरण्ययम् ॥

3. Thou art that God, Whose both hands of knowledge and action, through Thy grand Majesty, wield commendable power, that spreads wide on the Earth. (1773)[5]

---

[1]See verse 438.
[2]See verse 453.
[3]See verse 354.
[4]Trio-Earth, Atmosphere, and Sky.
[5]God has been described as Dwijanmā, i.e., doubly born in this verse and the previous one, as God is realizable by the joint efforts of two forces, the body and Om, as fire is kindled by rubbing together the two pieces of wood.

IV

१. आ यः पुरं नार्मिणीमदीदेदत्यः कविर्नभन्यो३ नार्वा । सूरो न ररुक्वां छतात्मा ॥

1. That God, Who lends consciousness to this citadel-like body, the residence of soul and mind, is ever Vigilant, Omniscient, pervading the heart like air, fast like a steed, brilliant like the Sun, and present in innumerable souls. (1774)

२. अभि·द्विजन्मा त्री रोचनानि विश्वा रजाᳲसि शुशुचानो अस्थात् ।
होता यजिष्ठो अपाᳲ सधस्थे ॥

2. Just as fire is kindled by rubbing together the two pieces of wood, so is God realised by stressing together the body and Om. He, illuminating the trio, is present in all the worlds. The same God, worthy of adulation by all, the greatest Sacrificer, manifests Himself in the universe, the place where knowledge and action go hand in hand. (1775)

३. अयᳲ स होता यो द्विजन्मा विश्वा दधे वार्याणि श्रवस्या । मर्तो यो अस्मे सुतुको ददाश ॥

3. God, realisable through the exertion of the body and Om, as fire is kindled by rubbing together the two pieces of wood, is the Benefactor of humanity. He hath in His possession all commendable things worthy of selection. The mortal man who dedicates himself to Him gets good offspring. (1776)

V

१. अग्ने तमद्याश्वं न स्तोमैः क्रतुं न भद्रᳲ हृदिस्पृशम् । ऋध्यामा त ओहैः ॥

1. O fire, we kindle thee this day with hymns that extol thee, that carries the oblations to heaven, as a horse carries us to our destination, is serviceable like a Yajna (sacrifice), and dear to our hearts. (1777)[1]

२. अधा ह्यग्ने क्रतोर्भद्रस्य दक्षस्य साधोः । रथीर्ऋतस्य बृहतो बभूथ ॥

2. O God, Thou art the Promoter of a vast genuine knowledge and the Fulfiller of an auspicious, wise and judicious resolve! (1778)

३. एभिर्नो अर्कैर्भवा नो अर्वाङ् स्वार्ऌण ज्योतिः । अग्ने विश्वेभिः सुमना अनीकैः ॥

3. O Bounteous God, bright like the sunlight, through these our praises, come Thou to meet us, with all Thy beauties! (1779)

VI

१. अग्ने विवस्वदुषसश्चित्रᳲ राधो अमर्त्य । आ दाशुषे जातवेदो वहा त्वमद्या देवाᳲ उषर्बुधः ॥

1. O fire, grant wondrous wealth to a charitably-disposed person, who rises

[1] See verse 434.

early in the morning. O inextinguishable fire, present in all created objects, grant consciousness today to the organs of this man, with the rise of the sun! (1780)[1]

२. जुष्टो हि दूतो असि हव्यवाहनोऽग्ने रथीरध्वराणाम् ।
सजूरश्विभ्यामुषसा सुवीर्यमस्मे धेहि श्रवो बृहत् ॥

2. O God, Thou art, the Leader of all Yajnas (sacrifices), worshipped by all scholars, the Sustainer of the entire universe, and Omnipresent. Accordant with Prāṇa and Apāna, and with refined intellect, grant us heroic strength and vast knowledge! (1781)

VII

१. विधुं दद्राणꣳ समने बहूनां युवानꣳ सन्तं पलितो जगार ।
देवस्य पश्य काव्यं महित्वाद्या ममार स ह्यः समान ॥

1. Age overpowers even a young person, who is the doer of deeds and the killer of many foes in a battle. Look at the high wisdom of God, through Whose greatness, he who died yesterday is living today. (1782)[2]

२. शाक्मना शाको अरुणः सुपर्ण आ यो महः शूरः सनादनीडः ।
यच्चिकेत सत्यमित्तन्न मोघं वसु स्पार्हमुत जेतोत दाता ॥

2 God is Almighty through His own strength, Refulgent, a nice Helper, Great, the Goader of all, Eternal, and Self-Sufficient. Whatever He knows and makes the sages know, is true and not useless. He is the Conqueror of all the habitable worlds, and the Giver of glory to the souls. (1783)[3]

३. एभिर्ददे वृष्ण्या पौꣳस्यानि येभिरौक्षद्वृत्रहत्याय वज्री ।
ये कर्मणः क्रियमाणस्य मह्न ऋते कर्ममुदजायन्त देवाः ॥

3. God keeps under His control many manly powers, the showerers of happiness through these forces of nature. God bestows knowledge through these forces to remove the ignorance of men. The learned, realising the truth of the grand, practical sustenance of the universe by God, overcoming the bondage of action attain to salvation. (1784)

VIII

१. अस्ति सोमो अयꣳ सुतः पिबन्त्यस्य मरुतः । उत स्वराजो अश्विना ॥

1. Here is ready this divine joy. Forces of deliberation, illumined knowledge, and resolve appreciate it. (1785)[4]

---

[1]Today means every day. This man means the person who rises early in the morning. See verse 40.

[2]See verse 325. Soul is immortal. It leaves one body and assumes another. This verse amply establishes the doctrine of the transmigration of soul.

[3]Conqueror means Master.

[4]See verse 174.

२. पिबन्ति मित्रो अर्यमा तना पूतस्य वरुण: । त्रिषधस्थस्य जावत: ॥

2. Mitra, Aryaman and Varuṇa, realise in Iḍā, Pinglā and Sushumnā divine joy, which purified through mind is the begetter of knowledge. (1786)[1]

३. उतो न्वस्य जोषमा इन्द्र: सुतस्य गोमत: । प्रातर्होतेव मत्सति ॥

3. Just as the Hota-priest is delighted in the morning after performing Homa, so is also the soul of a spiritually advanced Yogi certainly pleased by drinking the divine joy coupled with knowledge. (1787)

IX

१. बण्महा॒ असि सूर्य बडादित्य महा॒ असि ।
महस्ते सतो महिमा पनिष्टम मह्ना देव महा॒ असि ॥

1. Verily, O King, the goader, thou art great, truly, O King, the levier of taxes, thou art great. O mighty King, thy majesty is great. O praiseworthy King, thou art great by thy greatness! (1788)[2]

२. बड् सूर्य श्रवसा महा॒ असि सत्रा देव महा॒ असि ।
मह्ना देवानामसुर्य: पुरोहितो विभु ज्योतिरदाभ्यम् ॥

2. Yea, O God, Thou art great in fame and knowledge. O Refulgent God, Thou art verily great. O God, through Thy greatness Thou makest the learned breathe. Thou verily art the lover of mankind, Ubiquitous and an Unconquerable Light! (1789)

X

१. उप नो हरिभि: सुतं याहि मदानां पते । उप नो हरिभि: सुतम् ॥

1. O God, the Lord of rapturous joys, come to Thy eulogiser from amongst us with Thy All-pervading attributes. Come to Thy eulogiser from amongst us with Thy All-pervading attributes! (1790)[3]

२. द्विता यो वृत्रहन्तमो विद इन्द्र: शतक्रतु: । उप नो हरिभि: सुतम् ॥

2. Soul, the extinguisher of sins, and the doer of numerous deeds, is known as the master of two forces, i.e., knowledge and action. May it drink the juice of joy born of the organs of senses. (1791)

[1]Mitra, Aryaman and Varuṇa are three classes of Yogis. He whose intellect shines like the sun is called Mitra. He who conquers the forces of nature, is the master of the organs of senses, and remains mentally steadfast is called Aryaman. He who is calm like the ocean and vast space, is pure in mind and realises the true nature of the soul is called Varuṇa. Iḍā, Pinglā and Sushumnā are the three arteries in which the Yogis concentrate their vital breaths.
[2]See verse 276.
[3]See verse 150. Repetition is for the sake of emphasis.

३. त्व॒ँ हि वृत्रहन्नेषां पाता सोमानामसि । उप नो हरिभिः सुतम् ॥

3. O God, the Dispeller of ignorance, Thou art the Guardian of all these souls in the universe. Fill with all sorts of knowledge our soul purified with Yogic practices! (1792)

XI

१. प्र वो महे महेवृधे भरध्वं प्रचेतसे प्र सुमतिं कृणुध्वम् । विशः पूर्वीः प्र चर चर्षणिप्राः ॥

1. O men, glean knowledge for the grand soul, that exalteth its glory. Entertain noble sentiments towards God, a Teacher, full of knowledge. O soul, the imparter of knowledge to the learned, thou lovest those who are devoted to the fulfilment of their ideal ! (1793)[1]

२. उरुव्यचसे महिने सुवृक्तिमिन्द्राय ब्रह्म जनयन्त विप्राः । तस्य व्रतानि न मिनन्ति धीराः ॥

2. The learned manifest through Veda the praise of God, the Sublime, the Far-pervading. The sages never violate His statutes. (1794)

३. इन्द्रं वाणीरनुत्तमन्युमेव सत्रा राजानं दधिरे सहध्यै । हर्यश्वाय बर्हया समापीन् ॥

3. Vedic verses establish God, Who illumines the universe and possesses infinite knowledge, for acquiring patience and forbearance. O man, urge Thy kinsmen to glorify God, Who pervades all worlds and souls! (1795)

XII

१. यदिन्द्र यावतस्त्वमेतावदहमीशीय । स्तोतारमिद्धिषे रदावसो न पापत्वाय रँसिषम् ॥

1. If I, O King, were the lord of riches ample as thine, I would give them, O King, who scatterest wealth; to the saint and never to the sinner! (1796)[2]

२. शिक्षेयमिन्महयते दिवेदिवे राय आ कुहचिद् विदे ।
   न हि त्वदन्यन्मघवन्न आप्यं वस्यो अस्ति पिता च न ॥

2. Each day would I enrich the man, who is charitably disposed, in whatsoever place he be. O God, no kinsman is a better shelter than Thee. No father is a better guardian than Thee! (1797)[3]

XIII

१. श्रुधी हवं विपिपानस्याद्रेर्बोधा विप्रस्यार्चतो मनीषाम् । कृष्वा दुवाँस्यन्तमा सचेमा ॥

1. O God, accept the call of a venerable, learned Yogi, firm like a rock.

[1]See verse 328.
[2]See verse 310.
‘l’ refers to a learned person.
[3]‘I’ refers to God. In the first half of the verse God reveals His resolve to bestow riches on a charitable person. In the second half a devotee expresses his firm faith in the guardianship of God.

Thou knowest the state of the mind of a learned person who lauds Thee. As a friend, residing in the intellect, receive these adulations! (1798)

२. न ते गिरो अपि मृष्ये तुरस्य न सुष्टुतिमसुर्यस्य विद्वान् । सदा ते नाम स्वयशो विवक्मि ॥

2. I know and ne'er forget the hymns and praises of Thee, O God, the Conqueror, the Friend of the Yogis. Thy self-refulgent name I ever utter! (1799)[1]

३. भूरि हि ते सवना मानुषेषु भूरि मनीषी हवते त्वामित् । मारे अस्मन्मघवं ज्योक्क: ॥

3. Among mankind many are the ways of Thy worship, O God, and many a time a pious sage invokes Thee. O Almighty God, be never distant from us! (1800)

XIV

१. प्रो ष्वस्मं पुरोरथमिन्द्राय शूषमर्चत । अभीके चिदु लोककृत् सङ्गे समत्सु वृत्रहा । अस्माकं बोधि चोदिता नभन्तामन्यकेषां । ज्याका अधि धन्वसु ॥

1. Duly sing of the strength of this Glorious God, Who sets in motion the chariot of the universe, He sees all from the closest quarter of the heart. Standing by our side in life's struggles, He removes the coverings of ignorance. He imparts knowledge unto us. The weak bow-strings of our week internal foes like lust and anger break upon the sight of God. (1801)

२. त्वं सिधूं रवासृजोऽधराचो अहन्नहिम् । अशत्रुरिन्द्र जज्ञिषे विश्वं पुष्यसि वार्यम् । तं त्वा परि ष्वजामहे नभन्तामन्यकेषां ज्याका अधि धन्वसु ॥

2. O God, destroying the cloud, Thou makest the rivers flow down. Foeless, Thou art known as the Friend of all. Thou tendest well each choicest thing. Therefore we draw us close to Thee. The weak bow-strings of our weak internal foes like lust and anger break upon the sight of God! (1802)

३. वि षु विश्वा अरातयोऽर्यो नशन्त नो धिय: । अस्तासि शत्रवे वधं यो न इन्द्र जिघांसति । या ते रातिर्ददिर्वसु नभन्तामन्यकेषां ज्याका अधि धन्वसु ॥

3. O God, destroyed be all our feelings against charity. May our intellects develop. Thy bolt, Thou castest at the foe, who would smite us dead. Thy liberal bounty gives us wealth. The weak bow-strings of our weak internal foes like lust and anger break upon Thy sight! (1803)

XV

१. रेवां इद्रेवत स्तोता स्यात् त्वावतो मघोन: । प्रेदु हरिव: सुतस्य ॥

1. O God, the Lord of the rotating planets, the praiser of a rich man becomes rich in this world, the praiser of Thee, unique in knowledge and riches will certainly become highly learned and rich! (1804)

[1]When clouds are dispersed, it rains, and rivers being filled with water flow down.

२. उक्थं च न शस्यमानं नागो रयिरा चिकेत । न गायत्रं गीयमानम् ॥

2. Doesn't a learned King understand the praise uttered by an ignorant person, or the song of praises that is sung? He understands them. (1805)[1]

३. मा न इन्द्र पीयत्नवे मा शर्धते परा दाः । शिक्षा शचीवः शचीभिः ॥

3. Give us not, O God, as a prey unto the violent or the disrespectful, grant us knowledge, O Mighty God, with Thy powers! (1806)

XVI

१. एन्द्र याहि हरिभिरुप कण्वस्य सुष्टुतिम् । दिवो अमुष्य शासतो दिवं यय दिवावसो ॥

1. O King, the imparter of life's comforts, give us pleasure through thy officials, who convey thy behests. Listen thou to the nice eulogy of that Wise God, the Lord of bliss! (1807)[2]

२. अत्रा वि नेमिरेषामुरां न धूनुते वृकः । दिवो अमुष्य शासतो दिवं यय दिवावसो ॥

2. Just as a wolf shakes with terror a sheep, so does the soul subduing these breaths control the mind. O soul, thou dweller in happiness, attain to the knowledge of this God, the Refulgent Lord! (1808)

३. आ त्वा ग्रावा वदन्निह सोमी घोषेण वक्षतु । दिवो अमुष्य शासतो दिवं यय दिवावसो ॥

3. O God, may a spiritually advanced, learned preacher, singing Thy praise, attain to Thee in this world, through Vedic knowledge. O soul, attain to salvation, revelling in that Refulgent Lord! (1809)

XVII

१. पवस्व सोम मन्दयन्निन्द्राय मधुमत्तमः ।

1. O joyful Yogi, full of glory and knowledge, exert to achieve God! (1810)

२. ते सुतासो विपश्चितः शुक्रा वायुमसृक्षत ॥

2. The accomplished Yogis, the seers of God, the doers of pure acts, attain to God. (1811)

३. असृग्रं देववीतये वाजयन्तो रथा इव ॥

3. Like chariots fighting and conquering, the tranquil Yogis, equipped with knowledge, bent on spiritual elevation continue exerting for the attainment of God. (1812)

[1]See verse 225.
[2]See verse 348.

XVIII

१. अग्निꣳ होतारं मन्ये दास्वन्तं वसो: सूनुꣳ । सहसो जातवेदसं विप्रं न जातवेदसम् ।
य ऊर्ध्वया स्वध्वरो देवाच्या कृपा ।
घृतस्य विभ्राष्टिमनु शुक्रशोचिष आजुह्वानस्य सर्पिष: ॥

1. I deem fire as an instrument for Yajna (sacrifice), the giver of wealth, the son of strength, the diffuser of knowledge with its light, like a sage who spreads his learning. The luminous fire, the reformer of the Yajna, the messenger to the forces of nature like air etc., rises up with its strength, with the lustre of the white-coloured heated clarified butter, when it is put into the fire in the form of oblations. (1813)[1]

२. यजिष्ठं त्वा यजमाना हुवेम ज्येष्ठमङ्गिरसां विप्र मन्मभिर्विप्रेभि: शुक्र मन्मभि: ।
परिज्मानमिव द्याꣳ होतारं चर्षणीनाम् ।
शोचिष्केशं वृषणं यमिमा विश: प्रावन्तु जूतये विश: ॥

2. O Omniscient, Refulgent God, with Vedic verses and learned thoughts, which expatiate on Thy greatness, we remember Thee ; Most Excellent and Superior to all souls. These souls, seeking Thy shelter, for the attainment of salvation, achieve Thee, All-pervading, Lustrous, the Giver of bounty to mankind, the Controller of all luminous planets like the Sun etc., and the Showerer of all joys! (1814)

३. स हि पुरु चिदोजसा विरुक्मता दीद्यानो भवति द्रुह्न्तर: परशुर्नं द्रुह्न्तर: ।
वीडु चिद्स्य समृतौ श्रुवद्नेव यत्स्थिरम् । निष्षहमाणो यमते नायते धन्वासहा नायते ॥

3. Verily God, with His blazing power, is Refulgent far and wide. Like an axe that cuts the trees, He cuts the bondage of the body. At Whose realisation the stout and strong bondage of the body is cut asunder like a jungle or water. Subduing all the opposing forces of the world, He regulates the universe. He enters the battlefield of the world like a skilled archer, but is not caught in its snare. (1815)[2]

---

[1]See verse 465. Giver of wealth: Those who use fire in industrial concerns amass wealth. Son of strength: Fire is firoduced by rubbing together with full strength the two pieces of wood, hence fire is figurative ly termed as the son of strength.

[2]Just as trees in a jungle are burnt to ashes by coming in contact with fire, or water heated by fire disappears in the shape of steam, so does soul attain to salvation by coming in contact with God, and cut asunder the fetters of the body. God creates, sustains and dissolves the universe. He is not inactive, but remains above the snares and wiles of the world to which an ordinary mortal falls a prey.

Chapter 2

I

१. अग्ने तव श्रवो वयो महि भ्राजन्ते अर्चयो विभावसो ।
बृहद्भानो शवसा वाजमुक्थ्या ॐ३ दधासि दाशुषे कवे ॥

1. O All-pervading God, great are Thy fame and strength. The fires in the shape of Sun blaze forth on high. O Thou Refulgent God, grant us knowledge revealed through the Vedas. O Wise God, out of Thy munificence Thou givest knowledge to Thy devotee, who dedicates himself to Thee, as a preceptor to his devoted pupil! (1816)[1]

२. पावकवर्चाः शुक्रवर्चा अनूनवर्चा उदियर्षि भानुना ।
पुत्रो मातरा विचरन्नुपावसि पृणक्षि रोदसी उभे ॥

2. O God, with purifying, brilliant sheen, with perfect sheen, Thou mani-festest Thyself in the heart. Just as a son residing with his parents protects them, so dost Thou guard both Heaven and Earth! (1817)[2]

३. ऊर्जो नपाज्जातवेदः सुशस्तिभिर्मन्दस्व धीतिभिर्हितः ।
त्वे इषः सं दधुर्भूरिवर्पसश्चित्रोतयो वामजाताः ॥

3. O God of unfailing strength, Omniscient, be gratified with our praises and Vedic recitations. Various sorts of noble well-bred learned persons, possessing a fine intellect, depend upon Thee, for fulfilment of their desires! (1818)

४. इरज्यन्नग्ने प्रथयस्व जन्तुभिरस्मे रायो अमर्त्य ।
स दर्शतस्य वपुषो वि राजसि पृणक्षि दर्शतं क्रतुम् ॥

4. O Immortal God, spreading forth Thy glory, with Thy dignities give us wealth. Thou shinest out as Ruler over all, with Thy beautiful power, and nourishest this handsome world created by Thee! (1819)

५. इष्कर्तारमध्वरस्य प्रचेतसं क्षयन्त ॐ राधसो महः ।
राति वामस्य सुभगां महीमिषं दधासि सानसि ॐ रयिम् ॥

5. I laud God, Who orders the sacrifice (Yajna) of this mighty world, Who is Wise, Who hath great riches under His control, and is the Bestower of nice, attainable objects. O God, Thou givest auspicious, plenteous food, Thou givest wealth to be shared by all! (1820)

६. ऋतावानं महिषं विश्वदर्शतमग्नि ॐ सुम्नाय दधिरे पुरो जनाः ।
श्रुत्कर्ण ॐ सप्रथस्तमं त्वा गिरा दैव्यं मानुषा युगा ॥

6. Men have set before them as guide, for acquiring happiness, God, the Embodiment of true knowledge, strong, the Seer of all. O God most Famous,

[1]See Yajur 12-106.
[2]See Yajur 12-107.

possessing Vedas as Thy ears, devout, contemplative couples magnify Thee
with Vedic praise-songs! (1821)

II

१. प्र सो अग्ने तवोतिभिः सुवीराभिस्तरति वाजकर्मभिः । यस्य त्वⒶ सख्यमाविथ ॥

1. O fire, he, whom thou choosest as friend, overcomes all obstacles, aided
by thy heroic safeguards, and deeds of power. (1822)[1]

२. तव द्रप्सो नीलवान् वाश ऋत्विय इन्धानः सिष्णवा ददे ।
त्वं महीनामुषसामसि प्रियः क्षपो वस्तुषु राजसि ॥

2. O soul, competent to fill the heart with joy, the ever-flowing delight is
an afforder of shelter, beautiful, and a dweller in vital breaths; being kindled,
it is taken up by the mind. Thou art the dear friend of venerable, bright intellects. Like the night that assuages all sufferings, thou manifestest in all
objects the strength that destroys afflictions! (1823)

III

१. तमोषधीर्दधिरे गर्भमृत्वियं तमापो अग्निं जनयन्त मातरः ।
तमित् समानं वनिनश्च वीरुधोऽन्तर्वतीश्च सुवते च विश्वहा ॥

1. Him, duly coming, as their germ the plants have received: this Agni
have maternal waters brought to life. So, in like manner, do the forest trees
and plants bear him within them and produce him evermore. (1824)[2]

IV

१. अग्निरिन्द्राय पवते दिवि शुक्रो वि राजति । महिषीव वि जायते ॥

1. The soul, for the attainment of God, purified through discernment goes
unto Him. The soul shines far resplendent in salvation. The soul manifests
itself in different forms, just as a queen presents her-self to her subjects in
different apparels. (1825)[3]

---

[1]He who makes proper use of electricity in industrial concerns, overcomes all obstacles
in the way of worldly progress.

[2]Him refers to Agni, fire, Pt. Jaidev Vidyalankar interprets Agni as soul which is found
in trees, plants and vegetables. Many Vedic scholars, like the renowned scientist J.C.
Bose believe there is life in plants and trees, an idea which is coroborated by the Vedic
Sukti येन प्राणन्ति वीरुधः i.e., plants breathe through God's grace. Maternal waters:
waters which through their intensity and motion produce heat.

[3]Some Commentators have translated महिषि as a buffalo-cow. Just as a buffalo gives us
milk and butter, eating grass, so does the soul make the stream of joy flow for us.

V

१. यो जागार तमृच: कामयन्ते यो जागार तमु सामानि यन्ति ।
यो जागार तमयँ सोम आह तवाहमस्मि सख्ये न्योका: ॥

1. The hymns of Rigveda love him who wakes and watches ; to him who watches come the verses of the Sāmaveda. Nature says to him who wakes and watches, "I" rest and have my dwelling in thy friendship. (1826)[1]

VI

१. अग्निर्जागार तमृच: कामयन्तेऽग्निर्जागार तमु सामानि यन्ति ।
अग्निर्जागार तमयँ सोम आह तवाहमस्मि सख्ये न्योका: ॥

1. God is watchful, the humns of the Rigveda love Him. God is watchful, Sāma hymns approach Him. God is watchful, to Him says this soul, "I" rest and have my dwelling in Thy friendship. (1827)

VII

१. नम: सखिभ्य: पूर्वसद्भ्यो नम: साकंनिषेभ्य: । युञ्जे वाचँ शतपदीम् ।

1. Praise be unto the friendly souls, who have achieved salvation; praise be unto the learned living souls. I use the Vedic speech, full of hundred sorts of knowledge. (1828)

२. युञ्जे वाचँ शतपदीं गाये सहस्रवर्तनि । गायत्रं त्रैष्टुभं जगत् ॥

2. I contemplate in Yoga Samādhi Vedic speech full of hundred sorts of knowledge. I sing in Gāyatri, Trishtup, Jagati hymns, the Sāmaveda, that gives a thousand instructions. (1829)

३. गायत्रं त्रैष्टुभं जगद् विश्वा रूपाणि सम्भृता । देवा ओकाँसि चक्रिरे ॥

3. Gāyatri, Trishtup, Jagati hymns, arranged in different forms, have the learned made familiar friends. (1830)[2]

VIII

१. अग्निज्योतिर्ज्योतिरग्निरिन्द्रो ज्योतिर्ज्योतिरिन्द्र: । सूर्यो ज्योतिर्ज्योति: सूर्य: ॥

1. Agni is light, light is Agni, Indra is light, light is Indra, Surya is light, light is Surya. (1831)[3]

[1]An idle, inactive person cannot acquire the knowledge of the Vedas, nor can he master the forces of nature. An active, vigilant person alone can learn the Vedas, and becomes not a slave to the forces of nature, like an ignorant, lazy person, but becomes its master.

[2]Made familiar friends: literally made their nomes or places of delight; i.e., the learned have become accustomed to, and take delight in hymns, in the Gāyatri, Trishtup and Jagati metres.

[3]Agni, Indra, Sūrya and Jayoti are synonyms. They are primarily the names of God, and secondarily of the forces of nature.

२. पुनरूर्जा नि वर्तस्व पुनरग्न इषायुषा । पुननं: पाह्यँहस: ॥

2. O God, appear unto us again with joy, turn Thou again unto us with joy and life. Save us again from sin ! (1832)

३. सह रय्या नि वर्तस्वाग्ने पिन्वस्य धारया । विश्वप्स्न्या विश्वतस्परि ॥

3. O God, come unto us, in Thy beautiful, charming appearance, O God, satisfy us with Thy All-pervading, All-Controlling stream of joy. (1833)

IX

१. यदिन्द्राहं यथा त्वमीशीय वस्व एक इत् । स्तोता मे गोसखा स्यात् ॥

1. If I, O God, were like Thee, the single ruler over wealth, my worshipper would be rich in kine; then why not Yours. (1834)

२. शिक्षेयमस्मै दित्सेयँ शचीपते मनीषिणे । यदहं गोपति: स्याम् ॥

2. I would be fain, O Lord of power, to impart wealth to, and instruct the intelligent pupil, were I the lord of kine, laud and speech. (1835)

३. धेनुष्ट इन्द्र सूनृता यजमानाय सुन्वते । गामश्वं पिप्युषी दुहे ॥

3. O God, Thy Vedic speech, the revealer of truth, yields the milk of knowledge like a cow, and grants spiritual strength and truthful speech to a seeker after knowledge, and a student of Vedic lore, nourishing him in every way ! (1836)

X

१. आपो हि ष्ठा मयोभुवस्ता न ऊर्जे दधातन । महे रणाय चक्षसे ॥

1. Yea, streams of knowledge, Ye bring peace and bliss, so help Ye us to energy and make us fit to acquire charming knowledge. (1837)

२. यो व: शिवतमो रसस्तस्य भाजयतेह न: । उशतीरिव मातर: ॥

2. Ye streams of knowledge, give us in this world, Your most auspicious joy. Nourish us as longing mothers nourish their sons. (1838)[1]

३. तस्मा अरं गमाम वो यस्य क्षयाय जिन्वथ । आपो जनयथा च न: ॥

3. O waters, for the removal of which impurity ye impel us, for the removal of the same we speedily go unto ye. Give us children who make the right use of water ! (1839)[2]

[1]See Yajur 11.51.
[2]See Yajur 11.52.
Go unto Ye: Use Ye. Those who make a correct use of the water become healthy and strong-bodied.

XI

१. वात आ वातु भेषज॑ शम्भु मयोभु नो हृदे । प्र न आयू॑षि तारिषत् ॥

1. May the King arrange for the blowing of medicinal air, that may bring health to our body and delight to our heart. May he prolong our days of life. (1840)[1]

२. उत वात पितासि न उत भ्रातोत न: सखा । स नो जीवातवे कृधि ॥

2. Thou art our Father O God, Yea, Thou art our Brother and our Friend. So give us strength that we may live ! (1841)[2]

३. यददो वात ते गृहे॑ऽमृतं निहितं गुहा । तस्य नो धेहि जीवसे ॥

3. O God, that immortal knowledge, that is hidden in Thee, and remains under Thy control, give us thereof that we may live ! (1842)

XII

१. अभि वाजी विश्वरूपो जनित्र॑ हिरण्ययं बिभ्रदत्क॑ सुपर्ण: ।
सूर्यस्य भानुमृतुथा वसान: परि स्वयं मेघमृज्रो जजान ॥

1. The soul, assuming diverse forms, full of knowledge and strength, treading the noble path of righteousness, fully understanding the significance of actions, full of ʃbrilliance, completely realising its true nature, clothed at fit times with the lustre of ʃthe Sun, through self effort, attains to the Pure, Mighty God. (1843)

२. अप्सु रेत: शिश्रिये विश्वरूपं तेज: पृथिव्यामधि यत् संबभूव ।
अन्तरिक्षे स्वं महिमानं मिमान: कनिक्रन्ति वृष्णो अश्वस्य रेत: ॥

2. The multiform soul, lays its seed in waters. It then appears on the Earth. Establishing its greatness in the mid-air, it sings the glory of the strength of God, the Father of all. (1844)[3]

३. अय॑ सहस्रा परि युक्ता वसान: सूर्यस्य भानुं यज्ञो दाधार ।
सहस्रदा: शतदा भूरिदावा धर्ता दिवो भुवनस्य विश्पति: ॥

3. This soul, the supporter of heavens, nourisher of the inhabitants of the

---

[1]See verse 184. The King should prevent the pollution of air, and make arrangements for keeping it pure, so that his subjects be physically healthy, mentally sound and able to live long.

[2]Vāta may mean air as well. Air protects us like a father, nourishes us like a brother, helps us like a friend, and makes us enjoy a long life.

[3]Soul is of diverse forms, i.e., cattle, birds, men, insects, fish etc. It appears in waters as fish, whale, sea monster. On earth it appears in the shape of men, cattle and creeping insects. In the atmosphere the soul appears in the shape of various flying birds like crow, sparrow and vulture.

world, giver of ample gifts in hundreds, thousands, assuming thousand robes
that suit it, upholds also the light of Sun. (1845)[1]

XIII

१. नाके सुपर्णमुप यत्पतन्तं हृदा वेनन्तो अभ्यचक्षत त्वा ।
हिरण्यपक्षं वरुणस्य दूतं यमस्य योनौ शकुनं भुरण्युम् ॥

1. O King, good persons gaze upon thee, as they gaze, with longing in their
heart, on the fast moving Sun, spreading lustre in heaven, strong-winged,
golden-flanked, the envoy of air, the bringer of rain, residing in the home of
lightning, and powerful like a bird ! (1846)[2]

२. ऊर्ध्वो गन्धर्वो अधि नाके अस्थात्प्रत्यङ्चित्रा बिभ्रदस्यायुधानि ।
वसानो अत्कं सुरभिं दृशे कं स्वा३र्णो नाम जनत प्रियाणि ॥

2. The wise soul that controls the organs of senses, as the Sun does his
rays, manifestly wielding the wondrous, beautiful weapons of the Yamas
and Niyamas, assuming its handsome pervading nature, full of joy, for seeing
the Mighty God, Lustrous like the Sun, achieves stability on the path of
salvation, and evolves its lovely aspirations. (1847)[3]

३. द्रप्स: समुद्रमभि यज्जिगाति पश्यन् गृध्रस्य चक्षसा विधर्मन् ।
भानु: शुक्रेण शोचिषा चकानस्तृतीये चक्रे रजसि प्रियाणि ॥

3. When the wise soul, moving like a flowing stream, attains to God, the
Vast, Deep Ocean of joy, or stationed in the mercy of God, Worthy of special
acceptance, visualises Him, its Lord, with the eye of an aspirer after salvation,
then enjoying in its own bright splendour like the Sun, it fulfils its desires in
the third highest stage of salvation. (1848)[4]

Chapter 3

I

१. आशु: शिशानो वृषभो न भीमो घनाघन: क्षोभणश्चर्षणीनाम् ।
सङ्क्रन्दनोऽनिमिष एकवीर: शतं सेना अजयत् साकमिन्द्र: ॥

1. A prosperous King is swift, rapidly striking, terrific like a bull, the killer

---

[1]Robes means bodies.

[2]See verse 320. The sun has been compared to a bird. Sun is strong winged as it emits
powerful rays having great speed. It is golden-flanked, due to its brilliance when it
shines.

[3]Yamas: Ahimsa, (Non-violence), Satya (Truth), Asteya (Non-theft), Brahmcharya
(celibacy), Aprigraha (Renunciation).
Niyamas: Shouch (Purity), Santosh (contentment) Tapa (Austerity) Swādhyāya (study
of scriptures) Ishwar Pranidhāna (Resignation to the Will of God). These have been
spoken of as the weapons of the soul for achieving salvation.

[4]Griffith considers the original hymn in the Rigveda as most obscure. I see no obscurity
in the verse.

of foes again and again, an awe-inspirer among the people, an inviter of foes
to battle, free from sloth, a sole hero, who subdues at once a hundred armies.
(1849)[1]

२. सङ्क्रन्दनेनानिमिषेण जिष्णुना युत्कारेण दुश्च्यवनेन धृष्णुना ।
तदिन्द्रेण जयत तत्सहध्वं यूधो नर इषुहस्तेन वृष्णा ॥

2. Ye warriors, win the battle, overcome the foe, with the help of the King,
the subduer of enemies, ever watchful, victorious, eager to fight, steady,
patient, whose hand bears strong arrows ! (1850)[2]

३. स इषुहस्तैः स निषङ्गिभिर्वंशी सं स्रष्टा स युध इन्द्रो गणेन ।
सं सृष्टजित् सोमपा बाहुशर्ध्यू३ग्रधन्वा प्रतिहिताभिरस्ता ॥

3. The King rules with the help of the soldiers, who carry arrows and
swords. He waging war fights against the enemy's hosts. He is foe-conquering
and enjoyer of happiness. He is strong of arms, and keeps the bow erect. He
shoots the enemy with his well-discharged arrows. (1851)[3]

II

१. बृहस्पते परि दीया रथेन रक्षोहामित्राँ अपबाधमानः ।
प्रभञ्जन्त्सेनाः प्रमृणो युधा जयन्नस्माकमेध्यविता रथानाम् ॥

1. O King, the guardian of multitude of people, attack the foe with thy
military conveyances. Thou art the slayer of the unjust, the remover of foes,
the breaker-up of the enemy's forces, and their destroyer. Winning in war, be
thou the protector of our military conveyances, that are used on the Earth,
the sea, and in the air ! (1852)[4]

२. बलविज्ञायः स्थविरः प्रवीरः सहस्वान् वाजी सहमान उग्रः ।
अभिवीरो अभिसत्वा सहोजा जैत्रमिन्द्र रथमा तिष्ठ गोवित् ॥

2. O King, the knower of thy strength, firm, foremost fighter, mighty,
learned, victorious, all-subduing, the possessor of nice warriors, and military
intelligent employees, famous for strength, master of passion, mount thy
conquering conveyance ! (1853)[5]

---

[1]Pt. Jaidev Vidyalankara has ably and nicely applied this verse to soul as well. See
Yajur 17-33.

[2]This verse is also applicable to soul. See Yajur 17-34.

[3]See Yajur 17-35.
Pt. Jaidev Vidyalankara has applied this verse to soul, but the explanation is highly
far-fetched and I have therefore avoided mentioning it.

[4]See Yajur 17-36. For the ethical interpretation of the verse see Pt. Jaidev Vidyalankar's commentary.

[5]See Yajur 17-37 and Pt. Jaidev Vidyalankar's interpretation.

३. गोत्रभिदं गोविंदं वज्रबाहुं जयन्तमज्म प्रमृणन्तमोजसा ।
इमं सजाता अनु वीरयध्वमिन्द्रं सखायो अनु सं रभध्वम् ॥

3. O coeval, friendly warriors, show your zeal and courage, and quit yourselves as heroes, following this King, the cleaver of forests, strong-bodied,
armed with thunder-bolt, who quells an army and with might destroys it !
(1854)[1]

III

१. अभि गोत्राणि सहसा गाहमानोऽदयो वीरः शतमन्युरिन्द्रः ।
दुश्च्यवनः पृतनाषाडयुध्योऽस्माकं सेना अवतु प्र युत्सु ॥

1. May the King, who, with surpassing vigour pierces the families of the
enemies, is pitiless, heroic, full of righteous indignation, unconquerable by
foes, conqueror of the enemy's forces, unequalled in fight, protect our armies
in our battles. (1855)[2]

२. इन्द्र आसां नेता बृहस्पतिर्दक्षिणा यज्ञः पुर एतु सोमः ।
देवसेनानामभिभञ्जतीनां जयन्तीनां मरुतो यन्त्वग्रम् ॥

2. In a battle, the Commander, the leader of these armies, the conqueror
and demolisher of the enemies should march behind, the organiser of the army
should march in front. The leader of big bands should march on the right.
The encourager of the army should march on the left. The warriors swift like
air should mareh ahead. (1856)[3]

३. इन्द्रस्य वृष्णो वरुणस्य राज्ञ आदित्यानां मरुतां शर्ध उग्रम् ।
महामनसां भुवनच्यवानां घोषो देवानां जयतामुदस्थात् ॥

3. Musical instruments, to infuse valour and energy should be played upon
before the commencement of the battle, by the learned soldiers of the powerful Commander, and mighty King, who possess decent homes, lofty ideas,
are able to conquer the enemies, have led a life of celibacy for forty-eight
years, are highly learned and strong, full of terrible power. (1857)[4]

IV

१. उद्धर्षय मघवन्नायुधान्युत् सत्वनां मामकानां मनांसि ।
उद्वृत्रहन् वाजिनां वाजिनान्युद्रथानां जयतां यन्तु घोषाः ॥

1. O adorable Commander, the slayer of foes, make the weapons of our

---

[1]See Yajur 17-38; and Pt. Jaidev's interpretation.
[2]See Yajur 17-39.
[3]See Yajur 17-40.
[4]See Yajur 17-41.

soldiers flourish, excite the spirits of our warring heroes, increase the speed
of our horses, and let the din of conquering cars go upward! (1858)[1]

२. अस्माकमिन्द्र: समृतेषु ध्वजेष्वस्माकं या इषवस्ता जयन्तु ।
अस्माकं वीरा उत्तरे भवन्त्वस्माँ उ देवा अवता हवेषु ॥

2. May the Commander of the army aid us when our flags reach the enemy's forces. Victorious be the arrows of our army. May our brave men of
war prevail in battle. May learned persons protect us at the time of war!
(1859)[2]

३. असौ या सेना मरुत: परेषामभ्येति न ओजसा स्पर्धमाना ।
तां गूहत तमसापव्रतेन यथैतेषामन्यो अन्यं न जानात् ॥

3. O learned persons meet Ye the army of our enemies, that comes against
us in a jealous mood, with its might, and enwrap it harshly in the darkness
of the smoke arising out of the use of guns, so that they may not recognise
one another! (1860)[3]

V

१. अमीषां चित्तं प्रतिलोभयन्ती गृहाणाङ्गान्यप्वे परेहि ।
अभि प्रेहि निर्दह हृत्सु शोकैरन्धेनामित्रास्तमसा सचन्ताम्

1. O queen, the slayer of foes, organise the bands of thy army, that be-
wilders the hearts of the forces of the enemy, remain aloof from sin, convey
thy aim to thy soldiers, burn down the foes, whereby they may abide in utter
darkness with hearts full of griefs! (1861)[4]

२. प्रेता जयता नर इन्द्रो व: शर्म यच्छतु । उग्रा व: सन्तु बाहवोऽनाधृष्या यथासथ ॥

2. Advance, O heroes, win the day. May the Commander of the army pro-
vide Ye with shelter, food and clothes. Exceeding mighty be your arms, that
none may threaten or injure you! (1862)[5]

३. अवसृष्टा परा पत शरव्ये ब्रह्मसंशिते । गच्छामित्रान् प्र पद्यस्व मामीषां कं च नोच्छिष: ॥

3. O wife of the Commander-in-chief, expert in the art of archery, trained
by a learned person knowing the Vedas, on persuasion, go afar, encounter

[1]See Yajur 17-42.
[2]See Yajur 17-43.
[3]See Yajur 17-47. Darkness: the use of fiery weapons produces smoke, that envelops
the enemy's forces, and being blinded, one soldier cannot recognise the other. It may
also refer to the use of gases which darken the eyes of the soldiers.
[4]See Yajur 17-44.
Apva: According to Sāyaṇa, a female deity who presides over sin; according to Mahidhar, sickness or fear. According to Swami Dayānand, it means the queen who leads the
army of women and kills the foes. This verse advocates the formation of the army of
women.
[5]See Yajur 17-46,

the foes, achieve victory by slaying them. Let not even one of those distant foes be left alive! (1863)[1]

VI

१. कङ्काः सुपर्णा अनु यन्त्वेनान् गृध्राणामन्नमसावस्तु सेना ।
मेषां मोच्यघहारश्च नेन्द्र वयांस्येनाननुसंयन्तु सर्वान् ।

1. Let ravens and strong-pinioned birds pursue them. Yea, let that army be the food of vultures, O King, let no sinner out of them escape; let carnivorous birds fall upon them to devour them! (1864)[2]

२. अमित्रसेनां मघवन्नस्माञ्छत्रुयतीमभि । उभौ तामिन्द्र वृत्रहन्नग्निश्च दहतं प्रति ॥

2. O philanthropic, foe-slaying king and the leader of the army, Ye both, burn down the host of foemen, that cometh on us in a warlike fashion! (1865)

३. यत्र बाणाः संपतन्ति कुमारा विशिखा इव । तत्र नो ब्रह्मणस्पतिरदिति: शर्म यच्छतु ॥
विश्वाहा शर्म यच्छतु ॥

3. There where the flights of arrows fall like boys whose locks are unshorn, may the Commander, the protector of the big army, grant us shelter, may the entire Assembly adorned with members, grant us a happy home through all our days. (1866)[3]

VII

१. वि रक्षो वि मृधो जहि वि वृत्रस्य हनू रुज । वि मन्युमिन्द्र वृत्रहन्नमित्रस्याभिदासत: ॥

1. Drive the violent and the greedy away, break thou the jaws of the Oppressor, who impedes our progress. O foe-slaying King, quell the foeman's wrath who wants to enslave us! (1867)

२. वि न इन्द्र मृधो जहि नीचा यच्छ पृतन्यत: । यो अस्मां अभिदासत्यधरं गमया तम: ॥

2. O Commander of the army, win battles, humble the men who challenge us, send down to nether darkness, him, who seeks to enslave us! (1868)[4]

[1]See Yajur 17-45.
[2]'Them' refers to the soldiers of opposing army killed in the battle.
[3]See Yajur 17-48. Like boys: The arrows fall where they list, as boys before the Mundan Sanskar (tonsure ceremony) play about vigorously where they like. Roth separates Vishikhā from Kumarā and translates (where the arrows fly young and old) that is feathered and unfeathered. Swami Dayānanda interprets arrows to mean weapons and arms.
[4]See Yajur 8-44, 18-70.

३. इन्द्रस्य बाहू स्थविरौ युवानावनाधृष्यौ सुप्रतीकावसह्यौ ।
तौ युञ्जीत प्रथमौ योग आगते याभ्यां जितमसुराणां सह्हो महत् ॥

3. Strong, ever-youthful, unassailable, fair, unendurable, are the arms of the King. These first let him employ at the time of battle, wherewith the great might of atrociously cruel persons is overthrown. (1869)

VIII

१. मर्माणि ते वर्मणा च्छादयामि सोमस्त्वा राजामृतेनानु वस्ताम् ।
उरोर्वरीयो वरुणस्ते कृणोतु जयन्तं त्वानु देवा मदन्तु ॥

1. O valiant warrior, thy vital parts I cover with armour. May this calm, considerate King protect thee with efficacious medicine. May the exalted King give thee more than ample joy. May the learned be delighted in thy triumph over the wicked! (1870)[1]

२. अन्धा अमित्रा भवताशीर्षाणोऽह्य इव । तेषां वो अग्निनुन्नानामिन्द्रो हन्तु वरंवरम् ॥

2. Blind, O my foemen, shall ye be, even as headless serpents are: may the Commander kill each best of you when fire has struck you down! (1871)

३. यो नः स्वोऽरणो यश्च निष्ठ्यो जिघांसति ।
देवास्तं सर्वे धूर्वन्तु ब्रह्म वर्म ममान्तरं शर्म वर्म ममान्तरम् ॥

3. A relative of ours, who is a man of low character, and wants to kill us secretly from a distance, deserves to be tormented by all learned persons. God or Veda is my internal armour. May my pleasant armour be my protector! (1872)

IX

१. मृगो न भीमः कुचरो गिरिष्ठाः परावत आ जगन्था परस्याः ।
सृकं संशाय पविमिन्द्र तिग्मं वि शत्रून् ताढि वि मृधो नुदस्व ॥

1. O Commander of the army, like a dreadful wild tiger roaming in the mountains with a crooked pace, encircle the distant foes. Crush thou the enemies, whetting the streaming forth sharp bolt, thou subduer of the wicked through punishment, win battles! (1873)

२. भद्रं कर्णेभिः श्रृणुयाम देवा भद्रं पश्येमाक्षभिर्यजत्राः ।
स्थिरैरङ्गैस्तुष्टुवांसस्तनूभिर्व्यशेमहि देवहितं यदायुः ॥

2. O sociable learned persons, may we with our ears listen to what is good, and with our eyes see what is good. With limbs and bodies firm may we extolling God lead a life conducive to the good of the sages! (1874)[2]

[1]See Yajur 17-49.
[2]See Yajur 25-21.

३. स्वस्ति न इन्द्रो वृद्धश्रवा: स्वस्ति न: पूषा विश्ववेदा: ।
   स्वस्ति नस्ताक्ष्यों अरिष्टनेमि: स्वस्ति नो बृहस्पतिर्दधातु ॥
   स्वस्ति नो बृहस्पतिर्दधातु ॥

3. May the Master of vast knowledge, may Mighty God prosper us. May
the Nourisher of all, the Author of all the Vedas prosper us. May He, the
Giver of all comforts like the horse, prosper us. May God, the Lord of all
the elements of Nature, vouchsafe us prosperity. May God, the Lord of all
the elements of Nature, vouchsafe us prosperity. (1875)[1]

---

[1]The repetition of स्वस्ति नो बृहस्पतिर्दधातु is meant to indicate the end of the Veda.
See Yajur 25-19.
Just as a horse takes us from one place to the other and gives us pleasure, so does
God, give us happiness by fulfilling our wants.

GLOSSARY AND INDEX

abode of bliss, 13

Achhavaka, one among the seven priests who officiate in the sacrifice; the others are Hota, Maitra Varuna, Brahman Achhansi, Pota, Neshtha and Agnidhra, 174 fn.

Adhibhautik, material, physical, 40fn.

Adhidaivic, 40fn.

Adhvaryu, one of the four classes of priests, the other three being Hotri, Udgatri and Brahman; his prescribed duties being: measuring the ground, building the altar, arranging vessels, wood and water for the sacrifice, to light the fire, to fetch the animal and offer it; while performing these actions, he was enjoined to repeat the hymns of the Yajurveda, 8fn., 10fn., 30, 123, 206

Adhyatmic, 40fn.

Aditya(s), one of the names of the Sun; the plural refers to the twelve months of the year or to that class of deities consisting of Varuna, Mitra, Aryaman, Bhaga, Daksha, Amsha and one or two others, all of them being sons of Aditi; these deities are different from their cousins, the Viswe devas, the sons of Visva, a sister of Aditi, 16, 220fn.

Aditya Brahmachari, cf., Brahmachari, 171
aeroplanes, 235fn.

Agni, one of the three chief Vedic deities; he presides over the earth and the messenger between the worlds of men and gods: as fire 1fn; as God 141fn., 285, 286; as messenger, 116; as preceptor 124fn., 212fn., 220fn.

Agnidhra, cf. Achhavaka, the priest who kindles fire, 174fn.

Agnihotra, oblation to Agni; this is of two kinds: nitya, which is performed daily at dawn with milk, oil and sour gruel; the other, kamya i.e., optional, 271fn., 274

Ajna chakra, one of the six mystical circles or diagrams described by the Tantras, 158fn.

Anavas, 39fn.

Angara, name of a *Rishi*, 220fn.

Angiras, a celebrated *Rishi*, author of the hymns of Rigveda, a treatise on astronomy and a code of laws; he is the father of Agni, 5fn., 141fn.

Angirasas, descendants of Angiras, 141 fn.

Anna kosha, one of the five sheaths which form the various frames of the body enveloping the soul, the other four being Pran, Mana, Gyan and Vigyan koshas, 39fn.

Antriksha, the middle space between heaven and earth; the middle of the three spheres or regions of life, 3fn., 98fn.

Anu, son of Yayati and Sarmishtha, 42fn.

Anushtup metre; this consists of four feet or quarter verses of eight syllables each, 92, 157fn., 226fn.

Apam, 4fn.

Apana, one of the vital airs which moves downwards and passes out through the anus, 8, 33, 47, 48, 56fn., 56, 64, 65, 73, 74, 81, 97fn., 103, 104, 111, 117, 118, 123, 131, 142, 154, 157fn., 158, 166fn., 168, 170, 176, 208fn., 213, 214fn., 217, 220, 226fn., 227, 229, 257, 258, 267-269, 271, 273, 274, 278

archer, 37, 283

armies, 52, 74

armour, 66, 68

arrows, 290

Arth, worldly prosperity, 36, 85, 135fn.

Arthaveda, science of wealth subordinate to Atharvaveda, 154fn.

Aryama, one of the Adityas usually invoked with Mitra and Varuna, 38, 167, 279

Ashwina, heaven and earth, 27fn.

Asikini R, the Vedic name of Chenab river, 226fn.

assembly, 153fn., 293

Aswins, two Vedic divinities who appear in the sky in a golden chariot drawn by horses or birds, as forerunners of the dawn; they are the physicians of the

Gods; parents of the Pandva princes Na-
kula and Sahadeva, 269, 271, 273, 274

Atharvan, the priest who first initiated the
worship of fire: he was the first learner
and teacher of Brahma-vidya, he composed the Atharvaveda, 2fn., 28fn., 146fn.

Atharvaveda, 6, 154fn., 239

atmosphere, 14, 92, 97, 107, 132, 135, 140,
149, 210, 230fn., 243, 255, 256, 259fn.,
261, 271, 273

atoms, 94

Aufrecht (Professor), 55fn.

Aushija, name of a Rishi, 22, 23fn.
autumn, 95

axe, 147

axle, 53, 168

Ayu, the first-born son of Pururavas and
Urvasi and father of Nahusha, 137fn.

Ayurveda, a treatise on medicine attri-
buted to Dhanwantri; a supplement to
Atharvaveda, 53, 168

battle, 12, 83, 91, 101, 108, 174. 212, 228,
237, 238, 253, 290, 291, 294

battlefield, 101, 119, 146, 199, 209, 283

bay steeds, 64

bee, 250

Bharadwaj, author of many Vedic hymns
and father of Drona, the preceptor of
the Pandavas; he enjoyed a very long life
extending over Treta and Dwapara
Yugas, 6fn.

Bhog Yoni, 25fn.

Bhrigu, a Vedic Rishi; regarded as the
founder of the race of Bhrigus or Bhar-
gavas, in which Jamadagni and Parasu
Rama were born, 149fn.

Bhrigus, the descendants of Bhrigu, 148fn.

bin, 110

birds, 13, 37, 50, 57, 142, 143, 293

body, 22, 24, 35, 76, 85, 86, 97, 99, 119fn.,
126, 131, 134, 136, 142, 194, 206fn., 211,
214, 216, 217, 246, 251, 255, 256, 265, 266,
268, 269, 273, 277

Bose, J.C., 285fn.

bow, 84

bow-string, 281

Brahma, the first member of the Hindu
triad and progenitor of all the worlds,
147

Brahmachari, an unmarried religious
student who is to observe celibacy till
the completion of his formal studies, 54,

150, 151, 202, 224fn.

Brahmacha i-aditya, one who observes
celibacy for fortyeight years, 171

Brahma day, it consists of one thousand
Maha-Yuga or Manwantara, each being
equal to 4,320,000,000 human years, 240fn.

Brahman, one of the four principal
priests, the other three being the Hotri,
Adhvaryu and Udgatri; he was the most
learned of them all and was master of
the three Vedas; he was to supervise the
sacrifice and to correct mistakes, 8fn.,
10fn., 206

Brahman-Achhansi, one of the seven
priests who participate in the sacrifice,
the others being Hota, Maitra-Varuna,
Pota, Neshtha, Achhavaka and Agnidhra, 174fn.

Brahma night, the duration is the same as
the Brahma day i.e., 4,320,000,000 human
years, 240fn.

Brahma randhra, 'Brahma's crevice' in the
crown of the head, through which the
soul escapes after death, 158fn.

Brihad-Aranyak Upanishad, 68fn.

Brihaduktha Rishi, 11fn.

Brihat Sama, hymn composed in Brihati
metre, 27, 30, 35, 106fn., 107, 123, 221

Brihati metre, a metre of thirty-six
syllables, 157fn., 226fn.

Brihati verses, 260

Bull, 114, 196, 211, 232, 253

Calf, 33, 55, 86, 171

Car, 11, 12fn., 53, 55fn., 117, 119, 129, 168,
174, 195, 292

Car horse, 74

Carpenter, 135, 147

Chariot, 12fn., 83, 98, 99, 126, 174, 194,
201, 206fn., 209, 220, 221, 267, 273, 283

Charioteer, 7, 73

Chhand, prosody, 154fn.

Chhandogya Upanishad, 68fn.

Clarified butter, 283

Cloud, 71

Commander, 81, 83, 228, 291, 292, 294

Commander-in-chief, 153fn., 292

Corn, 110, 152, 224

Cow(s), 25, 52, 68, 82, 106, 147, 171, 196,
224, 232

Cowell, 40fn., 164fn.

Cowherd, 82, 155

Creator, 5, 7, 11, 14, 16, 97, 98, 117, 140,